LOGIC IN THE HUSSERLIAN CONTEXT

Northwestern University
Studies in Phenomenology
and
Existential Philosophy

LOGIC
IN THE
HUSSERLIAN
CONTEXT

Johanna Maria Tito

Northwestern University Press
Evanston, Illinois

1990

Northwestern University Press
Evanston, Illinois 60201

Copyright © 1990 by Northwestern University Press
All rights reserved. First published 1990
Printed in the United States of America

95 94 93 92 91 90   5 4 3 2 1

Library of Congress Cataloging-in-Publication Data

Tito, Johanna Maria.
   Logic in the Husserlian context / Johanna Maria Tito.
      p. cm — (Northwestern University studies in phenomenology and
existential philosophy)
   Includes bibliographical references and index.
   ISBN 0-8101-0966-2
   1. Husserl, Edmund, 1859–1938—Contributions in logic. 2. Logic. 3.
Transcendental logic. I. Title. II. Series: Northwestern University studies in
phenomenology & existential philosophy.
B3279.H94T55 1990
160—dc20   90-43344
                                                                CIP

To my teacher and friend,
Dr. Jakob Amstutz

Contents

Acknowledgments

I wish to express my gratitude to Dr. Jakob Amstutz for his continual feedback during my writing of this work. His encouragement and philosophical insights proved invaluable. Thanks go also to Dr. Jeff Mitscherling for his suggestions for improving this work.

I am indebted to my parents and brother who have encouraged my work and helped me in innumerable ways. Thanks go to my friend, Marea Carey, for her unwavering support and for cheering me on. To Danuta Kamocki I am grateful for encouragement and many hours of philosophical dialog.

Abbreviations

In this work sigla are used when either quoting from or referring to a text. Where applicable, reference to the English translation is given in parentheses, followed by reference to the original text in square brackets. B. Gibson's translation of *Ideas* was primarily used, but in the few instances in which F. Kersten's translation of this text were used, the letter "I" for *Ideas* is cited followed by the letters "FK." Below is a listing of the sigla in *alphabetical order*. This is followed by another listing of the sigla arranged alphabetically *according to author*.

The sigla in alphabetical order:

A   Carnap, R. *The Logical Structure of the World.*

AN   Freud, S. "A Note on the Unconscious in Psychoanalysis."

AS   Ross, W. D. (ed.) *Aristotle Selections.*

ASTP Duhem, P. *The Aim and Structure of Physical Theory.*

BN   Sartre, J.-P. *Being and Nothingness: An Essay on Phenomenological Ontology.*

BP   Freud, S. "Beyond the Pleasure-Principle."

BT   Nietzsche, F. *The Birth of Tragedy.*

C   Husserl, E. *The Crisis of European Sciences and Transcendental Phenomenology.*

CD   Freud, S. *Civilization and its Discontents.*

CHF Cairns, D. *Conversations with Husserl and Fink.*

CI   Ricoeur, P. *The Conflict of Interpretations: Essays in Hermeneutics.*

CL Chomsky, N. *Cartesian Linguistics: A Chapter in the History of Rationalist Thought.*

CM Husserl, E. *Cartesian Meditations.*

CNM Schmidt, A. *The Concept of Nature in Marx.*

CPR Kant, I. *Critique of Pure Reason.*

CWA Horowitz, J. *Conversations with Arrau.*

D Descartes, R. *Discourse on Method and Meditations.*

DEJ Amstutz, J. "Das Erkenntnisverhalten C. G. Jungs."

DF Fancher, R. *Psychoanalytic Psychology: The Development of Freud's Thought.*

DL Buber, M. *Daniel: Dialogues on Realization.*

DeM de Muralt, A. *The Idea of Phenomenology: Husserlian Exemplarism.*

DU Dummett, M. *Frege: The Philosophy of Language.*

DWP Landgrebe, L. *Der Weg der Phänomenologie.*

EI Freud, S. "The Ego and the Id."

EJ Husserl, E. *Experience and Judgment: Investigations in a Genealogy of Logic.*

EW Merleau-Ponty, M. *Essential Writings of Merleau-Ponty.*

F Friedman, R. M. "Merleau-Ponty's Theory of Subjectivity."

FB Strasser, S. "Feeling as Basis of Knowing and Recognizing the Other as an Ego."

FCW Koyré, A. *From Closed World to Infinite Universe.*

FLI Frege, G. *Logical Investigations.*

FMS Bettelheim, B. *Freud and Man's Soul.*

FTJ Bell, D. *Frege's Theory of Judgment.*

FTL Husserl, E. *Formal and Transcendental Logic.*

GA Frege, G. *Foundations of Arithmetic.*

GF Sluga, H. *Gottlob Frege.*

GG Payzant, G. *Glenn Gould: Music and Mind.*

GI Dodds, E. *The Greeks and the Irrational.*

HAP Ricoeur, P. *Husserl: An Analysis of his Philosophy*.

HEA Elliston, F., and P. McCormick (eds.) *Husserl: Expositions and Appraisals*.

HFL Bochenski, I. *A History of Formal Logic*.

H-J Huertas-Jourda, H. *On the Threshold of Phenomenology: A Study of Edmund Husserl's "Philosophie der Arithmetik."*

HNN Føllesdal, D. "Husserl's Notion of Noema."

HR Descartes, R. *The Philosophical Works of Descartes*, vol. 2. Translated by Elizabeth S. Haldane and G. R. T. Ross.

I Husserl, E. *Ideas: General Introduction to Pure Phenomenology*.

IK Kern, I. *Husserl und Kant*.

IL Veatch, H. *Intentional Logic*.

IOI Hintikka, J. *The Intention of Intentionality and Other New Models for Modalities*.

IRI Brand, G. "Intentionality, Reduction, and Intentional Analysis in Husserl's Later Manuscripts."

ITL Mitchell, D. *An Introduction to Logic*.

IVI Smith, D., and R. McIntyre. "Intentionality via Intensions."

K Nietzsche, F. *The Birth of Tragedy and the Case of Wagner*.

KK Kneale, W. and M. *The Development of Logic*.

KS Hartmann, N. *Kleinere Schriften*.

LI Husserl, E. *Logical Investigations*.

LP Ayer, A. *Logical Positivism*.

LSL Carnap, R. *The Logical Syntax of Language*.

M Camus, A. *The Myth of Sisyphus and Other Essays*.

MBF Tugendhat, E. "The Meaning of 'Bedeutung' in Frege."

MGL Solomon, R. C. *Morality and the Good Life*.

MR Barral, M. *Merleau-Ponty: The Role of the Body-Subject in Interpersonal Relations*.

MT von Kleist, H. "Über das Marionettentheater."

MUS Amstutz, J. "Der Mensch und das Sein."

N Freud, S. "On Narcissism: An Introduction."

NAS Langsdorf, L. "The Noema: An Analysis of its Structure."

NRH Perelman, C. *The New Rhetoric and the Humanities: Essays on Rhetoric and its Applications.*

NS Scheler, M. *The Nature of Sympathy.*

P Palmer, R. *Hermeneutics: Interpretation Theory in Schleiermacher, Dilthey, Heidegger, and Gadamer.*

PA Bambrough, R. (ed.) *The Philosophy of Aristotle.*

PE Zaner, R. *The Problem of Embodiment.*

PES Brentano, F. *Psychology from an Empirical Standpoint.*

PH Gadamer, H.-G. *Philosophical Hermeneutics.*

PhP Merleau-Ponty, M. *Phenomenology of Perception.*

PL Husserl, E. *Paris Lectures.*

PM Spiegelberg, H. *The Phenomenological Movement.*

PN Nietzsche, F. "The Spirit of Modernity."

POP Merleau-Ponty, M. *The Primacy of Perception.*

PTP Mohanty, J. N. *The Possibility of Transcendental Philosophy.*

PW Geatch, P., and M. Black. *Translations from the Philosophical Writings of Gottlob Frege.*

RM Rickman, H. *W. Dilthey: Selected Writings.*

RPL Rosenberg, J., and C. Travis. *Readings in the Philosophy of Language.*

S Merleau-Ponty, M. *Signs.*

SA Trilling, L. *Sincerity and Authenticity.*

SAT Stigen, A. *The Structure of Aristotle's Thought.*

SB Merleau-Ponty, M. *The Structure of Behaviour.*

SHL Bachelard, S. *A Study of Husserl's "Formal and Transcendental Logic."*

SO Angelelli, I. *Studies on Gottlob Frege and Traditional Philosophy.*

SW Pétrement, S. *Simone Weil: A Life.*

THN Hume, D. *A Treatise of Human Nature.*

TIHP Levinas, E. *The Theory of Intuition in Husserl's Phenomenology.*

TM Gadamer, H.-G. *Truth and Method.*

VM Fichte, G. *The Vocation of Man.*

WA Ross, W. *The World of Aristotle.*

Z Nietzsche, F. "Thus Spoke Zarathustra."

The sigla listed according to author:

DEJ Amstutz, J. "Das Erkenntnisverhalten C. G. Jungs."

MUS ————. "Der Mensch und das Sein."

SO Angelelli, I. *Studies on Gottlob Frege and Traditional Philosophy.*

LP Ayer, A. J. (ed.) *Logical Positivism.*

SHL Bachelard, S. *A Study of Husserl's "Formal and Transcendental Logic."*

PA Bambrough, R. (ed.) *The Philosophy of Aristotle.*

MR Barral, M. *Merleau-Ponty: The Role of the Body-Subject in Interpersonal Relations.*

FTJ Bell, D. *Frege's Theory of Judgment.*

FMS Bettelheim, B. *Freud and Man's Soul.*

HFL Bochenski, I. M. *A History of Formal Logic.*

IRI Brand, G. "Intentionality, Reduction, and Intentional Analysis in Husserl's Later Manuscripts."

PES Brentano, F. *Psychology from an Empirical Standpoint.*

DL Buber, M. *Daniel: Dialogues on Realization.*

CHF Cairns, D. *Conversations with Husserl and Fink.*

M Camus, A. *The Myth of Sisyphus and Other Essays.*

A Carnap, R. *The Logical Structure of the World.*

LSL ————. *The Logical Syntax of Language.*

CL Chomsky, N. *Cartesian Linguistics: A Chapter in the History of Rationalist Thought.*

D Descartes, R. *Discourse on Method and Meditations.*

HR ———. *The Philosophical Works of Descartes*, vol. 2. Translated by Elizabeth S. Haldane and G. R. T. Ross.

GI Dodds, E. R. *The Greeks and the Irrational.*

ASPT Duhem, P. *The Aim and Structure of Physical Theory.*

DU Dummett, M. *Frege: The Philosophy of Language.*

HEA Elliston, F., and P. McCormick (eds.) *Husserl: Expositions and Appraisals.*

DF Fancher, R. E. *Psychoanalytic Psychology: The Development of Freud's Thought.*

VM Fichte, G. J. *The Vocation of Man.*

HNN Føllesdal, D. "Husserl's Notion of Noema."

GA Frege, G. *Foundations of Arithmetic.*

FLI ———. *Logical Investigations.*

AN Freud, S. "A Note on the Unconscious in Psychoanalysis."

BP ———. "Beyond the Pleasure-Principle."

CD ———. *Civilization and its Discontents.*

EI ———. "The Ego and the Id."

N ———. "On Narcissism: An Introduction."

F Friedman, R. M. "Merleau-Ponty's Theory of Subjectivity."

PH Gadamer, H.-G. *Philosophical Hermeneutics.*

TM ———. *Truth and Method.*

PW Geatch, P. T., and M. Black (eds.). *Translations from the Philosophical Writings of Gottlob Frege.*

KS Hartmann, K. *Kleinere Schriften.*

IOI Hintikka, J. *The Intention of Intentionality and other New Models for Modalities.*

CWA Horowitz, J. *Conversations with Arrau.*

H-J Huertas-Jourda, J. *On the Threshold of Phenomenology: A Study of Edmund Husserl's "Philosophie der Arithmetik."*

THN Hume, D. *A Treatise of Human Nature.*

ABBREVIATIONS

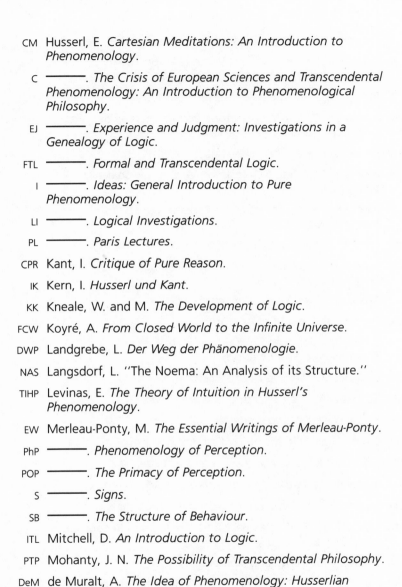

CM Husserl, E. *Cartesian Meditations: An Introduction to Phenomenology.*

C ———. *The Crisis of European Sciences and Transcendental Phenomenology: An Introduction to Phenomenological Philosophy.*

EJ ———. *Experience and Judgment: Investigations in a Genealogy of Logic.*

FTL ———. *Formal and Transcendental Logic.*

I ———. *Ideas: General Introduction to Pure Phenomenology.*

LI ———. *Logical Investigations.*

PL ———. *Paris Lectures.*

CPR Kant, I. *Critique of Pure Reason.*

IK Kern, I. *Husserl und Kant.*

KK Kneale, W. and M. *The Development of Logic.*

FCW Koyré, A. *From Closed World to the Infinite Universe.*

DWP Landgrebe, L. *Der Weg der Phänomenologie.*

NAS Langsdorf, L. "The Noema: An Analysis of its Structure."

TIHP Levinas, E. *The Theory of Intuition in Husserl's Phenomenology.*

EW Merleau-Ponty, M. *The Essential Writings of Merleau-Ponty.*

PhP ———. *Phenomenology of Perception.*

POP ———. *The Primacy of Perception.*

S ———. *Signs.*

SB ———. *The Structure of Behaviour.*

ITL Mitchell, D. *An Introduction to Logic.*

PTP Mohanty, J. N. *The Possibility of Transcendental Philosophy.*

DeM de Muralt, A. *The Idea of Phenomenology: Husserlian Exemplarism.*

BT Nietzsche, F. *The Birth of Tragedy.* Translated by F. Gilffin.

K ———. *The Birth of Tragedy and the Case of Wagner.* Translated, with Commentary, by Walter Kaufmann.

PN ———. "The Spirit of Modernity."

Z ———. "Thus Spoke Zarathustra." *The Portable Nietzsche.*

P Palmer, R. E. *Hermeneutics: Interpretation Theory in Schleiermacher, Dilthey, Heidegger, and Gadamer.*

GG Payzant, G. *Glenn Gould: Music and Mind.*

NRH Perelman, C. *The New Rhetoric and the Humanities: Essays on Rhetoric and its Applications.*

SW Pétrement, S. *Simone Weil: A Life.*

RM Rickman, H. P. (ed. & Translator) *W. Dilthey: Selected Writings.*

CI Ricoeur, P. *The Conflict of Interpretations: Essays in Hermeneutics.*

HAP ———. *Husserl. An Analysis of his Phenomenology.*

RPL Rosenberg, J., and C. Travis (eds.) *Readings in the Philosophy of Language.*

AS Ross, W. D. (ed.) *Aristotle Selections.*

WA ———. *The World of Aristotle.*

BN Sartre, J.-P. *Being and Nothingness: An Essay on Phenomenological Ontology.*

NS Scheler, M. *The Nature of Sympathy.*

CNM Schmidt, A. *The Concept of Nature in Marx.*

GF Sluga, H.-D. *Gottlob Frege.*

IVI Smith, D., and R. McIntyre. "Intentionality via Intensions."

MGL Solomon, R. C. *Morality and the Good Life.*

PM Spiegelberg, H. *The Phenomenological Movement.*

SAT Stigen, A. *The Structure of Aristotle's Thought.*

FB Strasser, S. "Feeling as Basis of Knowing and Recognizing the Other as an Ego."

SA Trilling, L. *Sincerity and Authenticity.*

MBF Tugendhat, E. "The Meaning of 'Bedeutung' in Frege."

IL Veatch, H. *Intentional Logic.*

MT von Kleist, H. "Über das Marionettentheater."

PE Zaner, R. *The Problem of Embodiment.*

Introduction

(a) ## Phenomenology as Transcendental Logic, the Science of Science

According to Husserl phenomenology is the science of the human soul (C 257, 264–65).[1] The essence of the soul, he maintains, is knowing (CM 156–57 [182–83]). Hence he also describes phenomenology variously as the science of rationality (C 338) and as transcendental logic, the science of science (FTL 13 [11], 231 [205]). Characterized in these ways phenomenology comes under attack from many schools of thought. For instance, today it is popular to maintain that one can speak of a philosophy that seeks to reveal a rationality common to all human beings only at the expense of the individual and that such a philosophy can at heart only be totalitarian.[2] According to the dictates of Husserl's phenomenology this belief is not only false but dangerous, for it promotes the very state of affairs that it denounces—totalitarianism.[3] After all, if humans do not have an inherent, essential rationality that can be mutually recognized, what compelling reason can be advanced for a liberal society? At best one might advance prudence as a reason, but that is surely the emptiest of reasons.[4]

As well, the claim that phenomenology is transcendental *logic,* science of the soul, is generally repugnant to logician and existentialist-humanist philosopher alike. To the former the claim sounds like a reversion to psychologism, the reduction of formal logical objects and laws to psychological (empirical) facts and laws. To the latter the claim merely reinforces the suspicion that phenomenology is a theoretical science, closed to Being and divorced from life. After all, questions of life and existence are questions of fact, and logic does not deal with matters of fact, but with matters of form only. That Husserl was a mathematician as well as a philosopher is taken as an indication that his phenomenological method is not unlike that of a pure mathematician—a disinterested method that abstracts from the "rough" elements of experience and considers only the unchanging, abstract forms of objects of experience. It is thought that Husserl views the world as a mathematical manifold and sees phenomenology as the geometry of the soul that will reveal this manifold.

Even certain phenomenologists will not be happy with the characterization of phenomenology as logic, for they think that phenomenology thereby loses its humanist-existentialist properties. They ignore the link between logic and phenomenology, even though Husserl developed the concept of "intentionality" out of the debate between psychologism and antipsychologism, and even though logic is the leitmotiv in his work. But ignoring the role of logic in phenomenology does not make the relation of phenomenology to life any stronger or clearer; it merely has the undesirable effect of taking away some of the rigor of phenomenology.

(b) ## Separation of the Universal and the Individual at the Root of a Crisis of Value

If Husserl talks about the universal or formal, it is not at the expense of the individual or of life. The universal and the individual are as inseparable as melody and rhythm in his view, and to stress one at the expense of the other is to belie human nature and court alienation. In fact, it is this separation of the universal, the rational, from the particular, from life, that lies at the root of the crisis Husserl speaks of in *Formal and Transcendental Logic* and the *Crisis*. In these two works Husserl describes the crisis that Europeans find themselves in as concerning "questions of the meaning or meaninglessness of the whole of this human existence" (C 6). According to Husserl, Europeans cannot see their place in a purposeful whole:

Men live entirely in a world that has become unintelligible, in which they ask in vain for the wherefore, the sense, which was once so doubtless and accepted by the understanding as well as by the will. [FTL 5 (5)]

Husserl maintains, then, that this crisis is at its most fundamental level a crisis of *value*. Europeans experience a loss of belief in those values previously determined by their view of humankind as part of a purposeful or meaningful whole, a view that gave meaning to their life.

Although the crisis Husserl describes, one felt on a massive or global scale, is the result of certain historical developments, such as the rise of technology with its disregard for value, and is precipitated by certain socio-political events that make one aware of the problematical nature of existence, such as the outbreak of World War I, the crisis is not by its *essence* a social phenomenon bound by particular historical or socio-political events. By its essence the crisis is much more pervasive that that, for it is related to the very constitution of humankind. Unlike much of their surrounding world, humans are not merely subject to natural and mechanical laws. They are not one event in a host of other events, but are also *witnesses*, onlookers, and are conscious of being such. This allows them to distance themselves from events, which, in turn, allows them to take their destiny in their own hands and to shape themselves. But this freedom to self-determination brings with it a sense of responsibility—it brings with it the question, *how* should I shape my life?

In the final analysis they [these ultimate questions of value] concern man as a free, self-determining being in his behavior toward the human and extrahuman surrounding world and free in regard to his capacities for rationally shaping himself and his surrounding world. [C 6]

It is because essence and fact have been separated that the question, "how shall I shape my life?," is left without an answer, for it rules out appeal to any essence one may have.

It must be understood that the problem is not merely one of having to choose between given values; it is one of establishing what, if any, the *criteria* of genuine value are. It is not that there are no values or standards of conduct to choose from, but rather there seems to be no satisfying *reason* for choosing one set of standards over an other. As mentioned previously, one may, of course, adhere to a set of rules or standards because it is prudent to do so or because they meet the necessities of daily life, but these are not *satisfying* reasons for choosing a set of standards. What seems to be needed is a justification beyond the facticity of one's particular life, a justification in terms of the whole beyond oneself and of which one forms a part. Hence the question of the criteria of value forces one to examine one's *total* existence. If the question is allowed to come to full consciousness—and frequently it is not—it can be nothing less than *radical*, for value itself, its ground and its meaning, is brought into question. The question, if it is *truly* a question, is experienced as an upheaval, as a *loss* of value, for in questioning the ground of value we suspend our belief in specific values. That is, questioning, if genuine, is by definition the very opposite of believing. Our confidence in specific values is shaken, for what we thought was absolute is now put into question. This has such an overwhelming effect on us because we feel we cannot live without (absolute) value grounded in or backed by reason. We feel we cannot live unless our life has meaning.

(c) ## The Crisis of Value as a Crisis of Reason

Generally one considers it the task of religion to address the question of the place of humankind within a purposeful whole—the Christian might think of God as the designer of the purposeful whole, for example—and one may think that the loss of belief in values that Husserl is speaking of is a loss of belief in religion. But this is not what Husserl means. The crisis is not of religion, at least not directly. The point at which humankind can no longer merely blindly believe in religion has already passed in the spiritual unfolding of Europeans according to Husserl—namely, the Renaissance. The crisis Husserl speaks of occurs in a state of spiritual development in which humankind has long since come to believe on the basis of *reason*. In fact, the crisis of value is a crisis of reason itself. It occurs at a point in time at which humankind has come to identify reason with science—that is, with science as it developed from its inception with Galileo and Newton, with science as a mathematization of nature (C 23). Humans turn to science to seek answers to these ultimate questions, but science does not address the question of the place of humankind in a purposeful whole, of the meaning of human life. *The loss of belief in values Husserl speaks of is the loss of belief in science or reason as a means to answering such questions:*

This belief that science leads to wisdom—to an actually rational self-cognition and cognition of the world and God, and, by means of such cognition, to a life somehow to be shaped closer to perfection, a life truly worth living, a life of "happiness," contentment, well-being, or the like—this great belief, once the substitute for religious belief, has (at least in wide circles) lost its force. [FTL 5 (5)]

As Husserl explains, because humankind believes on the basis of reason, and because science (reason) not only does not address these ultimate questions but considers them to fall outside its range of meaning, they remain unanswered. Humankind has, then, no way of dealing with those questions, which in a sense are most pressing to it. Reason is then seen in a limited capacity, for it does not seem to deal with ultimate questions. Reason is identified with science understood as a discipline concerned with the objective quantifiable aspect of nature and is thought not to deal with questions of the meaning of existence and life, which by their very nature tend to be subjective and non-quantifiable.

(d)   ## Science Rethought Must Answer the Crisis of Value

Because it seems to us that we cannot live without value, the question of the criteria of genuine value begs for some standard or norm of value. But where should one turn to seek the ground of value? As mentioned above, Husserl's answer is: to science. The question must be answered scientifically. Transcendental phenomenology is to reestablish human values by grounding the sciences in their unity (FTL 7 [7]). But how strange this claim seems, for according to Husserl the rise of science itself was in part responsible for the value-reason split, and according to him science does not deal with such questions. Husserl explains that seeking to rediscover human value by rediscovering the sense of science seems wrong, because science had nothing to say to humanity about humanity in its time of alienation or loss of value. It seems that science itself is, at least in part, responsible for human alienation, because it is concerned with either pure theory for its own sake—that is, with theory that does not reflect back on human existence as a whole—or with useful results. The question of human value appears to have no place in science.

While we would no doubt not want to do without the useful results of science, these do not in and of themselves tell us how to shape our lives. In other words, the paradigm of science is a narrowly construed pragmatics, one not sufficient as a guide to action. In that sense, science does nothing to help us and the rise of science can be seen as tantamount to the loss of value.

At the turn of the century artists especially lamented the rise of science and gave expression to this in their works. Hence the philosophical enterprise of discovering the sense of science as means of spiritual "salvation" was held under suspicion (C 137) for it seemed to entail exactly what it sought to remedy:

This way of looking at it makes it appear as if, once again, a new, purely theoretical interest, a new "science" with a new vocational technique, is to be established, carried on either as an intellectualistic game with very ideal pretensions or as a higher-level intellectual technique in the service of the positive sciences, useful for them, while they themselves, in turn, have their only real value in their usefulness for life. [C 136]

And:

Is it not the case that what we have presented here is something rather inappropriate to our time, an attempt to rescue the honor of rationalism, of "enlightenment," of an intellectualism which loses itself in theories alienated from the world, with its necessary evil consequences of a superficial lust for erudition and an intellectual snobbism? Does this not mean that we are being led again into the fateful error of believing that science makes man wise, that it is destined to create a genuine and contented humanity that is master of its fate? Who would still take such notions seriously today? [(C 289–90]

If this philosophical enterprise was held suspect in Husserl's time, it is much more so today. Science has drifted even further from its true sense—consider the moral dilemmas it presents us with—and the philosophic critique of scientific rationalism has proliferated. How can science, which poses a threat to the survival of humankind and which poses grave ethical problems, be said intrinsically to have questions of value at its center? How can it be said that we should turn to science for guidance in matters of value, including moral value, when science itself seems to be the source of so many moral dilemmas? Yet this is what Husserl seems to maintain when he advocates the ideal of philosophy as rigorous science.

How can we explain this? It is not the case that science in his day was closer to humankind; it is not the case that science was a source of humanity and culture in his time whereas it is not in ours. It was said above that Husserl maintains that the crisis of value is also a crisis of reason, of science. According to Husserl the science of his day, although high in practical value, has nothing to say to humanity about humanity (C 6). Yet he maintains that this is not because of the intrinsic makeup of science, but because science had strayed from its true sense (C 7). When he says that we should turn to science for moral guidance, he does not mean that we should turn to any de facto—that is, existing—science but he means, rather, that we must *rethink* science in order to find once again its true sense (CM 9 [50]), a sense that is, according to Husserl, the path to our humanity, to self-responsibility and even to God:

The present condition of European sciences necessitates radical investigations of sense. At bottom these sciences have lost their great belief in themselves, in their absolute significance. The modern man of today, unlike the "modern" man of the Enlightenment, does not behold in science, and in the new culture formed by means of science, the self-Objectification of human reason or the universal activity mankind has devised for itself in order to make possible a truly satisfying life, an individual and social life of practical reason. [FTL 5 (4–5)]

And:

Now, however critical and skeptical our attitude toward our scientific culture as it has developed historically, we cannot simply abandon it, with no more reason than that we lack an ultimate understanding of it and are unable to manage it by virtue of such an understanding—because, in other words, we are unable to explicate its sense rationally, to determine the true range of its sense, the range within which we can self-responsibly justify the sense of our culture and with our continued labor, make this sense actual. If we are not satisfied by the joy of creating a theoretical technique, of contriving theories with which one can do so much that is useful and win the admiration of the world—if we cannot separate genuine humanity and living with radical self-responsibility, and therefore cannot separate scientific self-responsibility from the whole complex of responsibilities belonging to human life as such— then we must place ourselves above this whole life and all this cultural tradition and, by radical sense-investigations, seek for ourselves singly and in common the ultimate possibilities and necessities, on the basis of which we can take our position toward actualities in judging, valuing, and acting. [FTL 5–6 (5)]

These excerpts from *Formal and Transcendental Logic* illustrate what an exalted status Husserl accords to genuine science. They illustrate also that according to Husserl the true range of the sense of science is "the range within which we can self-responsibly justify the sense of our culture, and with our continued labor, make this sense actual." Genuine science and genuine humanity are, then, for Husserl one and the same. It is clear that science in our time, as in Husserl's time, has lost its true sense. It is because science has lost its true sense that humankind is in crisis according to Husserl, and throughout all his writings he urges us to seek anew this sense.

(e) Transcendental Logic: Correcting
     Traditional Logic's Failure to be a
     Theory of Science

But what *is* the true sense of science and how do we go about rediscovering it? To have a sense of science means to have a theory of science. According to Husserl, a theory of science can be found already in Plato's thought. In Plato logic (dialectic) is concerned with the theory of science. Logic is the discipline whose task it is to seek the sense of science and to guide its development in light of this sense. Hence, if Husserl is correct, it is to logic that we must turn to seek a sense of culture and humanity.

How odd this sounds to the contemporary ear, for logic is not viewed today in that capacity. But then, according to Husserl, logic too has strayed from *its* true sense and no longer seeks the sense of science. Speaking about logic Husserl says the following:

Logic itself, however, has strayed utterly away from its own sense and inalienable task in recent times. [FTL 3 (3)]

And:

For this situation, as we have said, logic itself shares the blame—because, as may be added here, instead of keeping its eye unfalteringly on its historical vocation and developing as the pure and universal theory of science, logic itself became a special science. Its own final sense demanded that, reflectively, it make that final sense a theme for radical considerations and master the essentially differentiated strata of problems in the theory of science that predelineate the hierarchy of logical disciplines, in which alone the idea of a theory of a science—and science itself—can become actualized. But logic did not satisfy this, its own essential sense. [FTL 4–5 (4)]

In other words, the crisis of science is at heart a crisis of logic, for if science has strayed from its ideal it is because logic has failed to make this ideal explicit and has failed to guide the development of science accordingly. Instead logic has itself become a special science. Contemporary (traditional, objective) formal logic is not logic in its true sense: theory of science. What is needed is a discipline that will examine traditional de facto logic to reestablish *its* sense or idea. That discipline is phenomenology. Phenomenology works out the *Idea* of logic contained in de facto logic, but from which the latter has strayed. This constitutes a radicalization of traditional logic. In working out the Idea of logic, phenomenology attempts to bring out the true, that is, full sense of logic, and thus reestablish the sense of science. All of Husserl's phenomenology in effect *is* an attempt to rediscover the genuine sense of science as a means of reestablishing human value.

(f) How Science Strayed from its Ideal

The fact that Husserl speaks of science drifting or straying from its true sense, a sense that according to him, includes questions of value, suggests that he believes there was a time when science was closer to its true sense than it is now. Indeed, according to Husserl, science at its inception with Plato was close to its true sense and included a concern with value. In fact, science as we know it today—that is, a critical attitude of seeking legitimation for facts and theories by norms—was born with Plato out of questions of human value. More specifically, science developed with Plato as a response to the claim made by certain Sophists that we cannot have moral knowledge and that there are no rational standards or norms according to which we should shape our life.[5] Certain Sophists, of course, deny the possibility of *any* knowledge, for seeing that the natural science they take to be paradigmatic of true knowledge or rationality does not in fact yield knowledge, they become skeptics. But it is especially the Sophists' consequent denial of *moral* knowledge that is of concern to Plato. Because the Sophists believe that there are no universal rational norms according to which one should shape one's life, they advocate exercising concealed tyranny: self-development according to self-interest. This position is morally unpalatable to Plato, who responds to the Sophists by trying to show that knowledge or science in general is possible, which in turn entails the possibility of moral knowledge. He attempts to show the possibility of science as such by working out the *idea* of science:

Plato's logic arose from the reaction against the universal denial of science by sophistic skepticism. If skepticism denied the essential possibility of any such thing as "philosophy," as science, then Plato had to weigh, and establish by criticism, precisely the *essential possibility* of such a thing. If all science was called in question, then naturally no fact, science, could be presupposed. Thus Plato was set on the path to the pure idea. Not gathered from the de facto sciences but formative of pure norms, his dialectic of pure ideas—as we say, his logic or his theory of science—was called on to make genuine science possible now for the first time, to guide its practice. [FTL 1–2 (1–2)]

The idea of science that Plato establishes is that of a deductive system in which the ultimate premises are self-evident first principles (cf., e.g., *Rep.* 533c). In other words, "a science worthy of the name must justify each of its steps" (SHL xxxiii). In itself this idea of science does not relate to questions of value and self-responsibility. For it to do so it is necessary to place the ideal in context of Plato's metaphysics, in context of his theory about the nature of true (ultimate) Being. The way it stands, however, the ideal seems to be unconnected to any metaphysical system. Hence Bachelard writes that "one can characterize science in this way without presupposing any particular theory of science" (SHL xxxiii). But in Plato's doctrine this ideal is interpreted in a metaphysical manner—that is, in terms of his theory of ideas—which essentially links the ideal of science to value. According to Plato science yields knowledge of true Being and only the ideas have true being. The ideas are hierarchically ordered with, at their apex, as the highest idea, the idea of the Good. The Good is the direct cause both of the being of the ideas, of true being, and of any knowledge of them. Hence only the Good can be an ultimate first principle, and the ideal of science for Plato really reads: a deductive system in which the ultimate first principles are descriptions of the Good.

Only a science that has as its domain the ideas and ultimately the Good is *genuine* science, according to Plato.

That science is dialectic, philosophy itself.[6] Because science in this view starts and ends with the Good, it is at once concerned with value. Dialectic, at once knowledge of self in terms of the whole of existence, at once knowledge of one's place in the world, in other words, is not only not alienating but constitutes a radical enterprise of self-responsibility; it is a prerequisite for moral behavior.

At its inception, then, science was essentially linked with value. Husserl considers this a weak link, however, because of its metaphysical—that is, *speculative*—nature. Let it be noted here, to avoid confusion, that Husserl uses the term "metaphysics" in two senses. On the one hand, he means by metaphysical claims those that concern true Being, genuine value, genuine knowledge, and so forth, claims that are based on descriptive analyses. On the other hand, he uses the term in a pejorative sense to refer to claims that are but speculative portrayals of those ultimate dimensions of the world and experience—in other words, to refer to *speculation* as opposed to *description*.[7] Although Plato's link between science and value is a weak one because of its speculative nature, Husserl nevertheless considers Plato to be on the right path. It will be shown later[8] how Husserl aims to reveal the inextricable link between the ideal of science and value without invoking a metaphysics.[9] Hence, Husserl does not merely want to repeat Plato, but wishes to reinterpret him.

While in Plato value and science belong together insofar as science is the search for and grasp of the idea of the good, beautiful, and true, gradually in the history of thought this link becomes weakened. In Plato's thought, theory of science and science are aspects of one discipline. Theory of science reveals the ideal of science, which, in turn, serves to guide the development of science. This assures the link between value and science, because the theory of science reveals that science aims at true Being, which ultimately relates to the Good. But in Aristotle theory of science (logic) splits off as a separate discipline. This split is the beginning of the weakening of the science-value link. Even though, after having been suppressed in the Middle Ages, the Platonic ideal of science resurges in the Renaissance, the ideal undergoes a change in meaning due to the development of natural science. This development of natural science was it-

self made possible through a change in worldview. In the
new worldview episteme comes to mean knowledge of the
physical world as it is in itself, as opposed to how it appears
to humankind. This deepens the split between human value
and science.[10] While science with its practical results forges
ahead, philosophy, being concerned with value and meaning, is left behind. Philosophy fails to advance in any systematic way, its importance not apparent vis-à-vis the usefulness
of science.

It is to this crisis in philosophy that Descartes responds.
He tries to reunite value and science, philosophy and science, but inadvertently deepens the rift between them. Indeed, with Descartes Plato's ideal of science undergoes a
modification that changes the face of philosophy, a modification that ultimately leads rationality to suffer the fate of
rejection mentioned above; it leads to the loss of belief in
reason as a means to answering questions of human value.
While Descartes, like Plato, is advancing a rationality, his
ideal of science differs significantly from Plato's in that he
uses the Galilean model of science, according to which science is not intricately linked with value. Yet Descartes does
not seem to realize this, for in his mind the ideal of science
is somehow linked with value. The science that he *wants* to
develop is value laden. In fact it can even be said that
Descartes's primary concern is with value, his interest in
science as such being subordinate to value. Although he
shares the Galilean view of knowledge, he does not believe
that all being and therefore all knowledge is on a par.[11]
According to Descartes the highest type of knowledge is
ethics, and all other knowledge is but a preparation for
ethical knowledge. In other words, for Descartes all knowledge is ultimately concerned with value. He writes:

Thus, all philosophy is like a tree, whose roots are metaphysics,
the trunk physics and the branches which grow out of this
trunk are all the other sciences, which are reduced to three
principal ones, namely, medicine, mechanics and ethics, by
which I understand the highest and most perfect science
which, as it presupposes a complete knowledge of the other sciences, is the last degree of wisdom.
But as it is not from the roots or the trunks of trees that the
fruits are picked, but only from the extremities of their

branches, so the principal usefulness of philosophy depends on those parts which we can learn only last of all. [D 183–84]

According to Descartes, we achieve ethical knowledge through gaining knowledge of self. Through contemplating our selves we become aware of God, the ultimate cause of all Being (HR 152), the highest Good (HR 158–59). This in turn allows us to know our place in the world. Only this can lead one to correct action. Ultimately, then, self-knowledge, being the ground of value, is the highest type of knowledge, according to Descartes.

To prove the unity of science and value, then, Descartes must show that value and science are united at their source; he has to show that knowledge of the ego is at once the ground of value and the ground of science. But Descartes is unable to do either, for to meet this twofold aim he has to prove the existence of God, and his proofs for the existence of God are notoriously weak, presupposing what they aim to establish—namely, belief in God. If science is to be grounded in the ego, then all knowledge, including that of the external world, should flow from the ego. But Descartes can make the leap from knowledge of the ego's existence to knowledge of the world's existence only by invoking the veracity of God.[12] This requires him to prove God's existence. Hence the cognitive link between the ego and the world is tenuous in Descartes's system. His claim that self-knowledge is the highest type of knowledge, and the ground of value, is also dependent on his proofs for the existence of God. This is so because in his view self-knowledge is the highest episteme precisely because it is at once knowledge of God.

Furthermore, self-knowledge is supposed to be a type of knowledge of the world; it is supposed to reveal one's place in the world as well and how one is to act in the world. But this becomes dubious if the cognitive link between the ego and the world is tenuous. The claim that self-knowledge is the highest episteme, ground of value, then also becomes doubtful. Hence, Descartes is unsuccessful at uniting philosophy and science, in uniting value and science. It is because Descartes's entire program is dependent on his proofs for the existence of God, proofs that presuppose belief in God, that Husserl writes that "unnoticed prejudices directed his [Descartes's] meditations so that, viewed as a whole, they lacked the power to convince even his contemporaries" (FTL 7 [6]).

But Descartes does more than fail to unify science and value, science and philosophy. He inadvertently deepens the rift between them. This is so because, in accepting the Galilean model of science, Descartes inadvertently views the ego through this model. On this model, mind or ego is seen as part of the world, something to be studied in itself. But this means that the model cannot appreciate value, for value is not something in itself outside human experience but is typically human. Like Descartes Husserl will maintain that science is grounded in the ego, but he will argue that this is not the ego viewed through the model of objectivistic science. Husserl will argue as well that the ground or proof of the value of self-knowledge lies in the *structure* of mind itself, but that this structure cannot be appreciated through the model of Galilean/Newtonian science.

(g)   The Split between Philosophy and Science

That science could proceed without answering the questions of philosophy was taken as an indication that these disciplines were two distinct fields of study, and so philosophy and science go their separate ways. The Platonic and Cartesian ideal of philosophy as universal science falls. Science no longer concerns itself with metaphysical questions—that is, with ultimate questions of genuine being, genuine knowledge, genuine value, and so forth, but is led on only by its useful results. Husserl explains that in turning away from metaphysical questions, science turns away from questions of *reason*, for problems of *genuine* knowledge, *genuine* value, and so forth, are problems of the rational criteria for the identification of genuine knowledge, value, and so forth. That is, metaphysical questions are questions of the legitimation of knowledge claims, of claims concerning being and values, and asking for *legitimation* is an act of reason. To neglect these questions is to turn away from the demands of reason:

It [positivistic science] has dropped all the questions which had been considered under the now narrower, now broader concepts of metaphysics, including all questions vaguely termed "ultimate and highest." Examined closely, these and all the excluded questions have their inseparable unity in the fact that they contain, whether expressly or as implied in their meaning, the *problems of reason*—reason in all its particular forms. Reason is the explicit theme in the disciplines concerning knowledge (i.e., of true and genuine, rational knowledge), of true and genuine valuation (genuine values as values of reason), of ethical action (truly good acting, acting from practical reason); here reason is a title for "absolute," "eternal," "supertemporal," "unconditionally" valid ideas and ideals. . . . All these "metaphysical" questions, taken broadly—commonly called specifically philosophical questions—surpass the world understood as the universe of mere facts. They surpass it precisely as being questions with the idea of reason in mind. [C 9]

While for Plato reason or science pertains both to mind and world, when science splits off from philosophy a division of labor results. Science comes to study the world independently of mind; it no longer considers questions of mind to be intricately connected with its domain. Questions of mind are not only considered irrelevant to the progress of science, but are seen to impede the progress of science. But in excluding questions of mind from its domain, science excludes questions of reason as well, for reason is an aspect of mind. Philosophy comes to think of itself as the discipline dealing with mind. Indeed, when one considers the disconnectedness of the sciences and the humanities at our universities, one can in effect view the philosophy-science split as the mind-matter or mind-body split on an institutional level. But science can ignore questions of reason only as long as it engages in self-deception. Science can ignore questions of reason and mind only as long as it focuses merely on its results and turns a blind eye to questions about its own nature, as long as it fails to take itself as object of study, as long as it fails to become self-reflective. And science feels justified to focus on only its results because these have become the exclusive measure of its success. Philosophy, however, due to its *lack* of success, becomes a problem for itself (C 11) and so becomes all the more self-reflective. It becomes critical philosophy.

Were science to examine itself, it would see that science is inextricably bound to reason in terms of its origin (it is a product of human reason), in terms of its structure (science is a system of judgments ordered according to certain ultimate unifying principles and theories, ordered according to reason, in other words), and in terms of what it does.

In ignoring questions of reason, science becomes "fact minded" and strays from the ideal it had at its inception with Plato. This is why Husserl says that science did not always leave out questions of value and that "the positivistic concept of science in our time is, historically speaking, a *residual concept*" (C 9). No longer concerning itself with self-responsibility, no longer relating its results to human value, science becomes alienated and alienating. Its results, while not acknowledged to be human products, are considered to be capable of yielding a total worldview. This leaves no room for any model of human nature not based on the results of modern science. Science may not be interested in questions of mind or reason as part of its procedure, but it has implicitly judged the nature of mind by determining that it is to be studied by the method of natural science—that is, by the method whereby one studies any real object in the world. But this is to falsify human nature, for, as mentioned previously, humans are not like other objects in that they are observers and have a certain amount of freedom.

(h) ## Consequences of the Philosophy-Science Split: Differing Theories of Rationality

With the increasing power of science, philosophers have to take a new stand not only toward science, but toward their own discipline as well. They have to reassess both their role and that of science. What is of interest to us here is that these new stands reflect specific theories of rationality. The positions that develop are many and varied, and their respective views concerning the relation of philosophy to science are often far from univocal. Nevertheless certain dominant *trends* emerge. Some, such as Neurath, align themselves with science and come to view philosophy as a handmaiden to the sciences. In this view philosophy is not seen as a distinct discipline but as subordinate to science. While philosophy initially determines the language of science, viz., physicalistic language, once it has done this its task is completed and philosophy becomes obsolete according to Neurath. He writes:

All the representatives of the Circle are in agreement that "philosophy" does not exist as a discipline, alongside of science, with propositions of its own: the body of scientific propositions exhausts the sum of all meaningful statements. [LP 282]

And:

The physicalistic language, *unified language*, is the Alpha and Omega of all science. There is no "phenomenal language" beside the "physical language," no "methodological solipsism" beside some other possible position, no "philosophy," no "theory of knowledge" . . . there is only *Unified Science*, with its laws and predictions. [LP 293]

And:

But the objection to the expression, "philosophizing," is not merely a terminological one; the "clarification of the meaning of concepts" cannot be separated from the "scientific method," to which it belongs. The two are inextricably intertwined. [LP 283]

Others, such as Carnap, see philosophy as logic of science, not subordinate to science with obsolescence as its fate, as Neurath would have it, but as a discipline alongside science responsible for distinguishing scientific claims from nonscientific (metaphysical/speculative) claims. In *The Logical Syntax of Language* Carnap writes:

Apart from the questions of the individual sciences, only the questions of the logical analysis of science, of its sentences, terms, concepts, theories, etc., are left as genuine scientific questions. We shall call this complex of questions the *logic of science*. . . .

According to this view, then, once philosophy is purified of all unscientific elements, only the logic of science remains. In the majority of philosophical investigations, however, a sharp division into scientific and unscientific elements is quite impossible. For this reason we prefer to say: *the logic of science takes the place of the inextricable tangle of problems which is known as philosophy.* [LSL 279]

It must be understood, however, that when Carnap says that philosophy is the logic of science, he uses the term "science" not in the way in which Plato or Husserl do, as intimately connected with self-understanding, but in the sense of positivist science, science that studies facts independently of their relation to mind. Although the arbitrational role that Carnap assigns to philosophy places it above science, its domain is still the domain of positivist science. Hence Carnap's theory of reason aligns itself with the worldview of the scientist, which leaves out all concern with questions of mind as part of the procedure of science. Reason, then, is not seen as relating to self-understanding as it was with Plato, but is understood as the study of deductive systems independent of mind, as the study of formal logic. That philosophy does not deal with questions of human value is not seen as a lack by Carnap.

Still others, notably the existentialists, turn away from science, if not against it. But although the existentialists turn away from science, they have something in common with scientists: like the scientists, the existentialists reject rationality, considering it to be of limited human value. They, like the scientists, turn away from the Platonic ideal of the unity of mind and world in ratio. The reason for this is the following. The existentialists see that humankind is alienated and that this is in part the fault of science with its disregard for the question of what humankind is. They see more clearly than the scientists that the latter, in talking about their exalted "facts," are actually engaging in a rationality of sorts. These facts do not present the world, but are absolutizations of *one* way of encountering the world. Writes Camus:

I realize that if through science I can seize phenomena and enumerate them, I cannot for all that, apprehend the world. [M 20]

Now, rationality means various things, but whatever else it may mean, it also means being part of a whole. It is this aspect of rationality that puts it at odds with the concept of life, according to the existentialists. They maintain that one's life (livedness, lived moment) is itself unconditioned, that it cannot be placed in any context, for context or meaning is something that follows upon the fact of one's being alive. In other words, because it does not form part of an ordered whole, one's life is a *bare* fact, is arational, according to the existentialists, and may be the only genuine fact there is. In their view, then, science fails to present us with facts, for that which is part of an ordered whole is no longer a genuine fact.

No rationality can therefore deal with human existence, can give us self-understanding, according to the existentialists. Mind meets the world in existence, and this meeting is, contrary to Plato, not rational, but arational. It is not ratio that binds mind and world, as Plato would have it, but the absurd:

The absurd depends as much on man as on the world. For the moment it is all that links them together. It binds them one to the other as only hatred can weld creatures together. [M 21]

While we *desire* rationality—that is, a unifying worldview of which we would be a part—since all such views start and end with the brute fact of one's existence, according to the existentialists, we are denied a purely rational worldview. Life, while inviting desire for the rational, at the same time resists this desire. Because it cannot tell us about life, rationality serves only to falsify life, according to the existentialists, who instead exalt the notions of "play," "dance," and creativity" which are thought to do more justice to the structure of life.

(i) ## The Need for a New Rationality: Beyond Platonism

But, urges Husserl, if rationality has failed scientist and philosopher alike, it is because rationality has not yet been

properly understood. Both the objectivist and the existen-
tialist views dichotomize reason and life, each view emphasizing a different term of the dichotomy. Husserl,
considering this a mistake, wants to establish a new rationality by bringing out its true sense as *universal* science
(FTL 6 [6]). This new rationality would, as it were, fall mid-
way between the former two approaches.

It must be understood that when Husserl urges that we
rethink the true sense of science, he is not advocating
merely returning to the origin and regaining Plato's idea
of philosophy/science. What Husserl is proposing, rather,
is that we return to the ancient *motive* to philosophize, the
motive to seek the idea of philosophy/science, and reinterpret this ideal in light of the historical development that
philosophy and science have undergone, thereby giving it
a *new* sense. Hence Husserl says:

Rather—as the reestablishment of philosophy with a new universal task and at the same time with the sense of a renaissance
of ancient philosophy—it is at once a repetition and a universal *transformation* of meaning. [my emphasis] [C 14]

The aim is to establish a *new* rationality, not merely to
repeat the rationalist tradition. This is to be achieved by
bringing to light and working out the idea of rationality
implicit in the tradition but which the tradition itself did
not work out. It is picking up on something the tradition
"skipped," as it were. Thus in *Formal and Transcendental
Logic* Husserl establishes a new rationality by working out
the idea of logic implied in de facto logic.

It must be understood from the outset also that just as
the intended goal is not merely to repeat Platonism, neither is Husserl's method of working out the idea of logic
implied in de facto logic founded on an implicit acceptance of Platonic rationalism, for although it seems to express Plato's theory of participation—the theory of the
relation between fact and idea, according to which we
come to know the idea through its imperfect realization in
the fact—Husserl's notion of ideas differs significantly
from Plato's. For example, while it can be argued that for
Plato fact and idea are separate, the new theory of rationality that Husserl puts forth is one that unites life with

reason, fact with idea. Furthermore, although both Plato
and Husserl maintain the idea to be first and foremost latent, this has essentially a different meaning for the two.
According to Plato, prior to its incarnation the soul exists
in the realm of ideas and knows the ideas (Phaedrus
249B,C). At birth, however, they are forgotten by the
soul—they become latent, subject to recall in later life
(Phaedrus 250A,C,D; Meno 81C). Hence "latent" for
Plato means "forgotten."

In the *Crisis* Husserl too speaks of "the latent life of
depth" (C 120) and sometimes uses the term "unconscious" to describe the latency of ideas (e.g., C 237, EJ
279).[13] But while "unconscious" can mean material that
was once known and is now forgotten, it can also mean
material that has never been known, that has never been
subject to explicit awareness. One can, for example, perceive or draw inferences unconsciously (EI 216), where
what is perceived or inferred is *new* material. In other
words, unconscious material can be active material that *has
never been known,*—that is, has never been brought to explicit awareness. This is the sense in which ideas that guide
our development are latent or unconscious for Husserl.
Contrary to Plato, for whom ideas are known prior to life,
for Husserl ideas are *lived* before they are known.[14] It
would be illegitimate according to Husserl to speak, even
metaphorically, of a "point" divorced from incarnate life
at which the ideas are known.

Although for Husserl unconscious ideas of the life of
depth are initially not known, that is not to deny that they
can *become* known. In the *Crisis,* for example, Husserl
speaks of a "dimension of the living spirit that had to remain hidden" (C 118) but that "*can* be made accessible to
scientific understanding through a method of disclosure
appropriate to it" (C 119). However, this becoming aware
of ideas is not a matter of recalling something one had
prior knowledge of. The difference between Plato and
Husserl on this point, even if it is only a matter of emphasis, reflects a difference in their notion of objectivity.
When Plato says that the soul lives in the realm of ideas
prior to incarnation (Meno 81C) he is suggesting that this
realm exists independently of incarnate life.[15] If one thinks
that something is objective only if it has existential inde-

pendence of subjectivity, then maintaining the realm of ideas to exist independently of incarnate life is a way of ensuring the objective status of the ideas. Husserl, however, maintains that objectivity does not demand independence of the lived, incarnate dimension.[16] To say that the idea is first and foremost lived, as Husserl does, is to say that it is lived "in" someone. The ideas, unconscious at first, but which one tries to bring to explicit awareness, are "someone's." In other words, Husserl emphasizes one's lived *link* with the ideas. In so doing he stresses a personal, subjective dimension, despite which the ideas are objective.

The phrases "unconscious" and "life" used by Husserl to refer to ideas reflects the potency and dynamism that the latent ideas have in his view. To say that the unconscious idea is *lived* is to say that it exerts a force on behavior. For example, he refers to the idea of "the universally, apodictically grounded and grounding science" as "*the driving force of life* for the highest stage of mankind" (my emphasis) (C 338). Furthermore, the "region" of ideas, the transcendental realm, he describes as:

Spiritual functions which exercise their accomplishments in all experiencing and thinking, indeed in each and every preoccupation of the human world-life, functions through which the world of experience, as the constant horizon of existing things, values, practical plans, works, etc., has meaning and validity for us. [C 119]

Our actions, including those of a theoretical nature, such as the development of logic or science, are in part unconsciously guided by ideas, according to Husserl.[17] As with most unconscious material, one cannot become acquainted with the idea directly, but one must discern the idea from results, both practical and theoretical, that were motivated by it. This is why in *Formal and Transcendental Logic* Husserl seeks to come to know the idea of logic through an analysis of the tradition of logic deposited in the history of thought. His method there consists of a "teleological consideration of history" (C 73), reflecting his belief that history is the result of a doing implicitly guided by an idea (FTL 10 [9]). But the method of reading history as a text to be deciphered for its motivating idea is that of hermeneutics. In other words, in *Formal and Transcendental Logic* Husserl engages in a hermeneutics.[18]

Basically, then, Husserl's new rationality is one in which the "subjective" is reintroduced into science (logic), in which *science* is *humanized* and becomes our telos, a telos that Husserl describes as:

That of humanity which seeks to exist, and is only possible, through philosophical reason, moving endlessly from latent to manifest reason and forever seeking its own norms through this, its truth and genuine human nature. [C 15]

In *Formal and Transcendental Logic*, using a teleological-historical approach, Husserl finds that, although humankind came closest to its telos with Plato, it is not fully realized by Plato. Aristotle, in attempting to come closer to the telos, paradoxically strays further away from it. But according to Husserl there is contained in Aristotle's thought an implicit idea that, if followed through and developed, brings us once again closer to our telos. This is the ideal of pure science, not determined by any facts or any particular being, but open to all Being. This pure logic is not developed by Aristotle.

In what follows it will be shown how Husserl works out a pure logic according to the idea, theory of science, to achieve a universal mathesis consisting of a pure ontology, and how this is developed yet further by him into a pure theory of multiplicities: a theory of possible forms of theories and its correlate, the concept of a possible province of cognition that would be governed by a theory having such a form. It will be explained how this logic, which, it will be argued in chapter 7, has parallels with the logic of Frege, is not a pure logic, but still presupposes a world, albeit a possible world. To achieve a truly pure logic one needs to go deeper, to the pure transcendental ego where no world is presupposed, to a logic founded on the self-evidence of the pure transcendental ego. It will be argued that such transcendental themes are also found in Frege's work. These "subjective" considerations are necessary for logic to understand itself, according to Husserl, who maintains that the purely "objective" considerations found in traditional logic are alienating and preclude self-understanding. In the course of this work it will be shown on the one hand that the appeal to subjectivity does not entail psychologism; on the other hand that the notion of the pure transcendental ego as knowing is not an ideal construction, but one that can do justice to the speculative demands contained in the concept of life, that it can accommodate the phenomena of death, the unconscious, the body, desire, sexuality, and other selves. In effect, then, Husserl's characterization of phenomenology as an a priori apodictic science of essences is reconciled with his characterization of phenomenology as a concrete science of the life-world, and, correlatively, Husserl's claim that the phenomenological method involves intuiting a priori essences is reconciled with his claim that it involves the teleological-historical (hermeneutic) approach.

Because of its emphasis on subjectivity, Husserl's rationality/science is one deeper than that of objectivistic science. For Husserl knowing is not an activity opposed to or divorced from feelings and emotions, value, spontaneity, and creativity—characterizations usually attributed to the artistic mode.[19] It will be shown that phenomenology, to use de Muralt's phrase, "possesses an aesthetic structure." Husserl's science (phenomenology) shares elements of Nietzsche's new science (new rationality), a science in touch with life and open to Being, a science in which science and art merge. Because Husserl's notion of knowing (science) is open to and in touch with Being, knowing for him is an activity that heightens the sense of Being and increases Being,[20] leading to ecstasy.[21]

(j)   Approach of this Work

A few words about the approach and style of this work are in order. The reading of phenomenology presented in this work has been strongly influenced by the writings of André de Muralt and Suzanne Bachelard. According to de Muralt, Husserl was guided by an *implicit idea* of phenomenology, and all Husserl's writings constitute so many factual expressions of this idea. In the present work an attempt is made to bring to light certain aspects of the idea of phenomenology through an analysis of its adumbrations in Husserl's writings. In other words, a phenomenology of phenomenology is engaged in.[22] Applying the phenomenological approach to Husserl's work, then, means his writings will be treated as *continuous*—all Husserl's works are considered to be adumbrations of the implicit idea of phenomenology, the latter being a unity in a multiplicity. This approach, to quote de Muralt, involves suspending "the historical facticity of Husserl's intellectual life and, following the deepest intention of Husserlian method, work[ing] on the pure meaning of the doctrine" (DeM 6).

It is this approach of attempting to bring to light the idea of phenomenology that led to the focus on the theme of logic, for it involves looking for a unifying principle, a guiding idea or leitmotiv. That leitmotiv, it should be apparent from the introduction, is logic. The theme of logic is one that runs throughout the breadth of Husserl's philosophic career, from the early *Philosophy of Arithmetic* to his final *Experience and Judgment*. Even after *Ideas*, for example, which is generally thought to contain the heart of the phenomenological doctrine and which is not a work dealing explicitly with logic, Husserl returns to an explicit treatment of the notion of logic in his *Formal and Transcendental Logic*. An examination of the notion of logic in Husserl's writings will bring out aspects of the idea of phenomenology that generally remain latent.

The Idea of Logic Contained in the History of Thought and the Projection of this Idea to its "Limit"

Beyond Traditional Logic: Husserl's Aim to Develop a Truly Pure Logic

Logicians generally argue that formal logic is a *pure* science, by which they mean that it is a science that has nothing to do with factual matters. They maintain that formal logic is a science that is neither based *on* nor refers *to* factual matters. Hence, the realm of logic is considered to have nothing to do with "experience" or the "world," for these are both factual realms. By some the objects of formal logic are said to be *ideal* objects, such as propositions, functions, classes, and the like, or signs and expressions standing for these, such as sentences standing for propositions, predicates standing for properties, and the like; by others they are said to be meaningless symbols manipulated according to given formal rules. The claims of logic, which concern formal relations between these objects, are said to be *necessary*—that is, the denial of any such claim constitutes a self-contradiction:[1] it is inconceivable. The relations of matters of fact, however, are said to be *contingent*—the denial of a factual claim is not inconceivable. Consequently, logical truths are distinguished from factual truths in that the former are necessary truths while the latter are contingent truths; or, as it is also expressed, logical truths are analytic, as opposed to truths about the world, which are synthetic.[2] Hence, examining the relation between logic and the world, between

1

logic and experience, is frowned upon by the formal logician, for there is assumed to be *no* connection.

The belief that the realm of logic is radically distinct from matters of fact is a long-standing one in the history of thought, one that is *taken for granted*. Hume, for example, who instituted a radical skepticism that subjected all knowledge of factual matters to a great upheaval, did not extend his skepticism to logic, precisely because he assumed the truths of logic to be necessary truths, quite distinct from truths of fact. Kant, in turn, inherits this belief from Hume. Writes Husserl:

> How does it happen that he [Kant] regards a formal logic, with its apriority, as self-sufficiently grounded? How is it compre-hensible that he never thought of asking transcendental ques-tions about the sphere of formal logic, taken as a sphere in and for itself?
>
> That can be understood as a consequence of the above-mentioned *dependence on Hume implicit in Kant's reaction* against him. Hume directed his criticism to experience and the experi-enced world, but accepted the unassailableness of the relation of ideas (which Kant conceived as the analytic Apriori). Kant did the same with his counter-problem: He did not make his analytic Apriori a problem. [FTL 260 (230)]

It must be underscored that Husserl agrees that if logic is really a pure science, then its truths, logical truths, should not be derived from or based on facts. However, he insists that *assuming* or *claiming* purity and turning one's eye away from the world does not in fact produce pu-rity. Husserl maintains that, paradoxically, *because* the logicians have not analyzed the connection between logic and the world, between logic and experience, logic has not achieved its purity. The logicians have not seen that their logic implicitly presupposes a world. That is what Husserl calls a *positivistic science* (FTL 13 [12]), a science that harbors meaning consti-tuted by the subject, but which is not recognized by the subject as doing so. To gain purity in logic one must go *through* the world, according to Husserl; one must acknowledge the level in logic that presupposes the world, so that one can go beyond it to establish a truly pure logic in which no world is presupposed. By means of the phenomenological method Husserl aims to develop such a logic.

It must be understood that this does not mean that Husserl *rejects* traditional formal logic. Contrary to Ricoeur (CI 247–48), the phenome-nological attitude and the objective attitude, of which traditional formal logic forms a part, an attitude in which meaning is not traced to its source, have not been placed in opposition. Rather, thinking that traditional logic has not achieved true scientific status, Husserl aims "to provide an honorable status[3] for the traditional locutions [of formal logic] by new insights" (FTL 330 [289]). In other words, Husserl takes the demands contained in the concept of traditional formal logic seriously, especially the demand that logic be pure. He is in fact more extreme in adhering to the demand for purity than most proponents of traditional logic, purifying logic to the point where its traditional notions are strained.

(b) The Implicit Idea of Logic: Logic as a Theory of Science

Since reference to the world is *implicit* in the meaning of logic, according to Husserl, he attempts to make the meaning of logic explicit, thereby exposing its hidden presuppositions. In *Formal and Transcendental Logic* he determines the idea (meaning) of logic by considering the de facto science of logic, logic in its historical development. Understanding the idea of x (the whole) by means of the factual development of x (the part) is a teleological-historical, or hermeneutic, task. Husserl uses the teleological-historical approach[4] because in his view the science of logic is a categorial object (object of the understanding) (FTL 41 [36]) sedimented in the history of thought, one that continues to develop in time, its "end point" being an ideal point at infinity. Evidence for claims concerning the nature of this object, then, are the facts of the history of thought. Hence Husserl *must* appeal to de facto logic, the science of logic as he finds it deposited in the history of thought. What is the idea of logic revealed in the history of thought?

In accord with the general opinion on the matter, Husserl maintains that formal logic as a distinct discipline was established by Aristotle as the science of the assertive predicative judgment, as *apophansis*.[5] Aristotle does not use the term "logic"[6] for this science but calls it "analytics" (HFL 44). In fact Aristotle's analytics forms only part of a science much broader in scope than what we today consider to be formal logic. Whereas we consider formal logic to deal with the *formal* properties of judgments only, this broader discipline, expounded by Aristotle in the *Organon*, also considers nonformal properties of judgments—namely, the rules of judgment as employed in everyday dialog and public debating contests (rhetoric), what we would today perhaps call informal logic. But from the standpoint of present-day formal logic, the *Prior Analytics* and *Posterior Analytics* "contain Aristotle's most mature thought about logic" (KK 24). What motivated Aristotle to establish analytics? What function was this science to serve? What need did Aristotle feel that led him to found logic as a distinct discipline?

We know that Aristotle's philosophy is based, at least in part, on a critique of certain aspects of Plato's theory of Ideas. Unlike Plato, Aristotle does not believe that the ultimate reality is a distinct realm of ideas:[7]

> Again, it would seem impossible that the substance and that of which it is the substance should exist apart; how, therefore, could the Ideas, being the substances of things, exist apart? [*Metaphysics* 991b]

Aristotle goes so far as to say that "of the ways in which we prove that the forms exist, none is convincing" (*Metaphysics* 900b10). He is especially perturbed by the theory of forms because it can account neither for the phenomena of growth and change, nor for the supposed interaction between the Ideas and sensible particulars:

> Above all one might discuss the question what on earth the Forms contribute to sensible things, either to those that are eternal or to those that come into being and cease to be. For they cause neither movement nor change in them. [*Metaphysics* 991a10]

Of course, Aristotle's concern with movement and change arises from his concern with the study of nature, and he maintains that with the Platonic theory's inability to account for movement "the whole study of nature has been annihilated" (*Metaphysics* 992b5).

In light of Aristotle's reservations for Plato's theory of Ideas, it is not surprising that he does not accept Plato's method of dialectic as a method that yields truth, for dialectic *presupposes*, as much as it serves to prove, the theory of Ideas. As a scientific method, dialectic is a failure in Aristotle's eyes, for it is prejudiced as to the nature of Being. A truly *scientific* method concerned with revealing Being, however, should be neutral with respect to Being—that is, should be *open* to its nature. Such a method would not be dependent or based on any particular being, but receptive to all Being. In sum, what Aristotle objects to in Plato's method of dialectic is its implicit failure to respect Being—the theory of Ideas on which dialectic is based could not account for the marks of Being: growth and change—as well as its inability to *reveal* Being.

For Aristotle demonstration, not dialectic, is the method of science. Demonstration proceeds by means of the syllogism, and the study of the syllogism forms a major part of Aristotle's analytics:

> By demonstration I mean a syllogism productive of scientific
> knowledge, a syllogism, that is, the grasp of which is *eo ipso*
> such knowledge. [*Analytica Posteriori* 71b2 15–20]

There is evidence to suggest that Aristotle intended syllogistic demonstration to be the ontologically neutral method required for science.
That Aristotle intended demonstration to be a neutral method is indicated, for example, by the neutrality of the technical expressions employed in his logic and by the use of letters to stand for cores of
judgments. Aristotle's concern with neutrality of method is noted by
Bochenski:

> What emerges from the text is the complete neutrality of the
> technical expressions "term," "premiss," "syllogism," relative
> to any philosophical interpretation. For the premiss consists of
> terms, the syllogism of premisses, and the premisses are *logoi*,
> which can equally well mean utterances or thoughts or objec-
> tive contents, so that the way is open to a formalist, psychologi-
> cal, or objectivist interpretation. All these interpretations are
> permissible in regard to Aristotelian logic; the purely logical
> system excludes none of them. Guided by his original intuition
> the founder of formal logic so chose his terminology as to rise
> above the clash of interpretations to the level of pure logic.
> [HFL 45]

Husserl too notes that in the study of the syllogism, the tool of
science, Aristotle uses letters to stand for the cores of judgments, suggesting a desire for purity and neutrality:

> In the materially determinate statements taken as examples,
> Aristotle substituted algebraic letters for the words (terms) in-
> dicating the material: that which is spoken about in the state-
> ments, that which determines judgments as judgments relating
> to divers material provinces or single matters. [FTL 48
> (42–43)]

And:

> With this taking of the materially filled cores as indeterminate
> optional affairs—lingually, as indeterminate terms, S, p, and
> the like—the exemplicative determinate judgment becomes
> converted into the universal and pure form-idea: the pure con-
> cept of any judgment whatever that has, as the case may be,

the determinate judgment-form "S is p," the form "If S is p, the Q is r," or the like. [FTL 49 (43)]

It seems, then, that it was the desire to achieve neutrality, to establish a method free from presuppositions about the "matter" it was to judge, that led Aristotle to found logic. Stigen's reading of Aristotle supports such an interpretation:

If scientific discourse and argumentation itself were introduced by Aristotle as a new factor to be treated in relative independence of things and thoughts, it is natural that he should be the founder of logic, and the first to formulate detailed requirements of scientific arguments and principles, as well as of dialectical proofs and sophistical fallacies. [SAT 123, n. 1]

In other words, Aristotle's logic is motivated by a concern with science. But a stronger claim must be made: the motivating idea behind Aristotle's science of logic is a *theory* of science. As soon as one either has or intends to develop a science, one has an implicit *theory* of science. That is, in order to develop a science one must have a working idea of the object domain of that science, a working idea of a method for revealing the objects of that object domain, for achieving truth, in other words, and a working idea of "truth." These ideas all form part of a theory of science—that is, a theory of science is concerned with questions of object domain, methods of revealing this domain and its objects, questions of truth, and so forth. Aristotle's logic is motivated by an implicit theory of science and cannot be understood in isolation from such a theory. As such, Aristotle's logic implicitly *is* a theory of science.[8]

Although Aristotle aimed for purity in logic, he did not achieve it, according to Husserl. This is so because although in the *Metaphysics* Aristotle poses the *question* of the nature or essence of Being (as opposed to Plato's *assuming*, in Aristotle's eyes, the nature of ultimate realty), he, no less than Plato, is prejudiced as to the nature of Being. Aristotle reveals his predilection for *natural* science when he maintains that Being qua Being is primary substance, the concrete individual.[9] As the individual for Aristotle is an entity in the world, Husserl is led to say:

Aristotle had a universal ontology of realities only; and *this* was what he accepted as "first philosophy." [FTL 80 (70)]

Although Aristotle's logic seemed to *have* purity, as Bochenski observes, in that logoi or premisses (judgments) could "mean utterances or thoughts or objective contents, so that the way was open to a formalist, psychological or objectivist interpretation," nevertheless the judgment, whether construed as utterance, thought, or objective content, always reflects the structure of *reality* according to Aristotle, and reality is living nature for him:[10]

> Aristotle relates his analytics to the real world and, in so doing, has not yet excluded from his analytics the categories of reality.[FTL 49 (43)]

For this reason Husserl writes that Aristotle's formal logic "did not attain the full purity and breadth prescribed by its essence" (FTL 48 [42]).

Hence, while Aristotle believes his logic to be a pure method that reveals Being, because he has not freed his logic from being, but bases it on a prejudiced notion of being, he has not allowed logic to reveal its intrinsic nature, its purity. As long as logic remained wedded to the concern for truth, the domain of *pure* logic was kept from view. Only if one has a sense of the proposition in itself can one develop a purely formal logic, for in order to appreciate the purely formal dimension of the proposition one must be able to exorcise all material considerations. Because the judgment was understood in terms of primary substance or individual being,[11] Aristotle did not focus on the judgment in itself, the judgment qua judgment.[12] The Stoics, on the other hand, who, contrary to Aristotle, studied propositions and the relations between propositions more for their own sake and not primarily as a means for revealing the nature (essence) of reality—their logic developed out of a concern for dialog, or "everyday argumentative encounters" (HFL 113)—were able to develop a notion that comes close to that of proposition in itself—namely, the notion of *lekta* (FTL 82 [72]):

> Aristotle always remained at heart a pupil of Plato's, looking for essences, and accordingly asking himself the questions: "Does A belong to B?" But the Megarians start from the pre-Platonic question: "How can the statement *p* be refuted?" [HFL 108–9]

Consequently, although Stoic logic stemmed from that of Aristotle (HFL 108),[13] because of their focus—their focus on dialog concerns propositions par excellence—they developed a logic of propositions more formalized than the logic of Aristotle. The Stoics "understood formal treatment in a formalistic way, and laid the foundations for an exact semantics and syntax" (HFL 109).

It is only when the domain of the pure judgment, of pure logic, is revealed that logic can become a true science, for only then can one see its object and its nature, only then can one ground the science, making it a true science. Husserl explains how the concern for truth masks the different levels *within* logic, for example:

> Here it is a matter of a shifting of concepts and an equivocation that went on in the logicians' thinking, not for accidental but for essential reasons and that necessarily remained hidden, because they themselves pertained to the unity in respect of theme that characterizes the logicians' "straightforward" thinking, as directed to the critical evaluation of judgments according to the norm of *truth*. More precisely, they necessarily remained hidden because inquiry about the formal conditions for possibly *true* judgments necessarily proceeded on the systematic levels that we distinguished as theory of the forms of judgments, consequence-theory, and theory of truth. [FTL 178 (158)]

There is a paradox here. The concern for truth that leads to purity in logic also stands in the way of achieving that purity. Although pure apophansis stems from the motive of the theory of science, in order to achieve purity in apophansis this motive must be put aside. Since science is concerned with truth, and the study of the judgment in its purity leaves *all* consideration of truth behind, there is a move *away* from apophansis as a theory of science. Yet precisely this move is necessary to unite logic with its original motive, to work logic out as a theory of science. So, if in the aim for purity we have "left things behind," we know logic must return to things if it is going to become one with its motivational force, theory of science, for this is concerned with adequation to things.

Unless this motive is kept in mind, the result will be a pure logic removed from the world, a logic involving and dealing with a narrow domain, a seemingly impotent field of study. That is, if the idea of purity contained in Aristotle's logic is followed through and made the proper object of logic, it will lead to a narrow, limited domain. Its object will be the broadest concept of judgment, the judgment qua judgment, the judgment qua possibility (conceived in its purity). In other words, the logic implied in Aristotle's analytics is a very narrow field of study, one that up until Husserl's time had not been developed. Suzanne Bachelard suggests that it was in part the narrowness implied in its development that kept the logicians from developing logic in its purity:

> In our opinion, one can go so far as to say that it is a fear of recognizing its own limits that has, for so long a time, kept

formal logic from absolutely assuming its formal character.
[SHL 25]

But this narrow field turns out to be, not an end point, but an impetus for the further development of logic. Narrowness may seem to connote impotence, but the narrowness implied in Aristotle's logic is one that points *beyond* itself. It points beyond itself precisely *because* of its narrowness, its apparent limits, for it is the desire to go beyond the felt restriction that leads one to reexamine what motivated the quest for purity, for formalness, a motivation that led the discipline into its narrow domain. In that broader motive lies a way beyond the limitations one has been led to. That motive was the construction of a pure method open to Being, a method that could be developed only in connection with a theory of science, a theory concerning the question of what science or knowledge is, what Being is, and so forth. Seen in context of its motivational force, logic can be understood to *be* a theory of science. Once logic is understood explicitly as theory of science, it is seen that logic must go beyond its apparent limits, because it must, despite all its purity, deal with the world. Writes Bachelard:

> In fact the "limits" of formal logic are not restrictions that would give rise to a sense of impotence; they are rather determining factors which on the one hand enable us to carry out the formal program and on the other hand force us to see that there can be other logical tasks. "Formal logic cannot be the whole of logic: the full and—in a new and richer sense—formal theory of science." [SHL 25]

It is noteworthy that at the point in *Formal and Transcendental Logic* at which Husserl begins to develop the pure logic implied in Aristotle's analytics, it may seem as if Husserl no longer appeals to the history of logic but adopts an essentialist approach instead. There are two reasons for this. First of all, if Husserl appeals less to the history of logic at this point it is because the pure logic he envisions had not yet been developed.[14] Indeed, logic itself had made little progress beyond Aristotelian logic, for although a conception of a purely formal logic is commonplace in contemporary thought, at the time at which Husserl was writing the notion had not yet been developed.[15] Second of all, as Husserl works out the purely formal logic implied in the history of thought, he will at each step of the way *legitimate* the notions he develops. Legitimation is an indispensable part of the phenomenological method and involves bringing concepts to evidence by "giving birth" to them in an act of experience.

According to Husserl the grounds for any notion are located in one's experience, so "proof" for a given notion is achieved by isolating and focusing on the experience that gives rise to the notion in question.[16] Presupposed is that its giving rise was motivated by a reason. According to Husserl there are "deeply hidden subjective forms in which theoretical 'reason' brings about its productions" (FTL 34 [30]). Hence, one's actual cognitive doing, the re-creating of the originary experience, becomes one's legitimation. Of course, re-creating the originary experience is not the same as the original cognitive act; it is not mere repetition (FTL 177 [157]) for one is now aware that one is legitimating. In effect, it is a rebirth of the concepts in a living doing:

> They [investigations concerning the subjective in logic] all have the character of investigations fundamental to the *uncovering and criticism of the original logical method;* and indeed we can characterize them all likewise as *explorations of the method by which the "fundamental concepts" of analytics are produced originaliter*, in that evidence which assures us of their respective essences as identical and safeguarded against all shiftings. [FTL 180 (160)]

Hence Husserl calls such legitimation clarification "from the most original sources" (FTL 71 [63]). On a larger scale this original re-creating is the method of philosophy itself, according to Husserl, as will be discussed later (page 136). Because in legitimation the emphasis is on individual experience and not on the history of thought per se, one may mistakenly get the impression that Husserl has abandoned the teleological-historical approach. But in truth legitimation and the teleological-historical approach are both aspects of one approach, for whatever an examination of the history of thought yields, "the explication turns back to the intentionality of the *scientists* from whom the Objective stock of concrete scientific theory originated" (FTL 10 [9]). "The explication begins with the *theoretical formations* . . . and puts them back *into the living intention of logicians,*" writes Husserl (FTL 10 [9]).

This is where the distinction between an objective formal logic and a transcendental logic lies. According to Husserl the phenomenological method of grounding notions in subjective acts of experience is indispensable to developing a purely formal logic as a true *science,* for only this method will allow a radical grounding or legitimation of logic. When the tradition generally offers legitimations of logical concepts, it tends to do so with further reference to objective concepts, albeit of a higher level. Such an endeavor no doubt has its place, but according to Husserl this can never be "complete" legitimation.[17] It is the fear of psychologism, the fear of confusing act and content of act, that has led the tradition generally to base its proof only on "static" objective concepts:[18]

> If the general confusion was reduced to the extent that (over-coming the psychologistic confounding of them) one distin-guished *judging* from *the judgment itself* (the ideal formation, the stated proposition), it then was even less possible to set a senseful *problem concerning the subjective* as long as the peculiar essence of all intentionality, as constitutive performance, was not understood and therefore judicative intentionality in par-ticular was not understood as the constitutive performance in the case of the ideal judgment-formations—and, still more par-ticularly, the intentionality of evidential judging was not under-stood as the constitutive performance in the case of the ideal truth-formations. [FTL 206 (183)]

Husserl already uses this method of proving by doing in his *Philoso-phy of Arithmetic*, where it is criticized by Frege for giving rise to psycholo-gism (H-J 61, 62). To date the phenomenological method is still not generally accepted in formal logic for the same reason.[19] Husserl argues that while the type of evidence he offers in legitimating notions is *in a certain way* subjective, not all appeals to the subjective entail psychologism.

In *Formal and Transcendental Logic* Husserl proceeds according to this method of legitimation. In sections 12–15 of *Formal and Transcen-dental Logic* Husserl introduces three levels of logic—namely, morphol-ogy, consequence logic, and the logic of truth, which he subsequently substantiates by appeal to the evidence of "subjective" experience.

(c) The Three Levels of Logic—
Morphology, Consequence Logic, and
Truth Logic: Their Legitimation and
Limitations

As mentioned earlier, while the three levels of logic that Husserl intro-duces in *Formal and Transcendental Logic* are commonplace today, at the time when Husserl was writing they had not been articulated. The type of legitimation he offers for these distinctions, however, is typically phe-nomenological. It is the phenomenological approach with its emphasis on intentional striving (FTL 9 [8]), asking after "the unity of an aiming 'meaning' " (FTL 9 [8]), which will show the limitations of these three levels of logic.

We are all familiar with the phenomenon of being presented with a vague judgment that one subsequently makes distinct. It does not matter whether the vagueness is due to an unclarity in the utterance (FTL 56 [50]), as, for instance, when the words are mumbled, or, if there is clear articulation, due to an unclarity in the content, in the meaning of the words. Nor does it matter whether it is a judgment performed by another (FTL 69 [61]), or by oneself, as when something vague comes to mind (FTL 56 [50]). One may, for example, walk out on a film feeling vaguely disturbed, muttering "This film bothers me." One may then try to articulate what was disturbing about the film. It was not the acting; *it*, in fact, was quite good. But the characters were unsympathetic; they were unreceptive to each other. More specifically they epitomized a state of loneliness, a condition in which people exist side by side with no genuine interest in each other. The film offered no recourse from this state. It is this emotional wasteland that depressed one. In this case "I don't like the film" was a vague judgment, which was subsequently made distinct. When one makes a vague judgment distinct, one "has" something before one. One knows *this* is what is *meant*. One suddenly or finally "sees" it.

The criterion of distinctness is being able to *perform* the judgment, being able to bring the meant to mind (FTL 56 [50]) ("The characters were unreceptive to each other," "The film epitomized a state of loneliness," etc.). The distinct judgment is an *explicit* judgment. It is "an *explicit performance belonging to judicative spontaneity*" (FTL 56 [49]). By explicit performance is meant, among other things, "explicit subject-positing [the *characters* were . . .], of a positing-thereupon as predicate [. . . *unreceptive* to each other], of a passing on relating to another Object, which is posited separately [the film offered no recourse from this state . . .], or of any like process" (FTL 56 [49]). As Husserl writes:

> If the "vaguely," *"confusedly," judging process of meaning* something that comes to mind is followed by such a process of *explicit judging*, then we say, on the basis of the synthesis of fulfilling identification that comes about: The confused meaning or opinion *"becomes distinct";* now, for the first time, something is *"properly judged";* and the judgment, which previously was meant only expectantly, now is *properly* and itself *given*.
> [FTL 56 (49–50)]

So the distinct judgment is a *performance*, a *doing*. Insofar as we make vague judgments distinct many times a day without giving it a thought, the "movement" from vague judgment to distinct judgment is "automatic." But one can also make this movement *thematic.* One can thematize the process of making a vague judgment distinct. One can make this process the subject of analysis and ask what is implied in our making a vague judgment distinct. Making the confused judgment distinct implies that the meant, the distinct judgment, is evidence *of* something—namely, of the judgment in its vague, most basic form. It is implied that it is this (same) vague judgment that one has made distinct. The distinct judgment and the vague judgment are the *same* judgment (FTL 69 [61]). In other words, one realizes that there is something that remained the same from vague to distinct judgment, something one aimed at, an *objectivity* itself. After one makes the act of rendering a vague judgment distinct an object of thematic consideration, one gets a sense of the judgment as *object.*

In short, when our action of rendering a vague judgment distinct is made thematic, it is seen to imply a proposition-in-itself, P. Although in distinct judging one *aims* for the judgment itself, the ideal objectivity, one does not yet have an *explicit* notion of judgment-in-itself, judgment as object. An explicit notion of the judgment-in-itself is achieved only in a secondary act of reflection. In effect, then, *evidence* for the notion "judgment-in-itself" is a *performance*, a second-order reflective act that takes as its object the act of rendering a vague judgment distinct. In this second-order reflective act the notion "judgment-in-itself" is itself rendered distinct. This is why Husserl says that although the explicit judgment is evidence of an ideal objectivity, and although "this evidence is an original emerging of the judgment as it itself," it is "not yet an evidentially experiencing (act of) *seizing upon and regarding it thematically*" (FTL 60 [53]). The latter is a secondary act that leads to the realization that one is aiming for an object, the meant judgment, which remains the same from the vague to the distinct judgment.

The distinct judgment, then, is evidence of the vague judgment:

> With the transition, with the making distinct to oneself of what one truly meant in the vague judging process of meaning . . . with this transition the distinct judgment becomes given as an *evident mere explication of the true sense or meaning.* There comes to pass a coincidence of identity belonging to an originally peculiar type, which indicates a *fundamental type of "evidence."* This evidence, like any other (and "experience" in the widest conceivable sense), has its degrees of perfection and its idea— here indeed an ideal limit of perfection, at which the synthetic coincidence would in fact be absolutely perfect. [FTL 69 (60–61)]

This type of evidence, evidence of distinctness, is, in turn, differ-ent from evidence of clarity, the evidence *for* the distinct judgment being true or false (FTL 60 [53], 69 [61]). For example, "My brother John is in the navy" is a *distinct* judgment, but also a *false* judgment. Or, to use our earlier example, perhaps one has misjudged the film and some of the characters do in fact relate to each other in a meaningful way. Perhaps the film *does* show a way out of the emotional wasteland. One's distinct judgments are then false. It is because the distinct judgment gives one the judgment "in itself" and because it does not have to be true that Husserl says that the judgment itself does not have a claim to truth in-cluded in its essence, even though this is what we are naturally led to believe:

> It cannot even be said that, in the strict sense of the word, a
> *claim to truth* is included in the proper essences of judgments;
> and consequently it is incorrect to account this claim-concept
> part of the judgment-concept from the start. [FTL 196 (174)]

And:

> [The] predicate truth, or . . . falsity . . . is not a constituent
> mark of any judgment as a judgment. [FTL 197 (175)]

But not all vague judgments can be brought to distinction. "No triangle has three sides," for example, cannot be made distinct—that is, cannot be performed as a judgment. What is meant cannot be brought to mind; it cannot be "grasped" or "pictured." But does that mean it is not a judgment? On purely formal grounds there is no justification for say-ing that only a judgment that can be brought to distinction deserves to be called a judgment. The distinct judgment is evidence for the vague judgment. But if there is no evidence for a given judgment, and I cannot render it distinct, then nonetheless it is still a judgment. Although the vague judgment is not given in evidence, it, no less than the distinct judg-ment, is a proper judgment, for it is that which one worked on. The claim "no triangle has three sides" has the form P and not-P. The only criterion for ruling such a claim out as a judgment is its inability to be brought to adequation. But the criterion of possible truth or adequation is not strictly speaking a *formal* consideration. Hence Husserl says that while the *theme* or the interest of pure apophantics is the genus, distinct judg-ment—that is, "possible forms of true judgments" (FTL 53 [46]),[20] its *province* is the judgment in its broadest sense, the vague judgment, the judgment itself irrespective of any "ties" to reality or truth (FTL 70

[62]). Hence, while pure apophantics has as its "field" the judgment qua judgment, the judgment irrespective of any ties to reality, irrespective of any concern with truth, apophantics will be *interested* in a subsection of judgments—namely, in those whose forms could yield truth. This interest stems from logic's guiding idea, theory of science, which is concerned with truth.

The vague judgment, then, leads to an appreciation of the judgment qua judgment, the judgment in its purity, and from the standpoint of its *province* pure apophansis asks what formal conditions must be met for a judgment to be a judgment at all, in the broadest sense of the term. This leads to a categorization of different judgments according to their forms and the relation between these forms:

> The possibility of subsuming all judgments under pure concepts of configuration or form immediately suggested the thought of a descriptive classification of judgments, exclusively from this formal point of view: regardless, that is, of all other distinctions and lines of inquiry, like those concerning truth or non-contradiction. [FTL 49 (43)]

Thus simple and composite judgments are formally distinguished (FTL 49 [43]). The former are classified as singular, particular, or universal judgments; the latter as disjunctive, conjunctive, and causal, for example (FTL 50 [44]). Such a classification of judgments, if done systematically, leads to what Husserl considers the first level of formal logic—namely, morphology, a grammar of pure logic:

> Systematically consistent and clean execution of such a description would have permitted the sharp isolation of a peculiar discipline, first defined in the *Logische Untersuchungen* and characterized there as *theory of the pure forms of significations* (or *grammar of pure logic*). This theory of the pure forms of judgments is the intrinsically first discipline of formal logic, implanted as a germ in the old analytics but not yet developed [FTL 50 (44)]

Morphology, more than a static description of formation rules, of the relation between judgment forms, involves an appreciation of the *operations* by which judgments are generated from more fundamental forms, something not recognized by Aristotle, according to Husserl. The concept of *operation* introduced here is of great importance and more will be said about it in what follows:[21]

> If we have become attentive of the *point of view of "operation"*
> . . . we shall naturally choose the concept of operation as a
> guide in our investigation of forms; we shall have to conduct
> this research in such a way that it leads to an *exhibition of the*
> *fundamental operations, and their laws,* and to the *ideal construc-*
> *tion of an infinity of possible forms* according to these laws. [FTL
> 52 (46)]

An analysis of the operations whereby judgment forms are generated from simpler forms is undertaken for both simple and complex
judgments. In the case of simple judgments of apophansis, predicative
judgment certainties, the primitive form is "S is p," where "p"
designates a determination and "S" its substrate. In Husserl's view not
only is "S is p" achieved by an operation (FTL 52 [46])—namely, that of
"determining a determinable substrate"—but even "S" is achieved by
an operation, by an act of nominalization. Higher forms can be generated from the form "S is p" by an operation of reiteration. "S is p" by
reiteration yields "Sp is q," which yields by reiteration "Spq is r" and so
forth ad infinitum:

> This, moreover, should be emphasized expressly: *Every opera-*
> *tive fashioning of one form out of others has its law;* and this law, in
> the case of operations proper, is of such a nature that the gen-
> erated form can itself be submitted to a repetition of the same
> operation. *Every law of operation thus bears within itself a law of*
> *reiteration.* [FTL 52 (46)]

Hence the fundamental forms, says Husserl, are not side by side but are
graded one above the other.
    In the case of simple propositions, then, we look at the *internal*
structure of the proposition and see how forms are generated from more
basic forms. In the case of complex propositions, the component propositions are treated as unanalyzed totalities and the complex propositions are examined for connections *between* these to discover
fundamental forms of connection and how reiteration of these leads to a
generation of more complex propositions. Hence such formation forms
as the conjunctive and hypothetical Husserl calls fundamental forms,
"since they indicate *fundamental kinds of 'operations'* that we can under-
take with any two judgments or judgment-forms" (FTL 51, 52 [45]).
    It may seem a bit puzzling why Husserl would appeal to the inter-
nal structure of the apophantic judgment, "S is p," since it is something
he inherits from Aristotle, who thought it to reflect reality (FTL 49 [43]).

However, Husserl does not think that the structure is faulty, just Aristotle's *interpretation* of it. Frege too questions Aristotle's interpretation, but while Frege indicates his rejection of Aristotle's subject-predicate distinction by adopting different terms—namely, object-concept—Husserl retains the terminology but reinterprets it.

The second level of pure apophantics is consequence logic, the logic of noncontradiction. This level spells out the possible forms of true judgments, separate or in combination. It is still a purely formal level, for truth is not made thematic (FTL 54 [47], 55 [48]):

> In such inquiry one is *not yet concerned with the truth* of judgments, but is concerned *merely* with whether the judgment-members included in a whole judgment, no matter how simple or how complex it may be, are *"compatible" with one another or contradict one another* and thereby make the whole judgment itself a contradictory judgment, one that cannot be made "properly." [FTL 54 (47)]

The fundamental question of this level of logic is:

> *When, and in what relations, are any judgments—as judgments, and so far as mere form is concerned—possible within the unity of one judgment?* [FTL 64 (57)]

The third level of logic occurs when we make *truth*, adequation of the judgment to the affairs themselves, our theme (FL 65 [57]). While the first two levels ruled out nonsense and formal countersense, respectively,[22] it did not rule out material countersense or any other untruth (FTL 65 [57]). But, as Husserl says, one thinks of the judgment from the start as a vehicle for truth, as under the motive of cognitive striving. That seems to be its *function:*

> *Now* the judgments are thought of from the very beginning, not as mere judgments, but as judgments pervaded by a dominant *cognitional striving*, as meanings that have to become *fulfilled*, that are not objects by themselves, like the data arising from mere distinctness, but passages to the "truths" themselves that are to be attained. [FTL 65 (58)]

On this third level of logic one focuses on cognition, on the states of affairs that are judged, in short, on the "object" of the judgment. One realizes that any contradiction in the judgment rules out the possibility of adequation:

> *Truth* and falsity are predicates that can *belong only to a judg-*
> *ment that is distinct* or can be made distinct, *one that can be per-*
> *formed actually and properly.* [FTL 66 (58)]

Of course, in this realm we do not take a stand concerning the
actual truth or falsity of the judgment. What occurs here is that our perspective is altered, "new *thematic interests* emerge" (SHL 19). Instead of
focusing on mere judgments, we now focus on cognition:

> By attaining the formal logic of truth I do not *know* more—I
> *am* in another way. Hence I know better. I know that, beyond
> the questions to which the second discipline of logic is limited,
> there are other questions to be raised by another discipline.
> [SHL 19]

(d) Extension of the Idea of a Purely Formal Logic: Formal Ontology, Formal Apophansis, and Mathesis Universalis

From the perspective of truth logic, the judgment is seen in terms of its
original motive, that of cognitive striving, of coming to know the object.
And it is precisely science that aims to know the object. But if the judgment is a way of knowing the object, then knowing the object forms part
of the judgment's *essence*. Hence, a theory of judgment, logic, in other
words, should include a theory concerning the objects that judgments
aim at and concerning the relation between judgments and their respective objects, albeit from a formal perspective. In short, formal logic seen
from the standpoint of its motivating idea should consist not only of formal apophantics, a formal theory of the judgment, but it should include
also formal ontology, a formal theory of the object. Husserl explains that
what formal ontology is and how it relates to formal logic could not be
grasped until pure mathematics, algebra, had been developed. Only
then could mathematics be seen to be dealing not with number and
quantity per se but with relations between *any object whatever*—for example, relation of whole to part, identity, equality, unity, totality, property,
and so forth. To see pure mathematics as a formal ontology it had to be
unified (SHL 32). For example, while the determining concept in the theory of cardinal number is that of *unit* and in set theory that of *element*,
each is "any object whatever."

However, once pure mathematics is seen as formal ontology the relation between it and formal apophantics may not be immediately clear. At first one may be at a loss as to how to unite the two disciplines into one formal logic, for apophantic analytics and formal ontological analytics seem to be two distinct sciences, having different provinces— namely, judgment-forms and forms of objects, respectively. Upon analysis, however, their relation will be seen to be a close one. Judgments are *about* objects: they predicate properties or relative determinations of them. As well, all forms of objects, all the derivative formations of "anything whatever," make their appearance *in* the judgment and hence in formal apophantics itself. Formal apophantics and formal ontology both involve the same type of objects—namely, senses—ideal objectivities "produced" by subjective acts. As well, both pure syntax and pure mathematics are calculi.

Indeed, when looked at in this way formal ontology and formal apophantics seem *indistinguishable* as sciences (FTL 78–79 [69–70]; 110 [98]). And Husserl presents us with the following paradox: if we focus on formal apophantics as the science (theory) of science, then, since the aim of science is (knowledge of) the object, the domain of formal apophantics, strictly speaking, *is* formal ontology. Formal apophantics would become formal ontology. If, on the other hand, we focus on the fact that the objects that formal ontology considers are categorial objects and that categorial objects are always constituted in judgments, and, if we consider that *even though* the judgment aims at an object, the object is what it is only in the judgment, that judgments aim to determine an object province only given in the judgment, then formal ontology becomes formal apophantics. On a static level there is, in Husserl's view, no resolution to the problem. As will be shown next, resolution of the problem requires phenomenological considerations of the *aim*, or concern, of science. It requires a phenomenological approach because *aim* involves a subjective doing, and phenomenology, unlike traditional logic, can bring in "subjective" considerations.

Science embraces a *critical attitude*—that is, it wants to have *evidence* for its judgments. It is an attitude in which it is known that both the judgment and the evidence for the judgment may be wrong. Hence in the critical attitude the judgment is treated as *supposed*, as needing verification. The critical attitude, in short, treats the judgment as a *meaning* or *sense*. Nevertheless science per se does not *thematize* meaning or sense as such; logic does. Science aims to verify its judgments; it aims at the true judgment. It turns to logic to provide it with norms to help it do so (SHL 71), for science consists of judgments in a certain relation to each other—that is, judgments organized according to theories. Hence formal apophantics, working at the service of science, focuses on judgments qua judgments, with the implicit goal of verifying them. The apophantic focus is an intermediary one, at the service of the aim of science. The end focus is *knowledge of the object*.

And here lies the *difference* between pure mathematics and formal apophantics. Unlike pure mathematics, formal apophantics was always part of a broader concern with truth. Husserl maintains that this is why mathematics can become a mere game, and logic, in its true sense, cannot. The relation of logic to truth prevents it from becoming a mere game. But pure mathematics can be seen as formal ontology only if it is inserted into the broader concern with the possible forms that objects that *are* could take. In other words, formal apophantics and formal ontology are not reducible to each other but are both moments of science, of the endeavor to attain knowledge of the object. Here we have the reemergence of Leibniz's mathesis universalis. If logic, an enlarged logic, mathesis universalis, is the theory of science, it will envelop both formal apophantics and formal ontology.

But one can carry the idea of a pure science further. Science does not consist of an arbitrary combination of judgments. Rather the judgments of science are *unified*. In the case of pure, abstract sciences, such as pure geometry, this unity is determined by certain principles or laws. All the judgments of such a science can be derived from basic axioms, and the objects of abstract sciences are defined by these lawful operations. In such a science, truth is analytic consequence from a priori principles. Hence in abstract sciences such as pure geometry, or, as Husserl calls them, nomological sciences, axioms determine both the *province* and the *theory form*. This is why Husserl, when he speaks of the theory of multiplicities, means both the province and the theory of a nomological science. "A multiplicity is not only a mere 'set' (*ensemble*) of objects but rather a set determined specifically by the fact that it is subject to a form of nomological theory" (SHL 47). Hence a formal theory of science is also concerned with a theory of possible forms of theories, and with its correlate, "the concept of *any possible province of cognition that would be governed by a theory having such a form*" (FTL 91 [79]), something the mathematician calls a multiplicity (*Mannigfältigkeit*). While the lower level of logic deals with pure forms of significational expressions found *within* science (from the perspective of formal apophantics: judgment-forms, argument-forms, proof-forms, for example; from the formal ontological perspective: any objects whatever, any sets whatever and their relationships, etc.), the theory of multiplicities focuses on entire judgment systems, systems that make up the unity of a possible deductive theory. Any nomological science can be reduced to a theory form through formalization. The theory of multiplicities then appears as the

highest level of logical analysis, and constitutes a full, entire logical analytics (FTL 99 [87]).

In taking the idea of science to a theory of multiplicities, Husserl
has taken the idea of a pure (analytically formal) science to its limit. But
here the limit betrays a *lack*. It was said that it is our concern with truth,
with science, that allows us to unite formal apophantics and formal ontology in one mathesis universalis. From the perspective of a theory of
science, formal apophantics and formal ontology are correlates of one
science—namely, logic, theory of science. But although mathesis universalis is motivated by a concern with science, mathesis universalis cannot
finally be *the* theory of science, for it cannot account for *concrete* science;
in other words, it cannot talk about the world. Mathesis universalis is a
theory of nomological science.

But *in fact* we distinguish between concrete and nomological
sciences. The unity of concrete sciences, unlike that of nomological sciences, is not determined by axioms or laws, but by the *object*, and there
can be no question of deriving all the judgments of a concrete science.
Truth is not analytic consequence from a priori principles but adequation to the thing (DeM 72). But, Husserl urges, this distinction between
nomological and concrete science is not an analytic distinction, and so is
not one that can be made from the standpoint of pure analytics alone:

> Thus logic, as analytics, is *not equipped with any ready-made dis-
> tinction among sciences*, like the usual distinctions between con-
> crete (descriptive) and abstract ("explanatory") sciences or any
> other distinction that may be proposed. By its own resources it
> can attain only the cognition that, conceived with formal uni-
> versality, an open plurality, or "multiplicity," of objects is for-
> mally conceivable as having *this* particular determination: that
> it is a definite mathematical multiplicity and that, correlatively,
> the propositions conceived with formal universality as jointly
> holding good for it have a constructional (deductive) system-
> form. [FTL 103 (91)]

While mathesis universalis is motivated by a concern with science,
science that deals with true Being, it finally cannot be a total theory of
science, logic in the true sense of the word, for it cannot talk about the
world. But, paradoxically, as Husserl shows, even this pure analytic logic,
this mathesis universalis, which cannot speak about the world, still presupposes the world. This shall be explained in the next chapter. To Husserl this means that a deeper scientific attitude exists than that of
analytics. That deeper science is transcendental phenomenology.

2

That, and in What Way, the Judgment is Dependent upon Experience: The Need for a Theory of Experience in any Theory of Judgment

(a) Mathesis Universalis Presupposes the World and Experience

When logic is worked out according to the idea of purity under the guiding idea of theory of science, we end up with a logic that has elements in common with contemporary logic, specifically with that of Frege and Carnap. But, as will be argued in this chapter, according to Husserl this logic still presupposes not only the world but experience. The latter introduces a subjective element into logic. It will be seen that the judgment is governed by material conditions, that its sense is dependent on a certain material lawfulness, and that the judgment implies experience both as its ground and as its aim.

(b) That the Judgment Sense is Dependent on a Certain Material Lawfulness

Logic deals with judgment senses, albeit under the notion of theory of science. But the phrase "judgment sense" can be taken in two ways:

> Thus the concept of sense has, in the judgment-sphere, an essentially *double sense*. [FTL 217 (193)]

On the one hand, "sense of judgment" refers to the judgment *as a whole*. Understood in this way the judgments, "It is possible that the tree is in bloom," "It is certain that the tree is in bloom," and "It is not true that the tree is in bloom" all have different senses. On the other hand, "sense of judgment" can also refer, not to the total judgment, but to *part* of the judgment—namely, to the part Husserl calls the "matter" or "content" of the judgment. By the "matter" of a judgment Husserl means that part of the judgment devoid of belief (thetic) character. The matter of an act determines the object of consciousness and what it grasps it as. "It is the act's matter that makes its object count as this object and no other," writes Husserl (LI 589). The belief character of a judgment Husserl calls the judgment's "quality"; it is the manner in which an object is posited, the manner in which it is thought to exist—for example, in memory, in perception, in phantasy, and so forth. If one understands the judgment sense to be the matter of an act, the above judgments would all be considered to have the same sense, "the tree is in bloom," for the modal operators and the negation, being belief characters, would not form part of the sense of the judgments. The judgments would, however, have different qualities associated with them—possibility, certainty, and negation, respectively:

> As the *sense* of a statement, one can understand—
> Firstly, the corresponding *judgment*. But, if the person who makes the statement goes on from the simple certainty, "S is *p*," to the uncertain presuming, the considering probable, the doubting, the affirmation or the denying rejection, or the assumption, of the same "S is *p*," there stands out—
> Secondly, as the judgment-sense, the *"judgment-content"* as *something common*, which remains identical *throughout the changes in the mode of being* (certainty, possibility, probability, questionability, "actuality," nullity) and, on the subjective side, the changes in the mode of doxic positing. This *identical What* in the judgment—throughout the changing modifications of the primitive mode, doxic certainty—, this that, in the particular case, "is," or is possible, probable, questionable, and so forth, the *Logische Untersuchungen* apprehended as a non-self-sufficient moment in the judgment-modalities. [FTL 216–17 (192–93)]

The "matter-quality" distinction that Husserl applies to judgments is one he borrows from Brentano, who uses it to bring out the nature of intentionality. According to Brentano, intentionality, being related to an object, distinguishes a phenomenon as a mental phenomenon; it is the essence of mind. It, in turn, is made possible by "mere presentation," the content or matter of an act, Brentano maintains:

> Every mental phenomenon is characterized by what the Scholastics of the Middle Ages called the intentional (or mental) in-existence of an object, and what we might call, though not wholly unambiguously, reference to a content, direction toward an object (which is not to be understood here as meaning a thing), or immanent objectivity. Every mental phenomenon includes something as object within itself, although they do not all do so in the same way. In presentation something is presented, in judgement something is affirmed or denied, in love loved, in hate hated, in desire desired and so on. . . . We can, therefore, define mental phenomena by saying that they are those phenomena which contain an object intentionally within themselves. [PES 88–89]

According to Brentano my acts of perceiving the cherry tree, loving the cherry tree, fantasizing the cherry tree, dreaming of the cherry tree, all have in common the fact that they are directed to an object— namely, the cherry tree. This being directed to the object, "mere presentation," is the essence of intentionality in Brentano's view:

> Accordingly, we may consider the following definition of mental phenomena as indubitably correct: they are either presentations or they are based upon presentations. [PES 85]

While not all intentionality in Brentano's view is *mere* presentation, no particular *mode* of presentation is basic or fundamental to mental phenomena, according to him. Brentano defines intentionality as presentation independently of the mode of presentation; his definition of presentation cuts across modes of presentation (e.g., perception, phantasy, desire, loving), in other words. This leads Husserl to say that Brentano means by "mere presentation," or matter of an act, that part of an act devoid of belief character:

> Among cases of "mere presentation" we must include, following Brentano, all cases of mere imagination, where the apparent object has neither being nor non-being asserted of it . . . as well as all cases where an expression, e.g., a statement, is well understood without prompting us either to belief or disbelief. It is mainly by contrast with such a "belief-character," whose

addition perfects judgement, that the notion of mere presentation can be elucidated. [LI 599]

Writes Levinas:

> According to Husserl, by [re]presentation Brentano means the
> act which Husserl later calls a "neutralized act," whose nature
> consists in presenting a mere image of an object in which the
> object appears independently of any claim to exist or not exist.
> Any Humean character or "belief" is missing. The image floats
> before us without our deciding about its existence or non-exis-
> tence [TIHP 58]

Hence Husserl says that according to Brentano:

> *Each intentional experience—is either a presentation* [i.e., a *mere*
> presentation] *or based upon underlying presentations.* [LI 598]

Inasmuch as Brentano considers mere presentation to be the essence of mind, he applies the matter-quality distinction to *every* act of
consciousness and its products (to imagination, perception, recollection,
to name a few) and not merely to judging. Although the distinction is
here applied to judgments and will be evaluated in terms of judgment
theory, because the judgment is an example of intentionality in general
(FTL 263 [232]) according to Husserl,[1] it will be a means of evaluating
the distinction as a characterization of the essence of mind, or intentionality, in general.

Applying the matter-quality distinction to judgments, then, we
get two notions of judgment sense: in the first notion of judgment sense
the unity of matter and quality of the judgment is taken to be the sense of
the judgment; in the second notion of judgment sense only the matter is
taken to be the sense of the judgment. That the distinction between the
two notions of judgment sense is legitimate, that is to say, that it is not
spurious, can be seen from the fact that it is not immediately clear which
notion of judgment sense we are referring to when we say logic deals
with the judgment sense. Indeed, a case could be made for either notion
of judgment sense. The judgment senses with which logic deals are *meanings*. Hence, on the one hand, intuitively it seems correct to understand
by judgment sense the total judgment, that is, matter plus quality, since
expressions of quality—in our examples the modal operators and the
negation—seem to form part of the *meaning* of the judgment. On the
other hand, since logic, the science of judgments, is traditionally held to

exclude subjective factors from its domain, it seems that we should take sense of judgment to refer only to the matter of the judgment, for belief characters are generally considered to be subjective factors.[2] There seems, then, to be a narrow way to understand "judgment sense"— namely, as the matter of the judgment, as well as a broader way— namely, as the matter plus quality of the judgment. There are also other grounds for maintaining that there are two senses of judgment sense. The two notions of judgment sense stand in a specific relation to each other: the broader notion is dependent on the narrower. More specific- ally, the unitary effectibility of the judgment *content* is a condition for the effectibility of the total judgment itself:

> The unitary effectibility of the judgment-content is prior to, and a condition for, the effectibility of the judgment itself. Or: the ideal "existence" of the judgment-content is a presupposition for, and en- ters into, the ideal "existence" of the judgment (in the widest sense, that of supposed categorial objectivity as supposed). [FTL 217 (193)]

Furthermore, the narrower concept of judgment sense, the matter of the judgment, is restricted by specific conditions of meaningfulness. As will be explained next, it is by examining these conditions that logic can be seen to presuppose the world.

It is assumed in formal logic that every judgment that meets the rules of syntax and noncontradiction can be brought to adequation— that is, can be brought to evidence—and found to be either true or false. This is known as the law of excluded middle. This law is assumed to hold universally for all judgments. But Husserl shows this not to be the case. If the matter of the judgment fails to meet certain conditions of sense not specified either by the rules of syntax or by the law of noncontradic- tion, the law of excluded middle will not apply to it. Examples of such judgments are "the king is cloudy" and "this color plus one makes three" (FTL 216 [192]). These judgments meet the requirements of the rules of syntax. While the rules of syntax will rule out such a judgment as "king and or bald," it will not rule out the two sentences above, for they are syntactically sound. Nor are these judgments ruled out by the law of noncontradiction, for their senselessness places them above the law of noncontradiction. For sentences like these the law of noncontradiction simply does not hold. Because they are senseless, they cannot be made into distinct judgments and so cannot be brought to adequation. They are neither true nor false. As Husserl says, for such judgments the law of excluded middle does not hold, because *"the 'middle' is not excluded"*

(FTL 220 [196]). The rules of syntax and noncontradiction are rules that prevent the formation of nonsense (*Unsinn*) and countersense (*Wider-sinn*), respectively. Here, however, we are dealing with a third type of sense. What conditions restrict the sense of the judgment content? What determines the unity of the judgment content?[3]

By examining judgments that are beyond the law of excluded middle, Husserl comes to the conclusion that the condition of sense for the judgment content is related to the syntactical *stuffs*, that it is determined by the cores being *materially* related. For the judgment content to make sense, the cores must "have 'something *to do with each other*' *materially*" (FTL 219 [195]). In other words, the judgment presupposes a unified "world" (EJ 39):

> *Prior* to all judging, there is a universal experiential basis. It is always presupposed as a *harmonious unity of possible experience*. In this harmony, everything has "to do" materially with everything else. [FTL 218 (194)]

And:

> Thus, *in respect of its content, every original judging* and every judging that proceeds coherently, has *coherence by virtue of the coherence of the matters in the synthetic unity of the experience*, which is the basis on which the judging stands. [FTL 218 (194)]

And:

> Apriori the syntactical stuffs of each possible judgment and of each judgingly combinable judgment-complex have an intentional relatedness to the unity of a possible experience—correlatively to a unitarily experienceable materiality. [FTL 219 (195)]

It is only if the cores are related materially that the law of excluded middle applies to a judgment, for only such a judgment can make sense—provided, of course, that it also adheres to the rules of syntax and noncontradiction—and it is only if a judgment makes sense that it can be matched against experience and thereby be brought to adequation or negation:

> *If the principles of logic were to relate to judgments universally, they would not be tenable, certainly not the law of excluded middle. For*

all judgments that are "senseless" in respect of content violate
this law.

The principles, to make this evident first of all, *hold good* unconditionally *for all judgments whose cores are congruous in respect
of sense*—that is: all judgments that fulfill the conditions for
unitary sensefulness. For, in the case of these judgments, it is
given *a priori*, by virtue of their genesis, that they relate to a
unitary experiential basis. Precisely because of this, it is true of
every such judgment, in relation to such a basis, either *that it
can be brought to an adequation* and, with the carrying out of the
adequation, either the judgment explicates and apprehends
categorially what is given in harmonious experience, or else
that it leads to the negative of adequation: it predicates something that, according to the sense, indeed belongs to this
sphere of experience; but what it predicates conflicts with
something experienced. [FTL 220 (196)]

Judgments that fulfill the conditions for unitary sensefulness,
then, presuppose a unified world. Logic, being the science of such judgments, thus presupposes a unified world as well. It will not do to deny
that the law of excluded middle needs to hold for logic, for if logic is the
method and theory of science and has been developed according to the
idea of science, then the law of excluded middle must hold for it. After
all, a system that contains judgments that are neither true nor false or
are capable of being both true and false at one and the same time, is a
system from which anything can be derived, as Popper[4] has shown. In
short, such a system is one that violates the very ideal of science and
hence violates the very principles that govern the system. But given
purely formal considerations, the law of excluded middle does not without further ado hold. In other words, Husserl sees that logic is founded
on a presupposition of which it is not aware. It presupposes the world.
"All the judgments, truths, sciences, of which this logic speaks, relate to
this existing world" (FTL 224 [198]), writes Husserl. And that this world
presupposed by logic is a *possible world* makes no difference (FTL 224ff.
[199ff.]; EJ 39).

At first sight Husserl's claim that the condition of sense for the
judgment content is related to syntactical stuffs, that it is determined by
the cores being *materially* related, seems decidedly unformal-logical and
indeed even un*phenomenological*. According to this view the universal status of the laws of logic depend on material conditions, on the core stuffs.
This seemingly goes against traditional formal logic, in that it maintains a
sharp distinction between empirical and formal realms, considering formal logic to be concerned with form only. It considers logic to be a pure,

not an empirical, science. Logic, to be pure, cannot be based on material factors. Hence traditional logic considers only syntactical forms (EJ 25).

The claim sounds unphenomenological because it seems that sense or intentionality is made dependent upon material factors *given* to the ego, thus violating the principle that the ego is the founder of all sense. One might mistake this for a naive empiricism. In fact, it is highly likely that one will take this for a naive empiricism because "world" *has* the sense of being already "there" for us, of being given to us (EJ 30ff.). It *seems* as if Husserl is saying that the "S" and "p" are linked in the judgment because they are linked in the world, that the unity of the judgment is based on the unity of the world.[5] It seems as if he is saying that the world "automatically" presents "S" and "p" as linked, that the judgment merely reflects a material, empirical link, that it merely copies a link in the world. This would be contrary to the demands both of formal logic and phenomenology. And this is not what Husserl means, as will be explained below.

That the judgment presupposes a world was seen by analyzing a type of nonsense. But the judgment can also be shown to be dependent on experience. When viewed from the proper logical perspective, theory of science, the judgment will be seen to imply experience as its *ground* and as its aim.

(c)   That the Judgment Implies Experience as its Ground and as its Aim

Formal logic deals with the formal aspects of judgments. It treats the components of judgments as empty cores, as indeterminate "mere anythings whatever" (FTL 202 [179]). These empty cores enter into such laws of logic as, for example, those that deal with the generation of judgments from more basic judgments. But Husserl points out that "we must note the *relativity* in which these laws leave *the indeterminately universal cores*" (FTL 202 [179]). These cores may contain syntactical structures. For example, the "S" in the form "S is p" could be formally instantiated by "S which is a," by "S which is in relation to Q," or by "S which is a and b," and so forth. In each of these, in turn, "S" could contain syntactical structures. The same applies to the predicate "p": it may contain syntactical structures (e.g., "p which is q").

It has already been noted in chapter 1 how judgments relate hierarchically to each other. This hierarchical relation is one of judgments being generated from lower level judgments. "S which is p, is r" is generated from "S is p," for example. "P is q" is generated from "S is p" by nominalizing the predicate, to give another example. Understood in this way, all sense formation has a logical history of sense genesis (FTL 207 [184]).[6] When considering such a hierarchical ordering of judgments, one is automatically led to the a priori idea of ultimate judgments containing ultimate cores, cores containing *no syntactical structures:*

> But it can be seen a priori that *any actual or possible judgment*
> *leads back to ultimate cores* when we follow up its syntaxes; ac-
> cordingly that it is a syntactical structure built ultimately,
> though perhaps far from immediately, out of *elementary cores,*
> *which no longer contain any syntaxes.* [FTL 202–3 (180)]

For mathesis universalis these nonsyntactical cores are of no particular *interest* (FTL 203 [180]). They are merely implied by ultimate judgments. They are of no greater significance than the generated structures. However, when we step into the attitude of logic as theory of science—the true sense of logic, according to Husserl—these ultimate substrates take on great importance. In the attitude of logic as theory of science, it will be recalled, logic, the theory of judgments, was not intended to deal with mere senses, but was intended to deal with judgment senses *as a means to truth,* with knowledge of existents. It is only when, in the attitude of logic as theory of science, we are led beyond the judgment sense that these ultimate cores take on significance (FTL 203 [180]). It is then that we realize that these ultimate cores refer to ultimate *substrates,* individual *objects,* which, since the judgment is *about* them, are *prior* to all judging:

> The activity of judgment is considered . . . as an activity which
> is at the service of the striving for knowledge. Knowledge of
> what? Speaking quite generally, knowledge of what-is, of the
> existent [*das Seiende*]. But, if the striving for knowledge is di-
> rected toward the existent, if it is the effort to formulate in a
> judgment what and how the existent is, then the existent must
> already have been given beforehand. . . . The act of judgment
> requires something "underlying," about which it judges, an *ob-*
> *ject-about-which.* . . . [EJ 19]

And:

> To the reduction of judgments to ultimate judgments with an ul-
> timate sense, there corresponds a *reduction of truths:* of the
> truths belonging to a higher level to those belonging on the *low-*

est level, that is: to truths that relate directly to their matters and
material spheres, or (because the substrates play the leading role
here) that relate directly *to individual objects* in their object-
spheres—individual objects, objects that therefore contain
within themselves no judgment-syntaxes and that, in their exper-
ienceable factual being, are *prior to all judging*. [FTL 204 (181)]

Since these objects-about-which are prior to judging, they contain no judgment syntaxes: "the individuum is the primal object required by pure logic, the absolute of (pure) logic back to which all logical
variants refer" (I, section 15). The object-about-which, formalized as
"S," *must*, then, be an individual, for generality or plurality already involves syntactical formations, which are the result of a more primitive
logical act of taking several individuals together (EJ 26).

We saw that the laws of logic held only for those judgments in
which the cores were materially related. This shows that these individuals
presupposed by the judgment are assumed to form part of a related
whole or unity, part of a *world*. Hence Husserl writes:

That judgments (not judgment-senses) relate to objects signifies that, in the judgment itself, these objects are meant as substrates, as the objects about which something is stated; and
reductive deliberation teaches, as an *Apriori*, that *every conceivable judgment ultimately* (and either definitely or indefinitely) *has
relation to individual objects* (in an extremely broad sense, real
objects), and therefore has *relation to a real universe*, a "world"
or *world-province*, "for which it holds good." [FTL 204 (181)]

In other words, when we consider truth logic we are led to "individual
objects in their object-sphere" (FTL 204 [181]). Every conceivable judgment ultimately refers to objects in a universe and for logic these objects
are first in themselves. That is, for logic these objects have the sense of
existing beforehand.

It must be noted that, because judgments also *aim at* knowledge of
the existent, of these objects that are first in themselves, the existent,
which is the ground of the judgment, is, paradoxically, also its telos (FTL
205 [182]). In other words, according to phenomenology the judgment is
not the deepest level of either logic or phenomenology, for the judgment
presupposes and aims at objects in their object sphere. According to Husserl a world is a world that is *experienced by a subject*. Hence, when intentional analysis following the logical sense given in judgments is led back to
the individual in a unified world, it is led back to sense experience.

It must be stressed once again, however, that the material foundation of logic does not destroy the purity of logic for Husserl, for these material conditions are in turn grounded by a deeper (pure, transcendental) logic. Husserl maintains, against Hume, that experience itself is intentional, which means it has a logic. This logic consists in the lawfulness of the transcendental subject, that is to say, the intentionality of the pure transcendental ego. "Every object expresses a *rule structured within transcendental subjectivity*" (PL 21 [22]), writes Husserl.

(d)   Husserl's Critique of Brentano: Sense Experience as the Primary Intentional Act

According to Husserl, then, we *start* with sense experience. What Husserl considers to be the difference between his and Brentano's notion of intentionality can be immediately seen. According to Husserl by "experience" or perception Brentano means a quality added on to an intentional act. That is, if I have sense experience of the lion, if I experience the lion as real, then for Brentano "reality" is a quality added on to the matter of the judgment, "the lion." This is not so for Husserl. For Husserl "experience" is not a quality added on to an intentional act, but is part and parcel of the intentional act. For Husserl experience is the genetically primary act of mind. It is intentional and is a precondition for the formation of the matter of the judgment; it is already something "within" what Brentano calls "matter." In other words, while for Brentano matter is neutral—it has no quality associated with it—according to Husserl matter by its essence is not neutral but *always* has a quality associated with it. What Brentano considers to be "pure" matter is made neutral, according to Husserl, by an additional act of consciousness, neutrality itself being a quality.

     Since the original quality is that of sense-experience, all other qualities are modifications of the original quality, according to Husserl:

> For objectivities of every sort, *consciousness in the mode, giving them-themselves, precedes* all other modes of consciousness relating to them, all these other modes being genetically secondary . . . from these genetical points of view, *the intrinsically first judgment-theory is the theory of evident judgments, and the intrinsically first thing in the theory of evident judgments* (and therefore in judgment-theory as a whole) *is the genetical tracing of predicative evidences back to non-predicative evidence* called *experience*. [FTL 209 (185–86)]

And:

> *The primitive mode of the giving of something-itself is perception.*
> [FTL 158 (141)]

And:

> *In respect of its being, reality has precedence to every irreality whatso-*
> *ever*, since all irrealities relate back essentially to an actual or
> possible reality. [FTL 168–69 (150–51)]

And:

> Most fundamentally, *the experiential judgment—is nevertheless the*
> *original judgment.* [FTL 211 (187)]

Since all qualities are *modifications* of the original quality (perception), they bear the sense of the original quality within them—that is,
their quality is understood by reference to the original quality. Since the
original judgment is the judgment of experience, all subsequent judgments will have within them a reference back to the judgment of experience. This forms no part in Brentano's theory of intentionality.

Indeed, Brentano's position entails the following problem, according to Husserl. If, as Brentano maintains, presentation (mere matter), the essence of intentionality, has no quality associated with it, and if
presentation is the mark of intentionality par excellence, then quality,
which is in principle distinct from matter, cannot come from intentionality. But on what basis, then, does certain matter become qualified as
sense experience? What marks some presentation as experience, then,
must be something nonintentional; it must be something "beyond" consciousness, for intentionality is the *essence* of consciousness. In other
words, it must be something like Hume's *vivaciousness* of impression,
which gives rise to a datum of belief. This is the position Brentano is
inadvertently driven to, according to Husserl. It is for this reason that
Husserl says that Brentano to some extent, like Hume, presupposes a
notion of belief understood as a datum on the tablet of consciousness:

> Even Brentano's concept of judgment supposes such a datum
> [of passive belief on the tablet of consciousness]—at any rate,
> as his theory of internal consciousness shows, *it is not an activity*
> *emanating from the ego-pole* [my emphasis]. [EJ 61]

The position entails that something, a datum, "enters into" or "strikes" consciousness, which makes it "label" it as sense-experience. But experience and common sense (Hume notwithstanding) do not support this position, and consequently it is not tenable phenomenologically. First of all, the claim that experience involves something, an object, an experiential datum, alien to consciousness entering into consciousness is countersensical—it is patently *absurd*. Secondly, and this relates to the first point, the belief in experience is *not*, contrary to Hume, something that cannot be grounded.

(e) The Intentionality of Experience

Consciousness is a seeing, an apprehending. But it is more than this. It is not just actual "seeing," but also the *ability* to see (PL 25 [25]): anything I can apprehend but is not yet in my "view," to speak metaphorically, is already related to consciousness, for the "I can" is a mode of consciousness. "Alien" to consciousness would then mean alien to being apprehended, for consciousness is also the *ability* to apprehend. Hence, if something were truly alien to consciousness, it would not be graspable by consciousness, and we would not be able to talk about it (PL 32ff. [32ff.]). If I label something as alien, it must be something for consciousness in order for me to be able to label it "alien." And if it is something for consciousness, it is not alien to consciousness. Hence Husserl writes:

> As in everyday life, so too in science (unless, under the misguidance of "realistic" epistemology, it misinterprets its own doing) experience is the consciousness of being with matters themselves, of seizing upon and having them quite directly. But experience is not an opening through which a world, existing prior to all experience, shines into a room of consciousness; it is not a mere taking of something alien to consciousness into consciousness. For how could I make a rational statement to that effect, without seeing such a state-of-affairs and therefore seeing not only consciousness but also the something alien to consciousness—that is: *experiencing* the alien affair? And how could I objectivate such a state-of-affairs as at least a conceivability? Would that not be immersing myself intuitively in such a countersensical experiencing of something alien to experience? [FTL 232–33 (206)]

Objects may be outside my attention, but not outside consciousness. The phenomenon of, say, a "mere 'stimulus' which proceeds from an existent in the environing world, as, e.g., the barking of a dog which 'just breaks in on our ears' " (EJ 60), is already something within the stream of experience. The noise may be "alien" to—that is, beyond— my psychophysical being, but it is not alien to consciousness. It is, rather, found within the stream of consciousness. If something is considered to be beyond or transcendent to me, the object receives this sense from my consciousness:

> If what is experienced has the sense of *"transcendent" being*,
> then it is the experiencing that constitutes this sense, and does
> so either by itself or in the whole motivational nexus pertaining
> to it and helping to make up its intentionality.[FTL 233 (206)]

Consciousness itself is what allows for experience, and if an object is transcendent to me or imperfectly given, it is experience that tells me that this is so. In other words, experience itself is imbued with sense, a sense I can consult and explicate:

> The currently experienced (physical things, I myself, others,
> and so forth), the current More that could be experienced, the
> self-identity with which the experienced extends throughout
> manifold experiences, the pointing ahead by every sort of ex-
> perience on the different levels of originality to new possible
> experiences of the same (first of all, possible experiences of my
> own and, at a higher level, possible experiences belonging to
> others), to the style of progressive experience, and to what this
> would bring out as existing and being thus and so—each and
> all of these are included intentionally in the consciousness it-
> self, as this actual and potential intentionality, whose structure
> I can at any time *consult*. [FTL 233–34 (206–7)]

Hence, according to Husserl experience is not only the basis for any act of mere presentation, but experience is itself already intentional, and thus always accompanied by consciousness:

> If their genuine sense is brought out, the intentionality of
> predicative judgments leads back ultimately to the intentional-
> ity of experience. [FTL 210 (187)]

"Mere presentation" is not the deepest act of intentionality. Experience, which grounds mere presentation, itself has a *sense* that can be explicated in phenomenological evidence.

(f)   Husserl's Reinterpretation of
       Brentano: Objectification, not
       Presentation, as the Essence of
       Intentionality

Although Husserl criticizes Brentano's claim that the mark of intentionality is presentation, he is not so much rejecting Brentano's claim as rein-
terpreting it. As Levinas writes, "Husserl thinks that he can still preserve
Brentano's formulation in its entirety by considering another meaning
of the term '[re]presentation' " (TIHP 59). Presentation *is* the mark of
intentionality *if* by presentation is meant an act of objectification (TIHP
61). In other words, according to Husserl the essence of intentionality is
objectification, having an object before the mind:

> *Each intentional experience is either an objectifying act or has its ba-*
> *sis in such an act.* . . . If no act, or act-quality, not objectifying
> by nature, can acquire "matter" except through an objectify-
> ing act that is inwoven with it in unity, objectifying acts have
> the unique function of first providing other acts with pre-
> sented objects, to which they may refer in their novel ways.
> The reference to an object is, in general terms, constituted in
> an act's "matter." [LI 648]

While Husserl agrees with Brentano that consciousness is always
consciousness *of* an object, he argues that the object itself is something
already constituted by consciousness. In other words, presentation,
which gives us the matter or object, S with predicates, is the result of
predication, an act of judgment. In Husserl's view any "definition" of
consciousness must also take into account this most basic level of constitution, the constitution of the object itself in the stream of experience. If
the definition of mental phenomena is changed from "presentation" to
"objectification," then we have a definition that will also account for the
more basic level of constitution, constitution of the object itself. In other
words, the objectification that occurs in presentation is not the most
"primitive" or basic level of objectification, but is already a level of objectification quite high up, so to speak. Presentation, which is an act of
predication, logically implies an earlier level of objectification—namely,
nominalization, which is prepredicative and experiential. Nominalization is a single-rayed act (LI 459), which makes something the subject, S,
for a judgment. On the lowest level, in the sphere of original passivity,
nominalization is an act of "turning toward the object" (EJ 77), an act
through which the object begins to stand out for consciousness (EJ 77).

This presupposes a field of experience or a "horizon," as Husserl terms it, against which the object will stand out. The horizon is implied in nominalization and is part of intentionality.

An examination of experience confirms the existence of the act of nominalization. I can scan the environment without anything standing out for me, without my focusing explicitly on any object. I may, for example, enter a room and walk about without focusing on anything in particular. Even if some object catches my attention—music playing, for instance—and there is nominalization, a predicative judgment proper need not be formed. Only if I focus on the object explicitly will it become the subject of a predicative judgment and will there be true objectification (EJ 62). If I proceed, for instance, to focus explicitly on the music, I may wonder whether this is the gramophone playing or the radio, and who the composer might be. I find it is the radio. In an attempt to identify the composer, I may listen closely to the music, noting its lyrical quality and expressive harmonies. From the announcer I learn that it is Mahler's Symphony no. 2.

It is crucial to see that presentation logically implies an earlier level of objectification—nominalization—in order to achieve a correct understanding of intentionality. When we see that presentation logically implies a lower level of objectification, that there is a relation between the predicative and prepredicative levels respectively, we are drawn to examining this relation. We will then discover that the relation is not restricted to these levels, but that presentation also implies a *higher* act of objectification. We will discover that acts of objectification are *never* simple acts cut off from others, but are acts always implying further acts of objectification.[7] In other words, we get a *glimpse*[8] of the fact that intentionality, the relation of consciousness to the object, is not a static relation, but one of movement, that it is *dynamic*—intentionality is an interplay of levels of objectification.

Now, the relation between the levels of objectification is an *essential* one. The higher levels could not *be* without their relation to the lower, and hence they always have a reference back to the lower levels. The lower levels enter into all higher levels of intentionality. As has already been remarked, since the basic level is that of perceptual experience—experience of real being—*all* levels of intentionality refer back to sense experience and hence to sensual, real being. It must be appreciated, however, that intentionality is not to be identified with any of its levels, neither with its most basic level, sense experience, nor with any of its higher levels. Intentionality *is* not any one level, but is the relation between levels. More specifically, it is the act of actualizing the potential of any level. For this reason a static analysis and correlatively a static concept of consciousness, of intentionality or of the transcendental ego, will not do, for such an analysis will be piecemeal and hence unrepresentative of intentionality. The transcendental ego, the "organ" of intentionality, is not any one point or level; it is never "complete"; it is not an *object*, but a *function* (of actualizing).

In sum, the difference between Brentano's and Husserl's notions of intentionality is the following: whereas Brentano has a static notion of intentionality, Husserl defines intentionality dynamically as a process of actualizing the objectivity contained potentially at lower levels. And while intentionality is essentially related to experience or real being for Husserl, for Brentano it is not.

(g) The Nature of Objectification: Bringing "X" to Evidence

It was said, then, that Husserl's claim that logic is dependent upon material factors, and thus upon experience, does not threaten the purity of either logic or phenomenology, because for Husserl experience already bears an intentional, logical structure. What this means can be made clear by discussing the nature of objectification, because an act, including an act of sense experience, is intentional if it is objectifying (FTL 262 [232]).

To objectify is to bring an object before the mind. To have the object before the mind is to have evidence of the object—that is to say, to *have it in its embodiment, as it itself, in its presence*, in its being (PL 22 [22]). To have an object before the mind, to have evidence of the object and intentionality, these are all one and the same thing. Because of the importance of this claim, Husserl is cited here at length:

> *Category of objectivity and category of evidence are perfect correlates.*
> [FTL 161 (144)]

And:

> *The concept of any intentionality whatever*—any life-process of consciousness-of something or other—and *the concept of evidence, the intentionality that is the giving of something-itself, are essentially correlative.* [FTL 160 (143)]

And:

Evidence, as has already become apparent to us by the above explanations, designates *that performance on the part of intentionality which consists in the giving of something-itself (die intentionale Leistung der Selbstgebung).* More precisely, it is the universal pre-eminent form of "intentionality," of "consciousness of something," in which there is consciousness of the intended-to objective affair in the mode itself-seized-upon, itself-seen—correlatively, in the mode: being with itself in the manner peculiar to consciousness. We can also say that it is the primal consciousness: I am seizing upon *"it itself"* originaliter, as contrasted with seizing upon it in an image or as some other, intuitional or empty, fore-meaning. [FTL 157–58 (141)]

And:

Thus it points to an essential *fundamental trait of all intentional life.* Any consciousness, *without exception* [my emphasis], either is itself already characterized as evidence (that is, as giving its object originaliter) or else has an essential tendency toward conversion into givings of its object originaliter—accordingly, toward syntheses of verification, which belong essentially in the domain of the "I can." [CM 58 (93)]

We must before proceeding make clear two senses of "evidence," which if not distinguished may lead one to reject out of hand the claim that to have an object before the mind is to have evidence of that object, for while the claim is true for one sense of evidence, it is not true for the other. The distinction between the two senses of evidence, and corresponding to this, between the two senses of truth, is one Husserl explicitly makes (FTL 127ff. [113ff.]). Roughly speaking, one can distinguish two senses of evidence and truth by saying that one is *naive* and the other is *critical* (FTL 127 [113]):

The word *evidence* also takes on a *double sense* in connexion with these two concepts of truth: In addition to signifying the *original having* of a true or actual being *itself,* evidence signifies the property belonging to the judgment—as a supposed categorial objectivity (an "opinion" or "meaning")—when it fits, in original actuality (*Aktualität*), a corresponding actuality (*Wirklichkeit*). Thus evidence involves, in the latter case, that *original consciousness of correctness* which arises in the event of actual adequation. That consciousness is itself evidence in the first sense, with regard to the correctness; it is a particular case under the broader concept of evidence as the having of some-

> thing itself. Then, in a naturally amplified sense, a judgment is called evident, also with reference to the potentiality of bringing about its adequation. [FTL 128 (113–14)]

Let us illustrate this with an example from perception, for it is the easiest to deal with. When I see a glass standing in front of me on the desk, and I pick it up, feeling the coolness of the glass, I have in my sensory impressions of the glass (vision, touch, sound, etc.), evidence of the glass. This evidence is naive: I quite literally do not give it a *second thought*. However, if after taking a sip from its content, I go about my work and later, wanting to take another sip, I do not see the glass anywhere, I may begin to question whether perhaps I had had a glass there at all, and whether I was perhaps thinking of yesterday. I take a *scientific, critical* attitude toward the evidence I had of the glass. I form a judgment, the glass as supposed, as I seek to determine whether there had been a glass on my desk. That is, I do not live in the judgment directly, but instead treat the judgment *as* a judgment, and one to be verified at that. When, after looking about, I find the glass behind a pile of books I had absentmindedly stacked in front of it, I have renewed evidence of the glass, though this time the evidence is critical, not naive—it is explicit and an object of my explicit will or cogito.

This critical attitude is the beginning of a properly scientific attitude. In the scientific attitude, one's stance toward evidence is still more critical, for not only does one have explicit evidence, but one knows that the evidence itself may be misleading:

> The scientist, however, has long been apprised, not only that evidence has its degrees of clarity but also that it may be deceptive evidence. Consequently there exists for him the further distinction between *supposed and genuine evidence*. His judgments must be verified by genuine, by maximally perfect, evidence; and only as so verified shall they be admitted among the results of science as theory. This brings about a *peculiar judging procedure on the scientist's part*, a *zigzag* judging, so to speak: first making straight for the givenness of something itself, but then going back *critically* to the provisional results already obtained—whereupon his criticism must also be subjected to criticism, and for like reasons. [FTL 125 (111)]

Usually when we speak of evidence we mean the latter, critical sense of evidence. But Husserl uses the term evidence for both cases. Evidence *broadly* speaking is "the having of something itself"; it is actuality as an itself given (FTL 127[113]). This is evidence in the naive sense;

one has evidence but one does not know that one has evidence. The narrower sense of evidence is that of evidence for the judgment. It occurs in the critical attitude when we have evidence of the judgment "fitting" actuality and involves focusing on the judgment qua judgment, the judgment as supposed. So when Husserl says that being related to an object—that is, intentionality—is the having of evidence of the object, he means evidence in the *first* sense, for many intentional acts of consciousness are not *critical*, in the second sense of evidence.

(h) Naive Evidence: a Complex Phenomenon

When intentionality is "defined" as evidence, then, the term is used in its first sense to mean naive evidence, evidence that presents the object itself. Understood in this way, sense experience too is intentional. However, although naive, this first type of evidence is a *complex* phenomenon. Even the "first" level of experience is full of *sense*. This is so because perception or evidence of an object, whether the object is real or ideal, is never restricted to what is immediately *given*, to what is immediately before the mind. What is *given* of the object *always* points beyond itself to what is not-yet-given but can become given. For any object we have the *idea* of the perfect givenness, the complete determination, of the object, which always remains unrealizable:

> But *as "idea"* (in the Kantian sense), *the complete givenness is*
> *nevertheless prescribed*—as a connexion of endless processes of
> continuous appearing, absolutely fixed in its essential type, or,
> as the field for these processes, a *continuum of appearances* de-
> termined *a priori*, possessing different but determinate dimen-
> sions, governed by an established dispensation of essential
> order. [I 366 (297)]

Hence, part of the *sense* of the object is an *anticipation* of the "filling out of the object." In other words, what evidence we have of the object points to further *evidence* (EJ 331). Evidence is not an isolated phenomenon but is part of an intricate web of further evidences:

> The giving of something-itself is, like every other single inten-
> tional process, a *function* in the all-embracing nexus of con-
> sciousness. The effect produced by a single intentional process,
> in particular its effect as a giving of something itself, its effect as

evidence, is therefore not shut off singly. The single evidence, by its own intentionality, can implicitly "demand" further givings of the object itself; it can "refer one" to them for a supplementation of its Objectivating effect [FTL 159–60 (142–43)]

And:

Thus a great *task* arises, the task of exploring all these modes of the evidence in which the objectivity intended to *shows itself*, now less and now more perfectly, of making understandable the extremely complicated performances, fitting together to make a synthetic harmony and *always pointing ahead*[9] [my emphasis] to new ones. [FTL 161 (144)]

How to achieve further evidence is prescribed by the *type* of object one is confronted with. That is, the object, whether real or ideal, is never merely an object in general, but is always an object of a certain *type*: perceptual, imaginary, memory, etc. "The factual world of experience is experienced as a typified world" (EJ 331), writes Husserl. Being of a certain type, the object has predetermined properties, an internal horizon, a set of determinations that define the object's own nature and prescribe the way in which that object can be brought to further evidence. For example, I may from a distance notice a brightly colored spot in my flower bed. Presuming it to be a flower, but being unable to relate it to any of the specimens I have planted there, I would try to bring the object to further evidence. Because I am dealing with a real object, I would do so by a series of partially physical acts, because physical objects are always given via the body (C 106). That is, the internal horizon of the object dictates that this is a three-dimensional object of bodily character, which I can touch, see, smell, and the like. I may walk over to the flower bed, bringing the shape of the flower into focus, push the other plants aside so as to see the newly discovered plant, and perhaps feel the texture of its stem and leaves. If, on the other hand, I am trying to recall the title of a mystery I read some time ago, because I am dealing with an ideal object in memory, I may try to bring the object to evidence by various acts of recollection. The internal horizon of the object dictates that the object I seek to bring to evidence is a meaning that stands in relation to the entire work as a name or abbreviation. I may try to recall the cover of the book, the name of the main character, the setting of the story, recall the author's name, and so forth, in the hope of jogging my memory. Hence, although qua object all objects have certain universal properties of evidence in common (FTL 168[150])—their evidence is something that can be "seen" (FTL 153 [139]), something that is in principle repeatable (FTL 157 [140–41]), and something that can "become disclosed as deception" (FTL 156 [140])—different regions of objects nevertheless have different *types* of evidence (C 166; PL 24 [25]):

> For though, in characterizing evidence as the giving (or, relative to the subject, the having) of an object itself, we were indicating a universality relating to all objectivities in the same manner, that does not mean that the structure of evidence is everywhere quite alike.
>
> *Category of objectivity and category of evidence are perfect correlates. To every fundamental species of objectivities*—as intentional unities maintainable throughout an intentional synthesis and, ultimately, as unities belonging to a possible "experience"—*a fundamental species of "experience," of evidence, corresponds*, and likewise a fundamental species of intentionally indicated evidential style in the possible enhancement of the perfection of the having of an objectivity itself. [FTL 161 (144)]

And:

> *To every region and category* of would-be objects corresponds phenomenologically not only *a basic kind of meaning or position*, but also a *basic kind of primordial dator-consciousness* of such meaning, and, pertaining to it, a *basic type of primordial self-evidence*, essentially motivated through a primitive givenness that conforms to the basic divisions just referred to. [I 356–57 (288)]

The *type* of the object, then, establishes an *internal* horizon of the object (EJ 36). Since the object is never given in isolation but is always given in context—it always has a background, for example—it is also endowed with an *external* horizon, a "field" of co-given objects with which it stands in relation (EJ 33). In terms of the previous examples, the external horizon of the flowering plant consists of the other plants in the bed, the shrubs at the back of the bed, the bees flying in and out of the flower, but also my memory of going to the nursery this spring to buy new specimens, my memory of having received some divisions from my neighbor, which I planted there as well, and so forth. The external horizon of the mystery's title consists of the cover, the main character, the setting, my memory of having read a review of the book, my memory of signing the book out at the library, and so forth.

"Naive" evidence of the object, then, involves further evidence, in the form of internal and external horizons of the object. This all forms part of the sense of "object" and of the sense of how to actualize its evidence. Each object comes in a web of cognitive expectations. From the moment I experience an object it is part of a complex structure. Whether I choose to become aware of it or actualize it is another question altogether, but the object is understood as something I *can*, at least potentially or in principle, bring to evidence. This means that "object" is understood in terms of a *doing*, for actualizing is a *doing*, a performance. This is why Husserl describes evidence as a *performance:*

> *Evidence as an effective performance (als Leistung)* . . . like all other effective intentional performances, takes place as woven into systematically built performances and abilities. [FTL 283 (250)][10]

And:

> Ascending level by level from sensuous experience, one can acquire an understanding of *evidence as an effective performance (als Leistung).* [FTL 282 (249)]

As discussed above, such doings or performances can, depending on whether the object is real or ideal, consist of an abstract set of cognitive performances, such as acts of recollection, or may involve actual physical acts of the body—kinesthesis—such as seeing, touching, and so forth. Kinesthesis, which is fundamental to sense experience, is to be understood as a complex set of activities unified in its sense:

> All kinestheses, each being an "I move," "I do," [etc.] are bound together in a comprehensive unity—in which kinesthetic holding-still is [also] a mode of the "I do." [C 106]

Evidence, then, is part of a complex theme. Husserl urges that those who have traditionally understood evidence as a *feeling*, have failed to analyze the concept of evidence properly. He criticizes Hume, for example, for maintaining that perceptual evidence is a feeling resulting from a datum of vividness (FTL 157ff. [140ff.]). Evidence is not a static entity or an ungrounded feeling, be it of vividness or anything else. Rather, it is a part or moment of a *theme*, of *sense*. Hence, perceptual experience, the original giving of something itself, the original evidence, is *thematic*. We may not always make this theme explicit, or we may not develop it further, but even then we *passively believe* in this theme. As Husserl says, originary sense experience involves a passive belief. Passively we believe that we *have* evidence, that it is of a certain *kind* corresponding to the type of object we have before us, and that we can bring the object to further evidence. Although this attitude is passive, it is nevertheless warranted to speak of *belief*, for it involves taking a *stand* as is seen from the fact that we can be *wrong*. That is, error implies prior assent. Correction of one's passive belief can be surprising and painful, as anyone who has ever attempted to go through a sliding glass door mistakenly believed to be open will attest. In this case it was incorrectly believed that one had evidence (of the door being open). It is also possible to be mistaken about the *type* of evidence one has. One may, for example, think that one has sensory or perceptual evidence, while in fact one is hallucinating. In either case, however, correction of one's passive belief is not made on the basis of a mere datum. A mere datum cannot ever really be evidence, for by itself it would not *relate* to anything, and evidence proper is evidence *for* or *of* something. A hallucination, for example, is not distinguished from reality by its lack of vividness but by its inability to fit into a larger set of anticipations. Indeed, the hallucination may be *as* vivid as the perception of physical reality. Whether or not one is hallucinating is determined by a complex set of cognitive/kinesthetic performances. If on having a fever I believe that someone hands me a glass of water, I conclude that I have been hallucinating if I *cannot* drink the water, *cannot* feel relief of thirst, *cannot* feel the glass. Nor is a dream, for example, differentiated from reality by its lack of vividness. When dreaming, the dream *is* my reality. It is distinguished from reality proper only when, upon waking, I *can*, say, no longer see the villain pursuing me, *can* no longer see the winding streets that I ran down, but *can* see my room with its familiar surroundings, and so forth. Or, to refer to the previous example, while a bump on the forehead can be quite persuasive, this stimulus by itself is insufficient for me to judge that the door is closed. I judge that it is closed by the fact that I *cannot* enter the garden, that I *can* see a slight reflection in the glass after all, that I *can* slide the door open, and so forth. In short, the theory of the datum of vividness does not hold up under close scrutiny.

(i)   Extending the Notion of Judgment:
      The Judgment as Paradigmatic of
      Intentionality

The original act of perception, of experience, then, involves *assent or belief* (PL 23 [23]). This original belief, belief in being, is a naive certainty. It is either confirmed or shattered on the basis of one's ability to bring the object before one to evidence. Hence, one may be mistaken about one's belief, confirm it, be certain or uncertain about it, as, for example, when one wonders whether "X" is an object of perception or a mirage, and so forth. For this reason Husserl maintains that modalities pertain not only to the predicational sphere but to prepredicative experience as well:

> This beginning, moreover, is the place systematically, *starting from the judgment, to discover* that certainty and modalities of certainty, suppositive intention and fulfilment, identical existent and identical sense, evident having of something itself, trueness of being (being "actual") and truth as correctness of sense—that *none of these is a peculiarity exclusively within the predicational sphere, that, on the contrary, they all belong already to the intentionality of experience.* [FTL 209–10 (186)]

And:

> The so-called *modalities* of judgment, which constitute a central element of traditional formal logic, also have their origin and their foundation in the occurrences of prepredicative experience. [EJ 91]

These considerations lead Husserl to conclude that the prepredicative level of experience is *like* the judgment, the predicative level, in two respects: (1) it too is objectivating, and (2) it too is *thetic* or positional—that is, involves taking a stand, the making of a decision or assertion. It is, in other words, syntactical in a certain way:

> Even this founding experience has its style of syntactical performances, which, however, are still free from all the conceptual and grammatical formings that characterize the categorial as exemplified in the predicative judgment and the statement. [FTL 212 (188)]

And:

> The syntactical as such . . . makes its appearance already in the pre-predicational sphere. [FTL 212 (188) n.2]

For this reason Husserl extends the notion of judgment to *experience:*

> Thus one comes *from the experiential judgment*—more particularly, from the most immediate experiential judgment having the categorial form—*to experience* and to *the motive for that*

> *broadening of the concept of the judgment* already indicated by
> Hume's concept of *belief.*[11] [FTL 210 (186)]

And:

> If experience itself is accounted as judgment in the broadest
> sense, then this theory of experience is to be characterized as
> itself the first and most fundamental judgment-theory. [FTL
> 211–12 (188)]

Even sense experience, the basic level of intentionality, shares
properties of the judgment. What Husserl is arguing, in other words, is
that the predicative judgment displays properties of intentionality in
general, that the judgment is not only an *example* of intentionality, but is
paradigmatic of intentionality. Hence according to Husserl "the predicative judgment gains universal significance for psychic life" (FTL 263
[232]). More specifically, it is the link in the judgment between "S" and
"p" that expresses intentionality par excellence. The link expresses an
ego act of *actualizing* an object, that is to say, of bringing it to evidence; it
expresses an act of objectification. It does so more fully, that is, it is a
more actualized state, than the objectification that occurs on the
prepredicative level. This does not mean that the predicative level is
somehow "more intentional" than the initial objectifying acts of the
lower, prepredicative levels, or than the still lower level of time-synthesis
of the stream of experience, for, as remarked earlier, intentionality
properly speaking is not restricted to any one level, but is a relation *between* levels. This means, rather, that since the predicative level is a more
explicit level, the workings of intentionality can be *seen* there. In the
predicative level we can see intentionality starting to work itself out,
starting to actualize itself. By studying this level we can gain a *sense* of
both the arche and telos of intentionality, for, as noted previously, the
predicative judgment implies both earlier and later levels.

In order to appreciate how the link in the judgment between "S"
and "p" expresses intentionality par excellence, how it expresses an ego
act of actualizing the object, it is necessary to appeal to the phenomenon
of attention.

(j)   Attention

Husserl characterizes attention as "a quite general structure of consciousness *sui generis*" (I 246 [189]). He speaks of it metaphorically as a

"ray of light" (I 248 [191]), a "personal ray" (I 249 [192]), as " 'a mental glance' or 'glancing ray' of the pure ego, of its turning toward and away" (I 246 [189]). Husserl writes:

> In general, *attention* is a *tendency of the ego toward an intentional object*, toward a unity which "appears" continually in the change of the modes of its givenness and which belongs to the essential structure of a specific act of the ego (an ego-act in the pregnant sense of the word); it is a tending-toward realization. [EJ 80]

Attention is the property of a " 'wakeful' Ego" (I 107 [63]) that *actual*izes intentional experiences:

> If an intentional experience is actual, carried out, that is, after the manner of the *cogito*, the subject "directs" itself within it toward the intentional object. [I 109 (65)]

Attention, which belongs to the cogito, is never *absent* from the Ego. As with many of Husserl's distinctions, this one is made for the purpose of analysis. The distinction is not a "real" one: ego and its attention, while distinct, are *always* related:

> To the *cogito* itself belongs an immanent "glancing-towards" the object, a directness which from another side springs forth from the "Ego," which can therefore never be absent. [I 109 (65)]

And:

> The shaft of attention is not separate from the Ego. [I 249 (192)]

In short, attention, the ability to focus, is sui generis—*it is always there and belongs to the ego* as a "tendency . . . [which] emanates from the ego" (EJ 82). The Ego lives in and through this ray of light, which can be directed freely at will, at anything in the stream of experience. The ray always occurs in conjunction with other acts and so belongs to every ego-act in the pregnant sense of the word—for example, perception, memory, willing. Indeed, since it makes an object stand out, the ray forms part of the essence of the ego, for it is the means whereby the ego *objecti-*

fies, objectification being the very essence of intentionality, the very essence of the ego:

> [There is an essential connexion] between attention and intentionality—this fundamental fact that attention generally is nothing else than a fundamental kind of *intentional* modification. [I 250 (192) n.4]

By means of the phenomenon of attention it is possible to explain in what way the link in the predicative judgment expresses an act of objectification, an act of intentionality, in what way the predicative level is a higher, more actualized state of intentionality than the prepredicative level, and in what way all levels of intentionality are nevertheless "equally intentional." The lowest level of experience, "prior to" the direction of attention, is the constitution of the stream of experience. This is a temporal constitution:

> Thus, the sensuous data, on which we can always turn our regard as toward the abstract stratum of concrete things, are themselves also already the product of a constitutive synthesis, which, as the lowest level, presupposes the operations of the synthesis in internal time-consciousness. These operations, as belonging to the lowest level, necessarily link all others. [EJ 73]

Genetically the next level is one in which the ego turns its glance, its attention, toward some object within the stream of experience, setting it apart from the rest of the stream. This is receptive experience, and, as indicated earlier, it is implied by the judgment. The judgment points back to the prepredicative basis, "S." According to Husserl, while "S" is prepredicative, it is still the result of an activity of the ego, for "S" is made to *stand out* from its surroundings—it is, after all, the *subject* of predication. It results from an act of the ego's *turning-toward* something within the stream of experience and may include contemplation of the object's properties. On the level of receptive experience, then, the ego is already active. This act of turning toward of the ego, not the act of predication, Husserl considers the lowest, most basic, act of objectification.[12] In other words, the "start" of the judgment (the beginning of the striving for knowledge) is not automatically given within experience, but is the result of a specific *act* of the ego.

Although the ego *is* productive on this level, "it is not as yet a field of objectivities in the true sense of the term" (EJ 72). This is so because "an object is the product of an objectivating operation of the ego, and in the significant sense, of an operation of predicative judgment" (EJ 72). What Husserl means here is the following. Something is object for us if we can return to it in memory, if it is an "abiding possession." Making something an abiding possession involves an explicit act of the ego of which the predicative judgment is an expression. While in receptive experience we are faced with objectivities and it *is* possible to recall them, they have not become our deliberate abiding *possessions* (EJ 197) and so are not truly objects for us. Forming the predicative judgment "S is p" is the result of a further act of the ego set in motion by attention, an interest-producing activity:

> With this tendency [of attention] is awakened an *interest* in the object of perception as existent. [EJ 82]

The interest sets into motion an activity, a striving, to bring the object to givenness:

> In this firm orientation on the object, in the continuity of the experience of the object, there is an intention that goes beyond the given and its momentary mode of givenness and tends toward a progressive *plus ultra*. It is not only a progressive having-consciousness-of but a striving toward a new consciousness in the enrichment of the "self" of the object which is forthcoming *eo ipso* with the prolongation of the apprehension. Thus the tendency of the turning-toward continues as a tendency toward complete fulfillment. [EJ 82]

And:

> As has already been said in a general way, here also it is true that the inception of an act of turning-toward, of paying attention to what exists, puts into play an activity with a tendency, a striving. It is a striving toward realization, a doing which includes different forms of discontinuance and completion.[EJ 82]

Attention is a motive for looking, a motive for acting:

> The tendency is thus actualized in a manifold "doing" of the ego. Its aim is to convert the appearance (figuration) which the ego has of the external object into other and again other "appearances of the same object." [EJ 83]

Interest sets into motion not only a striving to bring the object to givenness, but, and this is what truly characterizes predicative objectivity from its prepredicative base, the will to "have" this object in its givenness *once and for all*. Judgments result from an act of *will*, the will of cognitive striving, the will to have knowledge of the object once and for all:

> In genuine cognitive interest . . . the ego wishes to know the object, to pin it down once and for all . . . the goal of the will is the apprehension of the object in the identity of its determinations, the fixing of the result of contemplative perception "once and for all." [EJ 198]

And:

> What is here important above all—this production of categorial objectivities in cognitive action is not the final goal of this action. . . . The goal of this activity is not the *production of objects*, but a *production of the knowledge of a self-given object*, therefore the possession of this object in itself as that which is permanently identifiable anew. [EJ 200]

This involves an "active" and abiding assent to the validity of the categorial object:

> This gives it the character . . . of an acquisition which still continues to be valid, which we still hold in our will. . . . I, the present ego . . . am in accord with the past act of will . . . I, the present ego, presently willing. [EJ 202]

Hence, active turning toward differs from receptive experience, which may also involve a turning toward, in that the former involves an act of will and results in the constitution of *true objectivities*—objects as abiding possessions. The act of turning toward that occurs in receptive experience, on the other hand, while an act of interest, is not yet an act of *will*, but is, rather, part of normal perception:

> We have also spoken of an *interest* which may be awakened along with turning-toward an object. It now appears that this interest still has nothing to do with a specific act of will. It is not an interest which engenders anything on the order of plans and voluntary activities. It is merely a *moment of the striving* which belongs to the essence of normal perception. [EJ 85]

Husserl nevertheless calls the lower act an act of interest because of the accompanying feeling of satisfaction that marks the actualization of the striving (EJ 85–86). This act of striving *can* become a true act of will, a will to knowledge, with deliberate positing of goals, and the like. Hence it becomes apparent that although intentionality may be the same throughout consciousness, it has its levels of *actualization*. Each lower level is the potential of a higher level—true intentionality being a point at infinity. This is why Husserl writes:

> The *interest in perception*, which guides receptive experience, is only the *forestage of the interest in cognition in the proper sense*. [EJ 197–98]

Interest in cognition, unlike interest in perception, involves the use of *will* to give rise to a *new* type of objectivity—namely, categorial objectivity, objectivity in the true sense of the term. Hence, although it is possible to *recall* an objectivity of receptive experience, what occurs on the next *higher* level is not a matter of *mere memory:*

> Such reproductions are then more than a mere memory of an earlier intuition. We return to what is reproduced as to an *acquisition*, actively produced in an act of will orientated toward this acquisition. As such, it is intentionally characterized. It is reproduced otherwise than in mere memory: *a modification of the will* is present, as with every acquisition. [EJ 201–2]

(k)   Genetic Analysis

The levels of objectification achieved by attention are the key to genetic analysis. According to Suzanne Bachelard, genetic analysis is "a new type of investigation characteristic of Husserlian phenomenology" (SHL 135–36), which gives "to Husserl's thought its horizon of originality" (SHL 136). Hence she writes that "its importance cannot be overemphasized" (SHL 136). When phenomenology asks after the meaning of a concept or phenomenon, it seeks to uncover the history of its logical genesis. In other words, for Husserl phenomenology *is* genetic analysis. Moving from higher to lower levels of sense, from higher objectivities to lower objective levels, from predicative to prepredicative experience, genetic analysis aims to expose levels of sense required for the concept or phenomenon in question to be functional at all. These levels of sense are levels of meaning that are currently *operative*. They are, in other words, *living* levels of sense. Hence when it is said that the earlier levels *imply* the later predicative levels, that the preobjective flow of experience implies both prepredicative and predicative objectivities, because this is a genesis of a logical nature, as Husserl never tires of pointing out, the lower levels are not "given up" or replaced by the later levels, as they would be in a psychological, temporal genesis. A more actualized level does not give up any of the lower levels in genetic synthesis as phenomenology understands it. According to temporal synthesis, earlier levels are taken up in later ones, of which they become a real part; the lower level always occurs first and *then* the second level occurs, at which point the former is taken up into the latter, leaving only the second level. According to genetic synthesis, on the other hand, while the lower levels are taken up into higher ones, and are needed for these, they are in no way given up; the lower levels do not become real parts of the higher levels, but remain temporally synchronous with the higher levels. In other words, in genetic synthesis components are distinct but temporally synchronous; earlier levels remain themselves while being taken up into higher levels.

To illustrate with an example, a psychological, temporal synthesis might deal with, say, how a child as a matter of fact was taught to count to three. It would reveal the actual steps taken in this procedure; the type of objects used, say, three sets of three objects, three crayons, three tops, three blocks, the manner in which they were presented, one object from each group was first presented as the phrase "*one* top," "*one* block," "*one* crayon" was uttered, next the second object of each set was presented and the phrase "*two* tops," "*two* crayons" was uttered, and so on until all three objects of each set had been presented. The actual process whereby the child learned to count does not form part of any counting the child later does. Genetic analysis, on the other hand, would reveal what notions were necessary for the act of counting to take place at all. It would reveal that counting presupposes the notion of "any object whatever," for instance. This notion remains ever-present in any act of counting. The notion of "any object whatever" itself is synthesized from lower levels of predicative and prepredicative experience, all of which remain ever-present in that notion.

To further illustrate with an example, one that will be returned to in chapter 6, the analysis of intersubjectivity moves from the objective conceptual sense of self and other, to a preobjective sense of self and other, and finally to that level of experience in which the sense of self and other merge, a level of intercorporeality. The lower levels remain ever-present as the ground of possibility of the higher levels.[13] In fact, as Merleau-Ponty describes, the lower levels may reemerge full blown in pathological phenomena.

But to understand *how* the earlier levels *imply* the later predicative levels, how the preobjective flow of experience implies both prepredicative and predicative objectivities without the lower levels being "given up" or becoming replaced, in order to understand how we can speak of a more actualized level that does not entail the giving up of the lower levels, we must again appeal to the distinction Husserl makes between the ego and its *attention*. Attention is a notion fundamental to phenomenology. As Husserl says, "this function of the wandering glance, which alternately enlarges and restricts its mental span, signifies *a special dimension of correlative modifications noetic and noematic*, of which systematic study on essential lines is one of the fundamental tasks of general phenomenology" (I 249 [192]). Without it Husserl could not execute his phenomenology, for without appealing to attention it is impossible both to account for and to perform genetic analysis and synthesis. Higher levels of sense are made possible by attention, for they result from acts of objectification, which, as was described above, come about by attention. Furthermore, all other levels can remain active because of the nature of attention, for by means of attention it is possible to "make a break" and to objectify while yet staying within a unity. Attention makes it possible to execute something *new*, a new objectivity, within the unity of one stream of experience. It allows components to be at once distinct and temporally synchronous. The focusing of the ray is temporal, but what happens next, the "looking" and its results, although occurring in time, do not come *after* the stream of experience (the lowest level, genetically), but merge with it: "the beam also is a phase of experience" (I 247 [190]). While the higher levels take up the objectification of the stream, its results also become part of the stream. The ray itself, of course, remains free to move through the various levels. The lower levels are *ever-present* realities for the ego and are in fact its field of potentiality.[14] Hence, the ego's attention makes possible a diversity within a unity. It allows both higher and lower levels to be co-present within one stream of experience. The stream of experience is ever-present, and the ego's attention can act on that stream; it can modify it, create out of it, retain its creations as part of the stream, and free itself for further acts (I 249 [192]).

(I) The Material Dependency of Judgment Cores Understood Phenomenologically

It can now be explained how the claim that the link between the cores in the judgment are conditioned by material factors, that they must have something to do with each other materially, that they reflect a unified coherent world, is to be understood phenomenologically. The material factor, the unified world, is itself intentional in nature—it is itself constituted by the transcendental ego. Although both the judgment and what it presupposes—namely, a unified world—are intentional objects, with the formation of the judgment we nevertheless have the creation of a *new* type of objectivity. This is so because intentionality involves *levels* of objectification. The higher levels of intentional constitution produce a new type of objectivity.[15] Specifically, in judgments in which the subject is determined by an adjective, *categorial objects* are created. Categorial objects are objects of the *understanding;* they are truly products of an act of mind qua mind. In the categorial object, cognition is deposited so that it becomes an abiding possession:

> Thus it is a matter here of objectifying achievements of a new kind, not merely of an activity *attached* to the pregiven and receptively apprehended objectivities; rather, in predicative knowledge and its deposit in the predicative judgment new kinds of objectivities are constituted, which can then themselves be apprehended again and be made thematic as logical structures, i.e., as what we call *categorial objectivities*, since they arise from the *kategorein*, the act of declarative judgment, or also (since judgment is certainly an activity of the understanding) *objectivities of the understanding*. Thus the work of cognition, this higher stage of activity, must, in contrast to receptivity, be characterized as a *creative spontaneity*, itself already productive of objects. [EJ 198–99]

Because the categorial judgment refers to the world, it is almost natural to think that categorial objectivities belong to the order of the world and are, as it were, "ready-made." In fact, however, the judgment creates a *new* type of objectivity. When a categorial mistake is committed, it is not a matter of the judgment not "mapping" onto the world. We are not dealing here with a straightforward mapping relation at all. According to Husserl, the judgment that *yields* knowledge of the world is not a straightforward reflection of the concrete world it presupposes, the world as experienced. The judgment transforms the base, as it were. While the judgment is *about* the concrete world and refers to it, the judgment is not the same type of objectivity as the world it is about. The world the judgment presents is not of the same "order" as the world it is based on. The latter is a prepredicative, and to some extent, preobjective "object"; the former a predicative, categorial object. Hence, in Husserl's view while the unity or link of the judgment relates to and in a way reflects the unity of the world it presupposes, the link or unity of the judgment is nevertheless of a *different* type than the unity of the concrete world.

It was said, then, that the unity of the judgment reflects the nature of intentionality, the nature of mind qua mind. It follows that according to Husserl the study of the judgment is at once a study of mind, of intentionality. Hence, a theory of judgment should include far more than what formal logicians have included under it (FTL 263 [233]). First of all, since the first judgment is the experiential judgment and all judgments implicitly contain a reference back to prepredicative experience as part of their sense, the theory of the judgment must include a theory of experience (FTL 264 [233–34]). Secondly, since the judgment, understood properly as relating to experience, is paradigmatic of all conscious life, of all intentionality, the study of the judgment could have a far greater *significance* than traditional logic attributes to it.

But introducing a subjective experiential factor into logic to many formal logicians spells the threat of psychologism, the reduction of logical laws to empirical, de facto laws. To avoid psychologism it must be demonstrated that when speaking of the laws of logic, even when grounded in experience, it is not a matter of describing what the psyche as a matter of fact does, but rather a matter of describing necessary laws. That, however, brings with it further problems. First of all, it must be shown that it is possible to maintain that the laws of logic are necessary, without falling into a kind of Kantian idealism in which the ego imposes a necessity on experience. This will be dealt with in chapter 3. Second of all, it must be shown that the necessary status of the ego can accommodate life phenomena, phenomena that would seem to destroy the absolute or pure status required of an ego that is the source of logical laws. Chapter 4 addresses this issue. Thirdly, it must be shown how the necessity of mind does not destroy facticity in general. This is discussed in chapter 5.

3

What Kant's Transcendentalism Missed: Life

Husserl's Transcendentalism versus Kant's

It has been argued, then, that intentionality is either the having of an object in evidence or the bringing of an object to evidence, and that different object regions have different types of evidence. It has been argued also that forming a judgment is an act of bringing the object or state-of-affairs to evidence and that the "rule" for achieving this evidence is dictated by the *idea of the type of object* in question. In a way, then, forming a judgment is an act of making the implicit explicit.[1] But it is important to understand the very special way in which Husserl means this, for this sounds like a typical rationalist/idealist position according to which the idea precedes or has priority over the real. Indeed, it sounds as if Husserl were saying that the idea prescribes how to make the object real, for having the object in evidence is having it *really* before one, and how to achieve evidence is dictated by the *idea* of the object. But it is fundamental to see how Husserl differs here from the rationalist/idealist tradition in general, and especially how he differs from one of its representatives—namely, Kant.

Kant's theory too is one according to which the concept precedes reality. In *The Critique of Pure Reason* Kant writes:

> Pure concepts . . . have their source in the understanding
> alone, *independently of sensibility.* [CPR 160 (B 144)]

And:

> We shall therefore follow up the pure concepts to their first
> seeds and dispositions in the human understanding, in which
> they lie prepared, till at last, on the occasion of experience,
> they are developed, and by the same understanding are exhib-
> ited in their purity, freed from the empirical conditions attach-
> ing to them. [CPR 103 (B 91)]

Kant claims that pure concepts on coming in contact with sense-impressions give rise to judgments about the world. Husserl, then, may readily
be mistaken for a Kantian, for it seems as if Husserl were saying that
forming a judgment involves nominalizing a sense-datum (the given) as
"S," applying to this the idea of object (an "X" with predicates) to get
the judgment "S is p."

Furthermore, Husserlian phenomenology may in general be confused with Kantianism because each is known as a transcendental philosophy, "a philosophy which, in opposition to prescientific and scientific
objectivism, goes back to knowing subjectivity as the primal locus of all
objective formations of sense and ontic validities, undertakes to understand the existing world as a structure of sense and validity, and in this
way seeks to set in motion an essentially new type of scientific attitude
and a new type of philosophy" (C 99). In other words, a transcendental
philosophy is one that attempts to overcome *all* objectivism, both prescientific and scientific.

Objectivism may be briefly characterized as the failure to recognize sense or ontic validity as being the result of a constitutive act of the
ego. It occurs when we mistake something "emanating from" the ego for
something "foreign to" the ego, when we mistake a sense or ontic validity constituted *by* the ego for something *given to* the ego. In its extreme
form objectivism results in the claim that objects (in its broadest sense,
the world) as described by science have absolute being and are the
ground of all being (C 68), including the being of the ego.[2] Objectivism is
considered undesirable because it lessens the ego's power and its self-
responsibility. Hence the aim is to overcome it. Insofar as both Kant and
Husserl attempt to overcome objectivism, they both have a transcendental philosophy.

But confounding Husserl's transcendentalism with that of Kant
would be a mistake. In *Formal and Transcendental Logic* Husserl stresses

that although Kant's theories "are *implicitly theories of intentional constitu-tion*" and are for him "a source of profound stimulations" (FTL 258 [228]), still Kant, unlike Husserl, did not achieve a *pure* transcendental phenomenology. Indeed, Husserl describes the character of Kant's advancement of a system of transcendental philosophy as being "half-way" (FTL 258 [228]) and claims that Kant is "far from accomplishing a truly radical grounding of philosophy" (C 99). In other words, Husserl overcomes objectivism in a way that Kant does not. While Kant still retains traces of objectivism in his philosophy, Husserl is able to overcome all objectivism in a *pure* transcendental phenomenology thanks to a "genuinely radical meaning of the opposition between objectivism and transcendentalism" (C 100), a radical meaning that he is able to achieve only by taking into account *life*. To show how Husserl differs from Kant it will be necessary to consider those of Kant's predecessors who influenced him most directly—namely, Descartes, Hume, and, to a lesser extent, Locke.[3]

(b) Historical Considerations: The Failure
of Husserl's Predecessors to Achieve a
Notion of the Pure Ego

According to Husserl, in maintaining the ego to be the founder of all sense, Descartes, Hume, and Kant *all* stand on the threshold of phenomenology.[4] Yet all fail to enter the region of phenomenology, and what prevents them from doing so is in all three cases the same: their concept of the ego. What differentiates phenomenology from the philosophies of Descartes, Hume, and Kant is its view of the *ego*. That the latter concept is the linchpin in transcendental philosophy should come as no surprise. After all, transcendental philosophy aims to ground all knowledge in the pure *ego*, in that level of the ego where *nothing* is taken for granted. According to transcendental philosophy, genuine science is built on that pure basis. Naturally, if the pure basis is not reached, if the synthesis of science occurs too soon, the demand of transcendentalism has not been met and a true (pure) transcendental philosophy cannot be established. The ego that Descartes, Hume, and Kant consider to be the pure ego, the ground of *all* sense, is not the pure ego at all, but is an ego constituted *by* the pure ego; it in fact contains levels of meaning constituted by the pure ego. Their failure to recognize this means that they do not overcome objectivism, for they consider certain meaning and concepts[5] to be given *to* the ego, whereas in fact they are constituted *by* the ego.[6] They work with these concepts without saying how they come about in the ego; they leave these concepts *ungrounded*. Not having taken their analysis to the *source* of meaning, they do not have the radicalism demanded by transcendentalism.

In part the inability of these philosophers to achieve a sense of pure ego is due to the then prevalent view of the ego as a "place" where thoughts occur, analogous to space being a place where events occur. According to this view, internal experience is analogous to external experience. Husserl terms the tendency to parallel "internal" and "external" experience, to treat psychic problems as having the same sense as problems concerning physical nature and to treat them by the same method (FTL 210 [187]), the naturalistic and sensualistic view of the ego:

> The way leading to the whole inquiry concerning origins, an inquiry that must be taken collaterally, as belonging to pure psychology and transcendental philosophy . . . that way remained for centuries untrod. This was an entirely understandable consequence of naturalistic and sensualistic aberration on the part of all modern psychology based on internal experience. This aberration not only drove the transcendental philosophy of English empiricism into that well-known development which made it end in countersensical fictionalism; it also arrested the transcendental philosophy of Kant's Copernican revolution short of full effectuation, so that the Kantian philosophy could never force its way through to the point where the ultimately necessary aims and methods can be adopted. [FTL 255 (225–26)]

Such a naturalistic, sensualistic concept of the ego can be found in all three philosophers, Descartes, Hume, and Kant, and in each case it is related to a mind-body, idea-reality split.

(c) ## Descartes's Failure to Adhere to his own Demand of a Radical *Epoché*: The Mind-Body Split and the Appeal to God

According to Husserl, Descartes was the first to approach phenomenology in his attempt to prove the ego in its rationality to be the founder, the absolute ground, of all sense, of all knowledge, and, on the basis of this, to establish philosophy as a universal science. By a radical skeptical *epoche* Descartes wants to find the absolute, indubitable ground of all knowledge, "a foundation of immediate and apodictic knowledge whose self-evidence excludes all conceivable doubt" (C 75). On the basis of this he wants by self-evident steps to build up a genuine science. Husserl points out, however, that what is new in Descartes that makes him the first to approach phenomenology is not the fact that he instituted an *epoche*, for this is something the ancient skeptics (starting with Protagoras and Gorgias, according to Husserl) (C 76) and St. Augustine[7] had achieved as well, but it is, rather, "the original Cartesian motif: that of pressing forward through the hell of an unsurpassable, quasi-skeptical epochē toward the gates of the heaven of an absolutely rational philosophy, and of constructing the latter systematically" (C 77). That is, while the skepticism of the ancients was a negative skepticism, "oriented negativistically toward the practical and ethical (political)," as Husserl phrases it, Descartes's skepticism is positive in nature, for it aims to give rise to truth.

As well, and indeed consequently, Descartes's skepticism is more radical than that of the ancients. While the ancient skeptics deny *episteme*, that is, scientific knowledge of what is in itself, according to Husserl, "the 'Cartesian epochē' . . . encompasses expressly not only that validity of all previous *sciences* . . . but even the validity of the pre- and extrascientific *life-world*, i.e., the world of sense-experience constantly pregiven as taken for granted unquestioningly and all the life of thought which is nourished by it—the unscientific and finally even the scientific" (C 76). Hence Husserl says that "the 'Cartesian epochē' has in truth a hitherto unheard-of radicalism" (C 76). While the ancient skeptics may have applied the *epoche* to the world *as an object of knowledge*, doubting that knowledge of the absolute nature of the world as it is in itself was possible, Descartes doubts the world *as an object of sense-experience;* he doubts the world as an object of everyday experience. In attempting to prove the ego to be the founder of all sense by applying a radical *epoche* not just to scientific knowledge, but to the *life-world*, and in attempting to establish a universal science on the basis of this, Descartes approaches phenomenology. But according to Husserl, Descartes is nevertheless unable to penetrate into the realm of phenomenology, because of his view of the ego. As will be explained next, this view results from his failure, despite all his good intentions, to adhere to his own demand for radicalism in executing the *epoche*.

Descartes's radical *epoche* leads finally past the life-world, past the world of everyday experience, to one certitude upon which all knowledge will be erected—namely, the ego of the ego-cogito. Writes Husserl:

> For Descartes . . . I, the ego performing the epochē, am the
> only thing that is absolutely indubitable, that excludes in prin-
> ciple every possibility of doubt. [C 78]

Contrary to Ricoeur (CI 227), the certainty of the ego's being
does not foreclose the question of the nature of the ego's being, even for
Descartes. Husserl notes that Descartes *does* ask himself "what *kind* of an
ego it is, whether the ego is the human being, the sensibly intuited human being of everyday life" (C 79). Descartes, too quick to answer his
own question (C 82), says that it is not the living body, for it, like all
physical objects, is "ruled out" by the *epoche*. According to Husserl, this
answer is prejudiced: it is motivated by Descartes's acceptance of the
Galilean belief that reality presented by the senses is misleading and cov-
ers up an in-itself, a purely physical reality, which is mathematical and
the subject matter of pure thought.

In other words, Descartes treats the physical body like any other
object of the physical, sensible world on the Galilean model—namely, as
a *pure* physical object. Hence, the ego Descartes is left with after applying
the *epoche* to the body "is the *residuum of a previous abstraction* of the pure
physical body" (C 80). But conceiving the ego as the residuum of an
abstraction from the pure physical body is to give a prejudiced view of
the ego's nature, for it is to characterize it strictly *in terms of the physical
order*, albeit negatively, and not at all in terms of its own nature, whatever
that turns out to be—that is, the ego that is the residuum of such an
abstraction "according to this abstraction, at least apparently, is a complement of this body" (C 80).[8] According to Husserl, there are various
ways of being an ego, and "none of its ways can be severed from the
others" (C 108) without distorting the nature of the ego, for "throughout all their transformations they form a unity" (C 108).

One of the ways of being an ego is through the "bodily I" (*die
leibliche Ichkeit*) (C 108), which is the I of the living body. It is a mistake to
treat the physical body like any other object given by the senses, as a pure
physical object, for the body has a "unique ontic meaning," according to
Husserl, in that unlike pure physical objects, the body is perceived as
living by me:

> In a quite unique way the living body is constantly in the per-
> ceptual field quite immediately, with a completely unique ontic
> meaning, precisely the meaning indicated by the word "organ"
> (here used in its most primitive sense), [namely, as] that
> through which I exist in a completely unique way and quite im-
> mediately as the ego of affection and actions, [as that] in which

I hold sway quite immediately, kinesthetically—articulated into
particular organs through which I hold sway, or potentially
hold sway in particular kinestheses corresponding to them. [C
107]

The body is never experienced as just pure body, but always as subject-
object, according to Husserl:

I . . . find my *animate organism* as *uniquely* singled out—namely
as the only one—that is not just a body but precisely an animate organism . . . the only Object 'in" which I *"rule and govern" immediately.* [CM 97 (128)]

To describe the ego strictly as *residuum* of an abstraction of the pure
physical body, then, is to deny the living physical aspect of the ego's nature, and ultimately to falsify the ego's essence.

The ego achieved through Descartes's abstraction is not a pure
apodictic ego. While Descartes has correctly isolated the "center" of
apodicticity, the ego cogito, he fails to understand its nature, because he
is blinded by a *Weltanschauung* that should have been included in the
epoche. According to Husserl the Galilean worldview that Descartes
adopts should also have been bracketed by the *epoche,* for this forms part
of the *Weltanschauung* of the ego, one that in the long run prejudices the
ego's self-understanding:[9]

Is Descartes here not dominated in advance by the Galilean
certainty of a universal and absolutely pure world of physical
bodies, with the distinction between the merely sensibly exper-
ienceable and the mathematical, which is a matter of pure
thinking? Does he not already take it for granted that sensibil-
ity points to a realm of what is in-itself, but that it can deceive
us; and that there must be a rational way of resolving this [de-
ception] and of knowing what is in-itself with mathematical rationality? But is all this not at once bracketed with the epochē,
indeed even as a possibility? It is obvious that Descartes, in
spite of the radicalism of the presuppositionlessness he demands, has, in advance, a *goal* in relation to which the break-
through to this "ego" is supposed to be the *means.* He does
not see that, by being convinced of the possibility of the goal
and of this means, he has already left this radicalism behind. It
is not achieved by merely deciding on the epochē, on the radical withholding of [judgment on] all that is pregiven, on all
prior validities of what is in the world; the epochē must seri-

ously *be* and *remain* in effect. The ego is not a residuum of the world but is that which is absolutely apodictically posited; and this is made possible only through the epochē, only through the "bracketing" of the *total* world-validity; and it is the only positing thus made possible. [C 79]

According to Husserl, the ego obtained through Descartes's abstraction is not one to which doubt no longer applies—it is one to which one can still apply the *epoche*, for it is full of meaning: it has an idea of the external world according to the Galilean model, has an idea of God, has an idea of others and of culture, and has an idea of itself vis-à-vis all of the aforementioned. In short, Descartes has left the psychological self intact. Husserl, on the other hand, maintains that the *existence* of the world, God, others, culture, and so forth, is not all that should have been subjected to doubt, but also the very *meaning* of these, *what* they *are* for the ego and how they come about in the ego. This is what Husserl means when he writes the following:

Is not the epochē related to the totality of what is pregiven to me (who am philosophizing) and thus related to the whole world, including all human beings, and these not only in respect to their bodies? Is it not thus related to me as a *whole* man as I am valid for myself in my natural possession of the world (*Welthabe*)? [C 79]

By "whole man" Husserl means here the psycho-physical self, and by "as I am valid for myself in my natural possession of the world" Husserl means my *Weltanschauung*, for a *Weltanschauung* is a way of possessing the world. What Husserl is saying here, then, is that the *epoche* should be applied not only to the physical aspect of the self—namely, the body as object—but to the psychological self as well, of which my *Weltanschauung*—that is, my conception of the world and, since I am a being in this world, my conception of my ego as a being in this world—forms a part.

Hence Husserl maintains that the act of "abstracting" the ego from the body is itself motivated by the *Weltanschauung* of the Galilean model of the natural scientist, by the "psychologist's way of looking at things, on the natural ground of the world as pregiven and taken for granted" (C 80). Descartes does not ask what the world is for the ego or how its sense comes about, because, according to the Galilean worldview he adopts, the ego is *cut off from the world*. It is of course true that the Galilean worldview acknowledges that the body reveals the world through the senses, but this forms no part of the view's understanding of the essence of the body; no provision is made for the special nature of the body as "door" to the world, or as a means whereby I have access to the world. Because Descartes has abstracted the ego from the body, the ego is considered as something that is the "opposite" of a pure physical thing, and hence the world is not given directly to the ego, for unless the ego and body are in some way inseparably "one," the ego has no immediate access to the world. This is why Descartes needs to invoke God's benevolence as a guarantee of the ego's knowledge of the world. In other words, if the ego is seen as radically distinct from the body, as in the Galilean worldview, the world will be considered to be completely independent of the ego. The inextricable bond that exists between the ego and the world according to the phenomenologist—that of the ego as constituter of the world—is denied in this view.

Yet according to this model the world is believed to be that which is "there" beforehand, the ground of all being, an in-itself. Hence the ego which is "in" the body must also on this view find its ground in the world—it too must be *part* of the natural order, *even though it was held to be radically distinct from the purely physical*. The reasoning is fallacious, yet Descartes's philosophy exhibits such thinking, for, while the ego is considered by him to be radically distinct from the world, still he maintains that the ego is to be studied by psychology, a science of the natural order.[10] In failing to subject the ego fully to the *epoche*, Descartes inadvertently substitutes the psychological ego for the pure ego. He implicitly assumes the ego to be a "place" where thoughts and ideas occur, and assumes these thoughts and ideas to be events that take place *in* time. Consequently Descartes understands the study of the ego to be a study of psychological facts.

The consequence of not applying the *epoche* to the psychological ego is the absurd position in which what is supposed to *ground* the objective sciences, the ego, is itself subject *to* the objective science of psychology, for the ego that is the ground of Descartes's science is the psychological ego:

> That Descartes, however, persists in pure objectivism in spite
> of its subjective grounding was possible only through the fact
> that the *mens*, which at first stood by itself in the epochē and
> functioned as the absolute ground of knowledge, grounding
> the objective sciences (or, universally speaking, philosophy), ap-
> peared at the same time to *be* grounded along with everything
> else as a legitimate subject matter *within* the sciences, i.e., in
> psychology. Descartes does not make clear to himself that the
> ego, his ego deprived of its worldly character [*entweltlicht*]

through the epochē, in whose functioning *cogitationes* the world
has all the ontic meaning it can ever have for him, *cannot possibly* turn up as subject matter *in* the world, since everything that
is of the *world* derives its meaning precisely *from these functions*—including, then, one's own psychic being, the ego in the
usual sense. [C 81–82]

To overcome the circularity of subjecting that which is to ground
the objective sciences, the ego, *to* the objective sciences, Descartes
should have taken the method of objective science, rationality, and
grounded *it* fully in the ego. To do this he should have subjected the
belief in the ego's inherent rationality to the *epoche*. That Descartes maintains the ego to be essentially rational follows from his intention to establish a universal *science* on the ego; that is, from his intention to develop a
science using only the resources of the ego itself. Indeed, inasmuch as
science proceeds by reason, Descartes could only ground science in the
ego if he assumed the thinking of the ego fundamentally and essentially
to proceed according to the dictates of reason; if, in other words, he
considered the ego to be essentially rational. But this assumption is not
questioned by Descartes. More specifically, Descartes *uses*, but does not
question, the notion of judgment, and the laws and procedures of logic,
including deduction. Had he questioned the assumption of the ego's rationality as does Husserl, he would have seen the need to ground rationality and would have been led to the pure ego.

It is for this reason that Husserl maintains that although Descartes was on the path to phenomenology, it is his failure to adhere to his
own demand for radicalism that prevents him from gaining access to the
pure ego, and thereby from entering the realm of phenomenology (CM
25 [64]):

In the foundation-laying reflections of the *Meditations*—those
in which the epochē and its ego are introduced—a break in
consistency occurs when his ego is identified with the pure soul
[i.e., ego as residuum of an abstraction from the pure physical
body]. [C 80]

And:

For Descartes, the *Meditations* work themselves out in the por-
tentous form of a substitution of one's own psychic ego for the
[absolute] ego, of psychological immanence for egological im-

manence, of the evidence of psychic, "inner", or "self-presen-
tation" for egological self-perception; *and this is also their
continuing historical effect up to the present day* [my emphasis]. [C
81]

According to Husserl, it was Descartes's "haste to ground objectivism
and the exact sciences as affording metaphysical, absolute knowledge"
that prevented him from setting himself "the task of systematically inves-
tigating the pure ego—consistently remaining within the epoché—with
regard to what acts, what capacities, belong to it and what it brings
about, as intentional accomplishment, through these acts and capacities" (C 82).

Paradoxically, Descartes's philosophy gives rise to *two* branches of
philosophy commonly considered to be diametrically opposed to each
other: rationalism and empiricism. Both the rationalism and empiricism
that follow Descartes take over the transcendental theme of returning to
the ego as the ground of knowledge. Both also take over the worst in
Descartes—namely, Descartes's misunderstanding of the nature of the
apodictic ego, of the ego as residuum of an abstraction from the body. In
short they take over Descartes's mind-body split. However, the empiri-
cists and rationalists are distinguished by this: while the latter believe in
the possibility of knowledge of a transcendent in-itself, the former eventually come to deny such possibility and adopt a skepticism similar to that
of the ancient skeptics.

It is ironic that Descartes by his original insight did not want to
split ego and object (object in its broadest sense being "world"), for he
was implicitly guided by a notion of intentionality: by the idea that every
cogitatio has its cogitatum (C 82)—that is, that the ego always *implies* an
object, hence that there can be no radical ego-object split. But since the
concept of intentionality is not made explicit, it cannot properly guide
him nor can he investigate it. Had he made this notion explicit, he would
have been led to the question of rationality, for in its broadest sense
intentionality involves problems of *reason* and *understanding* (C 82): intentionality, the ego's being related to its object, is an act of believing
and has its modes of confirming, disconfirming, of truth and of falsehood. In short, Descartes would have been led to question the nature of
rationality, and that in virtue of which the ego is rational at all—namely,
evidence.[11] Had Descartes made explicit his concept of intentionality,
he would have been led to the true nature of the ego, not as residuum of
an abstraction from the pure physical body, but as the ground of rationality.

(d)   Locke, Berkeley, and Hume: Heirs to
       Descartes's Transcendental Motive,
       Heirs to Descartes's Mind-Body Spilt

Any notion of intentionality that Descartes may have had implicit in his philosophy is lost with Locke (C 82). Locke takes over Descartes's view of the soul as residing in the body, as residuum of an abstraction from the body. The motive of a return to the ego as ground of all knowledge remains, but with one difference: whereas in Descartes's theory the ego could know the reality that transcended it (the world in itself, substance), in Locke's theory the transcendent, the in-itself, substance, can never be known by the ego. All that we know, according to Locke, is what is given internally *in* the soul. That which is transcendent to the soul is a *je ne sais quoi*. This theme is carried further in Berkeley, according to whom it is not only not possible to know a reality, an in-itself transcendent to the ego, but according to whom there *is* no such thing. In his view, the transcendent reality, the *je ne sais quoi* found in Locke's theory, is but a philosophical invention (C 82).

It is Hume who carries this line of thought to its extreme. For Hume not only is "substance" a philosophical invention, but so are *all* objective categories (e.g., cause and effect, substantial self), prescientific as well as scientific. This leads Hume to reject the possibility of knowledge of matters of fact—it leads him to reject the possibility of science, in other words, for the latter is given through objective categories. This position, in which the possibility of empirical knowledge is denied, is of interest here because it is at once a theory of the nature of the ego. A brief outline of the way in which he arrives at his position follows next.

(e)   Hume's Pushing the Transcendental
       Motive to its Extreme: The Ego
       as Sole Arbiter

According to Hume, knowledge is marked by a type of certitude found in judgments of logic and mathematics. Such judgments express relations between ideas; they express *necessary* connections between ideas. Hence, in Hume's view, knowledge is given in judgments expressing necessary relations between ideas. In so-called knowledge of the world, such necessary relations are presumably expressed in judgments of cause and effect. The objective category of cause and effect is thought to express a necessary connection: we assume the effect *must* follow upon the cause.

But Hume asks: What *evidence* do we have for the necessary nature of this connection, for the link between cause and effect? Using his "copy-principle" as criterion of evidence, Hume is unable to find any evidence for the "necessity" of this link. He maintains that experience is fundamentally a series of sense-impressions, and that what we term knowledge of fact is a connection of representations derived from these sense-impressions. But the connections between these representations are made on the force of what is *usually* the case, not on what *must* be the case. Hence, they are in no way *necessary* connections. Belief in the necessary nature of the link between cause and effect is groundless. Since judgments of cause and effect express no necessary relations, they express no certitude, and, consequently, do not constitute knowledge claims,[12] according to Hume.

Hume does not end his "attack" on empirical knowledge there. Once again with the aid of his copy-principle he shows that *all* objective categories (such as substance, substantial self), and not merely the category of cause and effect, are groundless. Hence Hume maintains that knowledge of the world is not possible, and he falls "into the countersense of a 'philosophy of as-if' " (FTL 257 [227]). Science or knowledge is not possible, for it deals with only fictional concepts; hence it presents us with an "as-if" reality.

Now, the important thing to note concerning Hume's philosophy, in Husserl's opinion, is that Hume's final position, however unphenomenological it sounds, is a consequence of his taking very seriously the transcendental impulse to see the ego as founder of all sense. According to Husserl:

> He [Hume] was the first to *treat seriously the Cartesian focusing purely on what lies inside:* in that he began by freeing the soul radically from everything that gives it the significance of a reality in the world,[13] and then presupposed the soul purely as a field of "perceptions" ("impressions" and "ideas"), such as it is qua datum of a suitably purified internal experience. [FTL 256 (227)]

But what is even more surprising, in light of the fact that Hume, unlike Descartes, had no concept of intentionality, and that he is generally acknowledged to be a proponent of sense-data empiricism, a position Husserl battled all his life, is that in Husserl's estimation Hume carries the transcendental motive of a return to the ego further than anyone prior to him, including Descartes and even Kant (C 262). Hume's transcendental move is more radical than Descartes's, in other words.

This is so not merely because he, unlike Descartes, frees the ego from all objective categories, but also because he was the first to make the problem of transcendental philosophy *concrete*:

> Hume's greatness (a greatness still unrecognized in this, its most important aspect) lies in the fact that, despite all that, he was the first to grasp the universal *concrete problem* of transcendental philosophy. In the *concreteness* [my emphasis] of purely egological internality, as he saw, everything Objective becomes intended to (and, in favorable cases, perceived), thanks to a subjective genesis. Hume was the first to see the necessity of investigating the Objective itself as a product of its genesis from that *concreteness* [my emphasis], in order to make the legitimate being-sense of everything that exists for us intelligible through its ultimate origins. Stated more precisely: The real world and the categories of reality, which are its fundamental forms, became for him a problem in a new fashion. [FTL 256 (226–27)]

In making the problem of transcendental philosophy concrete, Hume enables the problem of transcendental philosophy to reach a new *depth;* he is able to see, more clearly than Descartes, what questions transcendentalism must answer and along which lines it must do so. In this way Hume points the way to a correct understanding of the transcendental ego.

A few words are in order concerning the way in which Hume goes beyond Descartes in executing the transcendental motive, and, more specifically, concerning what is meant by making the transcendental problem *concrete*.

It is undeniable that in a *certain* sense Descartes has a more phenomenological *attitude* than Hume, in that he is fundamentally guided, albeit implicitly and somewhat inconsistently, by a notion of intentionality. That is, Descartes is able to see beyond the "parts," ego-God-world, to the unity they imply: he sees that the ego implies a sense of objectivity and of God. The ego implies a sense of objectivity because the ego, in order to be, must be self-aware, and it can be self-aware only by contrast to something that resists it—namely, an object, which in its broadest sense is the world. In the ego's self-awareness, God is given, for God is given in apodictic truth, and self-awareness is the apodictic truth of one's own being. But, as mentioned earlier, Descartes's insight is a sweeping intuition in need of anchoring, for at times, indeed at the most crucial moment when he is about to answer the question of the nature of the apodictic ego, he loses sight of his intuition. This causes his writings to be a curious blend of depth and superficiality. Descartes should have asked what this fact that the ego and object are given at once, this intentionality, says about the nature of the ego. It has already been suggested that this would have led him to question "rationality" and "evidence," which in turn would have revealed the true nature of the apodictic—that is, transcendental—ego. Instead Descartes lets his insight into intentionality slip, and, assuming a gulf between the ego and the world, needs to appeal to the benevolence of God in order to bridge this gulf. Without God's benevolence the ego could not *know* the world (D 149). In short, "evidence" for the object is not immediately given to the ego, but mediately through God.

In maintaining this Descartes has strayed from the transcendental demand that all knowledge ultimately be grounded directly in the ego. He has strayed from the transcendental demand that the *ego* be the ground of evidence. One should not have to appeal to the benevolence of God for knowledge of the object if one is truly going to ground knowledge in the ego. One should appeal to *reason*. At *most* the appeal to God's benevolence is an intermediate step, which itself will be explained by reason, and so should not form part of the final expression of how the ego can have knowledge of the object. But the appeal to benevolence itself betrays a dependency on *revelation*. That is, while Descartes proves God's perfection by appeal to reason, that perfection implies benevolence does not immediately follow. It is, rather, something known from revelation, the acceptance of which itself requires faith. Hume, however, adheres to the transcendental demand to the end, for he asks what *concrete* evidence the ego has for the object. That is, he asks what proof the living ego *here and now* in direct experience has for the object:

> But idealism was always too quick with its theories and for the most part could not free itself from hidden objectivistic presuppositions; or else, as speculative idealism, it passed over the task of interrogating, concretely and analytically, actual subjectivity, i.e., subjectivity as having the actual phenomenal world in intuitive validity—which, properly understood, is nothing other than carrying out the phenomenological reduction and putting transcendental phenomenology into action. [C 337]

Hume does not consider that which is not directly *given* to the ego to be evidence. Revelation is not evidence in his view, for it requires faith. In other words, Hume, pushing the transcendental demand to its extreme, can legitimately ask what evidence there is for revelation, for faith in God. *Everything* is to be grounded in the ego. This is so for Husserl as well; he too maintains that God is something constituted by the ego, that "God" finds its sense in the ego, and he points out that this is in no way to commit a blasphemy. Hume, then, is truer to the transcendental motive. It is his *question* of what concrete evidence the ego has for the object that can set us on the path to working out explicitly the nature of the transcendental ego. It is just that his *answer* is disappointing. Using his copy-principle as criterion for evidence, he is unable to find any sense-impression corresponding to such objective concepts as "object," and he concludes that objective concepts are groundless; that they are without evidence altogether; that they are fictions. That is, on seeing that the ego has no *external* evidence for these ideas but is the source of these ideas, instead of looking for the evidence or ground of these ideas "in" the ego, something that would have led him to intentionality and phenomenology, he concludes that these ideas are completely *without* evidence, that they are ground*less*. This leads him to the absurd position of a "philosophy of as-if" (FTL 257 [227]). But it is precisely this absurdity that motivates us to go beyond Hume. In other words, Hume's philosophy will lead us closer to phenomenology in both a direct, positive way, and an indirect, negative way. On the positive side he leads us to phenomenology, to the extent that he pushes the transcendental move to its extreme in asking for the ego's concrete evidence for objective categories. On the negative side he leads us to phenomenology in that his philosophy leads to an absurd position, which will force us to reexamine the concrete facts at that point where his philosophy gives way to absurdity and to seek another answer to Hume's question of the ground of the objective categories.

(f) Kant's Inability to Purge his Notion of the Transcendental Ego of Objectivistic Elements

And this is precisely what Kant does. Following Hume's "transcendental turn," Kant in effect[14] asks what evidence the ego has for the legitimacy of the objective categories. Kant "in effect" asks this because actually he asks how we can know that judgments of fact are knowledge—how we can in principle be *assured* of their truth. But this is tantamount to asking for the legitimacy of objective categories, for judgments of fact are composed of them. The legitimacy of judgments of fact, then, depends on the legitimacy of the objective categories. The question of the legitimacy of the objective categories and judgments of fact is essentially the question of how we know that these objective categories and judgments of fact "match" something in experience, how we know that they represent reality. When Hume says that judgments concerning the world are fictions he means that they do not "match" experience, that there are no sense impressions corresponding to the objective categories. There is for Hume, then, a judgment-experience split. And this is the problem that Kant addresses when he addresses the problem of objective categories, when he addresses the problem of the epistemic status of judgments of fact. Writes Husserl:

> Hume had made him [Kant] sensitive to the fact that between
> the pure truths of reason and metaphysical objectivity there re-
> mained a gulf of incomprehensibility, namely, as to how pre-
> cisely these truths of reason could really guarantee the
> knowledge of things. [C 93]

But for Kant the fact that evidence for the objective categories cannot be found in experience is not an indication that these categories are fictions. Kant attempts to show that evidence for them cannot be found *in* experience because they allow for the very possibility *of* experience. "The categories," writes Kant, "are the conditions of the possibility of experience, and are therefore valid *a priori* for all objects of experience" (CPR 171 [B 161]). Experience already "makes use of" the categories, as it were:

> Kant now undertakes, in fact, to show, through a regressive
> procedure, that if common experience is really to be experi-
> ence of *objects of nature*, objects which can really be knowable
> with objective truth, i.e., scientifically, in respect to their being
> and nonbeing, their being-such and being-otherwise (*So-und-
> Andersbeschaffensein*), then the intuitively appearing world must
> already be a construct of the faculties of "pure intuition" and
> "pure reason," the same faculties that express themselves in
> explicit thinking in mathematics and logic. [C 94]

While judgments of fact were fictions for Hume, since they did not "match" what was given in experience, for Kant judgments of fact already express the ego's relation to the world, since the objective categories of which they are composed make experience possible. Any judgment about the world (which *is* experience of the world, in Kant's view) comes about, according to Kant, when sense-impressions (which by themselves are not knowledge, but are uninformed) and pure concepts (which without sense-impressions are empty) "meet," as it were. Writes Kant: "the categories are not in themselves knowledge, but are merely forms of thought for the making of knowledge from given intuitions" (CPR 253 [B 288]). The categories themselves, according to Kant, "come from" the ego.

A brief outline of the argument whereby he claims that the categories "stem from" the ego follows. Kant says that the categories stem from the understanding:

> The understanding alone [is] their [the a priori concepts']
> birth place. [CPR 103 (B 90)]

The understanding, in turn, is made possible by the original unity of apperception. That is, the very function of the understanding, combination or synthesis, presupposes unity.[15] Hence the original unity of apperception is ultimately what makes the categories possible. Kant makes it quite clear that the original unity of apperception, which allows for the understanding, is not to be confused with the *category* of unity, for the latter stems from the understanding:

> This unity, which precedes *a priori* all concepts of combination,
> is not the category of unity; for all categories are grounded in
> logical functions of judgment, and in these functions combina-
> tion, and therefore unity of given concepts, is already thought.
> Thus the category already presupposes combination. We must
> therefore look yet higher for this unity (as qualitative), namely
> in that which itself contains the ground of the unity of diverse
> concepts in judgment, and therefore of the possibility of the
> understanding even as regards its logical employment. [CPR
> 152 (B 131)]

This unity of apperception is, rather, the "unity of consciousness," "the pure original unchangeable consciousness" or *"transcendental appercep-tion"* (CPR 136 [A 107]) It is the *"a priori* ground of all concepts" (CPR 136 [A 107]). This unity finds expression in the representation "I think," a representation that must be able to accompany every intuition or thought, according to Kant (CPR 153 [B 132]). For Kant, then, as for Hume, the categories have their source in the ego.

But while the categories are ungrounded and hence fictitious for Hume, for Kant they find their *ground* in the ego. Kant will try to show by his "regressive method" (C 114) *how* the categories are grounded, thereby showing their legitimacy. By thus demonstrating their legitimacy he shows how knowledge is possible. But here Kant runs into difficulties, partly because he has inherited from Hume some concepts that will not *allow* him to work out the problem of the grounding of the objective categories. First of all, Kant accepts the Humean notion of knowledge as certainty, the type of certainty exhibited in mathematics and logic. This will force Kant to find a *nonempirical* source of knowledge of the world, for only the nonempirical is capable of giving the type of certitude that Hume and Kant think marks knowledge. Since judgments about the world are formed by means of objective categories, this means the source of the objective categories must be pure:

> Since they [the categories] are *a priori* concepts, and therefore independent of experience, the ascription to them of an empirical origin would be a sort of *generatio aequivoca*. [CPR 174 (B 167)]

Hence the ego that is the source of the categories cannot be the empirical ego but must be the *pure*, transcendental, ego. Indeed, this is why Kant stresses that the original synthetic unity of apperception is a *thought*, not an intuition, for if it were an intuition, it would not be free of empirical admixture:

> In the synthetic original unity of apperception I am conscious of myself, not as I appear to myself, nor as I am in myself, but only that I am. This *representation* is a *thought*, not an *intuition*. [CPR 168 (B 157)]

If the "I" of the "I think" were the natural soul, it would be in space and time, and its structure/function would be determined according to the forms of space and time. In that case evidence for the categories would be within space and time. This was Hume's standard of evidence and it meant that that which grounds the categories was something "in" space and time. Hume found nothing in experience to correspond to the objective categories. For this reason Kant must hold that the original synthetic unity of apperception is free from all impressions of the senses:

> This is the concept or, if the term be preferred, the judgment "I think." As is easily seen, this is the vehicle of all concepts. . . . But it can have no special designation, because it serves only to introduce all our thought, as belonging to conscious-

> ness. Meanwhile, however free it be of empirical admixture
> (impressions of the senses). . . . [CPR 329 (B 399–400)]

And again:

> For, it must be observed, that when I have called the proposi-
> tion, "I think," an empirical proposition, I do not mean to say
> thereby, that the "I" in this proposition is an empirical repre-
> sentation. On the contrary, it is purely intellectual, because be-
> longing to thought in general. [CPR 378 (B 423)]

Hence, although Kant realizes that the proposition "I think" is an empirical proposition—I can only think "I think" once I have as a matter of fact thought—that is, "I think" is something I can find out only empirically—he holds that the "I" is not in any way empirical. It must, then, be pure thought.

To successfully show how the categories originate in the pure transcendental ego, then, Kant will have to show the difference between the transcendental and empirical ego. But he will have difficulty doing this, for according to him we can have no *knowledge* of the pure transcendental ego—that is, *all* knowledge involves the combination of intuition and categories, and the transcendental ego, in view of its purity, cannot be made intuitively clear. It cannot be revealed by the self-evidence of inner perception because according to "the Kantian doctrine of inner sense . . . everything that can be exhibited in the self-evidence of inner experience has already been formed by a transcendental function, that of temporalization (*Zeitigung*)" (C 114). The transcendental ego can neither be known nor experienced, according to Kant (CPR 246 [B 277]).[16]

And there is another concept that Kant takes over from Hume that prevents him from achieving a proper understanding of the pure ego—namely, his notion of inner-perception. Kant, like Descartes and Hume before him, views self-evident inner perception as self-perception of the naturalized soul (C 115). Kant cannot *concretely* distinguish, and hence cannot *clearly* distinguish, transcendental subjectivity from the "soul which is made part of nature and conceived of as a component of the psychophysical human being within the time of nature, within space-time" (C 115). Hence if he attempts to make intuitively clear how objective categories are grounded in the transcendental ego by appeal to inner-perception, he inadvertently grounds them in the objective soul. Kant cannot effect a true transcendental philosophy, he cannot show *how* the objective categories are grounded in the transcendental ego, because he cannot free himself from the popular view of the ego.

Hence, while Kant has gone beyond Hume and has come a step closer to transcendental philosophy in maintaining that the objective categories are not *fictions* but are required for the very possibility of experience, still Husserl's complaint against him is that these objective categories remain, as in the case of Hume's philosophy, *groundless*. The categories of science are "in" mind, but what grounds them, from where do we "get" them?

> There is some complaint about the obscurities of the Kantian philosophy, about the incomprehensibility of the evidences of his regressive method, his transcendental-subjective "faculties," "functions," "formations," about the difficulty of understanding what transcendental subjectivity actually is, how its function, its accomplishment, comes about, how this is to make all objective science understandable. And in fact Kant does get involved in his own sort of mythical talk, whose literal meaning points to something subjective, but a mode of the subjective which we are in principle unable to make intuitive to ourselves, whether through factual examples or through genuine analogy. [C 114]

Part of Kant's problem with grounding the objective categories results from his description of the "I think." According to Husserl, Kant's conception of the "I think" renders it completely incomprehensible and *powerless*. Presumably the "I think" that accompanies all thought and intuition *precedes* all thought and intuition, the empirical merely being the "condition of application" of thinking "I think" (CPR 378 [B 423]). But what does it *refer* to, and what makes it ever-present? How does it come to attach itself to all thought and intuition? Now, although Kant says that the "I" of the "I think" cannot be an object of knowledge, he *does* on the one hand term the "I think" a *thought*. But it is a thought that "can have no special designation, because it serves only to introduce all our thought" (CPR 329 [B 399–400]). In that case it is a thought that in itself has neither reference nor sense. But how then is it to serve as unifying agent? That is, how, by what *motive*, will it ever "attach" itself to all intuition and thought? Let us stress that the difficulty rests not with saying that the "I" of the "I think" has no special designation—this is what Husserl maintains as well—but with maintaining that and, *further*, that it is a purely intellectual "entity," for then it has no inherent link with intuition and thought—it has nothing to "anchor" it to the empirical. According to Husserl the "I" of the "I think" must immediately be related to the sensible. Indeed, if the "I" were a thought, since the "I think" precedes all intuition and thought, it would precede itself; it would make itself possible. Such a "system" could never "get off the ground." The "I think" must be *immediately* given and secured. For Husserl the "I," while pure, is not without significance. It refers to an ever-present experience.

When Kant maintains that the "I" makes experience possible, he is working with a very special concept of experience. By experience Kant means *objective* thinking, *knowledge*. "Experience is an empirical knowledge," writes Kant (CPR 208 [B 218]). Hence for Kant experience is knowledge and already involves objective categories. Indeed, Kant's "problem" is the possibility of *science*—that is, it is "the problem of rational natural science which primarily guides and determines Kant's thinking" (C 97). But according to Husserl our scientific way of knowing the world is a specialized act of mind, one "higher up" than our general experience of the world. Not all experience, in Husserl's opinion, is scientific knowledge. In fact, science itself *presupposes* a world in which we live, a world thought to be there beforehand. Without this presupposition, science makes no sense and could not advance:

> It belongs to what is taken for granted, prior to all scientific thought and all philosophical questioning, that the world is— always is in advance—and that every correction of an opinion, whether an experiential or other opinion, presupposes the already existing world, namely, as a horizon of what in the given case is indubitably valid as existing, and presupposes within this horizon something familiar and doubtlessly certain with which that which is perhaps canceled out as invalid came into conflict. Objective science, too, asks questions only on the ground of this world's existing in advance through prescientific life. Like all praxis, objective science presupposes the being of this world, but it sets itself the task of transposing knowledge which is imperfect and prescientific in respect of scope and constancy into perfect knowledge—in accord with an idea of a correlative which is, to be sure, infinitely distant, i.e., of a world which in itself is fixed and determined and of truths which are *idealiter* scientific ("truths-in-themselves") and which predicatively interpret this world. To realize this in a systematic process, in stages of perfection, through a method which makes possible a constant advance: this is the task. [C 110–11]

While experience and knowledge are the same for Kant, in that both are subject to the objective categories, for Husserl there is a level of experience that has not yet been subjected to the objective categories, a level of experience that is the *ground* of the objective categories. The "I" is such an experience, an experience that is preobjective, and is not *knowledge*. According to Husserl the "I" refers to an ever-present experience.

More specifically, this "I" refers to the *living* body. Husserl writes that "our living body . . . is never absent from the perceptual field" (C 106). Such a position is unthinkable for Kant, for according to him "body" refers to that which is an object of outer sense (CPR 329 [B 400]). But here Kant makes the same mistake that Descartes does. "Body" does not refer to only that which is an object of outer sense, nor mind exclusively to inner sense. "Body" as immediately sensed is *subject*, not object; "body" *is* sensing. The body is not given only through outer sense, as when one observes one's hands or hears one's voice, for example, but body is also sensed immediately as subject or as "inner" as, for example, when I inhale, blink my eyes, swallow, when I feel hungry.

One could not call this sensing an intuition in Kant's sense of the word, for intuition for Kant is *of* an object, and the above refers not to the sensing *of* an object, but refers to *sensing itself*—that is, to myself *as* sensing. This "I," then, is not an impression free from empirical admixture; it is an impression of the senses. The "I" refers to a condition, not to an object—namely, the condition of immediate, always present, feeling or sensation of "inner." Not only is this condition always present—that is, not only is it always "there"—but it defines for us our temporal present. This "I" is not an empty thought; it refers to something. Nor is it a pure thought a priori in the mind, but is born within experience; it is made up of and comes from one's experience. All experience is experience of this abiding body; every act of cognition will reflect this position or condition. According to Husserl, "we are concretely in the field of perception, etc., *and in the field of consciousness* [my emphasis], however broadly we may conceive this, through our living body" (C 108).

This is why Husserl differs radically from Kant. The transcendental ego is not a pure thought for Husserl, but is *lived*. There can be no question of sense-impressions coming into contact with pure concepts of the transcendental ego. Nor will Husserl say that the transcendental ego "contains" the idea, as will be explained later in greater detail. The transcendental ego *is* the pure idea in Husserl's view. But if the transcendental ego is the pure idea, it *is* also reality. *All* reality is for the transcendental ego, is relative to the transcendental ego, according to Husserl. The transcendental ego allows for reality. Hence in Husserl's view the transcendental ego is that in which reality and idea are *one*. While in the philosophies of both Hume and Kant there was some form of idea-reality split—it will be recalled that there was a judgment-reality split in Hume's philosophy, and a category-sense-impression split in Kant's philosophy—in Husserl's philosophy there is *no* idea-reality split in any form whatsoever (EJ 330).[17] The idea (the eidetic idea, not the concept) of the object makes for the reality of the object and vice versa.[18] By real object we mean an object we *can* touch, hear, see, and so forth.[19] This project of "can do" requires or involves the idea. In turn the idea *is* of the real object.

Now, the transcendental ego is both arche and telos. Its telos is that of perfect self-awareness. This it could not achieve without the object, for the transcendental ego in itself is "transparent." It follows that the transcendental ego could not *be* without the idea (and hence the reality) of the object. The *fact* of our living then becomes ground of the transcendental ego. Hence Husserl's claim that phenomenology is *description*. While Kant has to ground the categories in an ego devoid of experience, for Husserl they are grounded in terms of the *life* of the transcendental ego; they are grounded in the being and structure of the transcendental ego that *is life* (life here is not to be confused with Kant's notion of experience). Life, not experience, becomes the ultimate basis of the legitimation of the categories.

Kant "skips over" this life-world—it is not something he puts to question; it is not considered in his theory. When Kant asks how we can know the world, he means by "world" the world given by *science*, a world that *presupposes* the world of everyday life. Hence Kant's questioning does not take place on the most basic level, and hence his philosophy cannot become a true transcendental philosophy. Kant has the transcendental ego constituting objective (scientific) thought directly—that is, by bypassing *life*. The transcendental ego, which Kant takes to be the pure ego, harbors meaning of which Kant is not aware. It harbors meaning of the transcendental ego *as* living. Kant has, then, purified the ego too readily—and this is not *genuine* purification. Purifying the transcendental ego means getting at a presuppositionless basis. But one cannot without further ado *declare* that a certain level of the ego is to be presuppositionless. Meaning must be *faced* to purify the ego. The pure transcendental ego is the ground of *meaning*, so meaning must be the guide to the pure transcendental ego; one must, as it were, strip successive layers of meaning. None can be skipped. Since the transcendental ego that Kant considers to be pure implicitly harbors a sense of life, purification must go through the sense of life.

This is where Husserl's philosophy differs from Kant's. While "from the very start in the Kantian manner of posing questions, the everyday surrounding world of life is *presupposed* [my emphasis] as existing" (C 104), Husserl's transcendental philosophy examines this presupposition and the meaning it harbors. Husserl's philosophy is explicitly concerned with the notion of "life," in other words. Indeed, according to Husserl a true transcendental philosophy must take "life" into account:

> It is the motif of inquiring back into the ultimate source of all the formations of knowledge, the motif of the knower's reflecting upon himself and his knowing *life* [my emphasis] in which all the scientific structures that are valid for him occur purposefully, are stored up as acquisitions, and have become and continue to become freely available. Working itself out radically, it is the motif of a universal philosophy which is grounded purely in this source and thus ultimately grounded. This source bears the title *I-myself*, with all my actual and possible knowing *life* [my emphasis] and, ultimately, my *concrete life* [my emphasis] in general. The whole transcendental set of problems circles around the relation of *this*, my "I"—the "ego"—to what it is at first taken for granted to be—my soul—and, again, around the relation of this ego and my so conscious *life* [my emphasis] to the *world* of which I am conscious and whose being I know through my own cognitive structures. [C 97–98]

There is another prejudice that Kant shares with both Descartes and Hume that stands in his way of achieving a proper understanding of the pure transcendental ego—namely, his blind acceptance of logic. All problems converge on this. To make this clear it is necessary to review briefly some of Kant's salient philosophical presuppositions:

(1) Knowledge is marked by certainty, the type of certainty exhibited in judgments of logic (a presupposition he shares with Hume).
(2) Everything in our experience has already been subjected to the objective categories—experience is knowledge, in other words.
(3) We have two representations of ourselves: " 'I,' as thinking, am an object of inner sense, and am called 'soul,' " and "that which is an object of the outer senses is called 'body' " (CPR 329 [B 400]).

As well, Kant does in a general way describe some aspects of the transcendental ego:

(a) The transcendental ego is the source of the pure categories and hence is the ground of *knowledge*. In light of (1) above, the transcendental ego is the source of that type of certainty exhibited in judgments of logic, and hence,
(b) The transcendental ego must in some way *be like* logical objects; it

must be pure, "thoughtlike" and "intellectual" (CPR 378 [B 423]; 168 [B 157]; 169 [B 158]; 247 [B 278]).

(c) The transcendental ego is not experienced (CPR 246 [B 277]).

(d) The transcendental ego is the ground of all meaning. This principle expresses Kant's transcendental motive of overcoming all objectivism.

From the above general philosophical principles and characterizations of the transcendental ego, it is clear that how Kant conceives of the transcendental ego is determined by how he conceives of knowledge, certainty, and purity. For Kant, as for Hume, the paradigm of this is *formal logic*. The transcendental ego for Kant is like a logical object (he calls it a judgment [CPR 329 (B 399)]). Now here we run into a conflict. His way of conceiving of the transcendental ego is determined by his conception of logic. Hence, unless he has a *purified* concept of logic, he will not have a purified concept of the transcendental ego. As long as his concept of *logic* remains objectivistic—that is, as long as it implicitly harbors meaning constituted by the transcendental ego—his concept of the *transcendental ego* remains objectivistic. But Kant does not realize that his logic is *not* a purified logic, that it is *objectivistic*, that it has a meaning constituted *by* the transcendental ego. Hence while Kant realizes he "wants" a logic purified by the transcendental motive, he is not working with such a purified logic. Husserl writes:

> *According to the words*, beginning with the definition and throughout the exposition, Kant's logic is presented as a science directed to the subjective—a science of thinking, which is nevertheless distinguished, as apriori, from the empirical psychology of thinking. But *actually*, according to its sense, Kant's purely formal logic concerns the ideal formations *produced by thinking* [my emphasis]. And, concerning them, Kant fails to ask properly transcendental questions of the possibility of cognition. [FTL 260 (230)]

And:

> As for Kant himself: clearly as he recognized (in the nuclear components of the Aristotelian tradition) the apriori character of logic, its purity from everything pertaining to empirical psychology, and the wrongness of including logic in a theory of experience, he still did not grasp the peculiar sense in which logic is ideal. Otherwise that sense would surely have given him a motive for asking transcendental questions. [FTL 261 (231)]

In other words, Kant does not appreciate the extent of the objective nature of logic (FTL 261 [231]), and so does not ask of it transcendental questions (FTL 258–59 [228–29]). According to Husserl, it is an anti-Platonism that prevents Kant from appreciating the objectivity of the ideal objects of logic (IK 55), and this in turn prevents him from asking transcendental questions concerning logic:

> But that [the failure to ask transcendental questions about logic] was because no one ventured, or had the courage to venture, to take the *ideality of the formations with which logic is concerned* as the characteristic of a separate, self-contained, *"world" of ideal Objects* and, in so doing, to come face to face with the painful question of how subjectivity can in itself bring forth, purely from sources appertaining to its own spontaneity, formations that can be rightly accounted as ideal *Objects* in an ideal "world." [FTL 260–61 (230)]

And:

> The definite aim [of purifying logic] could not be attached to the obscure need for logical inquiries directed somehow to the subjective until after that the ideal Objectivity of such formations had been sharply brought out and firmly acknowledged. For only then was one faced with the unintelligibility of *how ideal objectivities* that originate purely in our own subjective activities of judgment and cognition, that are there originaliter in our field of consciousness purely as formations produced by our own spontaneity, *acquire the being-sense of "Objects,"* existing in themselves over against the adventitiousness of the acts and the subjects. [FTL 263–64 (233)]

In Husserl's view, then, the transcendental set of problems that Kant applies to judgments of science should have been applied to judgments of logic as well:

> Accordingly the *transcendental problem* that *Objective logic* (taken no matter how broadly or narrowly) must raise concerning its field of ideal objectivities takes a position *parallel to the transcendental problem of the sciences of realities.* [FTL 264 (233–34)]

And this is what Husserl means by saying that "Kant's Copernican revolution [falls] short of full effectuation" (FTL 255 [226]); he means that Kant fails to extend the Copernican revolution that he effects in natural science to the realm of logic. Hence, Kant's description of the transcendental ego is based, however implicitly, on a model of an objectivistic logic, and this will not allow him to overcome objectivism. If a transcendental philosophy wants to arrive at the ego without presuppositions, it cannot use a model containing presuppositions for its descriptive purposes. The transcendental ego of Kant's philosophy is still an objective ego, for it is conceived on the model of a logic that is something *formed by* thinking, a "had" meaning. According to Husserl objectivism can be overcome only in *life*, the start of *all* meaning.

4

The Pure
Transcendental Ego,
Ground of Logic and of Life:
Where Psychology and
Phenomenology Meet

(a)   The Threat of Psychologism

In chapter 2 it was argued that the form of the judgment "S is p" reflects an act of objectification and that objectification is the essence of the transcendental ego. It was said also that objectification is an act of bringing the object to evidence and that the "rule" for doing so is the idea of the object (X with predicates). While this sounds like a form of Kantian idealism—it seems as if Husserl were saying that the judgment "S is p" results from nominalizing a sense datum (the given "S") and applying the idea of the object (X with predicates) to this datum—in chapter 3 it was explained how Husserl's position differs from that of Kant. While in Kant's theory there seems to be a category-sense-impression split—the transcendental ego somehow "has" the categories, which, on coming in contact with sense impressions, give rise to experience—for Husserl such a split is unthinkable. To have a sense-impression *is* to experience, in his view. For Husserl the transcendental ego *is* at once the idea of the object,[1] the center of experience and the center of life. But since the judgment reflects the essence of the transcendental ego, logic, the study of the judgment, is at once the study of the transcendental ego. Furthermore, since the transcendental ego is the center of experience; logic will involve not only a theory of experience,[2] but will also involve a theory of life, since it is always a living subject who experiences. Judgment, experience, life, and transcendental ego are all interwoven in Husserl's phenomenology.

The claim that one needs a theory of experience[3] in order to ground logic is one most logicians shun, for to them it implies a *dependency* of the judgment on experience, which in turn introduces a subjective factor in logic, for, as stated above, it is always a *subject* who experiences. To them this subjective factor spells the threat of psychologism, the doctrine that denies the objective status of logical laws and objects by reducing them to subjective, psychological acts. For example, when, as early as the *Philosophy of Arithmetic*, Husserl wanted to ground arithmetic and logic by reference to subjective acts—that is, by reference to experience—Frege criticized him for propounding a psychologism. But even at that time Husserl denied that he was advancing a psychologism. Husserl's point was and remained that explaining the logical by reference to subjective acts does not automatically imply psychologism. Whether or not psychologism is implied depends on how one conceives of the nature of the subjective act. According to psychologism psychic acts are *real* events (events in space and time) to be studied by psychology, an *empirical* science. Logical psychologism maintains that the laws of logic reflect the way the mind, the human psyche, as a *matter of fact* works; hence, it reduces logical laws to empirical laws. Describing logical psychologism Husserl writes:

> The Data for logic are real occurrences belonging to the sphere of psychology; and, as such, according to the usual view, they would be unambiguously determined within the universal causal nexus of the real world and explainable by causal laws.
>
> But this later point may be left out of consideration. Our main concern here is the *equating of the formations produced by judging* (and then, naturally, of all similar formations produced by rational acts of any other sort) *with phenomena appearing in internal experience*. This equating is based on their making their appearance "internally," in the act-consciousness itself. Thus concepts, judgments, arguments, proofs, theories, would be psychic occurrences; and logic would be, as John Stuart Mill said it is, a "part, or branch, of psychology." This highly plausible conception is *logical psychologism*. [FTL 154 (137–38)]

Understood in this way, logical psychologism is an empiricism, as opposed to a rationalism/idealism, which maintains that mind contributes something a priori *to* experience and knowledge.

But here a paradox confronts us. As will be discussed below, Husserl charges Kant with psychologism. But Kant's philosophy is generally said to be an idealism. Furthermore, Hume, who believes in the a priori status of logical laws—he unquestioningly takes these to be paradigmatic of knowledge[4]—and who generally is thought to be an empiricist, Husserl labels an idealist (FTL 166 [148])! This paradox is resolved, however, once one sees that logical psychologism is but a facet of a broader notion of psychologism:

> The extraordinary broadening and, at the same time, radicalizing of the refutation of logical psychologism, which we have effected in the foregoing investigation, have brought us an extreme *generalization of the idea of psychologism*, in a *quite definite—*but not the only*—sense.* Psychologism in this sense is to be distinguished by the circumstance that some species or other of possibly evident objectivities (or even all species, as in the case of Hume's philosophy) are *psychologized*, because, as is obvious, they are constituted in the manner peculiar to consciousness—that is to say: their being-sense is built up, in and for subjectivity, by experience or other modes of consciousness that combine with experience. That they are "psychologized" signifies that their objective sense, their *sense as a species of objects* having a peculiar essence, is *denied* in favor of the subjective mental occurrences, the Data in immanent or psychological temporality. . . . The expression psychologism is more appropriate to any interpretation that converts objectivities into something psychological in the proper sense; and the *pregnant* sense of psychologism should be defined accordingly.
> [FTL 169 (151)]

In other words, Husserl *extends* the notion of psychologism. Logical psychologism, which denies the objective status of logical idealities, is but an aspect of a more generalized psychologism that denies the objective status of all idealities. Whereas logical psychologism applies to a restricted region of Platonic ideas, the broader psychologism applies to an extended region of Platonic ideas, as it were (FTL 166 [148]).[5] For example, the notion of real objects, as Hume realized, also involves idealities,[6] such as the idea of identity over time and the idea of substance (FTL 166 [148]). Something is objective—that is, transcendent to me—if it has its own abiding being (identity and substance). If one reduces ideal logical objectivities to subjective acts, then, if one is going to be consistent, one should reduce the idealities involved in the perception of real objects to subjective acts as well. Hume denies the objective status of the latter type of idealities, because there are no sense data corresponding to these ideas, sense data being the criteria of reality for him.[7] He considers these ideas fictions. That is why Husserl says that Hume denies the objective status of objects of perception. For Hume real objects make their appearance in mind and are reduced to data of mind; their objective, transcendent status is denied, for he considers the ideas that allow for that status to be fictions. But while Hume reduces idealities involved in perception of real objects to subjective acts, he does not so reduce logical idealities.

While logical psychologism is an *empiricism*, a psychologism that rejects the idealities of real objects leads to an *idealism* because, paradoxically, it is the ideal aspects of real experience that give real objects their objectivity and hence their reality. That is, acknowledging a real object involves the employment of ideas, such as that of extension, substance, the general idea of object (an X with predicates), and so forth. Strictly speaking, if one were consistent one would deny the objective status of all idealities if one denied the objective status of any, or make *all* idealities problematic if one makes *any* problematic. But if these philosophers are inconsistent it is due to their failure to see that logical and ontological concepts are perfect correlates (see chapter 2).

To avoid logical psychologism, then, it must be shown that logical laws are necessary laws, that they do not describe what mind as a matter of fact does. But showing that the laws of logic are in *some way* necessary although they are generated by mind, as Kant does when he shows that the categories are necessary for experience/knowledge to be possible at all, will not in itself overcome psychologism. While such an approach lends some necessity to logical laws, it does not make them truly a priori, for the logical laws that are necessary for experience/knowledge to be possible may still have been generated by the empirical psyche. The laws will not be a priori unless that from which they are generated is truly a priori, is a priori through and through. There can be no factual/empirical "residue," for something a priori cannot come from something empirical. In other words, to show that logical laws are generated from "mind," and are truly a priori, one needs to show that mind is truly a priori. Logical laws must be grounded in a structure that in no way is the empirical psyche. This means that mind, that from which logical laws are generated, must be necessary not in terms of something extrinsic to it— experience/knowledge in Kant's system can be said to be extrinsic to logical laws because the categories are prior to experience—but in terms of its *own being*. Mind must be *absolutely a priori*; its *being* must be necessary. This is what Husserl maintains. The being of the pure transcendental ego is a necessary being:

I myself, or my experience in its actuality am *absolute* Reality (*Wirklichkeit*), given through a positing that is unconditioned and simply indissoluble.

The thesis of my pure Ego and its personal life, which is "neces-sary" and plainly indubitable, thus stands opposed to the thesis of the world which is "contingent." All corporeally given thing-like entities can also not be, no corporeally given experiencing can also not be: that is the essential law, which defines this necessity and that contingency.

Obviously then the ontic necessity of the actual present ex-periencing . . . is the necessity of a fact (*Faktum*), and called "necessity" because an essential law is involved in the fact, and here indeed in its existence as such. [I 131]

This brings us face to face with a two-sided dilemma: it will have to be shown (i) how certain phenomena associated with the concept of life, which seem to threaten the necessary and absolute status of the transcendental ego, in fact are compatible with the absolute, pure, sta-tus of the latter, and (ii) in what way mind is necessary in terms of its own being without destroying facticity. This first issue is addressed in the remainder of this chapter; the second is dealt with in the next chap-ter. This two-sided dilemma, then, is part and parcel of the problem of psychologism.

(b)   How Phenomena of Life Seem to Threaten the Pure Status of the Transcendental Ego

Phenomenology is differentiated from previous philosophies and specif-ically from realism and idealism by the fact that it acknowledges both ideal and real objectivities as well as their essential interrelatedness. Ac-cording to Husserl the ideal and real, or eidos and fact, respectively, mutually imply one another. On this Husserl differs from the realists who deny objectivity of the ideal and from such idealists as Kant who maintain the eidos to be "separate" from the fact.

The essential relation of the eidos and fact is a core point of phe-nomenology. It has already been said that this relation corresponds to the transcendental ego, that the transcendental ego is the idea and the fact of the object, according to Husserl. But "object" is given via the body, via kinesthesis, the "states" whereby one holds sway in the body (C

107). Without kinesthesis one would not have a concept of object, according to Husserl. As Dorion Cairns writes:

> Husserl proceeded to develop his idea of kinaesthesis. The constitution of an object in perception depends not only on a certain *Verlauf* (course, flow) of sensational-hyletic data, but also upon a certain correlation with a certain type of kinaesthesis. Kinaesthesis differs form *Empfindung* (sensation) by having an intimate relation to subjective potentiality. The "I can" works directly on or with kinaesthesis, and brings about sensational and hence objective changes only indirectly. The identity of an object depends on a certain relation to the *"ich kann"* (I can). I asked Husserl whether, if, were it impossible for the body to have a reflex perception to itself (one hand touch the other, the eye see the hand, etc.) there would then be the possibility of the constitution of a world, or of a body. If, e.g., our only sense organ was an eye, would we have any sort of world? He answered no. [CHF 3–4]

Fact and eidos are *one* in the living body (*Leib*), and it is the living body that is the concrete transcendental ego in Husserl's view. It has been noted above that Husserl differs in this respect from Kant. For Husserl, unlike for Kant, the transcendental ego is *lived*;[8] the pure transcendental ego involves the living body (subject-object) for Husserl. Writes Gadamer:

> "Life" is also, and no less, the transcendentally reduced subjectivity that is the source of all objectifications. Husserl calls "life" that which he emphasizes as his own achievement in his critique of the objectivist naivete of all previous philosophy. It consists, in his eyes, in having revealed the unreality of the customary epistemological controversy between idealism and realism and, instead, in having thematized the inner relation between subjectivity and objectivity. This is the reason for his phrase "productive life." "The radical contemplation of the world is the systematic and pure interior contemplation of the subjectivity, which expresses itself in the 'exterior.' It is as with the unity of a living organism, which we can certainly examine and analyse from the outside, but can understand only if we go back to its hidden roots. . . . " Thus also the intelligibility of the subject's attitude to the world does not reside in conscious experiences and their intentionality, but in the anonymous "productions" of life. The metaphor of the organism that Husserl employs here is

more than a metaphor. As he expressly states, he wants to be
taken literally. [TM 220]

But this poses several problems. If logic is grounded in the transcendental ego, the " 'subjective-relative' a priori of the life-world" (C
140), then logic is grounded in the living body, since the transcendental
ego is the living body. But the body is the seat of desires, and as Freud
tells us, thought closely related to the body is not subject to the laws of
noncontradiction, and is not subject to objective time. An observation of
our dreams confirms this.[9] In other words, thought closely related to the
body is not subject to the structure of objective thought. Does this mean
that the "universal prelogical a priori through which everything logical,
the total edifice of objective theory in all its methodological forms, demonstrates its legitimate sense and from which, then, all logic itself must
receive its norms" (C 141) is itself essentially illogical, perhaps even determined by desire?

Furthermore, the body perishes; it is subject to death. Does the
claim that the transcendental ego is the living body violate the absolute a
priori status of the transcendental ego (C 28), which as absolutely a priori and nonfactual cannot perish? Husserl cannot maintain, as a large
segment of the philosophical tradition does, that the absolute subjective
a priori is an eternal soul that leaves the body at death. As discussed
previously,[10] in Husserl's view the eidos always implies the fact and so
cannot exist independently of the fact. How then are we to conceive of
the absolute subjective a priori, the absolute transcendental ego?

And there is yet another phenomenon that challenges the claim
that the transcendental ego is absolute Being—namely, the phenomenon of experiencing another human being. If the transcendental ego is
absolute Being, then how can there be "room" for other selves, since
these would presumably all be absolute Beings? The transcendental
ego's relation to the factual seems on the one hand to threaten its truly a
priori status, yet without the factual relation it becomes something mythical. These are pressing questions for transcendental phenomenology. If
phenomenology is to be legitimate, then it must both tell us something
and be true to the phenomena. The problems of life and death, of the
body, and of other selves are, then, not merely peripheral problems for
phenomenology, but core problems. They severely put to test the claim
that the transcendental ego is pure, absolute Being and a successful
treatment of these problems by phenomenology will determine its viability.[11] More specifically, the claim that the transcendental ego is pure yet
the center of life needs to be explained if psychologism is to be avoided
in Husserl's phenomenology.

(c)   Concrete Transcendental Ego (the
Living Body) "versus" the Pure
Transcendental Ego (the Eidos
Transcendental Ego); Fact : Eidos

What is really at issue here is how to conceive of the absolute transcendental ego. Husserl warns us that here the conceptual difficulties are the greatest, for we are asking for the most radical ground of being-sense.[12] Speaking about delving into the absolute, transcendental realm, Husserl writes:

> Nevertheless, these are the slightest difficulties compared to those which have their ground in the essence of the new dimension [the truly transcendental] and its relation to the old familiar field of life. Nowhere else is the distance so great from unclearly arising needs to goal-determined plans, from vague questionings to first working problems—through which actual working science first begins. Nowhere else is it so frequent that the explorer is met by logical ghosts emerging out of the dark, formed in the old familiar and effective conceptual patterns, as paradoxical antinomies, logical absurdities. Thus nowhere is the temptation so great to slide into logical aporetics and disputation, priding oneself on one's scientific discipline, while the actual substratum of the work, the phenomena themselves, is forever lost from view. [C 120]

At this juncture nothing is so crucial as clear vision, the only means of remaining true to the phenomena:

> How great the temptation is, here, to misunderstand oneself and how much—indeed, ultimately, the actual success of a transcendental philosophy—depends upon self-reflective clarity carried to its limits. [C 153]

At this point it is necessary to introduce a distinction that Husserl makes but that has not been generally recognized by Husserl scholars—namely, that between the concrete transcendental ego and the pure transcendental ego. Although the living body is the transcendental ego, it is not the *absolute* transcendental ego. The living body is what Husserl calls the *concrete* transcendental ego, and it is a "fact" related to an eidos. The individual's stream of experience or life is but a factual instance of the eidos transcendental ego, and it is in fact constituted by the latter. The *eidos* transcendental ego is the *absolute* transcendental ego:

> After the significant formulation of the idea of a transcenden-
> tal phenomenology according to the eidetic method, when we
> return to the task of discovering the problems of phenomenol-
> ogy, we naturally confine ourselves thenceforth within the lim-
> its of a purely eidetic phenomenology, in which the *de facto
> transcendental ego* [my emphasis] and particular data given in
> transcendental experience of the ego *have the significance merely
> of examples of pure possibilities* [my emphasis]. [CM 73 (107)]

And:

> The eidos itself is a beheld or beholdable universal, one that is
> pure, "unconditioned"—that is to say: according to its own in-
> tuitional sense, a universal not conditioned by any fact. . . .
> Each singly selected type is thus elevated from its milieu within
> the *empirically factual transcendental ego* [my emphasis] into the
> pure eidetic sphere. . . . In other words: With each eidetically
> pure type we find ourselves, not indeed inside the de facto ego,
> but *inside an eidos ego*; and constitution of one actually pure
> possibility among others carries with it implicitly, as its outer
> horizon, a *purely possible ego*, a pure possibility-variant of my *de
> facto* ego. We could have started out by imagining this ego to
> be freely varied, and could set the problem of exploring eideti-
> cally the explicit constitution of any transcendental ego what-
> ever. . . . Therefore, if we think of *a phenomenology* developed
> as an intuitively apriori science *purely according to the eidetic
> method*, all its eidetic researches are nothing else but *uncover-
> ings of the all-embracing eidos, transcendental ego as such*, which
> comprises all pure possibility-variants of my de facto ego and
> this ego itself qua possibility. Eidetic phenomenology, accord-
> ingly, explores the universal Apriori without which neither I
> nor any transcendental Ego whatever is "imaginable." [CM
> 71–72 (105–6)]

And:

> How can we make it more concretely understandable that the
> reduction of mankind to the phenomenon "mankind," which is
> included as part of the reduction of the world, makes it possi-
> ble to recognize mankind as a self-objectification of the tran-
> scendental subjectivity which is always functioning ultimately
> and is thus "absolute"? [C 153]

In other words, the concrete transcendental ego, the living human being, which is an instance of the essence "humankind," is a self-

objectification of the eidos transcendental ego (C 186). It is to be noted, then, that we are dealing with three "divisions" or "stratifications" of the ego. In addition to the pure eidos transcendental ego and the concrete transcendental ego, there is the concrete factual psyche with *its* corresponding eidos. That is, the concrete transcendental ego, the living body, has necessarily correlated with it factual, objective psychophysical phenomena, such as phenomena of desire, repression, alienation, and so forth, which are usually studied by empirical psychology:

> To the concrete transcendental ego there corresponds then the human Ego, concretely as the psyche taken purely in itself and [as it is] for itself, with the psychic polarization: I as pole of my habitualities, the properties comprised in my character. Instead of my eidetic transcendental phenomenology we then have an eidetic pure psychology, relating to the eidos psyche, whose eidetic horizon, to be sure, remains unexamined. If, however, it did become examined, the way to overcome this positivity would become open—that is, the way leading over into absolute phenomenology, the phenomenology of the transcendental ego, who indeed no longer has a horizon that could lead beyond the sphere of his transcendental being and thus relativize him. [CM 73 (107)]

It is only the eidos of the pure transcendental ego that is absolute. But this notion of the eidos being *absolute* is very difficult to conceptualize. Since the concrete transcendental ego and the empirical ego are self-*objectifications* of the pure transcendental ego (C 153), the latter being *pure subjectivity*, understanding the relationship between the pure transcendental ego and its objectifications, the concrete transcendental ego and empirical ego, involves appreciating the way in which Husserl conceives of the relation between objectivity and subjectivity *in general*. Gadamer describes the special way in which Husserl understands this relation of subjectivity to its objective elements:

> What Husserl means, however, is that we cannot conceive subjectivity as an antithesis to objectivity, because this concept of subjectivity would itself be conceived in objective terms. Instead, his transcendental phenomenology seeks to be "correlational research." *But this means that the relation [between subjectivity and objectivity] is the primary thing, and the [objective] "poles" into which it [subjectivity] forms itself are contained within it, just as what is alive contains all its expressions of life in the unity of its organic being* [my emphasis]. [TM 220]

Gadamer's description, that "the objective poles into which subjectivity forms itself are contained within it," applies equally to the pure
transcendental ego and its objectifications. That is, it was explained earlier how for Husserl the eidos and fact mutually "imply" one another,
how eidos and fact are necessarily related. This holds in the case of the
eidos transcendental ego also: the eidos transcendental ego implies the
concrete factual transcendental ego. It would be more accurate, then, to
say that the absolute transcendental ego is a *relation* of the eidos transcendental ego to the factual transcendental ego. In other words, the
pure eidos transcendental ego in a sense "contains" the concrete transcendental ego and the empirical psyche "within" it.

The *relation* between the transcendental and factual or empirical,
then, is difficult to conceptualize. But one of the most common errors to
guard against is to conceive of the transcendental as being the "true"
realm, as being *real* being, and to conceive of the empirical as the "false"
realm. As Merleau-Ponty cautions:

> The truth is that the relationships between the natural and the
> transcendental attitudes are not simple, are not side by side or
> sequential, like the false or the apparent or the true. [S 164]

The reduction that yields the transcendental was meant to understand
objectivity (C 189); it was not meant to downgrade as fake objectivity or
objective thought.

> Objective truth belongs exclusively within the attitude of natu-
> ral human world-life. . . . In the reorientation of the epochē
> nothing is lost, none of the interests and ends of world-life,
> and thus also none of the ends of knowledge. But for all these
> things their essential subjective correlates are exhibited, and
> thus the full and true ontic meaning of objective being, and
> thus of all objective truth, is set forth. [C 176]

The transcendental and the empirical or factual are *essentially related* for
Husserl; they cannot be reduced to each other. If the transcendental
were the "true" and the factual the "false," Husserl would be advancing
an idealism, the type of idealism he criticizes Kant for when the latter
"splits" the transcendental (the a priori), and the factual. As Merleau-
Ponty writes:

> We must not treat the transcendental Ego as the true subject
> and the empirical self as its shadow or wake. If that were their

relationship to each other, we could withdraw into the constituting agency. (PhP 426]

The pure transcendental ego is implied *by* the factual transcendental ego, not as a true realm, but as its *ground*. The pure eidos transcendental ego is the ground of the concrete transcendental ego.
Indeed, if the concrete transcendental ego really *is*[13]—"Human subjectivity also possesses being-value," writes Gadamer (TM 216)—then it
must be *thinkable*, for everything that *is* has an identity over time. But
that means it must have an eidos, for the eidos is that which allows an
object to be thought, to have identity over time (EJ 341). That means
that the concrete transcendental ego is a fact vis-à-vis an eidos, the pure
transcendental ego. In fact, the "divisions" of the ego, the pure eidos
transcendental ego, the concrete transcendental ego, the empirical ego
and its eidos, are all *essentially* interrelated, and must be understood rela-
tionally. They mutually imply each other. This means that the living
body, the concrete transcendental ego with its concrete psyche, must be
a function of the pure transcendental ego:

> The universal Apriori pertaining to a transcendental ego as
> such is an eidetic form, which contains an infinity of forms, an
> infinity of apriori types of actualities and potentialities of life,
> along with the objects constitutable in a life as objects actually
> existing. [CM 74 (108)]

Life, then, must be understood in relation to the pure transcendental ego; the concrete psychological phenomena must be shown to be
understandable in terms of the pure transcendental ego and vice versa.
In other words: to get at the pure transcendental ego, we cannot merely
posit an empty pure transcendental ego, but we must go *through* the living body with its objective correlates. As discussed previously, this is not
something Kant did—he "skipped" the life-world—but only in this way
does one avoid positing the transcendental ego as a mythical entity (C
153), for the lived phenomena are *evidence* for the transcendental ego.

Because the concrete objective phenomena correlated with the
living body are to be evidence of the absolute transcendental ego, Husserl says that *psychology* is the decisive field (C 203, 208) for transcendental phenomenology:

> Psychology is constantly involved in this great process of devel-
> opment, involved, as we have seen, in different ways; indeed,
> psychology is the *truly decisive field* [n.: i.e., decisive for the
> struggle between subjectivism and objectivism. For by begin-

ning as objective science and then becoming transcendental, it bridges the gap]. [C 208]

But, even if we can see that the concrete transcendental ego implies the pure transcendental ego, still we must show *how* the latter is the ground of the former. This means that phenomenology must be able to discuss the pure transcendental ego's relation to the concrete transcendental ego, of which the factual or empirical psyche is a "component." It must be able to explain how the pure transcendental ego involves the *concrete* transcendental ego, including life and death, if it is truly to deal with psychologism. The remainder of the chapter deals with these issues.

(d)   The Pure Transcendental Ego and Death

The absolute transcendental ego, then, is best described as being a correlation between the eidos transcendental ego and factual transcendental ego, the living body. In other words: the body as fact is not radically separate from the pure transcendental ego, but is a necessary part or aspect[14] of its being. But the body is subject to death. Despite this, however, the absolute status of the pure transcendental ego is not threatened. The *factual* transcendental ego is not only life; it is also death. Death is a necessary aspect of the concrete, factual transcendental ego, for life involves movement, growth, and decay, all of which could not occur without death. Death, as it were "makes room for" life. In the words of Buber:

> My existence . . . was the bed in which two streams, coming from opposite directions, flowed to and in and over each other. . . . What I *knew* was the stream coursing downward alone, but what I *was* comprehended the upward one . . . coming-to-be and passing-away, these two did not alternate with each other like building up and breaking down; they lay side by side in endless embrace, and each of my moments was their bed. It was foolish to limit death to any particular moments of ceasing to be or of transformation; it was an ever-present might and the mother of being. Life engendered being, death received and bore it; life scattered its fullness, death preserved what it wished to retain. [DL 130–31 (66)]

Life in effect implies death, feeding off death, while at the same time overcoming it. This is perhaps what Freud means when he says life *aims* at death (BP 160). Hence, not only does death not destroy the being of the pure transcendental ego, but it "ensures" its being, for death allows for the *facticity* of the concrete transcendental ego that forms a necessary part of the pure transcendental ego.

This means that death, being part of the factual transcendental ego, is something *for* the pure transcendental ego and is included in the *epoche* (C 188). It must be appreciated, however, that in maintaining death to be something for the transcendental ego, Husserl is *not* in any way denying the reality of death. Death is a *reality* for the pure transcendental ego, and by including "death" in the *epoche* Husserl means only that its meaning must be phenomenologically clarified. Nor does he maintain that at death "I" become, or withdraw into, the pure transcendental ego, the immortal soul. We can *never* withdraw into the pure transcendental ego. In other words, he does not maintain that death brings the onset of our real being and that life, being only apparent or false being, is inferior to death. Such a position would tend to preach abstinence in life and encourage a turning away from life, for it would see death as superior to life. But this is not Husserl's position. Husserl's position is, rather, in accord with that of Nietzsche when he criticizes philosophies that preach superiority of death with their concomitant denial of life (Z 156–58).

While death is not superior to life, neither is it inferior to life. Life and death are on a par, as it were. Death is as much a part of our Being as is life. Hence we must embrace both fully. That is not to say that Husserl denies immortality, for saying that death is part of the absolute transcendental ego's Being *is* to affirm immortality. "The spirit alone is immortal," writes Husserl (C 299). Rather, it is to say that Husserl denies immortality in the "conventional" sense. Since death is not superior to life in Husserl's view, it brings no automatic guarantee of something, a promised heaven, beyond life. "What life did not accomplish, death too will not produce," writes Buber (DL 131 [67]). In other words, belief in immortality cannot take away from our responsibility here in life. One must still *do* something, one must "shape one's whole personal life" (C 338). What we *do* will make a difference, for, says Husserl, in our philosophizing we are "functionaries of mankind" (C 17). In this sense Husserl is also in agreement with Heidegger, according to whom, in the words of Amstutz, "Der Mensch ist vom Sein mit gewaltigen Aufgaben betraut" (MUS 8). But the question is, *what* must we do? "What should we, who *believe* [in the telos of rational philosophy], do in order to be able to believe?," asks Husserl (C 17). For Husserl, no less than for Fichte,[15] our task is not one of mere speculation, is not one of "mere academic oration" (C 16), but is one that involves our *concrete* being and a *concrete* doing:[16]

> What follows this is the ultimate self-understanding of man as being responsible for his own human being: his *self-understanding as being in being called to a life of apodicticity*, not only in abstractly practicing apodictic science in the usual sense but [as being mankind] which realizes its whole *concrete being* [my emphasis] in apodictic freedom by becoming apodictic mankind in the whole *active* [my emphasis] life of its reason—through which it is human; as I said, mankind understanding itself as rational, understanding that it is rational in seeking to be rational; that this signifies an *infinity of living* [my emphasis] and striving toward reason . . . that reason allows for no differentiation into "theoretical," "practical," "aesthetic," or whatever; that being human is teleological being and an ought-to-be, and that this teleology holds sway *in each and every activity and project of an ego* [my emphasis]. [C 340–41]

But to know what it is we must do, we must know what we are, for we have the freedom to shape ourselves, to actualize our potential nature (C 340f.). And this brings us to the question of the relation of the pure transcendental ego to life, for although it has been argued that death does not threaten the pure transcendental ego's absolute status in that it allows for the facticity of the concrete transcendental ego, a facticity of which the pure transcendental ego is the eidos, the relation between the transcendental ego and life must still be grasped.

(e) The Pure Transcendental Ego and Life

Husserl, following Brentano, maintains that our essence is intentionality. It is that which differentiates psychic phenomena, which are generally taken to constitute our subjectivity, from material phenomena. But we must understand the depth of intentionality for it to be the significant concept it was meant to be, and we can do so only if we appreciate its relatedness to life. A correct grasp of self, of subjectivity qua subjectivity, of pure subjectivity, means grasping intentionality vis-à-vis life. According to Husserl, if we fail to see intentionality as a concept related to life, we fall into an idealism or psychologism of the Kantian sort.

But the concept of life has proved to be notoriously troublesome for philosophies that sought to describe pure subjectivity. This is so because life involves the *body*[17] and body is not usually considered to be part of pure subjectivity. That is, pure subjectivity is generally thought to be mind (soul/spirit) or thought, which, although "in" the body, is nevertheless considered distinct from the body. The body is material; mind immaterial. It seems as if the biological/physical has its own motivation, structure, laws, and thought *its* own. Life is biological, psychophysical; it is growth, desire, sexuality, and decay. It seems to have a wellspring distinct from that of thought. The body is studied by empirical sciences, which are generally held to be subject to a methodology distinct from that used to study pure subjectivity. There is a conceptual tension here that is of great significance. On the one hand intuition tells us that life *is* that which is truly subjective, for life can only be seen from "within"—it is the subjective par excellence. As Gadamer writes:

> What is alive can never really be known by the objective consciousness, by the effort of understanding which seeks to penetrate the law of appearances. What is alive is not such that a person could ever grasp it from outside, in its living quality. The only way of grasping life is, rather, to become inwardly aware of it. [TM 223–24]

But on the other hand life involves the body, which is usually not considered as pure subjectivity. Indeed, philosophies of subjectivity, philosophies of mind, have not generally been able to meet the speculative demands contained in the concept of life. We may recall, for example, Aristotle's critique of Plato's theory of ideas. In Plato, pure subjectivity, the soul, is *like* the ideas. Yet the theory of ideas could not deal with the phenomena of life, according to Aristotle; specifically it could not deal with the phenomena of movement, growth and decay. The ideas are static and eternal, whereas life is dynamic.

But the same critique cannot be leveled against Husserl. In Husserl's system life at once involves the ideas, the *eideae*. That is why, according to Husserl, *any* objective science concerned with life can lead to pure transcendental phenomenology. Any empirical science, whether biology, ecology, psychology, or physiology, to name a few, can reveal the eidos by the essential fact-eidos relation and can become a *pure* phenomenology if it is led to the source of this relation: pure subjectivity. However, according to Husserl, of all the empirical sciences *psychology*, which also includes as its subject matter bodily phenomena such as the unconscious, desire, sexuality, is most likely to lead to pure subjectivity, for *it* already "makes the psychic, the specifically subjective . . . its chief theme" (FTL 38 [33–34]). Hence, although Husserl frequently says that pure transcendental phenomenology *is* transcendental logic, and although he does derive pure phenomenology from traditional logic, which in its traditional embodiment is also an objective science, it must not be thought that this is the only way into phenomenology (FTL 7 [7]). In the *Crisis* he suggests how to enter phenomenology via psychology.

That one can enter phenomenology equally well via logic or psychology suggests that in Husserl's view phenomenology is truly a blend of the formal and the concrete. Because both emphasize different aspects of phenomenology—one the more formal, the other the more concrete—both have their pros and cons as an entrance way. On the one hand, it is "safer" to proceed via logic, in that logic deals with the universal and aims at a purity (formality) that phenomenology aims at as well. The path of logic shows more readily than the path of psychology that the transcendental ego is necessary for *any* meaning, for *any* science, and shows the essential connection between meaning and science and the life-world.

The way of logic also reveals formal ontology, which in turn allows one to see the relation between the transcendental ego and all being. The reduction is in fact only truly radical via ontology, because it reveals transcendental subjectivity as the constituting source of all Being, both possible and actual. The shortcoming, however, is that since we are dealing with meaning (science) and knowledge, the connection between the transcendental ego and our concrete selves may not be clear, or may be missed altogether. To reveal that connection the path of psychology is more advantageous. Following that path shows the transcendental ego to be necessary for explaining concrete psychological phenomena. But the path of psychology, on the other hand, may fail to show the *universality* of the findings. It may not be apparent that the transcendental ego is necessary for any thought whatsoever; its enormous impact for mind in general may not be understood. That phenomenology studies mind qua mind, qua possibility, may not be clear, and if that is not clear, the impact for science (knowledge), for logic and for ethics, will not be appreciated. This may be overlooked because the psychologist tends to focus on minds (psyches) in the world. While psychologists necessarily must carry out the *epoche* (C 251–52), they may not carry the *epoche* to its extreme; that is, to the discovery of the pure transcendental ego.

(f) Pure Psychology as Pure
     Transcendental Phenomenology

It is possible, then, to enter phenomenology through psychology. It should not surprise us that we must go through an "empirical" discipline in order to see the pure transcendental ego, for the pure transcendental ego, being transparent, cannot be seen directly but must be seen through its objects:

> Yet not withstanding these peculiar complications with all "its" experiences, the experiencing Ego is still nothing that might be taken *for itself* and made into an object of inquiry on its *own* account. Apart from its "ways of being related" or "ways of behaving," it is completely empty of essential components, it has no content that could be unravelled, it is in and for itself indescribable: pure Ego and nothing further. [I 214 (160)]

But what *may* be surprising is how close Husserl considers the link between psychology and phenomenology to be. Husserl maintains not only that psychology is the decisive field for overcoming the subject-object dichotomy in pure subjectivity (C 208), but that *true* psychology *is* pure transcendental phenomenology:

> The surprising result of our investigation can also, it seems, be expressed as follows: a pure psychology as positive science, a psychology which would investigate universally the human beings living in the world as real facts in the world, similarly to other positive sciences (both sciences of nature and humanistic disciplines), does not exist. There is only a transcendental psychology, which is identical with transcendental philosophy. [C 257]

And:

> Thus pure psychology itself is identical with transcendental philosophy as the science of transcendental subjectivity. This is unassailable. [C 258]

And:

> Thus pure psychology is and can be nothing other that what was sought earlier from the philosophical point of view as absolutely grounded philosophy, which can fulfill itself only as phenomenological transcendental philosophy. [C 259]

Let us note carefully the claim here. True psychology, which studies the body in its psychosomatic aspects (desire, sexuality, etc.) *is* pure phenomenology. Let us reflect on the full implications of this assertion.

It means that pure psychology is also pure transcendental logic, since pure phenomenology *is* pure transcendental logic.

That Husserl considers there to be such a close link between psychology and phenomenology only proves that the transcendental ego in his view is not divorced from the concrete, from life, that it is not merely an empty (formal) structure *von oben her*. In fact, it is because the Cartesian way into phenomenology posits a pure, as if empty, transcendental ego that Husserl dislikes the Cartesian way into phenomenology:[18]

> The "Cartesian way" . . . has a great shortcoming: while it
> leads to the transcendental ego in one leap, as it were, it brings
> this ego into view as apparently empty of content, since there
> can be no preparatory explication; so one is at a loss, at first,
> to know what has been gained by it, much less how, starting
> with this, a completely new sort of fundamental science, deci-
> sive for philosophy, has been attained. [C 155]

According to Husserl, in phenomenology the formal and the concrete blend into one science. This is because he intends phenomenology to be a descriptive science, a science of what *is*, and so it must in its purity be able to adequately handle the concrete. If the transcendental ego is not understood via its correlate, the concrete, then its significance will not be understood; the concept of the pure transcendental ego will be uninformative, and the whole enterprise of phenomenology will have lost its purpose, its raison d'être. Hence Husserl would disagree with Ricoeur when the latter maintains that "the reflecting philosopher cannot go beyond abstract or negative statements" and that the propositions the reflecting philosopher generates "are true, but lifeless" (CI 242). In Husserl's view the pure transcendental ego *must* be understood through the concrete, through life:

> The empty generality of the epochē does not of itself clarify
> anything; it is only the gate of entry through which one must
> pass in order to be able to discover the new world of pure sub-
> jectivity. The actual discovery is a matter of concrete, ex-
> tremely subtle and differentiated work. [C 257]

The pure transcendental ego runs through *all* **mental accomplishments and through** *all* **of life. It is that**

> which is *taken for granted*, which is presupposed by all thinking,
> all activity of life with all its ends and accomplishments.
> [C 113]

This is why, according to Husserl, both a true psychology and phenomenology end up with the pure, absolute, transcendental ego, the ground of all being-sense. But it should be possible to show this concretely: it should be possible to take a psychology and show the theory of intentionality to be at its core. In the next section the connection between psychology and phenomenology shall be worked out *concretely*. In so doing the relation of the transcendental ego to life shall be brought to light.

(g)   A Concrete Example: Psychoanalytic
      Theory and its Relation to Pure
      Phenomenology

But which psychology should we work with? Husserl would say with any that is true to the "facts," true to the phenomena:

> If empiricism had done more honor to its name by being thus
> [i.e., by being empirical][19] it could never have missed the phe-
> nomenological reduction, its descriptions would never have led
> it to data and complexes of data, and the spiritual world, in its
> own specificity and infinite totality, would not have remained
> closed.[20] [C 249]

In other words, to develop a true psychology, one must become an astute observer of the human psyche. One must "learn to see" (C 248).

One psychology that has developed out of a shrewd observation of human nature is Freudian psychology. His is an auspicious psychological doctrine to relate to pure transcendental phenomenology, for it deals with what is most problematic for a philosophy that considers consciousness to be the foundation of all being-sense[21]—namely, desire rooted in biological life.

Some philosophers, such as Paul Ricoeur, think that Freud's findings concerning the unconscious *contradict* phenomenology's basic tenet regarding the absolute status of consciousness. Writes Ricoeur:

> The contemporary philosopher meets Freud on the same
> ground as Nietzsche and Marx. All three rise before him as
> protagonists of suspicion who rip away masks and pose the
> novel problem of the lie of consciousness and consciousness as
> a lie. This problem cannot remain just one among many, for
> what all three generally and radically put into question is some-
> thing that appears to any good phenomenologist as the field,

foundation, and very origin of any meaning at all: consciousness itself. [CI 99]

And:

[Psychoanalytic theory] is an antiphenomenology which requires, not the reduction to consciousness, but the reduction *of*
consciousness. [CI 237]

According to Ricoeur, then, not only is this psychology *not* phenomenology, it even *contradicts* it. Ricoeur maintains that Freudian psychology challenges any philosophy of the cogito by maintaining that
"consciousness is not the principle, not the judge, not the measure of all
things" (CI 238). In taking psychoanalytic theory to demonstrate that
pure psychology is pure phenomenology, then, our challenge is a double
one, for not only is the connection between psychology and phenomenology not clear in this instance, but it seems threatened.

Freudian psychology deals with desire rooted in biological life. As
explained above, the concept of life is notoriously problematic for a philosophy of the subject. But let us note how Freud conceives of life. Even
as a nonpurified science—that is, even as a non-pure-phenomenological
science—Freudian psychology shows that life essentially involves *ideas.*
Freud saw that every drive or instinct is essentially ideational, that human biological life is *essentially* significant. According to Freud, the two
main instincts of life are Thanatos, the death instinct, and Eros, libido
(EI 224). From the following quotations it is clear that Freud considers
Thanatos and Eros to be essentially ideational, and that he understands
and "defines" life in terms of an opposition of *ideas:*

Starting from speculations on the beginning of life and from
biological parallels, I drew the conclusion that, besides the instinct to preserve living substance and to join into ever larger
units, there must exist another, contrary instinct seeking to dissolve those units and to bring them back to their primaeval, in-
organic state. That is to say, as well as Eros there was an
instinct of death. The phenomena of life could be explained
from the concurrent or mutually opposing action of these two
instincts. [CD 65]

And:

I may now add that civilization is a process in the service of
Eros, whose purpose is to combine single human individuals,

and after that families, then races, peoples and nations, into one great unity, the unity of mankind. Why this happens, we do not know; the work of Eros is precisely this. [CD 69]

Note how Freud describes Eros, life force, which is bodily, as a tendency to join living substance into ever larger units, and Thanatos as the opposite tendency. These forces are ideational, and the phenomena of life, Freud tells us here, can be explained from the concurrent or mutually opposing action of these instincts.

From the above it follows that an individual's sexuality, being a manifestation of Eros, is essentially ideational. This indeed accords with Freud's doctrine: in Freud's theory, sexual behaviour is essentially *meaningful*. In fact, according to this psychological doctrine, *the body is meaningful in its being, in its life*. Freud maintains furthermore that *cognitive* being, the *ego*, is at the service of life. Although the id is the source of the instincts, Eros and Thanatos, since the ego is a manifold aspect of the id, it too is essentially related to the basic ideas and instincts that make up Eros and Thanatos. Hence, self-preservation, which is part of Eros, belongs to the ego as well:

> The ego is subject to the influence of the instincts, too, like the id, of which it is in fact only a specifically modified part. [EI 223]

And:

> It [Eros or the sexual instincts] comprises not merely the uninhibited sexual instinct proper and the impulses of a sublimated or aim-inhibited nature derived from it, but also the self-preservative instinct, which must be assigned to the ego. [EI 224]

And:

> It seems a plausible view that this neutral displaceable energy, which is probably active alike in the ego and in the id, proceeds from the narcissistic reservoir of libido, i.e., that it desexualized Eros. (The erotic instincts appear to be altogether more plastic, more readily diverted and displaced than the destructive instincts.) From this we can easily go on to assume that this displaceable libido is employed in the service of the pleasure-principle to obviate accumulations and to facilitate discharge. . . . If this displaceable energy is desexualized libido, it might also be described as sublimated energy; for it would still retain

the main purpose of Eros—that of uniting and binding—in so
far as it helped towards establishing that unity, or tendency to
unity, which is particularly characteristic of the ego. If the intellectual processes in the wider sense are to be classed among
these displacements, then the energy for the work of thought
itself must be supplied from sublimated erotic sources. . . . [EI
226–27]

Freud obviously considers the human organism, psyche and
soma, as a meaningful whole, as a whole united in *significance*, for mind,
through its relation to the instincts, is related to the body, and the body,
because the instincts are ideational—significant—in their essence,[22] is
related to cognition. Hence the body has something thoughtlike[23] about
it, or, to use Merleau-Ponty's words, Freud shows that "in sexuality
[there are] . . . relations and attitudes which had previously been held to
reside *in consciousness*" (PhP 158). To cite Merleau-Ponty:

Thus sexuality is not an autonomous cycle. It has internal links
with the whole active and cognitive being, these three sectors
of behaviour displaying one typical structure, and standing in a
relationship to each other of reciprocal expression. Here we
concur with the most lasting discoveries of psychoanalysis.
Whatever the theoretical declarations of Freud may have been,
psychoanalytical research is in fact led to an explanation of
man, not in terms of his sexual substructure, but to a discovery
in sexuality of relations and attitudes which had previously
been held to reside *in consciousness*. Thus the significance of
psychoanalysis is less to make psychology biological than to discover a dialectical process in functions thought of as "purely
bodily," and to reintegrate sexuality into the human being. . . .
It would be a mistake to imagine that even with Freud psychoanalysis rules out the description of psychological motives, and
is opposed to the phenomenological method: psychoanalysis
has, on the contrary, albeit unwittingly, helped to develop it by
declaring, as Freud puts it, that every human action has a
"meaning," and by making every effort to understand the
event, short of relating it to mechanical circumstances. [PhP
157–58]

According to Merleau-Ponty, then, psychoanalytic theory, contrary to Ricoeur, not only does not contradict phenomenology, but
"helped to develop it by declaring, as Freud puts it, that every human
behaviour has a 'meaning' " and by declaring that concrete lived-being is
significant. According to this psychological doctrine, significance and life

are one, and this unity is expressed in desire, in the *desire* to unify and to self-preserve.[24] But this is to say that bodily being (life) is a *seeing*, for as Freud says, Eros is self-preservation as well as the tendency to unify oneself with others, and to do that, even to desire that, I must have *some* sense of self and other, however unthematic or nascent that sense. Without that minimum level of self-awareness, "I" could not fulfill the structure of life—I could not live. In my bodily life I am an intending and a projecting of myself. The body in its living being is a seeing: a seeing of self and of others. "The thing expressed [my being, which is self-assertion] does not exist apart from the expression [my bodily life]" (PhP 166).

To see myself is to have *evidence*[25] of myself and to *anticipate* further evidence, and my "first" evidence is my livedness, my living body. My body is the sign (of my being) for myself and for others, and it is the evidence (realization, actualization) of that sign (again, for myself and for others). In my act of life I *am* an incarnation of an idea, I am an actualization, I am a significance. I have meaning in my being:

> If we therefore say that the body expresses existence at every moment, this is in the sense in which a word expresses a thought. Anterior to conventional means of expression, which reveal my thoughts to others only because already, for both myself and them, meanings are provided for each sign, and which in this sense do not give rise to genuine communication at all, we must, as we shall see, recognize a primary process of signification in which the thing expressed does not exist apart from the expression, and in which the signs themselves induce their significance externally. In this way the body expresses total existence, not because it is an external accompaniment to that existence, but because existence comes into its own in the body. This incarnate significance is the central phenomenon of which body and mind, sign and significance are abstract moments. [PhP 166]

My being is a seeing. But we have previously said that consciousness is a seeing.[26] Hence being and consciousness have the same structure.

Husserl's point is that although the body is not yet an explicit cogito, it still warrants being termed "intentional," for intentionality is not equivalent to the explicit cogito. Intentionality also includes the implicit cogito. On this point Husserl criticizes Descartes, for whom cogito was synonymous with explicit cogito. While Husserl retains Descartes's dictum, *ego cogito, ergo sum,* he reinterprets the meaning of cogito to take account of both the implicit and explicit cogito. While the latter is *conceptual,* the former, the lived cogito, is preconceptual. The lived, implicit cogito is, however, meaning laden, for, while it is not conceptual, it *is* ideational, it involves the eidos.[27] But it must be understood that the eidos is not the concept of explicit thought (EJ 318). Being the ground of the concept, the eidos is prior to the concept and is that to which the concept refers:

> The eidos itself is a beheld or beholdable universal, one that is pure, "unconditioned"—that is to say: according to its own intuitional sense, a universal not conditioned by any fact. It is *prior to all "concepts,"* in the sense of verbal significations; indeed, as pure concepts, these must be made to fit the eidos.
> [CM 71(105)]

The eidos is conceptualized or thematized in the explicit cogito.

At first we have *lived-experience*, which is the ground of the explicit cogito. By directing *attention* to this lived-experience, the cogito is made explicit and eventually judgments are formed. These judgments are hierarchically ordered, with eidetic judging as the highest form of judging (EJ 319). But even *if* the cogito has as its telos the eidetic judgment (EJ 319), it requires the "lowest" cogito as its ground, as its source of evidence. Hence consciousness must pass through the world in order to see the eidos, for seeing the eidos *means* going through the world; the eidos cannot be seen directly. The body is, in other words, an indispensable moment of intentionality. It is "part of" intentionality.

But it must be kept in mind that when it is said that the body is a type of cogito, by cogito is *not* meant pure thought or spirit as in Hegel's system. It literally is bodily:

> The return to existence, as to the setting in which the communication between body and mind can be understood, is not a return to Consciousness or Spirit, and existential psychoanalysis must not serve as a pretext for a revival of spiritualism.
> [PhP 160]

In other words, intentionality is quite literally *the* founding act in Husserl's view, and this *is* compatible with Freudian psychology. Intentionality *grounds* life—it is needed for life. Hence, in Husserl's philosophy of the subject, the absolute status of intentionality or consciousness is not threatened by the phenomena that are the subject matter of psychoanalytic theory, such as the phenomena of life, the body, desire.

Furthermore, the theoretical constructs that psychoanalytic theory uses to deal with the phenomena of life are compatible with phenomenology. Specifically, the theoretical constructs of topography—that is, unconscious, preconscious, and conscious (henceforth abbreviated as Uncs, Pcs, and Cs, respectively), and of forces or roles—that is, id, ego, and superego, isolated by Ricoeur (CI 240) as contradicting phenomenology, are compatible with phenomenology. The theoretical constructs of topography and of roles or forces are thought to contradict phenomenology by Ricoeur because according to these consciousness is "displaced" from being omnipotent/omnipresent (fundamental/foundational) to being *one* of three "places" (CI 237–38, 240) of the mind. Ricoeur's claim that consciousness is displaced by the topographical constructs would be correct *if* by "consciousness" he meant the explicit cogito. The unconscious and preconscious deny the autonomy of the *explicit* cogito. But in Husserl's view intentionality (consciousness) is not restricted to the explicit cogito; it includes the implicit cogito. The former is merely a *manifestation* or an aspect of intentionality, of the cogito that is the foundation of all being-sense. The unconscious and preconscious do not deny the omnipotence of *intentionality*, but of the *explicit cogito* only. In Freudian theory, no less than in Cartesian and Kantian theory, mind or consciousness is identified with the explicit, wakeful cogito. In the Freudian topography of Uncs, Pcs, and Cs, by "consciousness" is meant the wakeful ego. Understood in this way, if we take "consciousness" in this division to mean the wakeful ego, the explicit cogito, then topography is compatible with intentionality.[28]

In fact, it can be argued that the distinctions between the unconscious, preconscious, and conscious are defined by descriptive phenomenological properties, that contrary to Ricoeur, the tripartite division is not one of *place* at all. According to Ricoeur:

> These "places"—unconscious, preconscious, and conscious—
> are in no way defined by descriptive, phenomenological prop-
> erties but as *systems*, that is, as sets of representations and af-
> fects governed by specific laws which enter into mutual
> relationships which, in turn, are irreducible to any quality of
> consciousness, to any determination of the "lived." [CI 237]

And:

> This preliminary abandonment is the prerequisite for the sepa-
> ration that exists between the field of all Freudian analyses and
> the descriptions of "lived" consciousness. [CI 237]

If we keep in mind that the wakeful ego is the result of *attention* directed at the stream of experience, the Uncs, that the stream of experience is unconscious with respect to the wakeful cogito, Freud's division can be seen to express a *relation* between attention and the stream of experience. This interpretation is supported by the text of Freud. From the quotation that follows it is clear that the distinction between Uncs and Pcs is described in subjective, lived terms and has been made on the basis of subjective, lived experience—namely, on the basis of *feelings* of resistance and repulsion that accompany the attempt at bringing certain material of the unconscious to consciousness. The distinction Uncs-Pcs is not one of *place:*[29]

> Every mental act begins as an unconscious one, and may either remain so or go on developing into consciousness, according as it meets with resistance or not. The distinction between preconscious and unconscious activity is not a primary one, but comes to be established after repulsion has sprung up. Only then the difference between preconscious ideas, which can appear in consciousness and reappear at any moment, and unconscious ideas which cannot do so gains a theoretical as well as practical value. [AN 51]

In other words, all mental processes start out unconscious, according to Freud, as for Husserl. However, by directing attention to the unconscious the ideas may either become conscious, or, if met with resistance at the preconscious level, may remain unconscious. Hence the topography is not, contrary to Ricoeur, "irreducible to . . . any determination of the 'lived' "[30] (CI 237).

Neither does the tripartite structure id, ego, and superego contradict phenomenology. The absolute consciousness phenomenology speaks about is not the ego of this division, for the ego of this division is itself constituted by the intentionality of the absolute transcendental ego. The claim that the ego of this tripartite division is constituted is in accord with Freudian theory. Fancher writes:

> In a totally immature system there would be no ego at all; there the incoming external stimulation would clash directly with the instinctual impulses of the id. It is out of just such clashes that the ego comes to be formed and to assume its role as mediator. [DF 204]

In Freudian theory, no less than in phenomenology, the genetically primary mental acts are unconscious, and out of these the ego as well as the superego (see chapter 6) are constituted. The unconscious, implicit cogito is, according to Husserl, a *productive* one, its mode of cognitive production being, not conceptual, as mentioned above, but associative (EJ 321). Here too Husserl is in accord with Freud, for whom the most "primitive" mode of cognition is association (compare the role of association in psychoanalytic theory and practice).

Freudian theory, then, a psychology that seemed to contradict phenomenology in that it deals with the phenomena of life, phenomena that have generally been difficult to deal with for a philosophy of the subject, is not only compatible with phenomenology, but *is* phenomenology in that intentionality lies at its core.[31] But it has been possible to relate phenomenology to the phenomena of life only by keeping the distinction between implicit and explicit ego in mind. To fail to keep this distinction in mind is to fail to appreciate the way in which Husserl unlike Descartes and Kant overcomes psychologism. Husserl maintains that Kant does not overcome psychologism, because he has taken the structure of the explicit cogito to be the structure of the transcendental ego.[32] But the structure of the explicit cogito is not ultimate, for it occurs within life. Hence, in confusing the explicit cogito for the pure transcendental ego, "life" is left outside the phenomenon of the transcendental ego, for according to that misunderstanding the transcendental ego occurs within life. That is, in that view the transcendental ego itself will be grounded on the facticity of life and will be a "fact" occurring in life, a fact left unexplained, and hence mythical, as Husserl calls Kant's description of the transcendental ego. In other words, Kant has not overcome the mind-body split; mind in Kant's theory is not integrated with the body. To overcome psychologism the transcendental ego must be the ultimate ground, for only then is any factual "residue" beyond the transcendental ego overcome. The transcendental ego must be a necessary structure for my *being*, for my being through and through (psyche and soma). For Husserl intentionality is necessary for my life, and, as well, intentionality involves life.

In the next chapter, on the hermeneutic circle, the following problem will be addressed. If the transcendental ego is necessary, and if it is an implicit cogito, the cogito proper being an explication of what was implicit in the transcendental ego, are we not dealing with a duplication in the explicit ego? Does this not mean all being-sense is *necessary*, thereby destroying *facticity*? That is, if the pure transcendental ego is absolute ground of all being-sense, if all being-sense is constituted by the pure transcendental ego, and if the explicit ego is nothing but an explication of that pure ego, is facticity not destroyed? While this objection has already to some extent been dealt with in this chapter, it will be addressed further in the next chapter.

Reconciliation of Husserl's Characterization of Phenomenology as a Philosophy of Essences and as a Teleological-Historical Discipline: An Answer to a Hermeneutic Critique of Phenomenology

(a)   Necessity versus Facticity

This chapter will concern itself with the question of necessity versus facticity.[1] More specifically it will examine the following question: If the
transcendental ego is absolute being, ground of all being-sense, and the
cogito proper but an explication of what was implied in the transcendental ego, is facticity not "consumed" by the necessity of the transcendental ego? Let us note that Husserl also describes the transcendental ego as
radical self-examination, a description that seems to run counter to that
of the transcendental ego as absolute. If the transcendental ego is by its
essence self-questioning, does this not imply that it is fundamentally factual and not necessary? It seems, then, that these two characterizations
of the transcendental ego rule each other out. Yet Husserl describes the
transcendental ego simultaneously as the absolute ground of meaning
and being, and as radical self-examination. It has been claimed that phenomenology as Husserl conceives of it[2] cannot maintain itself because
his concept of transcendental subjectivity as the absolute ground of being-sense contradicts his concept of transcendental ego as radical self-
examination.[3] It is claimed that the concept of transcendental ego as
radical self-examination leads to an infinite regress, which precludes the
absolute status of the transcendental ego, because something absolute
should be beyond question.

Clearly, the charge that Husserl's apparent contradictory ways of characterizing the transcendental ego undermine his phenomenology cannot be left unanswered, for it challenges the viability of phenomenology. But this question as to whether the essence of the transcendental ego is the absolute ground of being-sense or whether it is a self-questioning is the question of necessity versus facticity that arose in the discussion on psychologism. These questions, which represent two ways of looking at the same problem, form part of the tension involved in the larger issue of whether phenomenology can successfully deal with the phenomena of life. Both Suzanne Bachelard and David Carr pick up on Husserl's apparent contradictory ways of describing the transcendental ego, though in different ways.

According to Suzanne Bachelard phenomenology is subject to an infinite regress if it maintains that the transcendental ego is self-criticism. She believes that because of this infinite regress Husserl cannot maintain that phenomenology reveals the essence of an absolute transcendental ego, but is led to say that the understanding of the transcendental ego is in *flux* and that phenomenology reveals a *dialectic* between the transcendental ego and the forms in which it necessarily manifests itself:

> The Husserlian conception of transcendental subjectivity in fact falls before the objection of the "third man."
> Actually, Husserl is unable to maintain his conception of an absolute transcendental subjectivity. . . . It does indeed seem that Husserl did not remain in the perspective of absolute transcendental subjectivism and that he was "unconsciously oriented toward a dialectic." For our part . . . we would say . . . "toward a dialectic of reason and the structural form." [SHL 222]

And:

> It is not precisely a question of a dialectic between subjectivity and its "objective" products, its "contents"; one should rather speak of a duality between subjectivity and the forms in which it necessarily manifests itself. [SHL 223]

Bachelard observes (SHL 222) too that Husserl acknowledges the possible threat of an infinite regress but denies that phenomenology falls prey to it:

> All transcendental-philosophical theory of knowledge, as *"criticism of knowledge," leads back ultimately to criticism of transcendental-phenomenological knowledge* (in the first place, criticism of

transcendental experience); and, owing to the essential reflexive relation of phenomenology to itself, this criticism also demands a criticism. In this connexion, however, there exist no
endless regresses that are infected with difficulties of any kind
(to say nothing of absurdities), despite the evident possibility of
reiterable transcendental reflections and criticisms. [CM 152
(178)]

Carr's claims concerning the tension between facticity and necessity in Husserl's phenomenology are potentially more devastating than
those of Bachelard. He expresses his concerns in terms of Husserl's
methodology, for the strain between facticity and necessity, between the
notion of the transcendental ego as absolute being and transcendental
ego as radical questioning, results in a tension in methodology. The tension in methodology is one between two approaches in phenomenology—namely, between the "essential approach" and the "teleological
approach." The latter maintains that the nature of X works itself out in
its history according to an inherent teleology that is both its arche and its
telos. While we can attempt to determine X's nature through an examination of its history, it cannot be known at once, according to this view.
Hence in the teleological-historical approach the ego's nature is revealed only through an *ongoing* questioning of its nature, through radical self-examination, in other words. But this means that we would never
know what the nature of the ego is, for our findings would always be
open to further question. According to the philosophy of essence, on the
other hand, the ego has an essence that can be known a priori. According to both models, the ego has a necessary nature, but only according to
the latter model can this nature be known apodictically.

Carr claims that this tension in methodology causes a break in
Husserlian phenomenology. He maintains that the *Crisis* marks a turning point in Husserl's thought, that developments in the *Crisis* not only
undermine Husserl's earlier position, but constitute a *break* with his
prior position. Specifically, Carr maintains that in the *Crisis* Husserl suddenly adopts the teleological-historical approach and that the earlier
"philosophy of essences" as expressed especially in the *Cartesian Meditations* is thereby undermined, albeit tacitly. According to Carr, Husserl
abandoned the *Cartesian Meditations*, and this would provide an answer as
to why he did so.

In order to give an accurate representation of his position, Carr is
cited at length:

The question of historical genesis is explicitly banned from phenomenology per se in Husserl's writings up through the *Cartesian Meditations*. Yet in the *Crisis* it suddenly makes its appearance as something the author obviously thinks is important. [C xxxv]

And:

A glance suffices to convince us . . . that by comparison to the other "introductions" available in English—the *Ideas*, Volume I, and the *Cartesian Meditations*—the *Crisis* is radically different in format. . . .

The earlier works mentioned above are both characterized explicitly by a "Cartesian" approach. In them, Husserl begins by inviting his readers to reflect upon the world and upon one's own consciousness of and thought about the world and to see that a certain new attitude, embodied in certain methodological procedures, will enable us to answer the questions of philosophy, to solve or dissolve its problems. Here, by contrast, Husserl announces "a teleological-historical reflection upon the origins of our critical scientific and philosophical situation." [C xxiv]

And:

These two themes [of historical discussion and life-world] and their interconnection must be examined in order to assess the significance of the *Crisis* not merely as a document of its time but as a general statement of Husserl's phenomenology. Such an examination is all the more important in light of an opinion first expressed by Merleau-Ponty and since taken up by many of his followers, the view that these new dimensions of the *Crisis* introduce elements into phenomenology that strain to the breaking point, whether he fully recognized it or not, Husserl's philosophical program and undermine the results of his earlier works. If this view is correct, it provides an answer to the question of why the German version of the *Cartesian Meditations* was abandoned and Husserl embarked on such an unusual approach at the end of his life. [C xxx-xxxi]

Carr adds in a footnote:

One possibility is that Husserl developed a new idea of philosophical "science" that was radically different from or even incompatible with the earlier one; another is that the investigations of the *Crisis* and other manuscripts of the period *imply* a denial of scientific philosophy even though Husserl did not recognize it or would not admit it to himself. [C xxxi, n. 21]

And:

> In earlier works, discussions of other philosophers are not part of the introduction to phenomenology, strictly speaking, but form either a kind of "introduction to the introduction" or a series of asides. A constant strain throughout Husserl's career is his disdain for the tendency of some philosophers to conjure up a doctrine of their own simply by an ingenious dialectical combination of the doctrines of others. The true introduction to phenomenology—and thus to philosophy, for Husserl—is to be found precisely by turning *away* from the opinions of the philosophers and by turning *toward* "the things themselves" (*zu den Sachen selbst!*). In the *Crisis*, by contrast, as stated in the Preface, the teleological-historical reflection serves "in its own right" as an introduction to phenomenology. [C xxx]

A little further Carr writes:

> This historical discussion, as is generally agreed, is one of the truly new elements in Husserl's philosophy which make their appearance in the *Crisis*. [C xxx]

As well, Carr cites Merleau-Ponty in support of his position:

> It was in his last period that Husserl himself became fully conscious of what the return to the phenomenon meant and tacitly broke with the philosophy of essences. [*Phénoménologie de la perception*, 61n; in C xxx, n. 20]

Clearly to Carr there is a tension between Husserl's philosophy of essences and the teleological-historical approach.[4] The conflict that Carr believes to be present in Husserl's writings can be described in more detail as follows.

According to Husserl's philosophy of essence, phenomenology is the apodictic, a priori science of essences:

> *Pure or transcendental phenomenology will be established not as a science of facts, but as a science of essential being* (as *"eidetic"* Science); a science which aims exclusively at establishing "knowl-

edge of essences" (*Wesenerkenntnisse*) and *absolutely no "facts."*
[I 40 (4)]

And:

> Phenomenology is here to be established as a science of Essen-
> tial Being—as an *a priori*, or, as we also say, eidetic science. [I
> 41 (5)]

The essence "defines" what something is, it is the What of an Individuum (I 48 [5]) and can be seen by instituting a reduction (I 40 [4]).
To be more exact, phenomenology is ultimately concerned with the essence of the pure transcendental ego (I 102 [59]; 140 [94]; 160 [113]).
The latter is an *immanental* essence. To focus on immanental essences
one must institute a series of reductions (I 103 [59–60]). The first reduction excludes matters of fact and exposes essences, both transcendent
and immanent. The second reduction excludes transcendent essences[5]
and yields immanent essences only.[6] Only the latter are strictly speaking
indubitable and form the strict phenomenological region:

> Phenomenology embraces as its own all *"immanental essences,"*
> i.e., all those which become singularized exclusively in the indi-
> vidual events of a stream of consciousness, in fleeting single
> mental processes of any kind. Now it is of fundamental impor-
> tance to see that *not all essences* belong to that sphere, that just
> as in the case of individual objectivities the difference between
> *immanental* and *transcendent* objectivities obtains, so too it ob-
> tains in the case of the corresponding essences. . . . If we in-
> tend to develop a phenomenology as a *purely descriptive eidetic
> doctrine of the immanental consciousness-formations*, the occur-
> rences in the stream of mental processes which can be seized
> upon within the boundaries drawn by phenomenological exclu-
> sion, then no transcendent individuals and, therefore, *none of
> the "transcendent essences"* belonging within those boundaries
> are included. [I FK 137–38 (114)]

And:

> To phenomenology that proposes really to limit itself to the re-
> gion of pure experience, no transcendent-eidetic regions and
> disciplines can contribute, in principle, any premises at all.
> Since, then, it is our purpose, in conformity with the standard
> already referred to above, to give to phenomenology precisely

this purity of construction, and since issues of the greatest philosophical import depend on deliberately preserving this purity
throughout, we *expressly* sanction an *extension of the original reduction* to all transcendent-eidetic domains and the *ontologies*
which belong to them. [I 162 (114)]

What is more, the essence can be seen without the consideration
of facts, can be seen by pure imagination (EJ 329):

The Eidos, the *pure essence*, can be exemplified intuitively in
the data of experience, data of perception, memory, and so
forth, but just as readily *also in the mere data of fancy (Phantasie).*
Hence, with the aim of grasping an essence itself in its *primordial* form, we can set out from corresponding empirical intuitions, *but we can also set out just as well from non-empirical
intuitions, intuitions that do not apprehend sensory existence, intuitions rather "of a merely imaginative order."* [I 50–51 (12)]

And speaking of the method used in phenomenology, Husserl writes:

There are reasons why, in phenomenology as in all eidetic sciences, representations, or, to speak more accurately, *free fan-
cies*, assume a *privileged position over against perceptions*, and that
even in phenomenology of perception itself. [I 182 (130–31)]

According to the teleological-historical approach, however, we
discern the nature of something, not from imagination, but from the de
facto development (the history) of that something. For example, one
would discern the nature of the ego from an examination of its de facto,
historical development. Since something's de facto development is in
principle infinite, in its development the ego may change radically, and
with it our conception of its nature. But in what sense would the nature
or "essence" of the ego then be *absolute* or *apodictic*, and indeed, in what
sense would phenomenology, the science of the pure transcendental
ego, then be an apodictic science? Contrary to the philosophy of essences, the nature or essence of something cannot be known a priori
according to the teleological-historical approach, but can be "known"
only a posteriori. Hence, according to Carr, when Husserl adopts the
teleological-historical approach in the *Crisis*, this means that Husserl
does so at the expense of his philosophy of essence, thus creating a tension in his writings. Writes Carr:

Not only would a "philosophy of history" seem to find no justification in phenomenological terms; it might even directly contradict the results obtained by that method. [C xxxiv]

(b) Why Phenomenology Demands Both the Teleological-Historical and Essential Approach

It can be argued, however, that the tension is not there in Husserl's philosophy, at least not in the way Carr believes it to be. The tension does
not reflect the incompatibility of the teleological-historical and essential
approaches, but reflects, rather, the need to work out explicitly the in-
terrelation of the two approaches. If Husserl adopts the teleological-
historical approach, it cannot be at the expense of his philosophy of essences, for to make these two approaches incompatible with one another
is to deny the very possibility of phenomenology: the teleological-historical approach without a philosophy of essences leads to a radical skepticism, and a philosophy of essences without a teleological-historical
approach leads to dogmatism.

As discussed above, phenomenology ultimately aims at the essence of the pure, absolute transcendental ego. If phenomenology were
identical with the teleological-historical approach as Carr conceives of
the latter, phenomenology would infer the nature of the absolute transcendental ego from how the ego in its individual and collective states as
a matter of fact has developed—from the de facto ego *only*. But it would
then be impossible to really know the nature of the transcendental ego,
because it is that which *is* developing. It would be in a state of flux and it
would not be possible to speak of its essence, for an essence is unchanging. An analysis of how the ego or humanity as a matter of fact develops
cannot yield an essence of the ego or of humanity. As André de Muralt
says:

> Now, what does the descriptive experience of man yield? Does
> it immediately reveal the essence of man to us as a necessary a
> priori? No, it does not; instead it gives only man's becoming or
> development, his flowing realization, his life or exercise of exis-
> tence. This flowing reality cannot be defined by a concept de-
> limiting an essence. [DeM 370]

In fact, with every act of questioning itself, the ego's nature would
be affected (P 52). How could phenomenology, then, ever maintain the

transcendental ego to be that which questions itself, for even *that* claim concerning the ego would be open to question? Because its nature would not be fixed, it would be conceivable, for instance, that at some point in time the ego changed from a self-questioning being to a dogmatic, authoritarian being.

Furthermore, there would be the problem of whence the ego gets its norms that enable it to engage in a self-critique. One cannot say that the ego gets it from itself, for, being part of the ego, such norms would then be open to critique. In such a position we are led to an infinite regress. Saying that what is involved is a spiral effect, where a higher level always criticizes a lower level, will not obviate the problem either, for every level remains open to criticism, thus leaving the question of the norms according to which the criticism takes place. Bachelard expresses this clearly:

> If one does not lose sight of the fact that phenomenology is set up on different levels, one can conceive of a new transcendental investigation which relates the norms of the first phenomenological subjectivity to a higher subjectivity; more specifically, one can conceive of a new transcendental investigation which performs a "criticism of those evidences that phenomenology at the first, and still naïve, level carries on straightforwardly." But then one is presented with the danger of an endless regress. [SHL 221–22]

Yet if, as an absolute ground seems to demand, the norms are said to be beyond the transcendental ego, they would be "objective" and we would fall prey to objectivism, the very antithesis to phenomenology, as Bachelard explains:

> How can the constituting subjectivity criticize itself without using norms, hence without referring to an "Objectivity" which dominates it and reduces its authority? [SHL 221]

Hence without some apodictic norms "in" the transcendental ego, we fall prey to either a radical skepticism or an objectivism, both of which destroy phenomenology. If one takes phenomenology to be the kind of teleological-historical approach that Carr takes it to be, then Bachelard's claim that phenomenology falls before the third-man argument rings true. If, on the other hand, one takes phenomenology to be a philosophy of essence, which, contrary to the teleological-hermeneutic approach, rules out appeal to facts, then phenomenology becomes a *dog-*

matic doctrine, one that asserts principles or ideals irrespective of the facts, and this contradicts its claim to rationality. As can be seen from the quotation below, rationalism is a *form* of relativism, according to Husserl. Phenomenology therefore must find its place somewhere between these two approaches.[7] And indeed, this is what Husserl maintains:

> It is high time that people got over being dazzled, particularly in philosophy and logic, by the ideal and regulative ideas and methods of the "exact" sciences—as though the In-itself of such sciences were actually an absolute norm for objective being and for truth. Actually, they do not see the woods for the trees. Because of a splendid cognitive performance, though with only a very restricted teleological sense, they overlook infinitudes of life and its cognition, the infinitudes of relative and, only in its relativity, rational being, with its relative truths. But to rush ahead and to philosophize from on high about such matters is fundamentally wrong; it creates a wrong skeptical relativism and a no less wrong logical absolutism, mutual bugbears that knock each other down and come to life again like figures in a Punch and Judy show. [FTL 278 (245–46)]

In sum, the teleological-historical and essential approaches must be compatible if phenomenology is going to be true to its own dictates.

(c) The Hermeneutic Approach of *Formal and Transcendental Logic*

There *is* evidence to show that a teleological-historical approach did not suddenly make its appearance in the *Crisis* but was there in Husserl's earlier works alongside his philosophy of essences. Consider, for example, the following passages from *Formal and Transcendental Logic* in which Husserl *explicitly* describes the approach he will use in that work, and it will be seen that what he describes is a teleological-historical approach:

> So much by way of a most general characterization of the aim and method of this essay. It is, accordingly, an *intentional explication of the proper sense of formal logic.* The explication begins with the *theoretical formations* that, in a survey, are furnished us by historical experience—in other words: with what makes up the traditional Objective content of formal logic—and puts

them back *into the living intention of logicians*, from which they
originated as sense-formations. [FTL 10 (9)]

And:

Now, however, our only concern is to gain an understanding of
the essential character of historically existing logic, by means of
an explication of the intentionality determining the sense of
logic most originally. [FTC 46 (40)]

Husserl is attempting to determine the meaning aimed at in the
science of logic (the whole) by looking at de facto logic (the part). This *is*
a teleological-historical approach, also known as a *hermeneutic* approach.
Hermeneutics may be characterized as a model of understanding according to which the "object" to be understood is treated like a text to
be interpreted (RM 10). It essentially involves a process of understanding the whole in terms of the parts, and vice versa.[8] While the term was
revived by Dilthey, who used it to refer to a process of understanding
socio-historical phenomena (RM 5, 10) [i.e., hermeneutics was a crucial
ingredient of the methodology of human studies (RM 10)], the term has
since evolved to refer to the process of understanding in general. As
Palmer writes:

In *Wahrheit und Methode*, Gadamer brings hermeneutics to a
new level of comprehensiveness. Dilthey and Betti had both argued for a comprehensive general hermeneutics—for the *Geis-
teswissenschaften*. What about the natural sciences? Do they
require a different understanding? The general conclusion has
been that the interpretation of an historically transmitted text
requires an act of historical understanding quite distinct from
the understanding practiced by a natural scientist. Gadamer
leaves this distinction behind, for he no longer conceives of
hermeneutics as restricted either to a text or to the *Geisteswis-
senschaften*.
Understanding, says Gadamer, is always an historical, dialectical, linguistic event—in the sciences, in the humanities, in the
kitchen. [P 214–15]

Not only does Husserl adopt a hermeneutical approach in *Formal
and Transcendental Logic*, but he considers there the difficulty such an
approach may pose to his demand for radicalism, for an *absolute* (essential) science. He in effect raises the question Carr cites Ricoeur as posing—namely, "How can a philosophy of the *cogito*, of the radical return

to the ego as founder of all being, become capable of a philosophy of history?" (C xxxiv):

> Thus we are presupposing the sciences, as well as logic itself, on the basis of the "experience" that gives them to us before-hand. Because of this, our procedure seems not to be at all radical, since the genuine sense of all sciences—or, equivalently, the essential possibility of their existence as genuine and not merely supposed sciences—is the very thing in question. And this applies in the case of logic itself, which is said to be the science of science, taken universally, and to bring out with its theories—or, as existing historically, to have ostensibly brought out—precisely that essential possibility. Nevertheless, whether sciences and logic be genuine or spurious, we do have experience of them as cultural formations given to us before-hand and bearing within themselves their meaning, their "sense": since they are formations produced indeed by the practice of the scientists and generations of scientists who have been building them. As so produced, they have a final sense, toward which the scientists have been continually striving, at which they have been continually aiming. Standing in, or entering, a community of empathy with the scientists, we can follow and understand—and carry on "sense-investigation." [FTL 8–9 (8)]

While this does not constitute a "solution" to the problem of the compatibility of a teleological-historical approach and a philosophy of essences, it does show Husserl to be aware of the problem and show him to consider the approaches to be compatible.

(d)   Apodicticity versus Relativism

Since the conflict between essential philosophy and a teleological-historical approach is one of apodicticity versus relativism, an examination of Husserl's notion of apodicticity is in order. Note Husserl's words in the *Cartesian Meditations:*

> Meanwhile we have lost sight of the demand, so seriously made at the beginning—namely that an *apodictic* knowledge, as the only "genuinely scientific" knowledge, be achieved; but we have by no means dropped it. Only we preferred to sketch in outline the tremendous wealth of problems belonging to the

first stage of phenomenology—a stage which in its own manner is
itself *still infected with a certain naivete (the naivete of apodicticity)*
but contains the great and most characteristic accomplishment
of phenomenology, as a refashioning of science on a higher
level—instead of entering into the *further and ultimate problems
of phenomenology:* those pertaining to its *self-criticism*, which aims
at determining not only the *range* and *limits* but also the *modes
of apodicticity.* [CM 151–52 (177–78)]

Of particular interest to us is that Husserl is here putting the traditional
notion of apodicticity into question. In the *Crisis* as well Husserl says that
"apodicticity" is far from clear and needs to be reexamined:

What this apodicticity could ultimately be which would be decisive for our existential being as philosophers, is at first unclear.
[C 18]

The apodicticity that contradicts a teleological-historical approach is a narrowly (objectivistically) construed apodicticity in which
facticity, relative truth, is considered the opposite of apodicticity, absolute truth. But Husserl writes:

What if, even when we get down to the primitive phenomenological bases, problems of relative and absolute truth are still
with us, and, as problems of the highest dignity, *problems of
ideas* and of the *evidence of ideas?* What if the relativity of truth
and of evidence of truth, on the one hand, and, on the other
hand, the infinitely distant, ideal, absolute, truth beyond all relativity—what if each of these has its legitimacy and each demands the other? [FTL 278 (245)]

Here Husserl is suggesting that phenomenology embraces both
relativism and absolutism. While phenomenology is an a priori science, it
is not a dogmatic absolutism. It contains elements of relativism, but *not*
of a skeptical relativism.[9] What is implied here is that hermeneutics, associated with relativism, and phenomenology, thought to be a form of absolutism, are compatible. But this will become clear if Husserl's notion
of apodicticity is contrasted with that of Descartes, for the Cartesian type
of apodicticity *does* contradict hermeneutics. Those who think Husserlian phenomenology contradicts hermeneutics usually do so because
they think the phenomenological notion of apodicticity is the same as
that of Descartes.

(e) Husserl Rethinks Cartesian Apodicticity: Beyond a Feeling of Strict Necessity

While both Husserl and Descartes base their philosophies on the apodictic cogito, for Husserl this has a different meaning than for Descartes. Husserl reinterprets the Cartesian philosophy by rethinking the apodicticity of the cogito. In fact, phenomenology *comes about* by a rethinking of apodicticity:

> The up-and-down of the historical movements—newly strengthened empiricist sensationalism and skepticism, newly strengthened rationalism in the older scientific style, German Idealism and the reaction against it—all this together characterizes the first epoche, of the whole "modern period." The second period is the renewed beginning, as the reappropriation of the Cartesian discovery, the fundamental demand of apodicticity; and in this beginning, through the changed historical situation (to which all the fateful developments and philosophies of the first epoche belong), there arise forces of motivation, a radical thinking-through of the genuine and imperishable sense of apodicticity (apodicticity as a fundamental problem), the exhibiting of the true method of an apodictically grounded and apodictically progressing philosophy; and included within this the discovery of the radical contrast between what is usually called apodictic knowledge and what, in the transcendental understanding, outlines the primal ground and the primal method of all philosophy. It is precisely with this that there begins a philosophy with the deepest and most universal self-understanding of the philosophizing ego as bearer of absolute reason coming to itself. [C 340]

Phenomenology felt the need to rethink the apodicticity of the ego because Descartes's understanding of this notion left his philosophy with deep problems. That is, while in Descartes's system the Ego's being is assured because the ego "somehow" *has*[10] apodicticity, the being of objects other than the ego, of objects in general and the world in particular, poses a problem. To assure *their* being Descartes appeals to God's veracity. Husserl argues, however, that had Descartes looked at the *nature* of the ego's apodicticity he would have seen that there is no need to invoke anything beyond the ego to legitimate objects in general and the world in particular. But grounding the cogito's apodicticity is not something Descartes does. Although Descartes says that the ego-cogito is apodictic because it is a clear and distinct idea—that is, an idea, the denial of which constitutes an absurdity—he fails to investigate why this is so. In short: Descartes does not make his concept of apodicticity scientific. In Husserl's view Descartes's apodicticity is based on nothing more than a *feeling:*

> How can the subjective-psychic characteristic of *clara et distincta perceptio* (which is nothing other than what later theorists "describe" as the evidence-characteristic, as the evidence-feeling, the feeling of strict necessity)—how can it guarantee an Objective validity, without which there would be no truth for us? [FTL 280 (247)]

But phenomenology cannot be satisfied with this, for true rationality cannot be based on a *feeling* of "strict necessity."[11] In other words, the cogito's apodicticity, contrary to Descartes, is not a quality that cannot be analyzed.

(f) Grounding Apodicticity: Not All Objects Given in the Immanent Sphere are Immanent

Apodicticity is expressed in terms of evidence, and, as Descartes correctly saw, in terms of being—that is, it is impossible to say cogito and to say I *am* not:

> An *apodictic* evidence, however, is not merely certainty of the affairs or affair-complexes (states-of-affairs) evident in it; rather it discloses itself, to a critical reflection, as having the signal peculiarity of being *at the same time the absolute unimaginableness* (inconceivability) of their *non-being,* and thus excluding in advance every doubt as "objectless," empty. [CM 15–16 (56)]

Evidence of the being of X is apodictic if the nonbeing of X is in principle unimaginable. The being of all transcendent objects, as Descartes noted, can be doubted: their being is beyond me, so I may be mistaken about them. Accordingly, Husserl, like Descartes, includes all transcendencies in the *epoche* (I 137, 147). True apodictic knowledge occurs only when evidence and the object are as close as can be—namely, *when the act of evidence coincides with the object of evidence,* as happens in self-reference, the performance of the cogito. If my cogito is directed at my pure co-gito—that is, at the cogito in which all transcendencies are excluded, at the cogito qua cogito—I can imagine the nonbeing of all objects except one—namely, my own act of thinking—for even in imagining that I am not, I am. The cogito is apodictic because whatever else it is aware of, it is also always aware of itself and in self-awareness there is no "gap" be-tween the object of evidence and the evidence. It is, in short, an *imma-nent* object.

In the cogito I coincide with my evidence—in the cogito I *am* my own evidence:

> Every immanent perception necessarily guarantees the exis-tence (*Existenz*) of its object. If reflective apprehension is di-rected to my experience, I apprehend an absolute Self whose existence (*Dasein*) is, in principle, undeniable, that is, the in-sight that it does not exist is, in principle, impossible; it would be non-sense to maintain the possibility of an experience *given in such a way not* truly existing. The stream of experience which is mine, namely, the one who is thinking, may be to ever so great an extent uncomprehended, unknown in its past and fu-ture reaches, yet so soon as I glance towards the flowing life and into the real present it flows through, and in so doing grasp myself as the pure subject of this life (what that means will expressly concern us at a later stage), I say forthwith and because I must: I *am*, this life is, I live: *cogito*.
>
> To every stream of experience, and to every Ego as such, there belongs, in principle, the possibility of securing this self-evidence: each of us bears in himself the warrant of his abso-lute existence (*Daseins*) as a fundamental possibility. [I 130 (85)]

And:

> But *my* empathy and my consciousness in general is given in a primordial and absolute sense, not only essentially but existen-tially. This privileged position holds only for oneself and for the stream of experience to which the self is related; here only is there, and must there be, anything of the nature of imma-nent perception. [I 130 (85–86)]

My proof for the indubitable cogito, the ground of the apodictic cogito, is a living *doing*—a seeing. Cogito *is* a seeing (I 75 [36]) and the only way to see that is *by* seeing, by directing the ray of attention to my act of seeing as I see:[12]

> *Only in seeing can I bring out what is truly present in a seeing;* I must make *a seeing explication of the proper essence of seeing.* [FTL 159 (142)]

It has already been explained how this seeing is my Being.[13] The living doing involves an act of reflection directed at the stream of experience. This act of reflection can itself become the object of yet a higher act of reflection. The phenomenological method proceeds by such acts of reflection:

> The study of the stream of consciousness takes place, on its own side, through various acts of reflexion of peculiar structure, which themselves, again, belong to the stream of experience, and in corresponding reflexions of a higher grade can be and indeed must be made into objects for phenomenological analyses. For it is through analysis of this kind that the foundations of a general phenomenology are laid, and the methodological insight so indispensable to its development is grounded. [I 200 (147)]

The cogito, then, is indubitable because it has itself as immanent object. In the cogito, seeing and being coincide. This is why Husserl thinks that phenomenology when properly carried out is the surest of all sciences and is the truest science. Hence Merleau-Ponty's claim that "there is no apodictic self-evidence, the *Formale und Tranzendentale Logik* (p. 142) says in effect" (PhP xvi), is misleading. What Husserl means in that section of *Formal and Transcendental Logic* is that there is no *principle* we can appeal to that would reveal truth. Only an *act of seeing* will reveal truth.[14] Here Husserl's conception of philosophy is identical to that of Simone Weil's:

> The rigor and certitude of philosophical investigation are as great as they can be; the sciences are far from coming close to them. Should one conclude from this that philosophical reflection is infallible? Yes, it is infallible to the degree that it is actually carried out. [SW 406]

But "cogito" refers both to an act of mind and to the content or objects of such an act. The legitimacy of this distinction can be seen at once by considering that the act of mind remains identical throughout its differing contents. Whether I am thinking about the tree in the garden, the significance of a poem or about how to dispose of the chair I no longer want, all these are instances of thinking. According to phenomenology the structure of the act of the cogito is apodictic, not its content per se. The cogito as act is apodictic because it is the act that has itself as immanent object. This is why Ricoeur asserts that "what is beyond all doubt is the *act*" (CI 262–63).[15] Iso Kern states:

> An apodiktischen Momenten scheinen am *cogito* übrig zu bleiben: seine Zeit-form, seine Existenz, seine intentionale Beziehung auf den Gegenstandspol und seine Beziehung auf den individuellen Ichpol, sowie dieser Ichpol selbst. Kein Inhalt, den die Phänomenologie als universale Erfahrungstheorie in sich aufnimmt, ist absolut gegeben. [IK 211]

And Husserl writes:

> No matter how absolute the apodicitic evidence of the ego's existence may be for him, still it is not necessarily evidence for the existence of the manifold data of transcendental experience. [CM 28 (67)]

And:

> Rather there extends through all particular data of actual and possible self-experience—even though they are not absolutely indubitable in respect of single details—a *universal apodictically experienceable structure* of the Ego. [CM 28 (67)]

If it is difficult to see that what is apodictic is not the content of the cogito but the structure of the act of the cogito, this is because separating content from act is difficult due to the act by itself being transparent and only being visible via the content.

Although the cogito qua cogito is apodictic because it has itself as immanent object, this does not mean that all *objects* "in" this act are immanent objects. Transcendent objects are also indicated. Looking at the cogito one sees many modes of relating to an object, and correlatively many types of objects "in" the cogito. For example, as Descartes realized, cogito can mean: "I perceive, I remember, I phantasize, judge, feel, desire, will" (I 104 [61]), and corresponding to these there are memory objects, judgments, phantasy objects, real objects, and so forth. All these modes of the cogito can be seen to refer back to experience of a real world as the primary mode[16] (I 114 [130]), though this does not yet give us *assurance* of the *being* of the real world. Because the cogito is related essentially to many types of objects, transcendent as well as immanent,[17] Husserl says that the cogito reflects, not a self-contained *proposition*, but a sphere:

> Thus, during the universal epochē, the absolutely apodictic self-evidence "I am" is at my disposal. But within this self-evidence *a great deal is comprised* [my emphasis]. A more concrete version of the self-evident statement *sum cogitans* is: *ego cogito-cogitata qua cogitata*. This takes in all *cogitationes*, individual ones as well as their flowing synthesis into the universal unity of one *cogitatio* in which, as *cogitatum*, the world and what I have variously attributed to it in thought had and still has ontic validity for me. . . . In the epochē, all these determinations, and *the world itself*, have been transformed into my *ideae*; they are inseparable components of my *cogitationes*, precisely as their *cogitata*. Thus here we would have, included under the title "ego," an absolutely *apodictic sphere* [my emphasis] of being rather than merely the one axiomatic proposition *ego cogito* or *sum cogitans*. [C 77–78]

While the apodictic immanent sphere is the ground, the basis, transcendent objects are also indicated. But this does *not* mean that transcendence is reduced to immanence. It means, rather, that transcendence receives its sense from immanence. Transcendent objects are seen as transcendent *by* me due to immanence. Real objects, one type of transcendent objects, also get their sense from my being, from immanence. Hence, I am the living criterion of whether something is real, of whether the world is there.

That I do not have perfect evidence of real objects and the world is neither a shortcoming or failing of real objects, nor does it bring into doubt my criteria of reality, for by their very nature transcendent objects are objects of which I cannot be certain. Transcendent objects are not apodictic;[18] by their very essence they can be doubted (I 131 [86–87]). But the criterion of truth or error for these objects comes from my cogito. Hence there is no need to invoke God's benevolence to "prove" the existence of the world. *All* beings, immanent and transcendent, achieve their being-sense from my cogito. If anything is to be *grounded*, it must be so in the cogito.[19]

In Husserl's view, then, the indubitable "I am" at once expresses one's link with the object. The "I am" is the moment of plenitude that allows me to see being—that is, that allows me to have evidence of being. It is, in other words, an openness to being, both immanent and transcendent. Since it is the moment that provides me with evidence, the "I am" is the moment I must consult if I want to know *anything*. Even the apodicticity of the cogito must be *grounded* in the I am. Nor can I go beyond it to ground my knowledge of the world, say, by appeal to the benevolence of God, for even the benevolence of God must be grounded in the I am. If anything, the "I am" is already an expression of the benevolence of God.

For Husserl, unlike for Descartes, the apodictic ego-cogito is not something enclosed in itself, cut of from its objects, from the world and from others:[20]

> It is through this abstention that the gaze of the philosopher in truth first becomes fully free: above all, free of the strongest and most universal, and at the same time most hidden, internal bond, namely, of the pregivenness of the world. Given in and through this liberation is the discovery of the universal, *absolutely self-enclosed* [my emphasis] and absolutely self-sufficient *correlation between the world itself and world-consciousness* [my emphasis]. By the latter is meant the *conscious life of the subjectivity* which *always* has the world in its enduring acquisitions [my emphasis]. [C 151]

Also:

> In this manner it becomes clear that *the ego, taken concretely,* has a *universe of what is peculiarly his own,* which can be uncovered by an original explication of his apodictic "ego sum"—an explication that is itself apodictic or at least predelineative of an apodictic form. *Within* this *"original sphere"* (the sphere of original self-explication) we find also a "transcendent world," which accrues on the basis of the intentional phenomenon, "Objective world," by reduction to what is peculiarly the ego's own (in the positive sense, which is now preferred). [CM 104–5]

The cogito, which I am, *is a relation to the object*.[21] Cogito is a seeing (I 75–76 [36]), a having of evidence of the object. The object is an indispensable aspect of the cogito, as Husserl captures in his tripartite expression *ego cogito cogitatum*. For Husserl, if I am sure of the ego's being, I am sure of the being of an object.

In sum, according to Husserl and contrary to Descartes, apodicticity is based on more than a mere feeling and can be made thematic. When it is made thematic and grounded, it will be seen that apodicticity is not opposed to or cut off from facticity, but that it is the basis from which all objects and all facticity gain their validity and status as objects or facts. This leads Husserl to an apodictic science, which, unlike Cartesian philosophy, is not a deductive science divorced from facts.

(g) Phenomenology, not a Deductive Science Divorced from Facts, but an Eidetic Descriptive Science of the Act That I Am

Hence, while Husserl's program of grounding knowledge in the apodictic cogito *sounds* Cartesian, there is a radical difference between how they each understand such a program. Descartes, a child of his times, understands "science," according to the model of the exact mathematical sciences, to mean *deductive* science. On the deductive model of grounding science in the cogito, the cogito's *content* is apodictic. The content of the cogito is, in a higher act of cogito, *derived* from the cogito's more primary content, each step in the derivation being apodictic. For Descartes grounding science in the ego-cogito means *deriving* all knowledge from the cogito isolated from facticity. This means that it contradicts hermeneutics, for it rules out using facts as a source of knowledge in the way hermeneutics does. But Husserl does not accept the deductive model of science as the only one:

> It is only a misleading prejudice to suppose that the historical methods of the *a priori* sciences, which are *exact* ideal sciences throughout, must be accepted without question as the pattern for every new method of science, and especially for our new transcendental phenomenology—as though all eidetic sciences must show one type of method only, that of "exactness." Transcendental phenomenology as descriptive science of Essential Being belongs in fact to a *main class of eidetic science wholly other* than that to which the mathematical sciences belong. [I 193 (141)]

And:

> It is naturally a ludicrous, though unfortunately common misunderstanding, to seek to attack transcendental phenomenol-

ogy as "Cartesianism," as if its *ego cogito* were a premise or a
set of premises from which the rest of knowledge (whereby one
naively speaks only of objective knowledge) was to be deduced,
absolutely "secured." [C 189]

Phenomenology is not a deductive science, but a descriptive science (I 184 [132]) and grounding objectivity does not mean *deriving* it
from the cogito for Husserl. "The point is not to secure objectivity but to
understand it," writes Husserl (C 189). Objectivity is *given*. We need not
derive it, but need to understand the meaning objectivity presupposes.
As Simone Weil says:

> True philosophy does not build anything; its object is given to
> it—it is our thoughts; it only makes, as Plato says, an inventory
> of them. [SW 406]

To try to derive objectivity from the cogito, as Descartes does, is in effect
to *reduce* objectivity to the cogito. But Husserl says that objectivity cannot be reduced to immanence.[22]

In Husserl's notion of grounding, however, the *act* (of cogito) is
apodictic, not the content of the cogito per se. Phenomenology aims to
describe the essence (structure) of the *process* or *act* of thinking (I 191
[139]) taken in its *purity*. While the process reveals itself in its contents
(I 151 [104]), it is not to be confused with *any* of its contents. Hence,
phenomenology does not describe psychological events or states in objective space/time (I 215 [161]), in nature, because the latter are also
constructs, "contents" of pure mind:

> Were something still left over enabling us to grasp the experi-
> ences as "states" of a personal Ego, in and through whose
> changes self-identical personal properties were manifested, we
> could break up these apprehensions also, do away with the in-
> tentional forms which bring them into shape, and reduce them
> to pure experiences. *Even psychical states* point to the ordering
> conditions of absolute experiences in which they are consti-
> tuted and take on the intentional and in its way *transcendent*
> form *"state of consciousness."* [I 151–52 (105)]

And:

> *All* empirical unities, and therefore psychological experiences
> also, are *indicators of absolute systems of experience*, and show a

quite distinctive essential formation, besides which still other
formations are conceivable; all are in some sense transcendent,
merely relative, contingent. [I 152 (105)]

Phenomenology, then, distinguishes pure mental processes from
their contents, and aims to describe the former in their purity. It aims to
uncover the universal structure of pure mental processes (CM 28 [67]);
it attempts to determine the universal structure of acts of mind by examining the contents of mind, for the latter are indices pointing to pure
absolute consciousness (I 152 [105]):

Thus we describe and, in so doing, determine by *strict* concepts
the generic essence of perception taken universally or that of
subordinate species, such as the perception of physical things
and their determinations, the perception of animate beings,
etc.; likewise the essence of memory taken universally, empathy
taken universally, willing taken universally, etc. Prior to these,
however, are the highest universalities: the mental process
taken universally, the cogitatio taken universally, which already
make extensive essential descriptions possible. [I FK 168 (140)]

In effect, then, phenomenology goes from particular content of
mind to the universal that underlies all content and allows that content
to be. One recalls Nietzsche: "Read thine own life, and understand
thence the hieroglyphs of the universal life" (PN 340 [353]). But this
only proves that phenomenology is not a deductive science, for the relation of particular to universal is not one of implication. So, for example,
when Husserl in the *Philosophy of Arithmetic* shows that the notion of
number presupposes the universal notion "any object whatsoever"
(*Etwas*), he is not attempting to *deduce* the concept of number from consciousness, but is describing what is necessary for the concept of number
to be at all.[23]

It must be observed, however, that when phenomenology looks at
the pure mental process, it sees that essentially associated with it is a pure
subject:

Among the universal essential peculiarities pertaining to the
transcendentally purified realm of mental processes the first
place is due the relationship of each mental process to the
"pure Ego." Each "cogito," each act in a distinctive sense, is
characterized as an act of the Ego, it "proceeds from out of
the Ego," it "lives" "actionally" in the act. [I FK 190
(159–60)]

And:

> But if I perform the phenomenological ἐποχή (epokhe-absten-
> tion), the whole world of the natural setting is suspended, and
> with it, "I, the man." The pure experience as act with its own
> proper essence then remains as residue. But I also see that the
> apprehension of the same as human experience, quite apart
> from the question of existence, introduces various features
> which do not need to be there, and that on the other side no
> disconnecting can remove the form of the *cogito* and cancel the
> "pure" subject of the act. The "being directed towards," "the
> being busied with," "adopting an attitude," "undergoing or
> suffering from" has this *of necessity* wrapped in its very essence,
> that it is just something "from the Ego," or in the reverse di-
> rection "to the Ego"; and this Ego is the *pure* Ego, and no re-
> duction can get any grip on it. [I 214 (160)]

Hence, strictly speaking, phenomenology distinguishes between the
pure subject, pure mental process, and its contents (I 214 [161]). It aims
to be the eidetic science of the pure mental process, which belongs essentially to a pure subject, a pure ego:

> Accordingly, there are always distinguished—in spite of the
> necessary relatedness to one another—the *mental process itself*
> and the *pure Ego* pertaining to the mental living. And, again:
> [there are always distinguished] the *purely subjective moments of
> the mode of consciousness* and, so to speak, the rest of the *content
> of the mental process turned away from the Ego*. As a consequence,
> there is a certain, extraordinarily important two-sidedness in
> the essence of the sphere of mental processes, of which we can
> also say that in mental processes there is to be distinguished a
> *subjectively oriented* side and an *objectively oriented* side. [I FK
> 191 (161)]

But I *am* the pure Ego that lives in the stream of experience—that
is, I am not only an empirical ego but also a pure ego (C 184, 186). I *am*
the stream of pure consciousness that phenomenology describes in its
pure universality. In other words, the universals "used" in all understanding and experience are the universals of my act of being. These
universals are what I seek to have evidence *of* and are part of my act of
evidence. In short: they are immanent objects that can be known apodictically. The universals that phenomenology seeks can be grounded apodictically in the *I am*. Since I am the universals that phenomenology seeks

to describe, phenomenology is self-analysis (cogito). Apodicticity in phenomenology is achieved only in the *act* of doing phenomenology, in the act of cogito: the universals are grounded in the *act* of seeing. The universals that phenomenology describes are not constituted by the explicit cogito but are the basis of the explicit cogito, are what I *am*—are universal *fact*. For this reason Husserl calls phenomenology a *descriptive* eidetic science (I 184 [132]), a *material* (as opposed to formal) eidetic science (I 185 [133]), and a *concrete* eidetic-science (I 189 [136]).

It is now possible to explain why Husserl denies that the claim that the transcendental ego is self-criticism is open to an infinite regress. The claim that the transcendental ego is that which questions itself can be interpreted in two ways. It can mean either (1) that the transcendental ego questions itself, or (2) that the transcendental ego *is* a self-questioning. A diagram of the first and second interpretations respectively may make the difference clear:

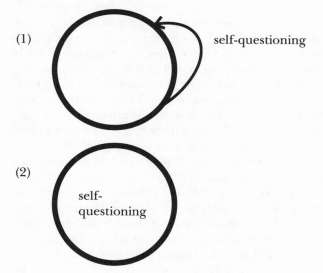

(1)   self-questioning

(2)   self-questioning

On the first interpretation, if the norms for the questioning are found in the transcendental ego, then they too are subject to questioning, in which case we have an infinite regress and phenomenology falls. If the norms are found beyond the transcendental ego, then we have objectivism, and phenomenology falls too. On the second interpretation, the norms are neither beyond the transcendental ego nor subject to questioning, but are "part of" the transcendental ego and the grounds of the self-questioning; that is, they are part of the self-questioning. While on the first model the transcendental ego has an identity outside the self-questioning, on the second model this is not so—the transcendental ego is self-questioning through and through. If the transcendental ego is *essentially* self-questioning, that means it *has* the norms, has a temporal aspect, has an atemporal pure subject, has a stream of experience with objects that are transcendent to it and which it seeks to know, and is itself in part transcendent.

The second interpretation accords with Husserl's theory. It is in keeping with the dicta of Husserlian phenomenology, according to which it is a contradiction to say that the transcendental ego gets its norms beyond itself, because there *is* nothing beyond the transcendental ego. According to Cartesianism, on the other hand, it is not a contradiction to say that the transcendental ego gets its norms from beyond itself, because there are "things" radically beyond the cogito—namely, the world, God, and others. On the second interpretation, the claim that the transcendental ego is self-criticism is not open to an infinite regress, because the claim is given in and based on the facticity of Being. That is where the regress ends: the regress ends with the fact of my Being, for my Being reveals itself to me as self-examination. My Being *reveals* itself as a stream of objects, both transcendent and immanent, and as involving a ray of attention that I can at will direct at the stream and its objects, which, because they are not totally given to me, I seek to bring to evidence. My Being *reveals* itself as a seeing of objects and as a seeing of self, for, if it is a seeing, its identity is self-seeing. I see that I am self-examination in the immediacy of my being. The norms used to criticize the self are not other than the transcendental ego, but are part of the transcendental ego, for the transcendental ego *is* self-criticism, which means it is at once ground, the striving to explicate the ground, and the norms. More specifically, the stream of experience is the ground; striving to explicate the ground occurs by means of attention and will; and the norms are found in the structure of that being of the transcendental ego.

In other words, what Husserl says about objectivity, that our task is not to *derive* it because it is given, but to understand it, applies also to subjectivity. The possibility of subjectivity as self-examination does not need to be proven, for it is given in Being. Phenomenology's task is "merely" to describe and understand what is involved in this process. If the transcendental ego is self-examination, that implies that it has norms, that it is in part a temporal Being, that I have some evidence—that is, direct contact with Being against which I assess claims, and so forth. And in questioning the latter claims I only "prove" them, for I would not, indeed, *could* not, question if I did not have *some* evidence,[24] if I did not have norms, and so forth. Nor can questioning these norms ever invalidate the norms, for every act of questioning applies the norms—the norms are the ground of all questioning. Even if my goal to achieve apodictic knowledge of myself cannot be met—even if I am constantly open to self-criticism—this does not deny the phenomenological claim that I have apodictic self-evidence, for I can criticize myself only if I have an apodictic ground—that is, some immediacy on which to do so. Even if I am always open to self-criticism, that does not make me fall prey to radical skepticism, for the very process of continual self-criticism implies I have in principle something (my Being) given to me and that I have norms.

What this shows is that Husserl's "model" of the structure of the transcendental ego is quite different from Descartes's model of the cogito. While the transcendental ego has properties similar to Descartes's cogito, because these properties find themselves in a structure different from that of Descartes's cogito, Husserl is able to overcome the difficulties and absurdities implicit in the Cartesian model of the ego, such as the isolation of the ego from the world, the apodicticity of the cogito contradicting the historicity (facticity) of the ego, and the cogito as self-examination leading to an infinite regress.

Since Husserl's concept of the transcendental ego as self-criticism implies that part of my being is historical, a hermeneutic approach is indicated. My Being (cogito) reveals that I do not know everything about myself, that while one aspect of "me" is apodictic and adequate—namely, the act of cogito—another is not:

> The Ego is *apodictically predelineated*, for himself, as a concrete
> Ego existing with an individual content made up of subjective
> processes, abilities, and dispositions—horizonally prede-
> lineated as an experienceable object, *accessible to a possible self-
> experience* (my emphasis) that can be perfected, and perhaps en-
> riched, *without limit* (my emphasis). [CM 28–29 (67)]

My transcendental ego is apodictic and adequate, my empirical ego is not. As empirical ego I am a *historical* process, which indicates the need for a teleological-historical approach:

> *Adequacy and apodicticity* of evidence *need not go hand and hand.*
> Perhaps this remark was made precisely with the case of tran-
> scendental self-experience in mind. In such experience the ego
> is accessible to himself originaliter. But at any particular time
> this experience offers only a core that is experienced "with
> strict adequacy," namely the ego's living present (which the
> grammatical sense of the sentence, *ego cogito*, expresses); while,

> beyond that, only an indeterminately general presumptive hori-
> zon extends, comprising what is strictly non-experienced but
> necessarily also meant. To it belongs not only the ego's past,
> most of which is completely obscure, but also his transcenden-
> tal abilities and his habitual peculiarities at the time. [CM
> 22–23 (62)]

Since the absolute transcendental ego is a process of self-examination, I am in part a *historical* process, for self-knowledge is, according
to the claim that I am self-examination, something I work or strive toward over time:

> This life, as personal life, is a constant becoming through a con-
> stant intentionality of development. What becomes, in this life,
> is the person himself. His being is forever becoming. [C 338]

A hermeneutic approach, then, is indicated in Husserl's model of
the cogito. And indeed there *is* a type of hermeneutics that incorporates
elements of Husserl's philosophy of essence. Husserl's philosophy of essence is not in conflict with hermeneutics in general, but only with a
specific type of hermeneutics. The tension Carr speaks of between essential philosophy and a teleological-historical approach, a tension between
absolutism and relativism, respectively, is parallel to the tension between
two branches of hermeneutics—that of Hirsch and Betti on the one
hand, and that of Heidegger and Gadamer on the other. The debate
between the two types of hermeneutics has been characterized succinctly
and clearly by Palmer in his book on hermeneutics[25] and throughout the
following sections frequent reference will be made to his work.[26]

(h)   The Hermeneutics of Betti and Hirsch
      versus Gadamer's Philosophical
      Hermeneutics

It must be noted that although the debate between the two camps of
hermeneutics is expressed in terms of "interpretation" and specifically
in terms of "interpretation of a work of art," "interpretation" is to be
understood as the model of *all* understanding. Since we *are* acts of understanding according to hermeneutics—this is so for phenomenology
as well, it might be added—even though it is expressed in terms of a
theory of interpretation of art, hermeneutics is at once a theory about
the nature of our Being, our ego or subjectivity.

In simplified terms, according to the hermeneutics of Betti and Hirsch, a work has an objective meaning of its own, a meaning that we aim to discover through our interpretation. One may term such a meaning the essence of the work; hence the alignment of this branch of hermeneutics with the philosophy of essence. This school of thought maintains that it is legitimate to speak of correct and incorrect interpretations of a work, and that there are norms that aid us in interpreting. According to the other branch of hermeneutics, the "philosophical hermeneutics" of Gadamer, the work has no "objective" meaning of its own, but has only a significance or relevance to our present situation, a significance the interpreter must discover and express. This type of hermeneutics, of which Palmer is a representative, stems from Heidegger's thought. According to it there are no objective criteria for interpreting a given work (P 63).

Clearly these two schools of thought are at odds. According to Betti and Hirsch, a hermeneutics that does not incorporate essentialism falls prey to relativism, to radical skepticism. Writes Palmer:

> In essence, Hirsch argues that if it is held that the "meaning" of a passage (in the sense of the verbal meaning) can change, then there is no fixed norm for judging whether the passage is being interpreted correctly. Unless one recognizes the "glass slipper" of the original verbal meaning intended by the author, there is no way of separating Cinderella from the other girls. This recalls Betti's objection to Gadamer's hermeneutics: that Gadamer does not provide a stable normative principle by which the "correct" meaning of a passage can be validly determined. [P 61]

Hence Betti and Hirsch maintain, for example, that "Gadamer is lost in a standardless existential subjectivity"[27] (P 58, 61). On the other hand, those, such as Palmer, who consider the hermeneutic approach incompatible with a philosophy of essences, do so because they consider the latter to involve a process of describing objective, static entities (essences) "above the flux of experience" (P 127), whereas they consider their own hermeneutics to be a radically "subjective" process, to be a "word event," as Palmer's terms it, using a phrase he borrows from Ebeling (P 65):

> Literary criticism is helped by oral interpretation to recall to itself its own inner intention when it takes (in a more conscious way) the definition of the "being" of a work not as static, conceptual thing, not an atemporal "essence" that has become a

thing as word-expressed concept, but rather as a being that realizes its power of being as oral happening in time. The word
must cease being word (i.e., visual and conceptual) and become
"event"; the being of a literary work is a "word-event" that
happens as oral performance. [P 18]

Paradoxically, in characterizing it in terms of word-event Palmer
considers his concept of hermeneutics to be *phenomenological*, though he
uses the term to refer to the philosophy of Heidegger and Gadamer,
rather than that of Husserl. The former he calls "hermeneutical phenomenology" (P 125). The hermeneutics of Hirsch and Betti, which is critical
of Gadamer's position, Palmer considers to be in alignment with at least
Husserl's early phenomenology, which he sees as a type of realism:

[Hirsch] affirm[s] that the verbal meaning is something independent, changeless, and determinate, which one can establish
with objective certainty. Such a conception of verbal meaning
rests on certain specifiable philosophical presuppositions,
mainly realistic, or perhaps those of the early Husserl of *Logical Investigations*, whom Hirsch quotes to the effect that the
same intentional object may be the focus of many different intentional acts. The object, in this latter case, remains the same,
an independent idea or essence. [P 63]

But Palmer's hermeneutics is *not* phenomenological in Husserl's
sense of the term. To make it so, he must incorporate exactly those elements in the hermeneutics of Betti and Hirsch he finds objectionable.
The hermeneutics of Betti and Hirsch, however, *is* compatible with Husserlian phenomenology generally and with Husserl's philosophy of essence in particular, but it is a mistake to consider either Husserl's
phenomenology or this type of hermeneutics to be a realism. To do so is
to fail to understand how Husserl overcomes psychologism and how he
understands the subject-object relation.

(i)   The Subject-Object Relation in
      Gadamerian versus Husserlian
      Hermeneutics and the Problem
      of Psychologism

The Gadamerian/Heideggerian school of hermeneutics, which considers essentialism to contradict its tenets, attempts to put forth a theory of

interpretation that overcomes the subject-object dichotomy of traditional metaphysics. In Palmer's words:

> It should be said at the outset that the subject-object model of interpretation is a realist fiction. It is not derived from the experience of understanding but is a model constructed reflexively and projected back onto the interpretive situation. [P 223]

And:

> To ask meaningfully about what happens when one understands a literary work means transcending the prevailing definition of the interpretive situation in terms of the subject-object schema. [P 224]

And:

> It is the service of Martin Heidegger in *Being and Time* to have opened up the ontological character of understanding in a way that moves radically beyond the older conception of it within the subject-object schema. [P 227]

It can be objected that overcoming the subject-object dichotomy of transcendental metaphysics is Husserl's concern as well. Although Palmer does cite Husserl as one of the first to attempt to overcome this dichotomy, he considers Heidegger the first to have done so successfully and considers Gadamer to have furthered this (P 216) by adding a Hegelian element to Heidegger's hermeneutics (P 215). According to Palmer, Husserl's attempt to ground all being-sense in transcendental subjectivity is a form of *subjectism*, which is but "the other side of" objectivism and an aspect of the old metaphysics. By subjectism Palmer means any philosophy that takes the human subject, whether as consciousness, will, spirit, or the like, as its ultimate reference point, and which thus regards the world as "measured by man":

> Subjectism is a broader term than subjectivity, for it means that the world is regarded as basically measured by man. In this the world has meaning only with respect to man, whose task is to master the world. The consequences of subjectism are many. First, the sciences take preeminence, for they serve man's will to master. Yet since in subjectism man recognizes no goal or

meaning that is not grounded in his own rational certainty, he
is locked in the circle of his own projected world. [P 144]

In other words, Palmer wishes to overcome traditional metaphysics quite literally by considering neither the subject nor the object as
foundational. Hence he deems Husserl to have been unsuccessful at
overcoming traditional metaphysics even though the latter criticizes objectivism, for Husserl considers transcendental subjectivity as being
foundational, and this, maintains Palmer, is subjectism. Heidegger, however, overcomes subjectism according Palmer by grounding being-sense
in Being, in human historical Being-in-the-world. Heidegger starts, not
with subjectivity, but with "the facticity (*Faktizität*) of the world" (P 227)
and grounds understanding "in the act of the world, the facticity of the
world" (P 228):

> Heidegger held that the facticity of being is a still more funda-
> mental matter than human consciousness and human knowl-
> edge, while Husserl tended to regard even the facticity of
> being as a datum of consciousness. [P 125]

For these reasons Palmer considers Heidegger's phenomenology to be
radically different from that of Husserl:

> Heidegger rethought the concept of phenomenology itself, so
> that phenomenology and the phenomenological method take
> on a radically different character.
>   This difference is epitomized in the word "hermeneutic" it-
> self. Husserl never used it in reference to his work, while Hei-
> degger asserted in *Being and Time* that the authentic
> dimensions of a phenomenological method make it hermeneu-
> tical; his project in *Being and Time* was a "hermeneutic of *Da-
> sein.*" Heidegger's selection of the term "hermeneutic"—a
> word laden with associations, from its Greek roots to its mod-
> ern use in philology and theology—suggests the antiscientific
> bias which forms a marked contrast to Husserl. The same
> strain is carried over into Hans-Georg Gadamer's "philosophi-
> cal hermeneutics," stamping the word itself with overtones of
> antiscientism. [P 125–26]

It is because Palmer wants to overcome objectivism that he denies
the objective status of a work, that he denies that it has "an essence" or
ideal meaning, whether that work be a work of art or the Ego. That is,
an ideal meaning is thought by him to be an essence, a "being-in-itself."

Instead, as explained above, Palmer reduces the work to an act of significance. But, as discussed in the next pages, in reducing the work to significance and overstepping ideal meaning, Palmer falls into psychologism,
his protestations to the contrary notwithstanding.

There are two reasons why Palmer fails to see that he has fallen
into psychologism.[28] First of all, Palmer is working with a definition of
psychologism that is far too narrow—namely, he thinks psychologism
occurs when (ideal) objects are reduced to *feelings*:

> To consider the above elements of the interpretative problem
> is not, as some might think, to fall back into "psychologism."
> For the perspective within which the charge of "psychologism"
> and the attitude of antipsychologism (presupposed in the
> charge) have any meaning assumes at the outset the separation
> and isolation of the object and then looks pejoratively at the
> "subjective" reaction as in the intangible realm of "feelings."
> The discussion presented here, however, has not dealt with
> feelings but with the structure and dynamics of understanding,
> the conditions under which meaning can arise in the interac-
> tion of reader with the text, the way in which all analysis pre-
> supposes an already shaped definition of the situation. Within
> the framework of such considerations the truth of George
> Gurvitch's observation is seen—that object and method can
> never be separated. Of course, this is a truth foreign to the re-
> alistic way of seeing. [P 26]

It is clear from the above quotation that Palmer thinks that psychologism occurs when one reduces the object to feelings. Because he
does not reduce the objects to *feelings*, Palmer thinks he has avoided
psychologism. But the definition of psychologism, at least as Husserl
uses it, is broader. Psychologism occurs when one reduces the object to
any subjective event, not merely to feelings. It occurs when one reduces
judgment to judging. In reducing the work to word-event, Palmer reduces judgment to judging. Husserl urges that while the two, judgment
and judging, are essentially related, they are nevertheless distinct, and
that to fail to keep these distinct is to propound either psychologism or
objectivism:

> We have already spoken of the difficulty of separating from
> psychological subjectivity the psychically produced formations
> making up the thematic domain of logic—the difficulty, that is,
> of regarding judgments (and likewise sets, cardinal numbers,
> and so forth) as anything other than psychic occurrences in the
> human beings who are doing the judging. [FTL 153 (137)]

And:

> The general confusion was reduced to the extent that (over-coming the psychologistic confounding of them) one distin-guished *judging* and *the judgment itself* (the ideal formation, the stated proposition). [FTL 206 (183)]

And:

> We noted in the first place the extraordinarily widespread dis-position of our time to *interpret the eidetic psychologically*. Even many who call themselves idealists have yielded to it; and in-deed, generally speaking, the influence of empiricist views on idealist thinkers has been a strong one. Those who take ideas or essences for "mental constructions," who with respect to the operations of consciousness through which "concepts" of colour and shape are acquired, drawn from intuited examples of things with colours and shapes, confuse the consciousness of these essences, colour and shape resulting from the momentary intuition, with these essences themselves, ascribe to the flow of consciousness as a real part of it what is in principle transcen-dent to it. But that is on the one hand a corruption of psychol-ogy, for it affects the purity of the empirical consciousness; on the other hand (and that is what here concerns us), it is a cor-ruption of phenomenology. [I 163–64 (116)]

Psychologism occurs when one reduces the object to subjective acts, ir-respective of whether these acts are feelings or not. Hence, unless Palmer is willing to speak of the meaning of a work, as opposed to merely its significance, unless he is willing to incorporate elements of essential-ism, he falls into psychologism.

A further misconception that Palmer has is his belief that "the attitude of antipsychologism . . . assumes . . . the separation and isola-tion of the object and then looks pejoratively at the 'subjective' as in the intangible realm of 'feelings,' " where by "separation and isolation of the object" Palmer presumably means separation and isolation of the object from the subject. But Husserl, a proponent of antipsychologism, neither looks at the subjective as an "intangible realm of feelings" nor maintains that the object exists in isolation from the subject. While Hus-serl urges that the logical object—that is, the meant, the judgment—is not to be *reduced* to the act that gave rise to it, he nevertheless urges that the two, the meant and the act of meaning, are essentially related. Hence, in Husserl's view any objective theory of meaning, such as logic, requires correlational research into the subjective act that gives rise to meaning. Since this point is important Husserl is cited at length:

> Logic . . . inquires in *two opposite directions*. Everywhere it is a matter of rational productions, in a double sense: on one side, as *productive activities and habitualities*; on the other side, as *results* produced by activities and habitualities and afterwards persisting. [FTL 33 (29)]

And:

> These Objective affairs [cognitional formations] all have more than the fleeting factual existence of what comes and goes as a formation actually present in the thematic field. They have also the being-sense of abiding validity; nay, even that of Objective validity in the special sense, reaching beyond the subjectivity now actually cognizing and its acts. They remain identical affairs when repeated, are recognized again in the manner suitable to abiding existents; in documented form they have Objective factual existence, just like the other objectivities of the cultural world. Thus they can be found in an Objective duration by everyone, can be regeneratively understood in the same sense by everyone, are intersubjectively identifiable, are factually existent even when no one is thinking of them.
>
> The opposite direction of logic's thematizing activity is *subjective*. It concerns the deeply hidden subjective forms in which theoretical "reason" brings about its productions. The first question here concerns *reason in its present activity*—in other words: that intentionality, as it flows on during its living execution, in which the aforesaid Objective formations have their "origin." [FTL 34 (30)]

And:

> The considerations just pursued give us access to an understanding of the *proper task of judgment-theory*, a discipline that, although much discussed, has remained rather fruitless, because it has lacked all understanding of the specific character of the investigations directed to the subjective that are necessary in the case of judgments, in the logical sense, and in the case of the fundamental concepts relating to these.
>
> 1. If the general confusion was reduced to the extent that (overcoming the psychologistic confounding of them) one distinguished *judging* and *the judgment itself* (the ideal formation,

the stated proposition), it then was even less possible to set a
senseful *problem concerning the subjective* as long as the peculiar
essence of all intentionality, as a constitutive performance, was
not understood and therefore judicative intentionality in particular was not understood as the constitutive performance in
the case of ideal judgment-formations—and, still more particularly, the intentionality of evidential judging was not understood as the constitutive performance in the case of ideal truth-
formations. [FTL 206 (183)]

Speaking of the meaning of a work of art does *not*, contrary to
Palmer, imply "objectivism" or realism, for one can maintain, as Husserl
does, that the meaning is constituted by the subject. Indeed, this is exactly the sense in which Betti and Hirsch speak of the meaning of a work.
Contrary to Palmer, they are not realists (P 60), but phenomenologists,
for while the realist maintains that the object exists independently of the
subject, both Betti and Hirsch insist that it is illegitimate to speak of the
object without a subject, as Palmer himself says:

> Betti by no means wishes to omit the subjective moment from
> interpretation, or even to deny that it is necessary in every hu-
> mane interpretation. But he does wish to affirm that, whatever
> the subjective role in interpretation may be, the object remains
> object and an objectively valid interpretation of it can reason-
> ably be striven for and accomplished. An object speaks, and it
> can be heard rightly or wrongly precisely because there is an
> objectively verifiable meaning in the object. If the object is not
> other than its observer, and if it does not, of itself, speak, why
> listen? [P 56]

And:

> Thus, as Betti observes, to speak of an objectivity that does not
> involve the subjectivity of the interpreter is manifestly absurd.
> Yet the subjectivity of the interpreter must penetrate the for-
> eignness and otherness of the object, or he succeeds only in
> projecting his own subjectivity on the object of interpretation.
> Thus it is fundamental and is the first canon of all interpreta-
> tion to affirm the essential autonomy of the object. [P 57]

Betti's position is one against psychologism. For Betti the object *is* objective, though vis-à-vis the subject. This is similar to Husserl's position.
But the second reason why Palmer believes he has avoided psy-

chologism is that he thinks he can avoid the subject-object distinction *altogether*. This is to be taken quite *literally*: in effect Palmer is trying *to get rid of the subject in hermeneutics*. This is contrary to Husserl's hermeneutics. He uses the example of Gadamer's writings on the phenomenon of "game" to describe the latter's hermeneutics as applied to art. "There are a number of significant elements in the phenomenon of 'game' which shed light on the way of being of the work of art" (P 171), writes Palmer. He adds that in the game "Gadamer had found a model which . . . can serve as a basis for substantiating the dialectical and ontological character of his own hermeneutics" (P 174). But what becomes clear is that on this model, as Palmer seems to interpret it, the subject becomes eradicated:

> The object of Gadamer's discussion of the concept of game or play in relation to art is to free it from the traditional tendency to associate it with activity of a subject. [P 172]

And:

> From the subjectivist point of view, the game is an activity of a subject, a free activity into which one wills to enter and which is used for his own pleasure. But when we ask what the game itself is, and how it comes to pass, when we take the game and not human subjectivity as our starting point, then it takes on a different aspect. A game is only a game as it comes to pass, yet while it is being played it is master. The fascination of the game casts a spell over us and draws us into it; it is truly the master over the player. The game has its own special spirit. The player chooses which game he will give himself to, but once he chooses he enters a closed world in which the game comes to take place in and through the players. In a sense the game has its own momentum and pushes itself forward; it wills to be played out. [P 172]

And:

> The "subject" of the experience of art, the thing that endures through time, is not the subjectivity of the one who experiences the work; it is the work itself. This is precisely the point at which the mode of being a game becomes important. The game, too, has its own nature independent of the consciousness of those who play it. [P 174]

The subject, it is to be noted, is being denied in *all* its forms—reason, freedom, love, spirit, will:

> How can thinking be defined in such a framework [i.e., the framework of subjectism]? Again, in presentational terms that go back to Plato. How can truth be conceived? In terms of correctness, certainty that the statement about something corresponds with the way the object is presented to us. This presentation cannot really be a self-disclosure of something, since it is caught up in the overpowering act of objectification by the subject. Therefore, says Heidegger, the great metaphysical systems become expressions of will, whether phrased in terms of reason (Kant), freedom (Fichte), love (Schelling), absolute spirit (Hegel), or will-to-power (Nietzsche).
>
> The will to power that is grounded in subjectism knows no ultimate value, only the thirst for more power. In the present day this expresses itself in the frenzy for technological mastery. [P 145]

Palmer thinks he does not fall into psychologism when he reduces the objective ideal meaning of a work to an event, because this *event* in his view is not that of a subject. While there *is* truth to what Palmer says, his claims need to be modified. It is one thing to say that the ultimate subject is not the psychological subject or to say that it is a *pure* subject, as Husserl does, but it is quite another to say that there is no ultimate subject. As it stands, Palmer seems to be denying the subject altogether.

(j) Consequences of Denying the Subject: Loss of Autonomy of Reason, Loss of Moral Responsibility

There are consequences to denying the subject that put this type of hermeneutics at odds with Husserlian hermeneutics. Because Palmer's hermeneutics is not based on the ultimate authority of the subject, there is a diminishing of personal responsibility in favor of adherence to authority and tradition:

> If there can be no presuppositionless understanding, if, in other words, what we call "reason" is a philosophical construction and no final court of appeal, then we must reexamine our relationship to our heritage. Tradition and authority need no

longer be seen as the enemies of reason and rational freedom
as they were in the Enlightenment and the Romantic period,
and into our own day. Tradition furnishes the stream of con-
ceptions within which we stand, and we must be prepared to
distinguish between fruitful presuppositions and those that im-
prison and prevent us from thinking and seeing. In any event,
there is no intrinsic opposition between the claims of reason
and those of tradition; reason stands always within tradition.
Tradition even supplies reason with the aspect of reality and
history with which it will work. Ultimately, Gadamer asserts,
the consequences of recognizing that there can be no presuppositionless understanding are that we reject the Enlightenment interpretation of reason, and both authority and
tradition win back a status they have not enjoyed since before
the Enlightenment. [P 183]

While on the one hand Palmer seems to be saying that reason is to
work hand in hand with authority and tradition, a claim not unaccept-
able to Husserl, on the other hand it seems that tradition and authority
are to have the "upper hand," as it were, a claim that has dire consequences and goes against all that Husserlian phenomenology represents.
Husserl considers the individual's free reason to be the path to self-
responsibility, which in turn he considers to be the key to human salvation and even immortality. In this sense, Husserl is a proponent of the
Enlightenment, albeit a *new* Enlightenment. While he considers the objectivistic rationalism of the Enlightenment (C 192) to be a mistake (C
290), he believes in the Enlightenment's aim of achieving self-responsibility through reason. The *New Enlightenment* in Husserl's view would
result from a reinterpretation of rationality, a reinterpretation that
would lead to a concept of rationality more in keeping with our deepest
nature. Husserl writes:

The rationalism of the Age of Enlightenment is now out of the
question; we can no longer follow its great philosophers or any
other philosophers of the past. But their intention, seen in its
most general sense, must never die out in us. For, as I emphasize once again, true and genuine philosophy or science and
true and genuine rationalism are one. Realizing this rationalism, rather than the rationalism of the Enlightenment, which is
laden with hidden absurdity, remains our own task if we are
not to let specialized science, science lowered to the status of
art or τέχνη or the fashionable degenerations of philosophy
into irrationalistic busy-work be substituted for the inextin-

guishable idea of philosophy as the ultimately grounding and universal science. [C 197]

And:

> I too am certain that the European crisis has its roots in a misguided rationalism. But we must not take this to mean that rationality as such is evil or that it is of only subordinate significance for mankind's existence as a whole. Rationality, in that high and genuine sense of which alone we are speaking, the primordial Greek sense which in the classical period of Greek philosophy had become an ideal, still requires, to be sure, much clarification through self-reflection; but it is called in its mature form to guide [our] development. On the other hand we readily admit (and German Idealism preceded us long ago in this insight) that the stage of development of *ratio* represented by the rationalism of the Age of Enlightenment was a mistake, though certainly an understandable one. [C 290]

This is not to deny that tradition and authority are important for Husserl, but it is to deny, rather, that they are foundational in his view. Tradition and authority are always for a consciousness, and it is *consciousness* that must inspire tradition and authority internally—that is, must bring these to life for the self. Without the active (inspired) relation of consciousness to tradition and authority, they will be but dead entities incapable of evoking anything but blind responses. In principle, respect for authority and tradition is based on the structure of Being, on the "I am,"[29] and it is consciousness that must supply the norms with which to evaluate tradition and authority, for by themselves they may be the bearers of evil—cf. Nazi Germany. There is once again a similarity to the philosophy of Nietzsche: the latter condemns a blind adherence to authority and tradition and praises an active, free adherence to tradition and authority, one that comes from a *plenitude* of one's Being—one that comes, not from a denial of self, but from an affirmation of self. Plenitude, which allows one to truly give to the other, comes from a celebration of self, which paradoxically allows one to become truly unselfish.

Palmer does not base hermeneutics on the authority of the individual's reason for this would constitute an instance of taking the subject as ultimate reference, a form of objectivism, a form of science. This is so presumably because any *concept* of the subject is, paradoxically, objective and this would falsify living subjectivity. But Palmer seems to have only one sense of science—objectivistic science. Science, for him, means technological mastery. Hence, when he says that a philosophy that takes the subject as ultimate reference gives predominance to science, he means that such a philosophy serves the human will to master, that it gives rise to technological mastery and a technological attitude.

But two objections can be raised against Palmer's position. First of all, not all science is objectivistic. Husserl does not have an objectivistic notion of reason. Reason is *lived*[30] according to him, and hence Husserl's notion of science is different than that of objectivistic science, reason and science being the same for Husserl. Second of all, it is incorrect to lump subjectism and technological science together. Husserl bases his science on consciousness precisely *in order to fight* the attitude that makes technological science the mode of grasping humanity.

But there are reasons to think that Palmer himself retains elements of objectivism in his philosophy. It was explained earlier that objectivism occurs when a phenomenon constituted by consciousness is not seen as such but as already formulated independently of consciousness. Consider, for example, the following quotation:

> How does the operation of language in understanding take
> into account the functions of will and desire in man? Gadamer
> would probably reply.first that his analysis in *Wahrheit und*
> *Methode* was of the event of understanding itself, not of the
> motivations for it or the personal affect surrounding it. [P 217]

Palmer's hermeneutics, in line with Heidegger's philosophy, is supposed to describe the essential human way of being-in-the-world—namely, understanding. But one wonders how *essential*, that is, how true to our Being, a hermeneutics is that does not account for desire or will, both of which are fundamental aspects of our Being-in-the-world. One is led to suspect that this hermeneutics is not in touch with the deepest source of Being, but is starting relatively "high up," that it is talking about understanding already cognitively advanced, and that a deeper act of understanding is needed to relate it to desire and personal affect. In fact, according to both Husserl and Merleau-Ponty, it is not possible to understand higher levels of cognition without considering the motivations or personal affect related to these, and this requires a deeper understanding, a deeper logos (PhP 365) than that of objective thought, and, it seems, deeper than a Heideggerian type hermeneutics as well. As will be discussed a little further on, according to Husserl cognition is inextricably linked with affect.

But it is revealing that, despite his vehement insistence that hermeneutics is not grounded in the subjective, Palmer himself is somewhat dissatisfied with the lack of discussion on personal affect as it relates to understanding. The quotation above, in which Palmer suggests what answer Gadamer would give to the question concerning desire in understanding, goes on to say:

> This may be so, but it would be very enlightening to know how Gadamer would answer this question. I believe that here again the dialectical character of Gadamer's hermeneutics as over against that of Heidegger would more adequately provide for *the contribution made by the person doing the understanding* [my emphasis] to the hermeneutical experience. This would valuably supplement and extend the final portion of the book dealing with the hermeneutical experience. [P 217]

Indeed, human nature in part is desire, and if Palmer's hermeneutics is to give us self-understanding, then it must be able to account for desire. Palmer is correct, however, in saying that Gadamer can in principle handle the question concerning desire better than Heidegger can, because of the Hegelian element Gadamer injects into his hermeneutics, for it allows the latter in principle to consider the subjective vis-à-vis the objective without falling into a reductionist position.[31]

If subjectivity is not considered fundamental but authority is, hermeneutics faces grave ethical problems, for, as Palmer himself admits, the individual will not be responsible:

> One notes the tendency in later Heidegger to describe understanding exclusively with a vocabulary of passive terms; understanding is no longer viewed as an act of man but as an event in man. There emerges a danger that man will be seen as a passive speck in the stream of language and tradition. [P 216]

And:

> It is difficult to resist asking what kind of ethics and doctrine of man are presupposed in Heidegger. Is man simply to live in a kind of responsive surrender to the call of being? And it would be of interest to put the same question to Gadamer. [P 217]

Palmer cites Jean-Marie Domenach's objection against a Heideggerian hermeneutics:

> A convergent undertaking [in philosophy today] seeks to re-

verse the order of terms under which philosophy has lived up to the present, and to negate the autonomous activity of consciousness. I don't think, I *am thought*; I don't speak, I *am spoken*; I don't deal with something, I *am dealt with*. It is from language that everything comes and to language that everything returns. The System, which is seized in the midst of itself, is proclaimed the master of man. . . . The System, a thinking that is cold, impersonal, erected at the expense of all subjectivity, individual or collective, negates at last the very possibility of a subject capable of expression and independent action. [P 216]

This is the same critique de Muralt has of the ontological aspect of Dufrenne's and Merleau-Ponty's theories:

Merleau-Ponty and Dufrenne represent the same philosophical position, one in ethics and the other in aesthetics. By insisting on the fact that human *operation* is essentially free, these writers come to suppress the freedom of *man*. Man thus becomes the bearer of a universal intentional teleology, just as scientists are bearers of the universal scientific knowledge interest which extends beyond each of them. This freedom is a curious freedom, one that hypostatizes human operation while preventing man from being truly responsible for it. I am not responsible for a work of which I am only the instrument. [DeM 367]

Palmer responds to the criticism by saying that a phenomenology that takes the life-world as foundational does not leave humankind out of account:

It must be said at once that the disembodied objectivity of a pure system that leaves man out of account stands at once worlds apart from any phenomenological approach, which takes as its foundation the life-world. [P 216]

Presumably Palmer is referring to Heidegger's notion of Being-in-the-world. But one cannot have it both ways. One cannot speak of a life-world and yet deny subjectivity, for it is a *subject* who lives. *Husserl's* phenomenology too takes the life-world as foundational and he is considered subjectivist by Palmer and Heidegger. What is perhaps required is not a denial of subjectivity, but a reinterpretation of it. Such a reinterpretation has already been adumbrated and will be substantiated in the chapter on other selves.

(k) Further Consequences of Denying the
     Subject in a Heideggerian Type
     Hermeneutics: Loss of Artistic
     Responsibility

There are further shortcomings to Palmer's hermeneutics, which Husserlian phenomenology is able to avoid. To explain these a distinction
must be drawn between consciousness, self-consciousness, and self-reflection. It was stated above that consciousness, whatever else it is aware
of, is also always aware of itself. Hence it might seem as if all three
phrases are interchangeable. However, in this work the term "self-reflection" is reserved for when consciousness explicitly makes itself the object
of its ray of attention. The term "self-consciousness" is not used, because it has negative psychological overtones. By a self-conscious person
is usually meant one who is more or less painfully aware of his or her
empirical ego. It describes an undesirable psychological state because
self-consciousness usually interferes with one's actions, especially with
artistic acts.[32] While the first two "states," consciousness and self-reflection, are indispensable to the artistic act, to one's relation to a "work,"
self-consciousness is not. Palmer, however, denies all three when he denies the role of subjectivity in the "work of art."

   According to Palmer not only does the work of art not involve
objective meaning, it involves neither the intention of the artist nor the
will or consciousness of the interpreter, whose relation to the work is one
of spontaneity, according to Palmer. Throughout his book Palmer uses
music to illustrate how philosophical hermeneutics conceives of the
"work." The example of music, however, illustrates just the opposite
that Palmer thinks it does. If Palmer were correct, then it would not be
necessary to inquire after the composer in order to play a given piece—it
would not be necessary to know whether one is playing Bach, Chopin, or
Beethoven, for example. At best, Palmer might adopt Gadamer's way
out of being left with no guidelines whatsoever for playing a given piece,
and say that we need to place the piece within the tradition in order to
play it well. But frequently tradition alone will not tell us how to interpret a work, for certain composers introduced radically new elements
into their works, which were atypical vis-à-vis the tradition. One thinks of
Beethoven. The tradition surrounding Beethoven will not itself tell one
how to perform Beethoven, for Beethoven broke with tradition.[33] While
the music he wrote was formed by a dialectical relation to the tradition, it
was not strictly speaking in keeping with tradition. That means that there
is a level of meaning "beyond" the tradition (which can later become

absorbed into the tradition), one that developed with the individual and bears his or her stamp, his or her intention or outlook.

As to Palmer's claim that the performer's relation to the work does not involve his or her will, consider the words of the renowned pianist Claudio Arrau:

> If the artist's gifts are exceptional, he will often show in his early years the qualities symbolized in the archetype of the Divine Child, which, as Jung describes it, "is a personification of vital forces quite outside the limited range of our conscious mind: of a wholeness which embraces the very depth of Nature. It represents the urge, the strongest, the most ineluctable urge in every being, namely the urge to realize itself. It is, as it were, an incarnation of the *inability to do otherwise* [Jung's italics], equipped with all the powers of nature and instinct, whereas the conscious mind is always getting caught up in its supposed ability to do otherwise."[34]
>
> This is the unconscious power of the child prodigy. But passing over from the divine innocence of unconscious security to the young manhood of conscious responsibility takes an act of supreme courage and heroism. For the young artist, it represents one of the most difficult periods of his life. He must pass through a great test. . . . First he must slay the terrible dragon (attain conscious understanding), then he must pass through the test of fire and water (with Sarastro, the force of conscious knowledge and commitment, as guide), and only then does he attain Pamina (his soul), and his heart's desire. In doing so, the dark terrible forces of the unconscious (Queen of the Night), which always seek to drag him down, sink into the deepest layers of his psyche from where he can then begin to draw his creative power, but this time mastered by his conscious mind. [CWA 241]

From Arrau's description we see the extent to which the self-reflective mind is involved in the creative process,[35] and how both will and courage are involved in this self-reflective process. The role of self-reflection in shaping the artist is a *lifelong* process, according to Arrau:

> This does not mean that from the age of fifty or so an artist begins to flag and accomplish less. Just the contrary happens if everything in his psychic development has gone well. His energy is as enormous as ever. Only now, if, as Jung describes it, the full process of individuation has taken place, or is taking

place—the process by which a man, through ever greater consciousness, effort, and wisdom finally attains his complete self-
hood in harmony with the cosmos—does he do his best and
most meaningful work. If this last task is achieved, it produces
a new wave of creativity arising from still deeper sources than
anything before. [CWA 243–44]

There is nothing in Palmer's description of the artist's relation to
the work to suggest any form of personal struggle, any form of personal
responsibility, of personal will. While it is true that the artist's relation to
his or her work may involve a state in which the subject and object are *one*
in the event (e.g., in certain performances)—that is, a state in which
among other things the artist is not self-conscious, a state that the pianist
Glenn Gould describes as "ecstasy"—this neither denies the consciousness of the artist nor the acts of will that led up to the achieving of that
"state." In describing the artistic process it is not legitimate to sever the
state of ecstasy from the process that led up to that "state," a process
that involved not only consciousness but self-consciousness—that is,
self-reflection—and that took place over a long period of time. Observe
the words of Gould:

The purpose of art is not the release of a momentary ejection
of adrenalin but is, rather, the gradual, lifelong construction of
a state of wonder and serenity. Through the ministrations of
radio and the phonograph, we are rapidly and quite properly
learning to appreciate the elements of aesthetic narcissism—
and I use that word in its best sense—and are awakening to
the challenge that each man contemplatively create his own
divinity. [GG 64]

Nor must it be thought that Arrau or Gould are exceptions, or that this is
peculiar to musicians. One thinks of the very long reflective development that Rilke underwent, for example.
    We know, on the other hand, how Husserl's concept of mind
stresses responsibility (C 340), how he speaks of the "heroism of reason"
(C 299). The process of conscious self-reflection that Arrau describes fits
in with Husserl's phenomenology. According to Arrau's description,
self-reflection, an act of objectification, is not only not antithetical to the
"word-event," it is indispensable to achieving the highest artistic performance. Self-reflection or objectification helps the artistic act come
about, which at its highest is inspired, alive, and deeply felt. This in effect
is Kleist's position in *The Marionette Theatre*:

We see that as in the organic world reflection becomes ever darker and weaker, so grace in proportion comes more brilliantly to the fore. But in the same way as the intersection of two lines on one side of a point, finds itself suddenly on the other side after passing through infinity, or as the image in a concave mirror, after having disappeared into infinity, suddenly reappears right in front of us, so in a similar manner does grace reappear, after knowledge has, as it were, passed through something infinite. At the same time grace appears in its purest form in a human body which either has an infinite consciousness or none at all, i.e., in a marionette or a god.

We must then, I asked, eat again from the Tree of Knowledge in order to return again to a state of innocence? Of course, he replied. Thus ends the last chapter of the world. [MT 141]

The act of objectification destroys or falsifies neither Being nor the artistic act. "Phenomenology possesses an aesthetic structure," writes de Muralt (DeM 368). Indeed, as de Muralt argues, without the notion of voluntary and reflected acts, the artistic act loses its value:

Without the freely voluntary and reflected act of the artist, it amounts to the same thing to say that the aesthetic creation is the necessary result of aesthetic exigency or that it is the product of chance. [DeM 372]

When Arrau talks of the unconscious power of the child prodigy undergoing lifelong reflection to increase the depth and beauty of his or her artistry, this is in line with Husserl's concept of how consciousness operates. For Husserl each level of thought is naive with respect to the next higher level, however rich, potentially or actually, the former is. This can be taken on the level of the individual or on the level of the history of thought. To illustrate the latter with an example, Plato's thought is naive with respect to Aristotle's, even though Aristotle's thought involves a misunderstanding of Plato's thought and even though, in Husserl's opinion, Plato's thought contained a greater truth than that of Aristotle. This greater truth is his view that logic, or, to use Plato's term, "dialectic," is one with philosophy, and not, contrary to Aristotle, a specialized science. Hence, when Aristotle makes logic a special science (FTL 7 [7]), he loses the deeper truth contained in Plato's thought. Yet paradoxically, this misunderstanding in the long run deepens our understanding of logic, for reflection will turn to the misunderstanding, and, correcting it, will gain an *explicit* and *deepened* understanding of logic. It will deepen our understanding because the explication will reveal meaning and connections that were previously only implicit. Hence Plato's thought is the ground, but in a condensed, implicit sense. The aim is to "return to" the original point, but in an enriched, reflective way, thereby *transforming* the origin. This is what phenomenology does also. Writes de Muralt:

> If we want to apply the Husserlian theory of the teleology of history . . . we might say that the Husserlian idea intentionally removes the historical dross from Plato's original intention and represents the true Platonic idea. [DeM 42]

And:

> As the reestablishment of philosophy with a new universal task and at the same time with the sense of a renaissance of ancient philosophy—it [phenomenology] is at once a repetition and a universal *transformation* [my emphasis] of meaning. [C 14]

This process holds for artists and their own creative development no less than for the philosopher dealing with the history of thought.[36]

It sounds as if according to Husserl we "have" an idea that guides us a priori, that shapes, perhaps even blindly drives, our behavior, and that we should come to know this idea. Here again is the tug between fact and necessity: Is our behavior predetermined by our telos? This sounds like a speculative theory about the nature of mind, in its individual and collective manifestations. But this is only seemingly so:

> The spiritual *telos* of European humanity, in which the particular telos of particular nations and of individual men is contained, lies in the infinite, is an infinite idea towards which, in concealment, the whole spiritual becoming aims, so to speak. As soon as it becomes consciously recognized in the development as telos, it necessarily also becomes practical as a goal of the will; and thereby a new, higher stage of development is introduced which is under the guidance of norms, normative ideas.
>
> Now all this is not intended as a speculative interpretation of our historical development but as the expression of a vital presentiment which arises through unprejudiced reflection. [C 275]

The description is phenomenologically sound; it is based on an analysis of the Being of the transcendental ego. Not only is the possibility of the historical movement of thought, both in its individual and collective manifestations, "contained" in the structure of the transcendental ego, but the *motive* to develop it is also given in the transcendental ego. The transcendental ego "contains" both the structure and the motive push for the development of thought, as will be explained next.

In terms of its structure, it has already been discussed how for Husserl consciousness can hierarchically relate to itself, each level of self-reflection being naive with respect to the next higher. In terms of motive, it has also been discussed how for Husserl the structure of the transcendental ego embodies motive: the transcendental ego is so structured as to imply further action, for it is seeing, and seeing is an act that is incomplete—neither myself nor the object is given completely—but that at the same time "contains" the possibility and rules of further completion. We *are* the part driven toward the whole. While in the moment of the "I am" I truly have apodicticity, I truly see and truly am, that moment indicates to me as well that I am not yet, but that I must bring myself to evidence. The latter constitutes the historical aspect of the self. As it were, the "I am" becomes the model and motivation for my cognitive life, for bringing to evidence, for it at once expresses the wish to increase my own Being. Being itself then becomes the motive for bringing to evidence.

Husserl would agree with Nietzsche when the latter, using musical dissonance as "the auditory analogue" of "the need to look and yet go beyond that look" (BT 143; K 140 [146]), says of humankind that it is an incarnation of dissonance (BT 145; K 143 [151]). Humankind is the need "to hear and at the same time to go beyond the hearing" (BT 143). One recalls also Sartre here: "Man is *the desire to be*" (BN 565). When I increase my seeing—that is, when I reflect—I increase my Being, for Being is seeing (as explained in chapter 4, this involves a physical element). From the beginning seeing is unified with Being and every act of seeing is incorporated into the primal stream of Being-seeing upon which I can reflect further. To reflect, then, is to magnify Being, to increase the intensity or being of Being, to increase power. This achieves its greatest intensity when thought examines itself—that is, when reflection makes the pure stream of experience its object. Again there is a similarity to the thought of Buber:

> Yes, this is what it means to realize: to relate life-experience to nothing else but itself. And here is the place where the power of the human spirit awakens and collects itself and becomes creative. [DL 69 (25)]

Buber speaks of this relating of life experience to itself as an act that "creates reality" in and through it (DL 69 [25]).

Hence, Being, which quite literally includes the body, the felt, itself points the way to reflection. Being propels and feeds itself in thought. In other words, reflection is a function of Being; it is Being asserting itself. Hence, reflection is self-assertion. Cupiditas, the tendency to self-assertion, is interwoven with our structure. On this level, then, the will is not a separate faculty, although it can later become the function of the explicit ego:

> We do not have a willing and, next to it, a perceiving, but in itself what is perceived is characterized as being produced voluntarily. [EJ 201]

And:

> We can form a *broader concept of interest* [a part of willing], or of acts of interest. Among such acts are to be understood not only those in which I am turned thematically toward an object, perceiving it, perhaps, and then examining it thoroughly, but in general every act of turning-toward of the ego, whether transitory, or continuous, every act of the ego's being-with (*inter-esse*). [EJ 86]

This first level, which is a type of will and structure, is felt, according to Husserl:[37]

> We have also spoken of an *interest* which may be awakened along with turning-toward an object. It now appears that this interest still has nothing to do with a specific act of will. It is not an interest which engenders anything on the order of plans and voluntary activities. It is merely a *moment of the striving* which belongs to the essence of normal perception. The reason we speak of interest here is that a *feeling* goes hand in hand with this striving, indeed a positive feeling, which, however, is not to be confused with a pleasure taken in the object. [EJ 85]

This first level is the source. This source, the living body, the felt, which Husserl calls the transcendental, is Dionysian, to speak in Nietzschean terms, which express very well what is at stake here. The way the Dionysian is described in the literature is similar to how Husserl describes the transcendental. Dionysus is the universal (K 128), basic ground of the world (K 143 [151]),[38] basis and origin of the word (K 129

[134]).[39] The reflective level, which is thought proper—that is, the concept, the word—is Apollonian (K 129). Apollo represents the individual; the cry to self-knowledge is Apollonian:

> As a moral Deity Apollo demands self-control from his people and, in order to observe such self-control, a knowledge of self. And so we find that the esthetic necessity of beauty is accompanied by the imperatives, "Know thyself," . . . [BT 34; K 46 (36)]

While these descriptions of Dionysus and Apollo are from Nietzsche's writings, Dodds describes the two in a similar fashion. According to Dodds, Apollo offers security through personal responsibility, while Dionysus offers liberation through self-abandonment (GI 76)—Dionysus "enables you for a short time to *stop being yourself*, and thereby sets you free" (GI 76). The Dionysian is the more powerful initially, because it is more immediate—it is felt. But if we hold off on a quick gratification of Dionysus, and instead reflect on Dionysus, we achieve a stronger, transformed, evolved Dionysus. What we achieve is an apollonization of Dionysus, which in turn is absorbed by Dionysus, the lived stream.

What is meant here comes close to something Nietzsche writes in *The Birth of Tragedy from the Spirit of Music*, where he describes the relation between the musical (Dionysian) and conceptual (Apollonian) elements of tragedy. This can be applied to life in general, to the relation between the Dionysian and Apollonian elements in life:

> If our analysis has shown that the Apollonian element in tragedy has utterly triumphed over the Dionysiac quintessence of music, bending the latter to its own purposes—which are to define the drama completely—still an important reservation must be made. At the point that matters most the Apollonian illusion has been broken through and destroyed. This drama which deploys before us, having all its movements and characters illuminated from within by the aid of music—as though we witnessed the coming and going of the shuttle as it weaves the tissue—this drama achieves a total effect quite beyond the scope of any Apollonian artifice. In the final effect of tragedy the Dionysian element triumphs once again: its closing sounds are such as were never heard in the Apollonian realm. . . . Dionysos speaks the language of Apollo, but Apollo, finally, the language of Dionysos; thereby the highest goal of tragedy and of art in general is reached. [BT 130–31; K 129–30 (135–36)]

And:

> When speaking of the peculiar effects of musical tragedy we laid stress on that Appollonian illusion which saves us from the direct identification with Dionysiac music and allows us to discharge our musical excitement on an interposed Apollonian medium. At the same time we observe how, by virtue of that discharge, the medium of drama was made visible and understandable from within to a degree that is outside the scope of Apollonian art *per se*. We were led to the conclusion that when Apollonian art is elevated by the spirit of music it reaches its maximum intensity; thus the fraternal union of Apollo and Dionysos may be said to represent the final consummation of both the Apollonian and Dionysiac tendencies. [BT 140–41; K 139 (145–46)]

And:

> Enchantment is the precondition of all dramatic art. In this enchantment the Dionysiac reveler sees himself as satyr, and as satyr, in turn, he sees the god. In his transformation he sees a new vision, which is the Apollonian completion of his state. And by the same token this new vision completes the dramatic act. [BT 56; K 64 (57–58)]

It must not be thought that because Nietzsche in places considers the Socratic spirit, rationalism, in other words, antagonistic to the Dionysian spirit and the destroyer of tragedy (BT 77; K 82 [79]),[40] phenomenology, also being a rationalism, cannot be harmonized with the Dionysian spirit. Nietzsche was not critical of all rationalism, for he believed in a "new rationalism," one that would be compatible with the Dionysian spirit. It could be argued that Husserlian phenomenology is such a new, reinterpreted rationalism.

Furthermore, one might note also Nietzsche's inconsistent characterization of Socrates, which ranges from scathing condemnation to high praise. On the one hand, his words in the *Birth of Tragedy* suggest that in Socrates are found the beginnings of such a new rationalism (BT 90; K 93 [92]). After all, Socrates espouses a theory of openness to Dionysus in the *Phaedrus* and in the *Ion* as well as in Diotima's speech in the *Symposium*, where unbridled receptivity to Dionysus is referred to as "Divine Madness."[41] On the other hand, Nietzsche maintains that the three Socratic maxims, "virtue is knowledge; all sins arise from ignorance; only the virtuous are happy" (BT 88; K 91 [90]) and his "scientific" attitude of maintaining that one can know nature (BT 94; K 97 [96]) and derive knowledge from a foundation by a logical deductive procedure, spell the death of tragedy (BT 88; K 91 [90]). But while these maxims are Socratic, the latter claims are more Cartesian than Socratic. Indeed, Socrates insisted that he knew only one thing—that he knew nothing. We are to take him quite seriously on this. Those who know that they do not know become seekers—they question. Nietzsche takes Socrates to be saying that he does not know *yet* but *will* know. But one can take Socrates to be saying that he *cannot* know, but can only ever seek to know. Hence, for Socrates, no less than for Lessing (BT 93; K 95 [95]), the search for truth has greater importance than truth itself. In other words, Socrates' seeing is also a nonseeing—he sees that he does not see.

In any case, the Apollonian dictum "know thyself" need not be considered as antithetical to tragedy. Surely the tragedy cited by Nietzsche himself, *Oedipus*, has as its theme precisely the need for and redeeming quality of self-knowledge, as Bruno Bettelheim observes:

> What forms the essence of our humanity—and of the play—is not being victims of fate, but our struggle to discover the truth about ourselves. Jocasta, who clearly states that she does not wish to discover the truth, cannot face it when it is revealed, and she perishes. Oedipus, who does face the truth, despite the immense dangers to himself of which he is at least dimly aware, survives. Oedipus suffers much, but at the end, at Colonus, he not only finds peace, but is called to the god and becomes transfigured.
>
> What is most significant about Oedipus, the Oedipal situation, and the Oedipus complex, is not only the tragic fate that we are all projected into deep conflicts by our infantile desires, but also the need to resolve these conflicts through the difficult struggles for, and the achievement of, self-discovery. [FMS 30]

This chapter attempted to show, then, that Husserl's characterization of the pure transcendental ego as the absolute ground of all being-sense is compatible with his characterization of the pure transcendental ego as radical self-examination. Phenomenology embraces both an essential approach and a hermeneutic approach. It was demonstrated that a purely hermeneutic approach à la Palmer, which excludes a philosophy of essences, cannot do justice to the creative acts of the ego. The next chapter examines whether the notion of the pure transcendental ego as absolute ground of being-sense can do justice to the phenomenon of intersubjectivity. In so doing, the connection between desire, value, and thought, between life and reason, will be worked out in more detail.

6

The Problem of the Other: A Resolution of Transcendental Solipsism

(a)   Nature and Relevance of the Problem

This chapter addresses the "problem of other selves." The nature of this problem is stated succinctly by Merleau-Ponty:

> How can an action or a human thought be grasped in the
> mode of the "one" since, by its very nature, it is a first person
> operation, inseparable from an *I?* . . . How can the word "I"
> be put into the plural, how can a general idea of the *I* be
> formed, how can I speak of an *I* other than my own, how can I
> know that there are other *I*'s, how can consciousness which, by
> its nature, and as a self-knowledge, is in the mode of the *I*, be
> grasped ιɴ the mode of the Thou, and through this, in the
> world of the "One"? [PhP 348]

The problem of other selves, then, may be characterized briefly as follows: How does the notion of "I," which denotes a private experience—namely—that of being conscious, of being alive, something *only* given directly from within—get transformed into the general idea of "I"? That is, how can I come to have a notion of "other I" or "other self," given that I cannot, by definition, experience another "I"?

Presumably Descartes gave rise to this problem when he said that mind and body are two distinct substances; the former, a mental sub-

166

stance, inhering in the latter, a material substance. Since consciousness in this view is construed as an interiority, the other remains actually inaccessible to me. One will presumably never encounter another consciousness directly, but will only be able to *think* another consciousness. Once again Merleau-Ponty expresses the problem clearly:

> If it [the body] is that object which the biologist talks about,
> that conjunction of processes analyzed in the physiological
> treatises, that collection of organs shown in plates of books on
> anatomy, then my experience can be nothing but the dialogue
> between bare consciousness and the system of objective corre-
> lations which it conceives. The body of another, like my own, is
> not inhabited, but is an object standing before the conscious-
> ness which thinks about or constitutes it. Other men, and my-
> self, seen as empirical beings, are merely pieces of mechanism
> worked by springs, but the true subject has no counterpart, for
> that consciousness which is hidden in so much flesh and blood
> is the least intelligible of occult qualities. [PhP 349]

According to this theory, original coexistence or intersubjective experience is denied: the other is identified by his or her body first as *object* and only subsequently as other person (consciousness/mind). Analogical reasoning, the process whereby I project my consciousness into the body of another in virtue of the other's body being the analogue of mine, is traditionally invoked to explain the transition from seeing the other as object to the seeing the other as person. But, as Merleau-Ponty points out, reasoning by analogy presupposes what it aims to explain:

> If it were really my "thought" that had to be placed in the
> other person, I would never put it there. No appearance could
> ever have the power to convince me that there is a *cogito* over
> there, or be able to motivate the transference, since my own *co-
> gito* owes its whole power of conviction to the fact that I am
> myself. [S 170]

Husserl makes the same point in the *Cartesian Meditations:*

> Therefore it is not as though the body over there, in my pri-
> mordial sphere, remained separate from the animate bodily or-
> ganism of the other Ego, as if that body were something like a
> signal for its analogue *(by virtue of an obviously inconceivable mo-
> tivation)* [my emphasis]. [CM 122 (151)]

Indeed, there seems to be no way out of the solipsism that is entailed by this view of the ego.

The problem of other selves is of significance to phenomenology[1] because it puts to the test the claim that Husserl's notion of pure transcendental ego can accommodate phenomena of life. If phenomenology cannot account for the experience of the other, it becomes questionable whether the notion of the pure transcendental ego can deal with life phenomena. Gadamer, for instance, wonders whether Husserl does "justice to the speculative demands contained in the concept of life" (TM 221), where specifically he questions whether Husserl can adequately account for the phenomenon of intersubjectivity and the understanding of the other "I":

> The immanent data in reflectively examined consciousness do not include the "Thou" in an immediate and primary way. . . . Husserl tried, through the most painstaking investigations, to throw light on the analogy between the "I" and the "Thou"— which Dilthey interprets purely psychologically through the analogy of empathy by means of the intersubjectivity of the communal world. He was sufficiently rigorous not to limit in any way the epistemological priority of transcendental subjectivity. But his ontological prejudice is the same as Dilthey's. The other person is first apprehended as an object of perception which then, through empathy, becomes a "Thou." In Husserl this concept of empathy has no doubt a purely transcendental meaning, but is still orientated to the interiority of self-consciousness and fails to achieve the orientation towards the functional circle of life, which goes far beyond consciousness, to which, however, it claims to return. [TM 221]

Gadamer speaks of Husserl's theory of the alter ego being orientated to the interiority of a self-consciousness. This is so, according to Gadamer, because of Husserl's tenet that consciousness intentionally constitutes all being, according to which the transcendental ego constitutes the alter ego. The other becomes constituted "in" me and is derived from the originary constitution of the ego-cogito. This is to deny original intersubjective experience in that what is original is the ego-cogito, the interiority of consciousness, as Gadamer states. But the other too is accordingly an interiority, a constituting transcendental ego. But how can I have access to such an interiority? How can it be given to me? How can I ever know any constituting activity other than my own transcendental ego to exist? This is precisely the problem of other selves, now encountered on a transcendental level. Hence, according to

Gadamer, we reencounter in Husserl's theory of intersubjectivity the very problem that he set out to solve in the *Cartesian Meditations*: Husserl's philosophy is caught up in a solipsism, albeit a transcendental solipsism. In the fifth chapter of the *Cartesian Meditations* Husserl himself raises the problem of transcendental solipsism:

> When I, the meditating I, reduce myself to my absolute transcendental ego by phenomenological epochē do I not become *solus ipse*; and do I not remain that, as long as I carry on a consistent self-explication under the name phenomenology? Should not a phenomenology that proposed to solve the problems of Objective being, and to present itself actually as philosophy, be branded therefore as transcendental solipsism? [CM 89 (121)]

And:

> But what about other egos, who surely are not a mere intending and intended *in me*, merely synthetic unities of possible verification *in me*, but, according to their sense, precisely *others*? Have we not therefore done transcendental realism an injustice. [CM 89 (132)]

And:

> Can we avoid saying likewise: "The very question of the possibility of actually transcendent knowledge—above all, that of the possibility of my going outside my ego and reaching other egos (who, after all, as others, are not actually in me but only consciously intended in me)—this question cannot be asked purely phenomenologically"? Is it not *self-understood* from the very beginning that my field of transcendental knowledge does not reach beyond my sphere of transcendental experience and what is synthetically comprised therein? Is it not self-understood that all of that is included without residue in my own transcendental ego? [CM 90 (122)]

Gadamer believes that it is because Husserl maintains that we have no direct perception of the other's interiority, that the latter is led to suggest that the other is first seen as object, and only subsequently, through analogical reasoning, is the other's "interiority," the other's consciousness, inferred.

The problem of the alter ego has an extensive impact on Husserl's philosophy, not only because it challenges the claim that phenomenology is a philosophy of life, but because it challenges some of the most basic tenets of phenomenology. This is why Gadamer says that the problem "threatens to burst asunder Husserl's framework" (TM 221) and why Ricoeur calls the problem of other selves the acid test for phenomenology:

> The constitution of the Other, which assures the passage to intersubjectivity, is the touchstone for the success or failure not only of phenomenology but also of the implicit philosophy of phenomenology.
>   All aspects of phenomenology, therefore, converge upon the problem of the constitution of the Other. [HAP 195]

In what way the problem of the alter ego tests the most basic tenets of phenomenology, in what way it is the acid test for phenomenology, is explained next.

(b)   The Problem of the Alter Ego: The Acid Test for Phenomenology

The insoluble dilemma of other minds has its origin in the ontological prejudice of Cartesianism.[2] Ontological prejudice occurs when being is *posited*, when we mistake sense or ontic validity constituted *by* the ego for something *given to* the ego. It is the ontological prejudice, the objectivism, of Descartes, in which being is reified and seen as an existent thing (CI 228), that renders the problem of other selves insoluble. That is, Descartes, in taking the ego to be a mental substance inhering in a physical body, in taking the being of the ego to be an existent thing, in other words, makes the alter ego something we can only infer; something we never see but only *think*. This commits him, in other words, to solipsism.

Husserl clearly states (CM 1 [43], 24 [63]) that his phenomenology was strongly influenced by Descartes's philosophy. Although he "corrects" Cartesianism by radicalizing it (CM 1 [43]), Husserl, like Descartes, grounds his phenomenology on the apodictic ego-cogito. But Ricoeur has shown that the ego-cogito of Descartes is not an innocent— that is, unprejudiced—assertion, but is one that reflects a specific metaphysics, based on an ontological prejudice. Ricoeur explains the nature of this ontological prejudice on which the ego-cogito is based:

It belongs to an age of metaphysics for which truth is the truth of existents and as such constitutes the forgottenness of Being. . . . The philosophical ground on which the cogito emerged is the ground of science in particular, but, more generally, it is the mode of understanding in which the existent *(das Seiende)* is put at the disposal of an "explanatory representation." The first presupposition is that we raise the problem of science in terms of research *(suchen)*, which implies the objectification of an existent and which places the existent before us *(vor-Stellung)*. Thus calculating man perhaps becomes sure *(sicher)*, gains certainty *(Gewissheit)*, of the existent. It is the point where the problem of certitude and the problem of representation coincide that the cogito emerges. In the metaphysics of Descartes, the existent was defined for the first time as the objectivity of representation and truth as certainty of representation. With objectivity comes subjectivity, in the sense that this being certain of the object is the counter part of the positing of a subject. So we have both the positing of the subject and the proposition of the representation. This is the age of the world as view or picture *(Bild)*. . . . We understand now in what sense the cogito belongs to the metaphysical tradition. The subject-object relationship interpreted as *Bild*, as picture, as view, obliterates, dissimulates, the belonging of *Dasein* to *Sein*. It dissimulates the process of this ontological implication. [CI 228–29]

This represents a metaphysics of presence, the view according to which Being is construed as the presence of what is present, as opposed to presence by clearing (PH 170).[3] The existent is understood, accordingly, in terms of objectivity of representation, and truth as the certainty of representation (cf. Hume and Kant: knowledge=truth=certainty). Truth, in other words, is seen as disclosedness, as opposed to being the interinvolvement of disclosure and concealment (PH 170). The truth of the ego is given by the absolute indubitability of the ego-cogito, the cogito being understood as representation. As mentioned in chapter 4, Ricoeur maintains that because of the emphasis on apodicticity, on certainty of representation, the *manner* of existence of the ego was not put into question. For this reason Ricoeur writes that according to Heidegger "it is the absolute certainty of the cogito which has foreclosed the problem of the meaning of the being of this entity" (CI 227). Apodicticity, in other words, becomes mistaken for adequation. Foreclosing the question of Being is ontological prejudice, because the ego's nature is not questioned far enough, to its "ground."[4]

But if Husserl, like Descartes, runs up against the problem of other selves, could it be because he has somehow inherited the very onto-logical prejudice of Descartes that he sought to overcome in phenome-nology? If so, the whole enterprise of phenomenology may be rendered suspect, for phenomenology claims to overcome *all* ontological preju-dice. It attempts to exclude all *positing* of being by exposing the truly given, by exposing the genetic primary level of Being, "the point" at which, genetically speaking, the ego "commences" constitution.[5] This it achieves by bringing phenomena to expression (PH 131) through re-peatedly instituting the transcendental reduction.[6] The repeated institu-tion of the transcendental reduction ultimately leads to the life-world, the very antithesis of objectivism (TM 218).[7] "The doctrine of life-world is intended to make the transcendental reduction flawless," writes Gadamer (PH 164).[8] According to Husserl, all ontological prejudice, both idealism and realism, are overcome in the concept of life-world. But if Husserl, like Descartes, runs up against the problem of other selves, it may, according to Gadamer, give support to Heidegger's criticism of Husserl's philosophical enterprise:

> Is Heidegger not right when he sees an ontological prejudice operative in Husserl's foundational structure, a prejudice that finally affects the whole idea of a constitutive phenomenology? [PH 169]

According to Gadamer, Husserl unwittingly incorporates a Carte-sian metaphysics in his phenomenology and his transcendental solipsism reflects this. It is important, then, to examine whether Husserl's phe-nomenology can deal with the problem of the alter ego. If it can be shown that Husserl's philosophy is able to deal adequately with the prob-lem of the alter ego, the claim that he shares Descartes's ontological prejudice cannot take hold here.

As this chapter will bear out, contrary to general opinion, a care-ful reading of Husserl's work reveals that phenomenology has the means to overcome the problem of the alter ego. The writings of Merleau-Ponty will be drawn on because, in phenomenological circles at least, he is generally credited with overcoming the problem of other selves by means of his theory of the living body, while on the whole it is not appre-ciated that this theory is already found in Husserl's writings. By the thesis of the living body, according to which consciousness is *essentially* embod-ied, Merleau-Ponty transposes the problem of the alter ego, for he de-nies the very mind-body split of objectivistic theories of consciousness that give rise to the problem of other selves. While it is true that Merleau-Ponty wrote more extensively and explicitly on the problem of the alter ego than did Husserl, the conceptual means whereby he overcomes the problem, especially the notion of living body, are contained in Husserl's thought, as Merleau-Ponty himself repeatedly indicates especially in his "The Philosopher and his Shadow." In "The Philosopher and his Shadow," where he is concerned with explicating the relation of his own theory of the living body to Husserl's thought, Merleau-Ponty isolates two central notions of Husserl's phenomenology that form the foundation of his theory of the living body. These are:

(1) Rejection of the notion of constituting consciousness—that is, "*Ideen II* brings to light a network of implications beneath the 'objective material thing' in which we no longer sense the pulsation of constituting consciousness" (S 166).[9] What Merleau-Ponty means is that in *Ideen II*, the "source" of constitution, the pure transcendental ego is seen, not as constituting *agency*, but as an *activity*.

(2) Overturning of "our idea of the thing and the world," and a resulting "ontological rehabilitation of the sensible" (S 166–67). Here he means that the emphasis is shifted from the constituted to the constituting. In other words, the emphasis is shifted from the thing, from being-in-itself, to prethetic, perceptual activity.

(c) How Husserl is Led to Overturning the Idea of Thing and World

The objective theory of consciousness, which underlies the problem of other selves, took root and blossomed with Descartes's theory of the ego-cogito. The philosophical ground on which the cogito, as Descartes conceives it,[10] emerged is the ground of *science* (CI 228) and, as will be explained next, Husserl's overturning of thing and world comes about via a critique of seventeenth-century science.

In *The Aim and Structure of Physical Theory* the physicist Pierre Duhem shows through an analysis of the history of science (ASTP 270) that science is implicitly guided by an idea that *motivates* it, and thus is necessary to it, but that, paradoxically, also falsifies the nature of physical science. The idea is that science will yield absolute knowledge of true being, of reality as it is in itself, that it will yield a consistent body of knowledge of reality-in-itself, a body of knowledge to which everyone would in principle assent. It is guided by the idea of cosmology, in other words. As discussed in the introduction, this idea forms part of the idea of science first explicated by Plato. Plato's idea of science leaves intact the basic ancient Greek presupposition or view of the world as cosmos, as an ordered, rational system, and of mind as reflecting this order—the mind can know the ideas because it is like them, according to Plato—a view in which to know the world is to know mind and vice versa. It was explained how, in Plato's science, value, mind, self-knowledge, and knowledge of the world are all related.

While the Platonic ideal of science resurges in the Renaissance after having been repressed in the Middle Ages, it undergoes a change in meaning due to the development of natural science, a change that itself is made possible by a change in worldview. The change is one from seeing the world as a finite, hierarchically ordered whole to viewing the world as an infinite system (C 22) in which all components are, or all being is, on a par. Hence, the ideal of universal science, science of true being, no longer means knowledge of a higher, transcendental realm, but knowledge of the physical universe. Koyré, whose position is similar to Husserl's on this in the *Crisis*, explains that this shift in worldview brings with it a loss of concern with value:

> This scientific and philosophical revolution . . . can be described roughly as bringing forth the destruction of the Cosmos, that is, the disappearance, from philosophically and scientifically valid concepts, of the conception of the world as a finite, closed, and hierarchically ordered whole (a whole in which the hierarchy of value determined the hierarchy and structure of being, rising from the dark, heavy, and imperfect earth to the higher and higher perfection of the stars and heavenly spheres), and its replacement by an indefinite and even infinite universe which is bound together by the identity of its fundamental components and laws, and in which all these components are placed on the same level of being. This, in turn, implies the discarding by scientific thought of all considerations based upon value-concepts, such as perfection, harmony, meaning and aim, and finally the utter devalorization of being, the divorce of the world of value and the world of facts. [FCW 2]

With this change of worldview, then, true knowledge—episteme—comes to mean knowledge of the physical world as it is in itself, as opposed to how the world appears to humans. But as Husserl notes, since subjective interpretations are essential to the empirically intuited world, these must be overcome in order to achieve a picture of the world as it is in itself. In the seventeenth century it seemed that the mathematical method of Euclidean geometry, the paradigm of exact knowledge, could provide empirical science with the exactness it required. By the time of the Renaissance the application of geometry to the earth and in astronomy had developed considerably. Because geometry aided "in bringing the sensible surrounding world to univocal determination" (C 29), it seemed as if geometry revealed reality independent of subjective perspective, that it revealed reality in itself. Husserl describes the idea this led to:

> Wherever such a methodology is developed, there we have also overcome the relativity of subjective interpretations which is, after all, essential to the empirically intuited world. For in this manner we attain an identical, nonrelative truth of which everyone who can understand and use this method can convince himself. Here, then, we recognize something that truly is. [C 29]

Geometry seemed to yield knowledge of true being, of being in itself. This led Galileo to the idea of extending this method to the whole of nature and of describing its objective being as prescribed by the ideal of universal science:

> *Must not something similar be possible for the concrete world as such?* If one is already firmly convinced, moreover, like Galileo— thanks to the Renaissance's return to ancient philosophy—of the possibility of philosophy as *epistēmē* achieving an objective science of the world, and if it had just been revealed that pure mathematics, applied to nature, consummately fulfills the postulate of *epistēmē* in its sphere of shapes: did not this also have to suggest to Galileo the idea of a nature which is constructively determinable in the same manner in all its *other aspects?* [C 33]

With the application of the mathematical method to the physical sciences, a distinction comes to the fore between the sensible thing and the physical thing, a distinction that later became known as secondary and primary qualities, respectively.[11] While physical objects achieve an exactness through participation in mathematical exactness, this participation is limited, for "there is . . . one part of the material object which physical-mathematical science cannot consider: the sensible qualities of the object (colour, sound, odor, etc.)" (DeM 240). Whereas mathematical exactness pertains to form only, physical objects are given to us "in a sensory fullness *(sinnliche Fülle)* which in some way 'fills' the 'form' that is abstracted by mathematical science" (DeM 240). These sensible qualities, then, fall outside the "new" precise science. The physical thing is considered to be the true object of science, the transcendent, extramental being; the sensible thing, the subjective element through which

transcendent being becomes known. Furthermore, a causal bond is instituted between physical and sensible thing: the physical thing is regarded
as the "efficient cause of the subjective data of perception." This model
leads to the view of the ego as a receptacle of sense data, and knowledge
as the representation of the world, a world that is a determined, ordered
whole, a rational systematic unity, a mathematical manifold:

> Through Galileo's *mathematization of nature, nature itself* is ideal-
> ized under the guidance of the new mathematics; nature itself
> becomes—to express it in a modern way—a mathematical
> manifold (Mannigfaltigkeit). [C 23]

As discussed in the Introduction, Descartes explicitly brings the
Galilean model to philosophy, for he too uses the model of the world as a
mathematical manifold and of science as knowledge of this mathematical
whole:

> After Galileo had carried out, slightly earlier, the primal estab-
> lishment of the new natural science, it was Descartes who con-
> ceived and at the same time set in systematic motion the new
> idea of universal philosophy: in the sense of mathematical, or
> better expressed, physicalistic, rationalism—philosophy as
> "universal mathematics." And immediately it had a powerful
> effect. [C 73]

It was explained in chapter 3 how Descartes, in accepting the
scientific model as *universally* valid, extends the model to the study of
mind. Descartes too, then, to a certain extent considers consciousness or
the ego as a receptacle of sense data, and the cogito as the representation
of the world. This model of the ego and cogito, which emerged on the
ground of science, is incorporated into Descartes's philosophy specifically, and into empirical philosophy generally. In the words of Merleau-
Ponty:

> The empiricist philosopher considers the subject x in the act of
> perceiving and tries to describe what happens: *there are* sensa-
> tions which are the subject's states or manners of being and, in
> virtue of this, genuine mental things. The perceiving subject is
> the place where these things occur, and the philosopher de-
> scribes sensations and their substratum as one might describe
> the fauna of a distant land. [PhP 207]

What emerges is a *schism* between subject and object, between the for-itself and the in-itself respectively, to use Merleau-Ponty's expression. The physical thing "transcends the *entire content* of the thing as it is given to us in the experience of its bodily presence" (DeM 242). Not only is empirical philosophy generally influenced by the natural scientific model of the ego, but even nonempirical philosophy, in its very criticism of the model, is influenced by it. Broadly speaking, this model of consciousness opens itself to two theories of human behavior, each, as it were, dealing with different sides of the same coin. On the one hand human behavior is construed as blind reactions to stimuli; on the other, it is construed as the execution of intentions. The former constitutes a realist/empiricist thesis, the latter an intellectualist/idealist thesis. According to Merleau-Ponty, the latter thesis merely constitutes the reversal of the former:

> Intellectualism certainly represents a step forward in coming to self-consciousness: that place outside the world at which the empiricist philosopher hints, and in which he tacitly takes up his position in order to describe the event of perception, now receives a name, and appears in the description. It is the transcendental Ego.[12] Through it every empiricist thesis is reversed: the state of consciousness becomes the consciousness of a state, passivity the positing of passivity, the world becomes the correlative of thought about the world and henceforth exists only for a constituting agent. And yet it remains true to say that intellectualism too provides itself with a ready-made world. For the constitution of the world, as conceived by it, is a mere requirement that to each term of the empiricist description be added the indication "consciousness of. . . . " The whole system of experience—world, own body and empirical self—are subordinated to a universal thinker charged with sustaining the relationships between the three terms. But, since he is not actually involved, these relations remain what they were in empiricism: causal relations spread out in the context of cosmic events. [PhP 207–8]

In believing in the being in itself of the world, then, science comes to split subject and object, and this split grounds the objectivist, causal theory of human consciousness. According to Merleau-Ponty, Husserl demonstrates that this distinction is not absolute by showing there to be a layer of experience in which this distinction becomes problematic (S 162). In the *Crisis* (part III A) Husserl explains that the world of science, which is the world of things in themselves *(blossen Sachen)*, is not the most basic mode of experience. Science and the scientific attitude did not always exist in the history of thought, but emerged and evolved; they sprang up out of a more basic mode of experience—namely, that of everyday experience, that of the life-world or the natural attitude. The life-world is prior to science, prior to the belief in a world in itself, prior to belief that the world can be considered independently from all subjectivity. Although the life-world is more basic than science and its attitude, although we in the natural attitude live in the life-world, the nature of the life-world is not immediately apparent to us, because the world of science with its beliefs is superimposed on it. Even if we are not scientists immersed in the scientific attitude, the tenets of science have seeped into the life-world and we are imperceptibly influenced by these. Even in the life-world we find "the scholastic dominance of objective-scientific ways of thinking" (C 129).

What *is* clear, however, is that the life-world, unlike the world of science, is not a *precise* world. In order to meet the ideal of a unified theory, of an exact science that glorified in universal assent, physical science had to be mathematicized: it represents the ideas it employs by *numbers*. The mathematization of physical science involves quantification: translation of concrete circumstances (facts) into numbers—into symbols. But quantification is abstraction or idealization (C 23, 48); it is representation of reality by signs and symbols,[13] and physical *theory* works on these symbols, these idealizations of reality, these approximations to reality, according to Husserl. Duhem makes the same observation as Husserl:

> An experiment in physics is the precise observation of phenomena accompanied by an *interpretation* of these phenomena; this interpretation substitutes for the concrete data really gathered by observation abstract and symbolic representations which correspond to them by virtue of the theories admitted by the observer. [ASPT 147]

In other words, whereas the theoretical fact is precise or exact, the practical fact is not. When formulating a theoretical fact about a given object, all irregularities of the object under study are ignored. To use an example given by Duhem, "the body studied [by physical science] is geometrically defined; its sides are true lines without thickness, its points true points without dimensions" (ASPT 133–34). The practical fact has none of this precision. Given an object in the life-world, "however sharp its edges, none is a geometrical intersection of two surfaces"

but its "edges are more or less rounded and dented spines," "its points
. . . more or less worn down or blunt" (ASPT 134).

As Duhem points out, scientists *acknowledge* this disparity between the precise and the imprecise, both in attenuating their descriptions of the practical by the theoretical fact by the words "approximate"
or "nearly" (ASPT 134) as well as by the use of *corrections* in experimentation. Only if it is understood that a practical fact is *not* the same as a
theoretical fact can the notion of correction in experimentation make
sense:

> If an experiment in physics were merely the observation of a
> fact, it would be absurd to bring in corrections, for it would be
> ridiculous to tell an observer who had looked attentively, care-
> fully, and minutely: "What you have seen is not what you
> should have seen; permit me to make some calculations which
> will teach you what you should have observed."
> The logical role of corrections, on the other hand, is very
> well understood when it is remembered that a physical experi-
> ment is not simply the observation of a group of facts but also
> the translation of these facts into a symbolic language with the
> aid of rules borrowed from physical theories. [ASPT 156]

Duhem, like Husserl (C 49, 51), also criticizes certain thinkers for
blurring the distinction between practical and theoretical fact, and taking the latter to be representative of the world in itself. Although science
is forgetful of the life-world, it remains the ground of validation of science (C 126) and indeed of any worldview or belief system; *all*
worldviews *presuppose* the life-world. Phenomenology wishes to describe
the life-world in its purity prior to any belief system, however. To do this
it must describe the structure of experience of the life-world qua experience (C 139):

> In opposition to all previously designed objective sciences,
> which are sciences on the ground of the world, this would be a
> science of the universal *how* of the pregivenness of the world,
> i.e., of what makes it a universal ground for any sort of objec-
> tivity. [C 146]

Phenomenology aims to describe "the world purely and exclusively *as*—
and in respect to *how*—it has meaning and ontic validity" (C 148).

While the life-world is intuitable within the natural attitude (S
163–64), we are nevertheless oblivious to or forgetful of it, not merely
because the tenets of science have been superimposed on it, but because

naturally the natural attitude involves a *practical* interest in the object, as de Muralt observes:

> The subject in the natural attitude is interested in the *Lebens-welt* in a quite concrete way, in the sense that man tries to sub-jugate the world and dominate it. [DeM 250]

To jolt our interest away from the object as practical means to jolt us into seeing the *Lebenswelt* qua *Lebenswelt*, Husserl institutes the *epoche* or transcendental reduction. What is required is a *"total* transformation of attitude, a *completely unique, universal epochē"* (C 148). Hence the transcendental reduction is quite radical, for it is an *epoche* "in regard to the totality of natural and normal life" (C 148). In the *epoche*, the being status of the world is *suspended*:

> We thus have an attitude *above* the universal conscious life
> (both individual—subjective and intersubjective) through
> which the world is "there" for those naively absorbed in ongo-
> ing life, as unquestioningly present, as the universe of what is
> there, as the field of all acquired and newly established life-in-
> terests. [C 150]

The result of the *epoche* is not a worldview or cosmology, for we focus not on the content—objects—of experience, but on the flow of experience itself. In this manner objects are considered not as objects in themselves (as *blossen Sachen*, being in itself), but as essentially related to a subject, as objects given in a flow of experience, as noemata. The world then appears as noema, the object of a transcendental experience:

> This is not a "view," an "interpretation" bestowed upon the
> world. Every view about . . . every opinion about "the" world,
> has its ground in the pregiven world. It is from this very
> ground that I have freed myself through the epoche; I stand
> *above* the world, which now has become for me, in a quite pe-
> culiar sense, a *phenomenon*. [C 152]

And from Merleau-Ponty:

> In other words, reduced thought concerns Nature as the "ideal
> meaning of the acts which constitute the natural attitude"—
> Nature become once more the noema it has always been, Na-
> ture reintegrated to the consciousness which has always consti-
> tuted it through and through. In the realm of "reduction"

there is no longer anything but consciousness, its acts, and
their intentional object. [S 162][14]

Since science is based on the distinction between subject and object, Husserl exposes a dimension of human experience in which objectivistic science with its causal theories has no jurisdiction. With the
opening up of this dimension, the myth of science having total explanatory power is exploded. It reveals an aspect of human nature for which
science cannot account—it brings to light the intentional nature of consciousness, for it results in placing emphasis on the constituting activity
of consciousness, as opposed to the thing's—the constituted's—alleged
causal relation to consciousness.[15] In such a fashion, human nature,
based on the essence of consciousness, is appropriated. According to de
Muralt, Husserl was concerned with exposing this dimension of experience throughout all his works, including *Formal and Transcendental Logic*,
though modifying the method whereby he brings this realm of experience to light (DeM 243).

(d)   How Overturning the Idea of Thing
and World Leads to the Notion of a
Constituting *Activity* in
Contradistinction to a Notion of
Constituting *Agency*, and How it
Leads to a Concept of the Living Body

As explained in chapter 3, it is precisely their failure to recognize and
treat the life-world as problematic that prevents Kant's philosophy from
being truly transcendental and prevents Descartes from explicitly reap-
ing the deepest insights contained in his philosophy. It prevents both
from freeing their notion of the ego of objectivistic elements.[16] According to Husserl, any objective element of the ego needs to be traced back
to its nonobjective constituting source; that is to say, it must be traced
back to the truly *transcendental* ego, the pure ego, which constitutes the
objective elements of the ego and the world. In other words, uncovering
the transcendental ego is not a novel contribution of phenomenology in
that Kant too realized that every cogito is the cogito of a transcendental
ego. Where phenomenology goes beyond Kant and makes a novel contribution is in taking its analysis a step further. Husserl sees that the ego
Kant and Descartes take as foundational is still empirical; it is not only
constituting but *constituted*. Husserl performs a reduction on that ego. In

so doing Husserl overcomes the notion of transcendental ego as constituting *agency* and secures a sense of transcendental ego as constituting *activity*. This is the second notion Merleau-Ponty identifies as contributing to the notion of living body. It is only in the *act* of living that objectivity is overcome. For Husserl the transcendental ego is *lived*, and is not merely an empty thought, as it was in Kant's philosophy. It was explained in chapter 4 that Husserl means this literally; in his view the transcendental ego involves the living body.

The notion of the living body, then, is crucial to Husserl's phenomenology for it is the means whereby phenomenology moves to the truly transcendental realm. And there can be no mistake about this: the notion of the living body is mentioned *explicitly* in the *Crisis*:

> The ego [is] functioning here in a peculiar sort of activity and habituality. In a quite unique way the living body is constantly in the perceptual field quite immediately, with a completely unique ontic meaning, precisely the meaning indicated by the word "organ" (here used in its most primitive sense); [namely, as] that through which I exist in a completely unique way and quite immediately as the ego of affection and actions, [as that] in which I hold sway quite immediately, kinesthetically—articulated into particular organs through which I hold sway, or potentially hold sway, in particular kinestheses corresponding to them. [C 106–7]

And:

> Thus, purely in terms of perception, physical body and living body (*Körper und Leib*) are essentially different; living body, that is [understood] as the only one which is actually given [to me as such] in perception: my own living body. How the consciousness originates through which my living body nevertheless acquires an ontic validity of one physical body among others, and how, on the other hand, certain physical bodies in my perceptual field come to count as living bodies, living bodies of "alien" ego-subjects—these are now necessary questions. [C 107]

And:

> [Being related] "through the living body" clearly does not mean merely [being related] "as a physical body"; rather, the expression refers to the kinesthetic, to functioning as an ego in

> this peculiar way, primarily through seeing, hearing, etc.; and
> of course other modes of the ego belong to this (for example,
> lifting, carrying, pushing, and the like).
>   But being an ego through the living body (*die leibliche Ich-*
> *lichkeit*) is of course not the only way of being an ego, and
> none of its ways can be severed from the others. [C 108]

Overturning of "thing" and "world," then, leads to the notion of a constituting *activity*, which, in turn, leads to the living body, a central notion
in Husserl's phenomenology.[17]

(e)   How Merleau-Ponty "Solves" the Problem of the Alter Ego

It is the absolute wedge between subject and object, between the for-
itself and the in-itself, embodied in theories of human behavior that
Merleau-Ponty, following Husserl, attacks in solving the problem of
other selves. Although the concepts whereby Merleau-Ponty solves the
problem of the alter ego are Husserlian, unlike Husserl he applies these
to the results of empirical studies in cognitive psychology. In the *Structure of Behaviour*[18] he shows through a painstakingly detailed analysis of
the results of experimental studies how traditional theories of consciousness and the body, the realist/empiricist thesis on the one hand and the
intellectualist/idealist thesis on the other, fail to account adequately for
behavior. Even the "lowest level" of behavior, reflexive behavior, cannot
be construed simply as a blind stimulus-response reaction, but is marked
by a sense bestowing, while the "highest level" of behavior, reflection,
remains marked by an opaque element,[19] something that remains hidden
from us, something we do not know. Consistent and plausible interpretation of experimental data tells us that behavior cannot be construed either as a thing or as an idea (SB 127), and shows that the distinction
between the for-itself and the in-itself is therefore not absolute, but that
behavior forms a bridge between these (SB 126). Here Merleau-Ponty in
agreement with Husserl denies a causal relation between subject and object. According to Merleau-Ponty, consciousness, the for-itself, is not absolutely distinct from its object, the in-itself—*one is not anterior to the
other*—hence their relation cannot be that of causality.
    In the *Phenomenology of Perception*, where Merleau-Ponty argues
against traditional theories of human behavior from a more phenomenological standpoint than in his earlier work, *The Structure of Behaviour*, he
formulates in a general and abstract way the shortcoming of the intellec-

tualist and empiricist theories of behavior by saying that both fail to answer Meno's paradox (see the quotation below for a statement of this paradox). It is precisely this bifurcation of the in itself and the for itself that lies at the heart of Meno's paradox:

> Whoever tries to limit the spiritual light to what is at present before the mind always runs up against the Socratic problem.
> *"How will you set about looking for that thing, the nature of which is totally unknown to you? Which, among the things you do not know, is the one which you propose to look for? And if by chance you should stumble upon it, how will you know that it is indeed that thing, since you are in ignorance of it?"*(my emphasis) [*Meno*, 80D]. A thought really transcended by its objects would find them proliferating in its path without ever being able to grasp their relationships to each other, or finding its way through to their truth. . . . We must define thought in terms of that strange power which it possesses of being ahead of itself, of launching itself and being at home everywhere, in a word, in terms of its autonomy. Unless thought itself had put into things what it subsequently finds in them, it would have no hold upon things, would not think of them, and would be an "illusion of thought." [PhP 371]

In other words, cognitive activity is paradoxically characterized by a *seeking* of something it does *not* know—the lack of knowledge is that which instigates or motivates cognitive activity—and at the same time *does* know—How else would it know when to terminate its activity? The former is an inconceivable state of affairs for intellectualism, while the latter is an inconceivable state of affairs for empiricism.[20] The cogito is, then, at once similar to and distinct from its object. The nature of cognitive activity itself "seen from the inside" thus would suggest that the distinction between the in-itself and the for-itself is not absolute, but is something overcome in cognitive activity.

The solution to Meno's paradox is at once the solution to the problem of other selves, for, as mentioned above, it is precisely the distinction between the in-itself and for-itself that also renders the problem of the alter ego insoluble. The paradox is overcome and the problem of the alter ego is transposed, according to Merleau-Ponty, if consciousness is no longer considered to be a mental entity distinct from yet residing in the body. With Husserl[21] Merleau-Ponty criticizes the views that treat and describe the body as pure object, as "a conjunction of physiological processes," as "a collection of organs shown in the plates of books in anatomy," and that treat consciousness as pure subject. The body is never really given to or experienced by us as pure object but as "an ob-

ject in which there is no distance between it and the subject" (F 230).
The body therefore is not an object in which consciousness resides, but *is*
in its livedness embodied consciousness.

For embodied consciousness Merleau-Ponty, like Husserl, reserves
the term "living body." It is in the living body that the alternative of the in-
itself and the for-itself is overcome (PhP 373) because the living body is
neither in itself nor for itself, is neither pure subject nor pure object, but
is, rather, at once subject *and* object. Mind-body dualism is overcome because consciousness is considered to be *essentially* embodied.

It is clear that Merleau-Ponty, like Husserl, goes beyond a repre-
sentational view of the cogito: consciousness is not primarily a reflective
activity distinct from the actual relatedness to things, but is a direct living
contact with things. The "I think" is at once a physical, perceptual relatedness to things via the living body. The living body is our immediate
epistemic contact with the world. Hence for Merleau-Ponty perception
is our inherence in things (PhP 350–51) and a theory of the body is at
once a theory of perception:

> Every external perception is immediately synonymous with a
> certain perception of my body, just as every perception of my
> body is made explicit in the language of external perception.
> If, then, as we have seen to be the case, the body is . . . an ex-
> pressive unity which we can learn to know only by actively tak-
> ing it up, this structure will be passed on to the sensible world.
> The theory of the body image is, implicitly, a theory of percep-
> tion. We have relearned to feel our body; we have found un-
> derneath the objective and detached knowledge of the body
> that other knowledge which we have of it in virtue of its always
> being with us and of the fact that we are our body. In the same
> way we shall need to reawaken our experience of the world as
> it appears to us in so far as we are in the world through our
> body, and in so far as we perceive the world with our body. But
> by thus remaking contact with the body and with the world, we
> shall also rediscover ourself, since, perceiving as we do with
> our body, the body is a natural self, and as it were, the subject
> of perception. [PhP 206]

We start neither with an in-itself (object) nor a for-itself (subject), for
both are given contemporaneously. In other words, the body is the
bearer of a dialectic (MR 173) between matter and spirit.

It can be intuited in what way the notion of embodied consciousness constitutes a solution to the problem of the alter ego. Since consciousness on this view is considered to be essentially embodied,

perceiving the other is no longer a problem. Because of embodiment, the other is no longer an "occult quality" whose existence I must hypothesize. I have assurance of the other's existence because I can now directly *perceive* another consciousness in its embodiment. I am in actual touch with the other:

> I overcome the impossibility of conceiving another for-himself for me, because I witness another behaviour, another presence in the world. . . . We can find others at the intentional origin of their visible behaviour. [PhP 432–33]

The above is Merleau-Ponty's way of dealing with the problem of the alter ego. Some have argued that the living body as Merleau-Ponty conceives of it is a notion foreign to Husserl's phenomenology, that according to Merleau-Ponty Husserl bases phenomenology on the pure transcendental ego, which is distinct from the living body. For instance, Zaner maintains that Merleau-Ponty's philosophy breaks with Husserlian phenomenology, that Merleau-Ponty abandons the *epoche*, because he believes the reflective method of phenomenology has no access to the prereflective level of experience:

> A genuine reflective withdrawal is for Merleau-Ponty intrinsically unable to grasp my body-as-lived. [PE 138]

And:

> The cards, however, are on the table: Merleau-Ponty simply rejects, without stating it, the Husserlian doctrine of epoche. [PE 142]

And:

> It is, in fact, only if one maintains to begin with that reflection is not able to apprehend this experience that *another* mode of access to it seems necessary. [PE 139]

Zaner maintains that the problem is with Merleau-Ponty's insistence that it is "only by *experiencing* my body-proper [living body] that I can *apprehend it as experienced by me*" (PE 138). According to Zaner, Merleau-Ponty's mode of access to unreflected, lived experience is unphenomenological, even "magical" (PE 140). But it has been argued throughout this work that for Husserl, no less than for Merleau-Ponty, I have access to the living transcendental ego only in the act of living.

Others have argued that while the pure transcendental ego represents an idealist element, the notion of living body reflects a realist element. Above it has been argued that the notion of living body found in Merleau-Ponty's writings is not only found explicitly in Husserl's writings, but that one can only appreciate the import of this notion if one understands how it is derived from phenomenological "dicta."[22] If one does not, one will be hard pressed to distinguish the concept of living body from any monism that claims that mind and body are one substance. Below it will be argued that the living body is not quite the *pure* transcendental ego and that without appeal to the pure transcendental ego, accessed only via the *epoche*, Merleau-Ponty cannot solve the problem of other selves. It will be argued below that Merleau-Ponty too has a sense of pure transcendental ego, and so has not abandoned the *epoche*. The pure transcendental ego is the basis of the living body and this is what is implied by Merleau-Ponty's identification of the two phenomenological dicta from which he develops his thesis of the living body.

(f)   "Embodiment" Insufficient to Solve the Problem of Other Selves: Appeal to the Pure Transcendental Ego

The notion of embodiment *seems* to be the way to overcome the problem of the alter ego, in that it is now possible to *see* the other's consciousness. But is this really a solution? Although the essence of consciousness is to be embodied, what I *see* or directly experience of the other is still "only" the objective body (body as object) and not the livedness of embodied consciousness (body as subject). As the *Crisis* states:

> Here my own living body alone, and never an alien living body, can be perceived *as* living; the latter is perceived only as a physical body. [C 107–8]

The livedness of the other's consciousness, even though embodied, *cannot* be directly experienced, for life, in its lived quality, precludes being seen "from the outside." "What is alive is not such that a person could ever grasp it from the outside, in its living quality," writes Gadamer (TM 224). If I could experience the other's livedness directly as livedness, I would no longer be experiencing an other, but I would *be* the other and hence "otherness" would fall away. As Husserl writes:

> Neither the other Ego himself, nor his subjective processes or
> his appearances themselves, nor anything else belonging to his
> own essence, becomes given in our experience originally. If it
> were, if what belongs to the other's own essence were directly
> accessible, it would be merely a moment of my own essence,
> and ultimately he himself and I myself would be the same. [CM
> 109 (139)]

Are we not at square one? How can I know that the other's body has a livedness if I cannot experience this livedness directly? It would seem as if we have not progressed one iota beyond our original problem. Are we not forced to appeal to reasoning by analogy in explaining how we gain awareness of the other qua other? Does Merleau-Ponty not beg the question, and is he not appealing to the traditional solution—namely, to the phenomenon of analogical reasoning—when, at the very point at which he proffers a solution to the problem of the alter ego, he writes:

> If I experience this inhering of my consciousness in its body
> and its world, the perception of other people and the plurality
> of consciousness no longer present any difficulty. If, for myself
> who am reflecting on perception, the perceiving subject ap-
> pears provided with a primordial setting in relation to the
> world, drawing in its train that bodily thing in the absence of
> which there would be no other things for it, then why should
> other bodies which I perceive not be similarly inhabited by
> consciousness? If my consciousness has a body, why should
> other bodies not "have" consciousness? [PhP 351]

This argument appears to be of the following form:

> My body is inhabited by a consciousness.
> There is another body like mine.
> Therefore, it too must have a consciousness.

This is unmistakably analogical reasoning. It *appears* from the above passage that according to Merleau-Ponty we start with a particular individual consciousness—namely, my consciousness—and reason from that to that of others; that is, "if my consciousness has associated with it a body and this is the only way I know my body and consciousness, then other bodies must have a consciousness." Hence, even after appeal to the notion of living body, Meno's paradox rears its head once again. I must at once be the same as and distinct from the object of knowledge, which in this case is the alter ego. I can know "consciousness" or "lived-ness" (living body) only subjectively—that is, through living it. In this sense consciousness or the self is particular, and in this sense we do and *must* start with the particular to have knowledge of consciousness. But this rules out the universality, "other selves," for it leaves us in the ego-centric predicament (solipsism).

The problem can be resolved only by appeal to the pure transcen-dental ego. In chapter 4 it was explained that the living body is the *con-crete* transcendental ego, and that it is necessary to do yet a further reduction to get at the *pure* transcendental ego. In other words, the no-tion of living body still has particular overtones—it is *my* living body, as is apparent from the fact that only I can suffer "its" death. Solving the problem of the alter ego requires more than the notion of *embodied* con-sciousness; it requires a conceptual element that is truly *universal*. As long as we start with the particular, individual self and try to *derive* the universal, other selves from it through analogical reasoning, for exam-ple, we remain committed to solipsism. To know other selves I *must* have a universal of self, of livedness, for without a universal I would not recog-nize others. Hence, for there to be others for me, I must, in my livedness, be *at once* particular *and* universal. That is to say, if I were absolutely distinct from the other, and hence absolutely unique, it would not be *possible* to perceive another ego, "another myself," for being unique there could be no other "myself." At the same time, I must be in *some* manner distinct from the other, for otherwise there would not be an *other* ego.

The solution to Meno's paradox as it applies to the problem of the alter ego, then, is the solution to the question as to the very *possibility* of other selves. What form the solution will take is expressed by Merleau-Ponty in the following passage from the *Phenomenology of Perception*:

> My life must have a significance which I do not constitute;
> there must strictly speaking be an intersubjectivity; each one of
> us must be both anonymous in the sense of absolutely *individ-*
> *ual* [my emphasis], and anonymous in the sense of absolutely
> *general* [my emphasis]. Our being in the world, is the concrete
> bearer of this double anonymity. [PhP 448]

From this passage we glean that the notion "I" (ego, self) must be *at once* (a) general and individual, or, phrased in term of Meno's paradox, must be *at once* universal and particular, and (b) anonymous—that is, anonymous particular and anonymous universal. In chapter 5 it was explained that the concrete transcendental ego needed the eidos transcendental ego in order to *be* at all. Every particular, in order to be, necessarily has a temporal dimension; this X that has been for however short a while, and will be or can possibly be again at a future time. "Every individual object can be thought more than once" (EJ 335), writes Husserl. Merleau-Ponty agrees with Husserl on this point: "It is through time that being is conceived" (PhP 430), he says. This temporal projection is the object's universality.[23] To be a particular, to be a fact, is *at once* to "participate" in an ideal or universal. According to Merleau-Ponty this is why Husserl insisted on the actual inseparability of fact and essence (S 173). The concrete transcendental ego, being in part particular, must also partake of an eidos:

> The transcendental ego is in a universal way the structure of
> the universal eidos "ego in general," the universal a priori
> without which no transcendental ego (neither I nor the Other)
> would be conceivable (CM 71ff. [105ff.]). [DeM 337]

In other words, a particular transcendental ego would not be conceivable or possible if it did not partake of a universal. Hence to say that the notion "I," the notion of the transcendental ego, must be both particular and universal, is no puzzle: it cannot be otherwise. This *universal* is the pure transcendental ego.

The eidos of the transcendental ego, of which the particular transcendental ego partakes, is anonymity. Writes de Muralt:

> In itself it [the transcendental ego] is simple, undivided, nu-
> merically identical, and empty of determinations. [DeM 328]

And in *Ideas* Husserl states:

> Aside from its "modes of relation" or "modes of comport-
> ment," the <Ego> is completely empty of essence-compo-
> nents, has no explicatable content, is undescribable in and for
> itself: it is pure Ego and nothing more. [I FK 191 (160)]

Since it is empty of determinations, the pure transcendental ego is anonymous.[24] It has no determinations, because it is not a thing or substance. In the words of Merleau-Ponty:

Subjectivity is neither thing nor substance but the extremity of
both particular and universal. [S 153]

So, if Merleau-Ponty is able to resolve the problem of the alter
ego through the concept of the living body, it is because he has not rejected the eidos, the pure transcendental ego. It is perhaps not as clearly
stated as in Husserl that one must do a reduction on the living body, but
it is nevertheless clear that Merleau-Ponty has done this reduction.
Hence, when Merleau-Ponty speaks of the "living body" he acknowledges the pure transcendental ego. The living body is not identical with
pure transcendental ego but neither is it *not* the pure transcendental
ego, for it needs the pure transcendental ego for its being; hence, the
pure transcendental ego is "in" or "founds" the living body. Merleau-
Ponty has not abandoned Husserl's phenomenology on this point. Indeed, to radically split the pure transcendental ego and the living body
would be a Platonism,[25] and to identify them would be an empiricism, or
an idealism.

(g)   Why Reasoning by Analogy is not
        Involved: The Husserlian Notion
        of Pairing

It is now possible to explain why reasoning by analogy is not involved
when in seeing the other's body I recognize him or her to be another
ego. The perception of individuals (particulars) involves universals
(types). To perceive an individual *is* to perceive it as a type, to place it
under a universal, even if that universal has not been made *explicit* (EJ
332). This is a one-step affair. We do not have an individual first and
subsequently a universal. The individual or particular *is* via the universal.
This relation of particular and universal underlies and makes possible a
process Husserl terms *association*. It is through association that I recognize another individual as belonging to the same type. Association is a
process that occurs passively, according to Husserl (EJ §16):

> The fact that all objects of experience are from the first experi-
> enced as known according to their type has its basis in the sedi-
> mentation of all apperceptions and in their habitual continued
> action on the basis of associative awakening. Association origi-
> nally produces the *passive* [my emphasis] synthesis of like with

the like, and this not only within a field of presence but also through the entire stream of lived experience, its immanent time, and everything which is constituted in it. [EJ 321]

It must be underscored, however, that the way in which Husserl uses the term "association" is not the same way as the way in which behavioral psychology uses the term when it refers to stimulus-response behavior. For the latter a stimulus is an external element that evokes a blind (automatic) response; that is, a stimulus is not considered as imbued with meaning *by* the subject. Husserl, on the other hand, insists that association is an *intentional* act, an act of *meaning* on the subject's behalf, albeit a passive one.[26] It is made possible by a still deeper intentionality— namely, time-synthesis. It is because everything in the stream of experience is connected a priori by virtue of its relation to the originary "now" that association can occur passively. Hence, according to Husserl association is:

That mode of passive synthesis founded on the lowest syntheses of time-consciousness. [EJ 177]

And:

What in a purely static description appears to be likeness or similarity must therefore be considered in itself as being already the product of the one or the other kind of synthesis of coincidence, which we denote by the traditional term *association*, but with a change of sense. It is the phenomenon of associative genesis which dominates this sphere of passive pregivenness, established on the basis of syntheses of internal time-consciousness.

The term "association" denotes in this context a form belonging essentially to consciousness in general, a *form of the regularity of immanent genesis*. That association can become a general theme of phenomenological description and not merely one of objective psychology is due to the fact that the phenomenon of *indication (Anzeige)* is something which can be exhibited from the point of view of phenomenology. (This insight, worked out as early as the *Logical Investigations*, already constitutes there the nucleus of genetic phenomenology.) Every interpretation of association and its laws which makes of it a kind of psychophysical natural law, attained by objective induction, must therefore be excluded here. [EJ 74–75]

Association is *passive*. It is not an active logical process—it is not an *inference*, in other words. It has an immediacy to it that inference does not have. It is *this* type of process that is involved in recognizing an alter ego, according to Husserl. From my own being I have a tacit sense of universal ego, on the basis of which I can associate, using the term in *Husserl's* sense, to others. That is, however tacitly, the way in which I essentially conceive of myself is at once how I essentially conceive others to be. Since I never perceive my own body purely as object, I never perceive the other's body purely as object. Likewise, it is because I do not experience myself as pure subject that I am able to recognize an alter ego through the objectivity of *his* or *her* body, which by its *essence* has a livedness. Hence, when I perceive the other's body as object, it is not as pure object, but it is *at once* an object-subject, or living body. In short, perceiving an other qua other, although involving my perceiving the other's objective body, does not involve analogical reasoning, but is a "one-step affair." It is subsuming a particular under a universal. It is for this reason that Merleau-Ponty in the quotation below speaks of a "*flash* of meaning" making my incarnation substitutable with that of another. Analogical reasoning, on the other hand, involves a sequential process of reasoning:

> The body proper is a premonition of the other person, the *Einfühlung* an echo of my incarnation, and . . . a flash of meaning makes them substitutable in the absolute presence of origins. [S 175]

It is no more difficult for me to recognize an other than it is for me to recognize a table. The former case, however, involves recognizing traits or properties that I know because I myself *am* those traits:

> I say that there is a man there and not a mannequin, as I see that the table is there and not a perspective or an appearance of the table.
> It is true that I would *not* recognize him (an other ego) if I were *not* a man myself. [S 170]

And:

> The body over there, which is nevertheless apprehended as an animate organism, must have derived this sense by an *apperceptive transfer from animate organisms*. [CM 110 (140)]

It is only the nominalism of empiricism that must appeal to reasoning by analogy, for, assuming an absolute wedge between the categories of the for oneself and for the other, it starts with the individual totally distinct from the universal.

It is unfortunate that in section 50 of *Cartesian Meditations* Husserl uses the phrase " 'analogizing' apprehension" (CM 111 [140]) when referring to the process whereby one recognizes an alter ego, for this has led some to believe that Husserl is explaining the process of recognizing an other by analogical reasoning. But Husserl states explicitly that this is not so:

> It is clear from the very beginning that only a similarity connecting, within my primordial sphere, that body over there with my body can serve as the motivational basis for the *"analogizing" apprehension* of that body as another animate organism.
> There would be, accordingly, a certain assimilative apperception; *but it by no means follows that there would be an inference from analogy* [my emphasis]. *Apperception is not an inference, not a thinking act* [my emphasis]. [CM 111 (140–41)][27]

He goes on to say that the type of apperception he is speaking of here occurs "at a glance" (CM 111 [141]), and in section 51 he narrows the process of recognizing the other down to the associative process of *pairing:*

> *Ego* and *alter ego* are always and necessarily given *in an original "pairing."* [CM 112 (142)]

Husserl explains that pairing, a form of association, is a universal property of the ego:

> *Pairing*, occurrence in configuration as a pair and then as a group, a plurality, is a *universal* phenomenon of the transcendental sphere (and of the parallel sphere of intentional psychology); and, we may add forthwith, as far as a pairing is actually present, so far extends that remarkable kind of primal instituting of an analogizing apprehension—its continuous primal institution in living actuality—which we have already stressed as the first peculiarity of experiencing someone else. Hence it is not exclusively peculiar to this experience. . . .
> Pairing is a *primal form of that passive synthesis* which we designate as *"association,"* in contrast to passive synthesis of "identification." [CM 112 (142)]

Furthermore, pairing is thought by Husserl to occur *immediately*, despite his saying the following:

> Neither the other Ego himself, nor his subjective processes or his appearances themselves, nor anything else belonging to his own essence, becomes given in our experience originally. If it were, if what belongs to the other's own essence were directly accessible, it would be merely a moment of my own essence, and ultimately he himself and I myself would be the same. [CM 109 (139)]

And:

> A *certain mediacy of intentionality* must be present here, going out from the substratum, "primordial world," (which in any case is the incessantly underlying basis) and making present to consciousness a "there too," which nevertheless is not itself there and can never become an "itself-there." [CM 109 (139)]

What Husserl means in the above quotations is that, although I see immediately that it is another subject, I do not experience the other's subjectivity in *its* immediacy, for if I did I would *be* the other. Hence Husserl does not mean to deny that the act of recognizing the other is immediate.

(h) ## Relating Husserl's Theory of Intersubjectivity to Freudian Ego Psychology; Rationality of the Empirical Ego Essentially Intersubjective

The problem of other selves occurs on the level of conceptual thought, on the level of identity of self, on the level of the empirical ego. But according to both Husserl and Merleau-Ponty there is a level that is deeper than the personal ego—namely, that of the transcendental ego, on which the problem is resolved. Husserl maintains that the transcendental ego *constitutes* the empirical ego. Phenomenology is here once again in agreement with psychoanalytic theory. The ego is not what is first in the developmental history of the individual, ego psychology tells us. According to Freud the ego develops out of its nucleus, the perceptual system (EI 214), via memory. Husserl too maintains that the ego develops via memory from perceptual consciousness, which is the first consciousness, according to him (FTL 158 [141]). He, like Freud, maintains that through memories one's unique experiences are made into abiding possessions (cogitata), creating one's personality (CM 73 [107]; CM, section 32; CM 67 [101]). Hence these authors would agree with Dilthey's position according to which individuality cannot be taken to be primary. Gadamer writes:

> Individuality now is not a fundamental idea that is rooted in
> phenomena. Rather, Dilthey insists that all "psychological life"
> "is subject to the force of circumstances." There is no such
> thing as the fundamental power of individuality. It becomes
> what it is by asserting itself. [TM 200]

More specifically, Husserl maintains that the transcendental ego constitutes the empirical ego via the other through pairing. I cannot have a concept of self without having at the same time a concept of the other, for I am myself only in contrast with other selves:

> The Other [is] . . . phenomenologically a "modification" of
> myself (which for its part, gets this character of being "my" self
> by virtue of the contrastive pairing that necessarily takes place).
> [CM 115 (144)]

And speaking of pairing in general, of which constitution of self and other is an instance, Husserl writes:

> There takes place in the paired data a mutual transfer of
> sense—that is to say: an apperception of each according to the
> sense of the other. [CM 113 (143)]

In other words, I could never come to form a concept of self if I did not encounter an other qua other, if there were no awareness of other. This fact is incorporated in the Freudian theory of the structure of the psyche. According to Freud the ego cannot *be* except in relation to an internal representation of the other—the superego. More specifically, Freud maintains that the ego is an energetic structure formed in relation to superego and id, and that the libido or strength of the ego cannot develop unless there is a superego, and indeed one that is neither too strong nor too weak:[28]

As has been said repeatedly, the ego is formed to a great extent out of the identifications taking the place of the cathexes
on the part of the id which have been abandoned; the earliest
of these identifications always fulfill a special office in the ego
and stand apart from the rest of the ego in the form of a superego. [EI 227]

And:

The development of the ego consists in a departure from the
primary narcissism which results in a vigorous attempt to re-
cover it. The departure is brought about by means of the dis-
placement of libido to an ego-ideal imposed from without,
while gratification is derived from the attainment of this ideal.
[N 121]

From these quotations it is clear that Freud maintains that the
ego is not ready-made, but develops through formation of a superego.
The superego forms through a process of identification and internaliza-
tion; one identifies with the other and internalizes his or her values. The
superego is the other internalized, in other words. The superego is necessary for the ego to actualize; it is the latter's ground of possibility.[29]
According to Husserl, then, neither the concept of self nor that
of other is first, where by "concept" is meant the "had" concept (EJ
318), the concept as object, as abiding possession of consciousness. The
concept of other, and paradoxically that of self, develop out of a *feeling*
of *otherness*. That is, association, Husserl said, is not a thinking act (CM
111 [141]). It is rather an affective (feeling) act:

All prominences in a field, the articulation of the field according to likenesses and differences and the group-formation arising from it, the coming-to-prominence of particular members
from a homogeneous background: all this is the product of associative syntheses of a manifold kind. But these are not simply
passive occurrences in consciousness; rather, these syntheses of
coincidence have their own affective power. We say, for example, of that which, in its nonsimilarity, stands out from a homogeneous background and comes to prominence that it "strikes"
us, and this means that it displays an *affective tendency* toward
the ego. [EJ 76]

Husserl speaks of the data in the sphere of association *having a sensitive
effect on the ego* (EJ 77), of its *forcing itself against the ego* (EJ 77), of its

obtruding on the ego (EJ 77). By calling this reaction of the ego an affective or feeling one, Husserl does not mean to deny that it is without a structure or meaning, that it is without a rationality. He means to indicate, rather, that there are ways of experiencing, that there are modes of rationality, that are not *objective*, that are not subject to the objective ratio of science, but that allow the objective—that is, wakeful—cogito to develop:[30]

> We must, therefore, distinguish:
> 1. The tendency which precedes the *cogito, the tendency as stimulus* of the intentional background-experience and its differing degrees of strength. The stronger this "affection," the stronger the tendency to give way to it, to bring about the apprehension. As already mentioned, this tendency has its two sides:
> *a) The obtrusion on the ego*, the attraction which the given exerts on the ego.
> *b)* From the side of the ego, *the tendency to give way*, the being-attracted, the being-affected, of the ego itself.
> From these tendencies *antecedent* to the *cogito* can be distinguished:
> 2. The turning-toward *as compliance with* the tendency, in other words, the transformation of the character of the tendency of the intentional background-experience in which the *cogito* becomes active. The ego is now turned toward the object; it has *of itself* a tendency directed toward the object. [EJ 78]

And:

> The accomplishment of the turning-toward is what we call *the being-awake of the ego*. More precisely, it is necessary to distinguish being-awake as the factual accomplishment of an act from being-awake as potentiality, as the state of being able-to-accomplish an act, a state which constitutes the presupposition of the actual accomplishment of the act. To be awake is to direct one's regard to something. To be awakened means to submit to an effective affection. [EJ 79]

Initially there is only the continuous feeling of my *living* will or desire to unify and to "self"-preserve, in which thought lies only dormantly rooted and at whose service it will begin to work. This desire is Eros.[31] It is warranted to speak of *desire* here, for Eros has a *goal* or *aim* as well as a push to achieve the goal. It is a *feeling of living* desire because at this point the will or desire is not yet an object for, an abiding possession of, the ego. But it must be underscored that desire is a *structure*, so when it is said that feeling or desire is the genetically first level of lived-experience it is not being denied that structure is operative.[32] What is meant, rather, is that *structure* can be experienced prethetically as well as thetically. Again we find a parallel with psychoanalytic thought:

> The body and its emotional equipment . . . constitute first sources of meaning; they provide the emotional—or in Werner's terms, "physiognomic" character of reality. Thus they offer foundations for reason when this comes forward as a positive force giving rise to new structures—structures that are based on purposeful action and objectifying knowledge. [FB 304]

Initially all I *am* is this living desire, so if something is to speak to me, if something is to make an impact on me, it will have to do so through my desires. It is through desire that thought is set into motion, that I come out of myself to become aware of a world beyond me, and come into myself—that is to say, become a reflective self, a self in the true sense of the word. *The emergence of self is the emergence of reflective thought and vice versa.* More specifically, it is through frustration of desire that I become aware of myself and concomitantly of others, for it is only if I am disturbed in my continuous path of being, of living desire, that thought is shocked into action by being thrown back on itself. If the living desire is disturbed, thought is motivated to do what it was destined to do—namely, to self-actualize, to pull itself out of its dormant state to become aware of itself and of the world beyond itself, making of both an object, all in the service of desire.

This is in keeping with the terminology Husserl uses in *Experience and Judgment* where he speaks of the datum's forcing itself against the ego as a cause of the ego's turning-toward, of becoming wakeful or reflective. Thought thrown back on itself, reflective thought, is at the same time pulled out of itself and forced to go beyond itself. In descriptive psychological terms one might say that through lack of gratification I become aware of my limitations, I begin to define myself (*fines* = boundaries, limits) and am at the same time thrust on the path of seeking to restore the sense of continuity that has been disrupted, to restore my strength. The latter necessitates thought to go into the world and to make of it an ally. This, once again, is in harmony with Freudian theory. According to Freud the ego develops out of the perceptual system and its running concern will be to know reality. He maintains that the ego is one's point of contact with reality, with the outside world:

> The ego is essentially the representative of the external world, of reality. [EI 222]

The ego can effectively make of the world an ally only if it makes its acquaintance with the world an *abiding* possession (*cogitatum*), to which it can return and which it can set in relation, and so forth.

Because the other, at least to begin with, is the agent that causes either the fulfillment or frustration of my desires, *it is the other who occasions the awakening of reflective* (objective) *thought*. And this is how thought on becoming reflective necessarily comes to understand itself, as something confronting and being confronted by an other (FTL 237–38 [210]). For thought cannot in the beginning understand itself as pure thought, but must understand itself in terms of its rootedness in desire. Thus when it comes to think of itself, it does so in terms of the structure of desire—namely, as something vis-à-vis the other. When thought thrown back on itself gives rise to the notion of self, it does not take itself merely as object, but always as *object seen*, actually or potentially, *by the other*. Hence, being object-seen-by-the-other is not merely an accidental property of self, but is an essential property of self, *as well as of reflective thought*. (We might recall in this context Plato's notion of thought as inner *dialog*.)

(i)   Intersubjectivity and Rationality of the
       Empirical Ego as it Relates to the
       "Solipsism" and Rationality of the
       Pure Transcendental Ego

It can be appreciated that the phenomenon of other selves is deeply intertwined with the whole of phenomenology. Phenomenology is a rationality and studies rationality, and we have seen that in its essential structure the rationality of the wakeful ego is intersubjective[33] through and through, from the "lowest level," at which experience of the other sets the wakeful ego in motion, to the highest level at which the cogito willfully has the other in view:

> Phenomenology . . . finally understands itself as a reflective

functional activity in transcendental intersubjectivity. [FTL 275 (243)]

The following objection may spring to mind. Although phenomenology is a rationality, it is said to be a *new* rationality. What is new is its *transcendental* perspective of rationality. While the rationality of the *wakeful* ego is essentially intersubjective, the pure transcendental is also the nonwakeful ego.[34] The latter is genetically prior to the objective rationality of science, the rationality of the wakeful ego, and is also preintersubjective, presubjective, *"solipsistic."* In what sense, then, is intersubjectivity essential to phenomenology? But it is necessary to point out once more that while phenomenology's contribution is the opening up of the anonymous, transcendental realm of preobjective rationality, emphasizing and exploring that level and thereby transforming rationality, preobjective rationality is not cut off from scientific rationality and intersubjectivity, which belong to the empirical realm. Zaner, for instance, seems to think that speaking of an anonymous constituting realm rules out the individual, empirical, realm:

> How does it happen that this seeing, when reflectively apprehended, discloses the sense that it is *"my* seeing"? How does "my" perception, and more importantly, "my" body, become "mine?" If the existence of the body-proper is truly anonymous, then why is not *my* body experienced by me as *yours*? If perception is truly generalized, then how does it happen that every perception is nevertheless necessarily unique, individual? [PE 220]

And:

> I submit that Merleau-Ponty has not clearly recognized the problems involved in the phenomenon, "my body qua mine," but has rather begged the entire question with his conception of the body as "anonymous" and "generalized." [PE 221]

Zaner asks: "If perception is truly generalized, then how does it happen that every perception is nevertheless unique, individual?" But it must be recalled that the anonymous, transcendental realm does not exist by itself. Phenomenology does not mean to oppose the transcendental to the empirical, and the rationality of the transcendental realm is not opposed to the rationality of the wakeful ego. In chapter 5 it was explained that phenomenology does not consider the transcendental, anonymous realm to be the true realm, and the objective, personal realm to be false. The intention is not to falsify or deny objective thought. Objective thought, or rationality, however, is forgetful of its origin, and in its forgetfulness it falsifies our understanding of experience and of ourselves *if* it considers itself to be the total ground or explanation of our experience. Reduction to the life-world is meant, not to deny objective thought, but to assign to objective thought its place and endow it with its relative validity (PhP 365). Phenomenology maintains that the rationality of the wakeful cogito is not the only or deepest rationality. It maintains that to understand the rationality of science we need to understand how it relates to the deeper rationality.

In fact, it is only a naive phenomenological reflection that leads to the transcendental realm and fails to see its relation to the empirical realm. This would constitute a *static* phenomenology. But Husserl urges that the first, of necessity, *naive*, phenomenological investigations need to be supplemented with a higher phenomenological reflection, a reflection that takes the first phenomenological reflection as its object. This higher reflection will reveal what we were doing on the lower level; it will reveal that we were led to the transcendental realm because we wanted to ground the empirical realm. Hence the higher-order phenomenological investigation reveals the transcendental realm *as related to the empirical*, and it reveals the transcendental realm to be the realm required by the empirical. This is the genetic phenomenological approach. This point is expressed clearly by Merleau-Ponty:

> We have discovered, with the natural and social worlds, the truly transcendental, which is not the totality of constituting operations whereby a transparent world, free from obscurity and impenetrable solidity, is spread out before an impartial spectator, but that ambiguous life in which the forms of transcendence have their *Ursprung*, and which, through a fundamental contradiction, puts me in communication with them, and on this basis makes knowledge possible. It will perhaps be maintained that a philosophy cannot be centred round a contradiction, and that all our descriptions, since they ultimately defy thought, are quite meaningless. The objection would be valid if we were content to lay bare, under the term phenomenon or phenomenal field, a layer of prelogical or magical experiences. For in that case we should have to choose between believing the descriptions and abandoning thought, or knowing what we are talking about and abandoning our descriptions. These descriptions need to provide us with an opportunity of defining a variety of comprehension and reflection altogether

more radical than objective thought. To phenomenology understood as direct description needs to be added a phenomenology of phenomenology. We must return to the *cogito*, in search of a more fundamental *Logos* than that of objective thought, one which endows the latter with its relative validity, and at the same time assigns to it its place. [PhP 364–65]

It is not a matter of choosing realms, for it is not possible to understand one realm without the other, according to phenomenology. If the first phenomenological reflections yield the transcendental realm, a further phenomenological reflection on that initial reflection, a reflection on *method*, a phenomenology of phenomenology, in other words, reveals what we were doing and how we were doing it—namely, grasping the objective rationality via the transcendental. Hence, while the first naive reflection yields a static transcendental realm, in phenomenology of phenomenology we are led to a *genetic* approach whereby we *relate* the transcendental to the empirical and in which relating the two realms becomes the *task:*

> The task of a criticism of transcendental self-experience . . . would belong to a higher stage, since it would presuppose that, first of all, we had followed the harmonious course of transcendental experiencing as it functions in a certain naive manner, that we had made inquiries about its data and described them in respect of their universal properties. [CM 29 (67–68)]

And:

> The scientific efforts for which we found the collective name, *transcendental phenomenology*, must proceed in *two stages*.
> In the *first* stage the *realm accessible to transcendental self-experience* (a tremendous realm, as we soon discover) must be explored—and, at first, *with simple devotion to the evidence inherent in the harmonious flow of such experience*, while questions pertaining to an ultimate criticism, intent on apodictic principles governing the range of evidence, are set aside. In this stage accordingly—a stage that is *not yet philosophical in the full sense*—we proceed like the natural scientist in his devotion to the evidence in which Nature is experienced, while for him, as an investigator of Nature, questions pertaining to a radical criticism of experience remain altogether outside the field of inquiry.
> The *second* stage of phenomenological research would be

> precisely the *criticism of transcendental experience* and then the
> criticism of *all transcendental cognition.* [CM 29 (68)]

And:

> We preferred to sketch in outline the tremendous wealth of
> problems belonging to the *first stage of phenomenology*—a stage
> which in its own manner is itself *still infected with a certain na-
> ivete (the naivete of apodicticity)* but contains the great and most
> characteristic accomplishment of phenomenology, as a refash-
> ioning of science on a higher level—instead of entering into
> the *further and ultimate problems of phenomenology:* those pertain-
> ing to its *self-criticism.* [CM 151 (177–78)]

In a self-critical approach of a phenomenology of phenomenology, it becomes clear that in order to make its concept of rationality
phenomenological, phenomenology has to show how the other is constituted by the transcendental realm, because its deeper rationality is understood in terms of the ratio of the wakeful cogito, which is an
intersubjective cogito. Hence, Husserl says:

> Reduction to the transcendental ego *seems* to entail a *perma-
> nently* solipsistic science; whereas the consequential elaboration
> of this science, in accordance with its own sense, leads over to
> a phenomenology of transcendental intersubjectivity and, by
> means of this, to a universal transcendental philosophy . . .
> transcendental solipsism is only a subordinate stage philosophi-
> cally. [CM 30 (69)]

The genetic phenomenological viewpoint, then, relates the transcendental realm to the empirical realm. But it must be stressed here, as
it was in chapter 5, that the relation between the realms is not a simple
one. Merleau-Ponty cautions:

> The truth is that the relationships between the natural and
> transcendental attitudes are not simple, are not side by side or
> sequential, like the false or the apparent and the true. [S 164]

The transcendental realm is that which is necessary for the being-sense
of the empirical realm. In terms of the problem of other selves, then, the
transcendental realm points to a fundamental basis without which objective notions of self and other would make no sense and would not be.

The preobjective and the objective are, in short, *essentially* interdependent:

> Intercorporeality (the pre-objective level of experience/living body) culminates in (and is changed into) the advent of *blosse Sachen* (things in themselves) without our being able to say that one of the two orders is primary in relation to the other. The pre-objective order is not primary, since it is established (and to tell the truth fully begins to exist) only by being fulfilled in the founding of logical objectivity. Yet logical objectivity is not self-sufficient; it is limited to consecrating the labors of the pre-objective layer, existing only as the outcome of the "Logos of the esthetic world" and having value only under its supervision. [S 173]

Nor must it be thought that the preobjective is the cause or means, and the objective the effect or end, for to do so would be once more to bifurcate them (S 173). Indeed, the preobjective—that is, the life-world or living body—is rather the condition of possibility of the objective:

> The body is nothing less than the things' condition of possibility. When we go from body to thing, we go neither from principle to consequence nor from means to end. We are present at a kind of propagation, encroachment, or enjambment which prefigures the passage from the *solus ipse* to the other person, from the "solipsist" thing to the intersubjective thing. [S 173]

As a condition of possibility of the empirical, the transcendental, the living body, is ever-present.[35] This means, moreover, the pure transcendental ego is ever-present as the condition of possibility of the empirical ego and that it is not a matter of competition between the two. The correspondence of the earlier, transcendental levels to the later, objective levels is one of forgetfulness, to use Merleau-Ponty's expression (S 173).[36] The thing in itself is constituted because intercorporeality is "forgotten," and it can be forgotten because thought aims at the objective:

> Logical objectivity derives from carnal intersubjectivity on the condition that it has been forgotten as carnal intersubjectivity, and it is carnal intersubjectivity itself which produces this forgetfulness by wending its way toward logical objectivity. Thus the forces of the constitutive field do not move in one direc-

tion only; they turn back upon themselves. Intercorporeality goes beyond itself and ends up unconscious of itself as intercorporeality; it displaces and changes the situation it set out from, and the spring of constitution can no more be found in its beginning than in its terminus. [S 173]

The transcendental is ever-present as the condition of possibility of the presence of objective being. It makes the objective possible through forgetfulness of itself (S 173). It is clear that we do not have merely a metaphysics of presence here, and that for Husserl Being is not construed as presence of what is present, as opposed to presence by clearing. We have, rather, a presence due to absence or forgetfulness. For Husserl, as for Heidegger, "forgetfulness of Being is not forgetfulness of the world" (PH 171), but is its ground of possibility. Nor, since the transcendental is a *condition of possibility* of the objective, do we have a mere dialectic, as Gadamer suggests (PH 170); absence is not a limit of being, but its condition of possibility.

The transcendental reduction, of course, is intended precisely to bring to the fore this forgotten level of experience. Hence in speaking of the anonymous solipsist—that is, transcendental—ego with its corresponding realm, we are neither denying the empirical ego, the ego of objective thought that culminates in the personal ego in the sense of unique cogito, nor intersubjectivity. What *is* being denied is the claim that we have this notion of the unique cogito to begin with. As Merleau-Ponty states:

> Consciousness of oneself as unique individual [cogito] whose place can be taken by no one else, comes later and *is not primitive* [my emphasis]. [POP 119]

It is the solipsist level that makes possible the phenomenon of intersubjectivity, that makes possible a *shared*—intersubjective—world. But it must be understood that transcendental solipsism is not the solipsism of a cogito or ego enclosed in itself. Transcendental solipsism is a solipsism or solitude of ignorance:

> True, transcendental solitude takes place only if the other person is not even conceivable, and this requires that there be no self to claim solitude either. We are truly alone only on the condition that we do not know we are; it is this very ignorance which is our solitude. The "layer" or "sphere" which is called solipsist is without ego and without ipse. The solitude from

which we emerge to intersubjective life is not that of the mo-
nad. It is only the haze of an anonymous life that separates us
from being; and the barrier between us and others is impalpa-
ble. If there is a break, it is not between me and the other person; it is between a primordial generality we are intermingled
in and the precise system, myself—the others. What "precedes" intersubjective life cannot be numerically distinguished
from it, precisely because at this level there is neither individu-
ation nor numerical distinction. [S 174]

In the transcendental solipsism there is awareness neither of the ego nor
of alter ego:

> The child does not live as an ego, but it lives as an us, in com-
> mon bond with its whole environment. [FB 300]

The child proceeds from a state of "neutral indistinction between self
and other." This is what Merleau-Ponty means when he asserts that
"transcendental subjectivity is inter-subjectivity."

Initially, then, there is no reflective awareness of self and hence
there is a state of mergedness, of *intercorporeality*, as opposed to a shared-
ness or intersubjectivity. The latter pertains to a state in which individua-
tion has been achieved—that is, which expresses a relation between
individual subjectivities. As stated previously, the initial mode of relatedness to the world and to others is based on an ignorance of self. It is
unreflectively *lived;* that is to say, it is emotional. Original empathy, *the*
basic mode of relatedness, is emotional, and based on an ignorance of
self, unlike adult empathy, which occurs between individuals.

The theory is once more in agreement with psychoanalytic psychology. In psychoanalytic theory it is held, for instance, that the emotional states, attitudes, and so forth, of the care-giver are communicated
to the very young infant by manner of touch, voice, and the like:

> According to Remplein (1966, p. 215) "it is beyond all doubt
> that the unconscious mind of the child responds to the par-
> ents' unconscious sets, attitudes and prejudices like a very sen-
> sitive seismograph. It responds to their peace and security,
> harmony and joy as well as to their irritability and anxiety,
> their quarrelling and temper." The concept of "contamination
> of feeling"[37] *(Gefühlsansteckung)* used by Max Scheler (1948)
> can be applied here. Scheler points to the fact that the process
> of contamination occurs beyond knowledge and intentions of
> the ego. [FB 301]

What is suggested by the above, then, is that something occurs that is akin to Scheler's "contamination of feeling" *(Gefühlsansteckung),* which he says takes place beyond explicit knowledge or intention of the ego (NS, chap. 1; 246). This is in accord with the way in which Freud describes the earliest type of interaction with others, the process of identification, which he says is "immediate" (EI 219) and occurs "prior to object cathexis" (EI 219). No analogical reasoning takes place. Since one is not self-aware on this level, it is an unconscious mode of being. According to Freud, the ego to begin with is not conscious, but preconscious and even unconscious (EI 210–11).

The gradual process whereby one goes from an undifferentiated state to a state of individuality will not be described in further detail here. For our purposes it is important to realize that everything passes from livedness to awareness, from nonreflective mergedness to a reflective intersubjectivity. Relatedness to the other is at first unreflectively lived, gradually becoming reflective until it culminates in the highest form of relatedness, that of linguistic dialog:

> In the experience of dialogue, there is constituted between the
> other person and myself a common ground; my thought and
> his are interwoven into a single fabric, my words and those of
> my interlocutor are called forth by the state of the discussion,
> and they are inserted into a shared operation of which neither
> of us is the creator. We have here a dual being, where the
> other is for me no longer a mere bit of behaviour in my tran-
> scendental field, nor I in his; we are collaborators for each
> other in consummate reciprocity. Our perspectives merge into
> each other, and we co-exist through a common world. [PhP
> 354]

The highest form of relatedness to the other, then, occurs when there is awareness of one's ego and that of the other, and occurs in linguistic dialog. Initially there is no sense of distinctness. The very young child does not see phenomena as "private": there is a oneness, and everything is considered accessible to all, as it were. The boundary between self and other gradually emerges. In the beginning, as it emerges, there is a "dizzying proximity to others." Self and other are confused, as is manifest in the phenomena of transitivity and syncretic sociability. These earlier, more fundamental levels of relating are, however, never lost, according to Merleau-Ponty. In a sense we always remain somewhat merged with others:

I borrow myself from others; I create others from my own thoughts. This is no failure to perceive others; it is the perception of others. [S 159]

Merleau-Ponty describes how in certain circumstances these earlier states of mergedness reemerge—in the phenomenon of love, and in certain pathological states, for example—and how this process of going from an undifferentiated state to a state of individuality or segregation is one that is never completely finished (POP 119).

(j)   Transcendental Phenomenology as
       Essentially Intersubjective

What follows from the above is that transcendental phenomenology is *essentially* intersubjective. Even the pure transcendental ego as ground of rationality is the potential for the self-other relation. The pure transcendental ego too is understood vis-à-vis the other, intersubjectively. To say that the transcendental ego is self-questioning is to say that it bears the structure self-other, for there are grounds and motives for questioning the self only if one does not quite coincide with oneself—that is, only if one is somehow also not-self, but other (object). Here we encounter again, as we did in chapter 4, that life and the cogito have the same structure—namely, that of subject-object or self-other. The pure transcendental ego too has this structure. The pure transcendental ego, life, and cogito all have the same structure and all are interconnected in phenomenology. The psyche is a correlation, and this correlation is at once the structure of life and the structure of cognition, for both cognition and life have the form analogous to self-other. Cognition has this form because we know (cogito) when we have evidence, when we *see*, and seeing is being witness (self) to the world (other).[38] Life has this form because life is always at some level self-assertion, which requires differentiation into self-other. In this sense, then, energy, libido, or life and cognitive structure or significance are intimately bound up with one another.

Here we see once more that the cogito is rooted in desire, for thought is quite literally motivated by prethetic experience, by desire, by Eros (self-preservation and unification). Thought was "born" out of desire and will always to a certain extent be determined by desire. All thought will have "in" it a connection to desire, however hidden that connection may become. And here is found the connection between science and value. Its rootedness in desire at once implicates thought in value, for our desires determine our values. Our "subjective affective states" are the immediate ground of our values. They validate or legitimate our choices. Knowledge is not a purely intellectual affair, but involves our subjective, affective states. Knowledge, according to phenomenology, is not representation, but *investment*.

It was said that thought, on becoming reflective, takes itself as object seen by others, that it takes on the structure ego-superego, for superego is the idea of the other's view of the ego. Differentiation into ego and superego, then, *is* reflection. But from what has been said it follows that the psyche would not differentiate itself on an abstract principle alone, but that thought has a motive for becoming or failing to become reflective—there is always something at stake. According to Freud the motive for internalizing the other, and hence the deeper motive for becoming reflective, is Eros, love of the other and fear of losing the other's love. "To the ego," writes Freud, "living means the same as being loved" (EI 233).[39] This is so because reflective thought, as mentioned previously, understands itself in terms of the other. It is welded to the other and needs the other for its being. Implicitly intuiting its indebtedness to the other, it will *tend* to love the other, though this may in fact prove difficult. Love of the other motivates the actualization of the differentiation of the psyche into ego and superego. Indeed, Freud claims that not only does living mean the same thing to the ego as being loved, but it means "being loved by the superego" (EI 233).

This is the reason why a celebration of self, as Nietzsche speaks of it, is essentially unselfish: the self is always vis-à-vis the other, and a celebration of self occurs when ego meets ego ideal, when it meets the superego's standards. The latter, it will be recalled, are the values of the *other* internalized. In other words, the concept of the ego resting in itself—as in idealism or realism, both of which treat the ego as a self-sufficient homogeneous, ready-made unit—is not a concept of life or energy. Such an ego has no life for it does not reflect movement. What breathes life or energy into the ego is the superego, something to which the ego can aspire or strive, a differential, for energy is created by a differential. Literally the superego inspires (inspire: breath into) the ego. The ego has its greatest surge of energy and indeed experiences its greatest sense of well-being when it achieves its ideal. It is a matter of life, potential significance, giving rise to significance, which in turn yields greater life. Cognition has the form of life and vice versa. Libido or life energy partakes of this cognitive form, for it is transformed so as to be freed or created by it. Once the psyche actualizes the self-other structure as ego-superego in a process that is cognitive at heart, the potential libido of the psyche is put at the disposal of the ego, which uses it for its work, as "energeia." There is no libido or life of the ego, hence no self-assertion, the principle of life, unless there is already significance.

There is ground for a morality here. Since, for the ego, being means being self-reflective—cogito ergo *sum*—and since this is made possible by the other, self and other are intimately connected. To hurt the other is then to hurt the self and vice versa.

In this chapter it has been argued, then, that Husserl's phenomenology can deal with the problem of other selves,[40] supporting the claim that Husserl's phenomenology does not share Descartes's ontological prejudice and supporting the claim that it can do justice to the phenomena of life. What needs to be shown next is that the specifically phenomenological concepts in transcendental logic, such as that of a constituting subjectivity, are in fact compatible with traditional formal logic, for it was said that phenomenology is a transcendental logic that developed by "going through" the tradition of formal logic. This concern shall be dealt with in the next chapter where Husserl's transcendental logic will be related to the formal logic of Frege, thereby demonstrating the connections between these two systems.

Frege and Husserl:
A Deepening of the Standard
Noema-*Sinn* Comparison
by Means of a
Transcendental Perspective

Transcendental Logic and
Contemporary Formal Logic

This chapter returns to an explicit treatment of the theme of logic. In chapter 1 it was explained that while transcendental logic constitutes a critique of traditional logic, it does not so much go against traditional logic as attempt to complete it by understanding its roots and origins (C 11, 14). In other words, although transcendental logic goes beyond the tradition, it is nevertheless best understood by going through the tradition (C 18).[1]

In the preceding chapters this was demonstrated by relating phenomenology to the concepts of logic found in the history of thought until the time that Husserl was writing. This chapter will relate phenomenology to a formal logic that developed contemporaneously with, though independently from, Husserl's transcendental logic—namely, the logic of Frege. In light of the fact that much of present-day formal logic is based on Frege's innovative ideas (e.g., quantification), that Frege's work is a cornerstone in present-day symbolic logic and semantics, comparing Frege's logic with Husserlian transcendental logic is a good choice. It amounts to comparing Husserlian transcendental logic to present-day formal logic.[2] It will be demonstrated that there are points of contact between traditional formal logic and Husserl's phenomenology. Specifically, it will be shown that neither the transcendental perspective nor intentionality is foreign to Frege's logic, lending credence to de Muralt's claim that "formal logic is the factical example which enables intentional analysis to anticipate the ideal examplar, transcendental logic" (DeM 355).

The Frege-Husserl connection is popularly known in two ways, namely (i) in terms of Frege's "devastating" critique of Husserl's alleged psychologism in the *Philosophy of Arithmetic*, which purportedly caused Husserl to alter his views, and (ii) in terms of the similarity between Husserl's notion of noema and Frege's notion of *Sinn*. With respect to the first, although Frege may have thought that he was attacking Husserl's psychologism, it does not follow that Husserl *was* committed to psychologism in his *Philosophy of Arithmetic*. There are grounds for maintaining that Husserl was not propounding a psychologism in that work, but that we find there the rudiments of his transcendental philosophy[3] and that Frege's criticism did not cause Husserl so much to abandon his views of the *Philosophy of Arithmetic* as to make his position more precise and less vulnerable to misinterpretation. Furthermore, it has recently been argued by Mohanty that Husserl developed many of the views embodied in that early work independently of Frege's critique. With respect to the similarity between noema and *Sinn*, comparisons deal with these notions in comparative isolation from the fuller theories of Husserl and Frege, respectively. But these notions constitute only a very narrow segment of their respective theories of meaning. Not only is Husserl's notion of noema truncated in these comparisons—due to the sometimes openly admitted ignoring of the transcendental reduction[4]—but, and this is perhaps a bit surprising, so too is Frege's notion of *Sinn*. It is pulled out of context as well. Once noema and *Sinn* are viewed in a broader context, a deeper connection between Frege and Husserl can be observed.

(b)   Husserlian Noema and Fregean *Sinn*

The person probably best known for making the comparison between Husserl and Frege is Dagfinn Føllesdal. A number of papers continuing this theme followed his 1969 article,[5] making the comparison by now commonplace. As stated above, the thesis that there are similarities between the theory of intentionality and that of intensionality is usually narrowed down to the claim that Husserl's notion of noema is similar to Frege's notion of *Sinn*. Authors who have made the noema-*Sinn* comparison maintain, for example, that just as for Frege the *Sinn* is a way of being directed to an object, the noema is said by Husserl to be the way of being directed to an object. Hintikka, for example, writes:

The only reasonable way of understanding Frege's statement in
the last analysis is to interpret the sense or *Sinn* as the *function*
which gives us the reference, by means of which we as it were
can find this reference. . . . It is not so far from Husserl . . .
for what Husserl was interested in was precisely those "vehicles
of directedness," the noemata, which enable us to intend or refer to objects. [IOI 235]

The comparison is a fair one. Both Frege and Husserl maintain
that *Sinn* is a way of relating or being directed to an object. Frege maintains:

It is natural, now, to think of there being connected with a sign
(name, combination of words, written mark), besides that
which the sign designates, which may be called the meaning of
the sign, also what I should like to call the *sense* of the sign
wherein the mode of presentation is contained. [PW 57]

Husserl writes:

Every noema has a "content," namely, its "meaning," and is
related through it to "its" *object*. [I 333 (267)]

However, while there is nothing wrong with comparing noema
and *Sinn* along this line, the way in which this relating or referring to an
object is generally understood in the literature does justice neither to
Husserl nor Frege. It is understood as a *"picking out"* of an object, and
this in turn is understood in terms of a *linguistic model* of referring.
Føllesdal, for example, maintains that "noemata are like linguistic Sinne
in most respects" (HNN 684). According to this model, the paradigm of
reference is the relation of a name to that extralinguistic entity it names,
or as it is sometimes called, the name/bearer relation. As Bell writes:

The reference of an expression is that extralinguistic entity
with which the expression has been correlated or which it picks
out. [FTJ 42]

Usually the extralinguistic entity "picked out" by the name is
taken to be an entity in the world. As Rosenberg and Travis write:

The question of *reference* is a specific instance of a general
philosophical concern about the relation of words and the

world—how is it possible to use *language* to talk about what is *not* language, the extralinguistic world? Indeed, one historically important tradition hoped to find in an adequate theory of reference the full answer to the question of word-world relationships. On this account, the theory of reference was to constitute a theory of *meaning* as well. Sentences are combinations of words; they are made up of words. Each word stands for or names an object. The meaning of the word is the object for which it stands. Thus language achieves extralinguistic import. In one variant or another, something like this theory has been a viable force in philosophy from Plato to the present. [RPL 163]

Hintikka too speaks of reference in terms of "picking out" an object:

> When one understands a singular term, one does not just know what it stands for. One also knows something about how its reference is picked out. [IOI 115]

But this is only one way in which to understand the theory of reference, and, as it stands, it is an incomplete account of the phenomenon of reference. As will be argued below, in the works of both Frege and Husserl there is to be found another notion of reference, one that is not based on the name-named paradigm.[6] It is in terms of this other model, and not the linguistic model, that the phenomena of *Sinn* and noema can best be understood.

The linguistic model is too static to fit either Frege's notion of *Sinn* or Husserl's notion of noema. The extralinguistic object to which *Sinn* relates, for example, is considered to be already "there." Although it is admitted that the noema and *Sinn* are entities related to the subject, that they are subject dependent, the subjective aspect of the relation is not discussed at any length. The subject's relation to *Sinn* is also treated in a more or less static manner. It is taken for granted that we somehow *have* the *Sinn* or noema, and by means of this *refer* to the object. What is focused upon is the purely "objective" side of the meaning entity, and its relation to the subject is not discussed. But, as explained earlier,[7] for Husserl there can be no hope of understanding the noema without understanding the nature of its relation to the "subjective" act—to the noesis.[8] Writes Husserl:

> The Eidos of the noema points to the Eidos of the noetic consciousness; both belong *eidetically* together. [I 265 (206)]

A little further he adds:

> A *parallelism* between noesis and noema does indeed exist, but
> is such that the formations must be described *on both sides*, and
> in their essential correspondence to one another. [I 266
> (207)][9]

It can even be argued that Husserl draws so much attention to the
noema only in order to reveal the constituting activity, the noetic activity, and, in the final analysis, to reveal specifically the pure noesis. The
noetic acts are intricate, and Husserl speaks of their intricacy being
"mirrored" in the noema, cautioning that this "mirroring" is not to be
taken as a simple side-by-side relation:

> These two doctrines of forms [of noeses and noemata] would
> not of course stand related to each other *in any sense as images
> in a mirror*, or as though they could pass over the one into the
> other through a mere change of signature, e.g., through simply
> substituting for every noema N the "consciousness of N." [I
> 265 (206)]

It is not possible to grasp the noema without considering its noetic relation, because the intricacy of the noesis is quite literally *taken up*
in the noema:

> Intentionalities in the noesis and noema rest on one another in
> *descending levels*, or rather *dovetail into one another* in a peculiar
> way. [I 269 (210)]

In other words, the noema for Husserl cannot be understood independently of a larger "cognitive" act.[10] If noema characterizes Husserl's phenomenology, it does so because it bears the mark of and
thereby reveals the activity of the constituting subject. When we focus
our attention on the noema in the phenomenological reduction, we are
supposed to see precisely this relation of objectivity, *any* objectivity, perceptual as well as the purely meant, to the constituting subjectivity.[11] We
are supposed to see the relation of constituted to constituting act, to
noesis, in other words.

De Muralt too argues that a proper phenomenological or transcendental understanding of the noema is one in which the complete
noema is understood to imply the corresponding noesis:

The complete noema thus appears as in itself intentionally implying the corresponding noesis, the complete constituted as
implying its constitution, the *cogitatum* as implying the *cogito*.
The genuine sense of the noema necessarily requires this implication, without which the noema is not transcendentally understood. [DeM 284]

Yet some of the seminal articles comparing Husserlian noema and
Fregean *Sinn*, such as that by Føllesdal and by Smyth and McIntyre, do
not include a study of the noesis. This is a result of failing to do the
transcendental reduction. As Langsdorf (NAS 8) also argues, Føllesdal
fails to perform the transcendental reduction. The same can be said of
Smith and McIntyre, who in their study on noemata in fact openly admit
to not being concerned with the reduction:

The performance of the epochē—the use of the phenomenological method—will play no role in our present efforts. [IVI
543]

Smith and McIntyre in fact maintain that noemata cannot only be
adequately understood without invoking the reduction, but that the reduction can be understood only via an understanding of noemata. They
assert:

The epochē, in fact, is an heuristic device whose purpose is to
acquaint us with noemata. But the method is neither comprehensive nor effective without an understanding of the nature
and role of the entities we are seeking by means of its use. [IVI
543]

The one exception is Jaako Hintikka, who does seem to appreciate the fact that the noemata are reached via the reduction. He writes:

The importance of the "phenomenological reduction" for the
practice of phenomenology . . . seems to me best explicable in
terms of the objective meaning entities, the noemata, which the
reduction is calculated to uncover. [IOI 231]

Disappointingly he goes on to say, however:

It has been argued recently, and quite persuasively, that the
very meaning of the phenomenological reduction can only be

understood in terms of the semantical and ontological status of noemata, not vice versa. [IOI 231]

His reference here is to the Smith and McIntyre article. Hintikka too ends up "concentrating on these meaning entities [the noemata] rather than on the technique allegedly needed to reach them" (IOI 231), and fails to see that the reduction shows the noema to be essentially linked to the noesis, that it shows the noema to point to an objectifying *act* that can be characterized.

In other words, the transcendental reduction is indispensable to executing phenomenology and to grasping the noema. An initial reduction gives us the meant qua meant, the *Sinn* of the noema. But unless the reduction is carried further, one is not engaging in a true transcendental philosophy. The reduction, continued to the point where it is seen that the meant qua meant is always the meant of a constituting subjectivity, is carried further still: it is applied to the constituting subjectivity, revealing the pure transcendental ego in terms of which all objectivities are to be understood. Only this yields a true transcendental phenomenology. Hence, the claim made by Smith and McIntyre is false. Neglecting the reduction prevents one from considering the complete noema, which leads to an objectivistic, and, from the transcendental phenomenological point of view, inadequate understanding of noemata, in which the connection to the noesis is neither seen nor understood.

(c)   Divisions within the Noema

While the divisions Husserl makes within the full noema, divisions that "mirror" the activities of the noeses, may be noted in the aforementioned papers, these divisions do not form part of the overall interpretation and in most cases are conflated. Husserl divides the noema into three moments: (i) a pure substrate of predicates, *"the pure X in abstraction from all predicates"* (I 337 [271]; (ii) a core or "characteristic nucleus" (I 338 [271])—also referred to by Husserl as "central 'nucleus,' " "the sheer 'objective meaning' " (I 246 [189]), "noematic Sinn," and "object simpliciter" (I 246 [189])—which is the X filled out by predicates: "a fully *dependable content* is marked off in every *noema* . . . a definite system of *predicates* . . . [which] determine the 'content' of the object-nucleus of the noema" (I 336–37 [270]); and (iii) a quality, the mode of presentation of the object—the object as seen, recalled, hallucinated, etc.: "an objective . . . has its ways of being given; its characters, its manifolds under which it is known in the complete noema" (I 250–51 [192]). All three moments together constitute the *complete* noema. Føllesdal appreciates the distinctions "within" the noema and initially likens *Sinn* only to the central nucleus of the noema, to the sheer objective meaning, the noematic *Sinn* (HNN 682). However, about one-third into the article he conflates the central nucleus—that is, the noematic *Sinn*—and the complete noema, attributing properties of *Sinn* to the complete noema.[12] This is surprising in light of the fact that Føllesdal himself cautions us about *Husserl's* inconsistent use of the term *Sinn*, using it sometimes to mean the full noema, and at other times to mean the objective meaning (HNN 681–82). But Føllesdal conflates the two where Husserl does not do so. For example, citing a passage in which Husserl is speaking about the noematic *Sinn* (HNN 684), Føllesdal generalizes Husserl's remarks about *Sinn* to the complete noema. His justification for doing so is the following:

> Since the other components of the noema are also "Sinn"
> components, the same presumably applies to them, and,
> thereby, to the whole noema. [HNN 684]

From this passage it is clear that Føllesdal believes that in general what is said about the noematic *Sinn* can be said about the complete noema. He does the same once again a little further on in the article when he cites a section of Husserl's manuscript "Noema und Sinn." In the section in question, Husserl characterizes *Sinn* as having the possibility of remaining the same in perception, meaning, and phantasy. It is clear that Husserl is talking about only *part* of the noema—namely, the sheer objective meaning, the central nucleus. Føllesdal once again, however, concludes that Husserl's discussion concerning *Sinn* in this passage "presumably applies to all components of the noema" (HNN 685). Now Husserl may indeed sometimes use *Sinn* alternately to refer to the complete noema and part of the noema, and it is possible that Husserl does this because the whole noema and a part of the noema have something in common, which the term *Sinn* applied to either attempts to express. But it does not follow that one can conflate the two in *all* cases, and certainly one should not do so where Husserl does not, as in the passages in question. If one does conflate the two terms, a reason for doing so, other than the one Føllesdal gives, should be advanced. Saying that the two notions have the same properties because they belong to the same complex is illegitimate.

Treating the complete noema as *Sinn* understood as noematic core, as Føllesdal as well as Smith and McIntyre do, amounts to treating the complete noema as an objective entity, for Husserl describes the core as "the sheer 'objective meaning' " (I 246 [189]). But Husserl does not understand the complete noema as an objective entity per se, for phenomenology is everywhere concerned with uncovering the original hidden constitutive activity of subjectivity. Because of this conflation of the noematic core and complete noema, Føllesdal's comparison of Frege and Husserl on *Sinn* is not completely reliable. The articles on this topic that follow Føllesdal's paper incorporate much of the latter's position, including the confusion just discussed. As a result the *complete noema* is underplayed. Smith and McIntyre in their paper "Intentionality via Intensions," for example, write the following:

> The noematic Sinn, because it prescribes the object of the act, is the most important component for Husserl's theory of intentionality. [IVI 545]

(d) "Quality" Indispensable for a Phenomenological Understanding of Noema

But in failing to focus on the full noema, attention is not directed to the noema's *quality*, an appreciation of which is indispensable for a correct grasp of Husserl's theory of intentionality.[13] It is above all this notion of *quality* or *character of the noema as inalienably belonging to the noema* that differentiates Husserl's theory of intentionality from that of Brentano, for example. Although Føllesdal realizes that Husserl's notion of intentionality differs from that of Brentano, he merely says that the difference is captured in the concept of "noema" (HNN 681). The claim, while true, is too general to be informative about the nature of this difference. Landgrebe argues that although the claim that Husserl has a unique conception of intentionality may be commonplace, it is nevertheless deserving of renewed attention:

> Das in der ganzen Entwicklung der Phänomenologie Husserls treibende Grundmotiv ist seine ihm *spezifisch eigene Konzeption der Intentionalität*. So sehr er selbst dies immer wieder betonte und so selbstverständlich das heute klingen mag, so sehr muss darauf hingewiesen werden, dass auch von seinen Schülern zumeist die Tragweite dieser Konzeption und die Konsequenzen, die sich aus ihr ergeben, verkannt wurden. [DWP 59]

Landgrebe argues (DWP) that although Husserl did not fully realize it, his own unique notion of intentionality is rooted in the *Philosophy
of Arithmetic* where it was misunderstood by Frege. In that work Husserl
found Brentano's concept of intentionality too narrow to be able to account for number. Although he tried to stay within the latter's theoretical framework, without being fully aware of it, Husserl had already gone
substantially beyond his teacher's notion of intentionality (DWP 15).
Husserl no longer conceived of the intentional act as an undifferentiated
act, but as a very specific *operation*, a very specific *striving*. Writes Landgrebe:

> In einer von Brentano abweichenden Weise ist also die Rede
> von Intentionalität wortlich genommen, ist sie gefasst als ein
> Intendieren, das von dem uneigentlichen zum eigentlichen
> Vorstellen hingeht, mit anderen Worten als ein Streben, das
> auf eine Leistung gerichtet ist, nämlich auf die Herstellung der
> eigentlichen Vorstellung. Der Unterschied zwischen eigent-
> lichem und uneigentlichem Vorstellen war freilich Brentano ge-
> läufig und spielte in seinen Analysen eine grosse Rolle. Aber es
> blieb bei der Feststellung dieser verschiedenden Arten inten-
> tionaler auf ein Objekt, die er voneinander abhob, man könnte
> sagen, in einer rein *statischen Weise*, ohne dass er das *Dynamis-
> che* des Übergangs, des Intendierens von dem bloss symbolisch
> Indizierten zur erfüllenden Veranschaulichung, zur ursprüng-
> lich gegebenden Vorstellung beachtet hätte. [DWP 14–15]

That Brentano's notion of intentionality is too restrictive for Husserl's purposes in the *Philosophy of Arithmetic* is not surprising when we
consider that the latter's account there of numbers involves appeal to
the process of *counting*, a highly specific process that intentionality as
undifferentiated act, as pure representation, cannot accommodate. And
Suzanne Bachelard notes how frequently Husserl compares the "operation" of intentionality to that of counting (SHL 66). As explained in
chapter 2 this operation of intentionality is one of bringing the object to
givenness. Intentionality is not merely the "having" of an object. In Husserl's words, it "does not consist in just holding the object presently before one" (I 263 [205]), but it is the *striving* to bring the object to
evidence, the striving to have it "originaliter."[14] It has been explained
also that this act can be characterized in detail, according to the type of
object that consciousness relates to, and according to the region of being
that the object belongs to, different regions having different types of
evidence prescribed in advance (I 356–57 [288]; C 166; PL 25). Evidence expresses a concern for truth, and bringing the object to evidence

is a striving for truth. This striving to bring the object to evidence, this striving for truth, is the essence of intentionality. It is this concern with truth that is expressed in the noema's quality.

(e) Quality of the Noema Expressive of the Striving for Truth

The quality or character of the noema expresses the manner in which the object is given to us—in perception, imagination, memory, and so forth. Specifying the manner of givenness indicates a concern with truth. That is, the type of presentation indicates the type of *evidence* required to bring an object to adequation, and we arrive at a classification of the type through attempting to bring the object to adequation. Just as an explicit sense of truth is arrived at negatively—one develops an explicit sense of truth only after one's passive belief, that is, naive, nonquestioning belief, in the truth of something has been frustrated[15]—so too the characters are arrived at *negatively*. Through failing to bring the object to adequation by means of perceptual evidence, we get a sense of object *not* perceived, but wished, recalled, hallucinated, and so forth. As explained in chapter 2,[16] Husserl's maintaining that all characters are modifications of perception reflects his belief in the primacy of perception. The striving for truth, for bringing the object to adequation, is always present, though it remains *implicit* until one encounters an error. Once error occurs, the object is qualified as real, fancied, dreamt, and the like, all of which expresses a concern for truth. As discussed in chapter 2, one becomes aware also of nuances that further bear evidence of a concern for truth—*probably* seen, *definitely* dreamt, and so forth:

> One recognizes further . . . that there is such a thing . . . as the consciousness of *"fulfilment of the intention,"* of authorizing and strengthening with special reference to the thetic characters, just as there are also the corresponding *opposed characters* of the *depriving of all authority and power.* [I 369–70 (300–301)]

The striving for truth, then, expresses itself in the quality of the noema. To discuss only the core of the noema is therefore to leave aside completely the notion of striving for truth, and this would be akin to Brentano's treatment of intentionality, not as a highly specified and specifiable act, but as an undifferentiated representation of object.

This, in one way or another, is what the authors comparing intentionality and intensionality in effect have done. They focus on the core of the noema only, thereby eradicating the difference between Husserl's and Brentano's notions of intentionality. While Føllesdal, for instance, claims that the notion of noema differentiates Husserl's and Brentano's concepts of intentionality, he sets out to understand the noema in such a way as to mask the difference between Brentano's and Husserl's notions of intentionality—that is, as *core* versus complete noema. Because noema is understood as core, these authors cannot account for the "filling out" of the noema, the process of bringing to evidence, nor do they see the importance for being able to account for this phenomenon so crucial to phenomenology.

McIntyre and Smith, for example, commenting on the shortcomings of their interpretation of noema as *Sinn*, state the following:

> There are important qualifications to this claim, dealing for the most part with the richness and evidential "fullness" of sensory intuition. But to allow for these here would be a *needless complication* [my emphasis] of our fundamental contention that noemata are intensions. It should be noted, however, that without further modification our present characterization of noemata is unable to account for evidential "fulfillment." (IVI 547, n. 10]

If, as they say, they cannot account for *perceptual* filling out without further modification of their account, there is reason to assume McIntyre and Smith cannot do so for any other type of filling out—for example, the filling out of irreal objects, for it involves appeal to the more complex notion of adumbration of irreal objects. It is fair to say, then, that their understanding of intentionality as intensionality is one that, as it stands, is unable to deal with the process of filling out, of bringing to evidence or truth. What McIntyre and Smith in fact are doing—and we find a clear instance of this also in Føllesdal's paper—is working with a notion of object as object already filled out.[17] In Føllesdal's understanding of intentionality there is no striving left—we have, as it were, "arrived."

(f) The Problem of Intentional Inexistence

Føllesdal maintains that Husserl considered his notion of noema to be a means of overcoming the problem of intentional inexistence. According to Føllesdal (HNN 680), the problem of intentional inexistence resulted from Brentano's thesis that "every mental phenomenon is characterized by the reference to a content, a direction upon an object," by what the Scholastics called "intentional inexistence of an object." He points out that according to Brentano even in hallucinating or in imagining, say, a centaur, consciousness is directed to an object. The problem in Føllesdal's words is the following:

> Whereas the view that the objects of acts are real leads to diffi-culties in the case of centaurs and hallucinations, the view that the objects are unreal, whatever that may mean, leads to diffi-culties in the case of many other acts, e.g., acts of normal per-ception: it seems that, on that view, what we see when we see a tree is not the real tree in front of us, but something else, which we would also have seen if we were hallucinating. [HNN 680]

According to Føllesdal, Husserl overcomes this problem by deny-ing that all acts have objects:

> Husserl resolved this dilemma by holding that, although every act is directed, this does not mean that there always is some ob-ject toward which it is directed. According to Husserl, there is associated with each act a *noema*, in virtue of which the act is di-rected toward its object, *if it has any* [my emphasis]. [HNN 681]

While Føllesdal does not specify or characterize the acts of con-sciousness not directed toward an object, he does provide an example of such an act—thinking of a centaur:

> When we think of a centaur, our act of thinking has a noema, but it has no object; there exists no object of which we think. Because of its noema, however, even such an act is directed. To be *directed* simply is to have a noema. [HNN 681]

What characterizes such an act? The thought of a centaur is one that cannot be perceptually filled out. It appears that Føllesdal thinks that if an act of consciousness has a content that cannot be perceptually filled out, then according to Husserl it has a noema but not an object. Certain acts of recollection, then, would also have a noema but no ob-ject, such as my recollection of Pedro, my dog that died many years ago. But how does the act of recollecting Pedro or of thinking of a centaur in its structure qua act of consciousness differ from my act of thinking of my actually existing, but absent, friend in Toronto? The former two acts cannot be perceptually filled out and the latter can, but that makes no difference to the nature of the acts qua acts of consciousness as they occur. It seems that Føllesdal is committed to saying that any content of thought that is not at the time at which it is thought given in immediate perceptual experience, which is not at the time of presentation perceptually filled out, has a noema but not an object. It seems that Føllesdal is committed to saying that, for Husserl, only if the object is what Husserl calls "perceptually filled out," is consciousness directed to an object. But this is not Husserl's position:

> *Every* [my emphasis] noema has a "content," namely its "meaning," and is related to its *"object"* [my emphasis]. [I 333 (267)]

That Husserl says that every noema is related to its object is not surprising, if we recall that the essence of intentionality according to Husserl is *object*ification. In thinking of a centaur or any irreal object, consciousness is directed to an object:

> Irreal objectivities . . . have the *essential property of all experiences* or evidences of whatever sort—that is to say: with the repetition of the subjective life-processes, with the sequence and synthesis of different experiences of the Same, they make evidently visible *something that is indeed numerically identical (and not merely things that are quite alike)*, namely *the* object, which is thus an object experienced many times, or, as we may also say, one that *"makes its appearance" many times* (as a matter of ideal possibility, infinitely many times) in the domain of consciousness. [FTL 162–63 (145)]

According to Husserl, while some acts of consciousness are intentional and not directed to an object, in the broadest sense of the term—namely, those acts that belong to what he terms "primary intentionality," such as the original time synthesis—*all* other acts of consciousness, including acts of imagination, hallucination, dreaming, and so forth, are directed toward an object. Husserl does not treat the intentionality of dreaming, hallucinating, and the like, any differently than that of perceiving a real object. All acts are directed toward an object, though different types of acts have different types of evidence—in the former case the objects are not perceptually filled out, in the latter they are. It is false to say, then, that Husserl differs from Brentano by claiming that in the case of acts of imagination, dreaming, and so forth, consciousness is not directed to an object. On this Husserl and Brentano agree: even in imagination consciousness is directed toward an object.

But not only is Føllesdal's interpretation not in line with Husserl's position, it runs into an insoluble difficulty, one that results from his failure to do the reduction. If consciousness in both its empty and filled states has a noema, but only in its filled state a noema *and* an object, Føllesdal is compelled to find a bridge from the noema to an extra-noematic object; he must account for how consciousness in its filled state gets from noema to object. In other words, in Føllesdal's theory there is a noema-object split. But such a split is unthinkable for Husserl, for the reduction is meant to reveal precisely that the object is *essentially* related to consciousness, that the object is always the object of a consciousness. "Noema" expresses this link between subject and object. When Føllesdal says that the mark of intentionality is not being directed to an object, but *having a noema,* he has to account for the noema's relation to the object when it has one, and he is thus, according to phenomenology, back at square one, for the noema was precisely to express the link of consciousness to the object. The problem arises because Føllesdal has reified the noema. The result is what Veatch (IL 15) calls confusing a formal sign for an instrumental sign. Of an instrumental sign, Veatch writes that "instead of being something which immediately represents its object to a knowing power, [it] is rather something which has to be known in itself first; and then from this knowledge one has to make some sort of inference to the object of which the idea is presumably a copy or resemblance" (IL 15).

The difference between empty and filled consciousness, then, is not that in one case consciousness refers to an object while in the other it does not. In both empty and filled consciousness there is reference to an object. The difference between empty and filled consciousness is rather, that in the latter the object is filled out by the hyletic data, while in the former it is not. Husserl does not run into the same difficulty that Føllesdal does because the hyletic data are not extranoematic elements to which a "bridge" must be spanned. In Husserl's theory only the telos, the object at infinity, which is the idea of the object completely filled out, is the whole; only the idea is independent, is concrete. All else—hyle, noesis, and noema—comprise *moments* of consciousness and cannot be taken as independent. In Husserl's theory no real break occurs between the "components" of consciousness including noema and hyle.[18] It is not possible to stipulate where hyle ends and noema starts, for the hyle remains ever present in *its original form* even "after" the noema has been conceived by the noesis. The noema *always* has a "lower level"—namely, the hyle, and always implies the hyle. Therefore there is no "gap" between noema and hyle that needs to be bridged.

What Føllesdal has inadvertently done is conflate the notions "object" and "real object." In imagining a centaur, consciousness *is* directed toward an object, only not a *real* object. But if for Husserl the mark or essence of intentionality is objectification, being directed toward an object, and if for Føllesdal consciousness is directed to an object only if there is a real object corresponding to the act of consciousness, then Føllesdal has inadvertently made *reality*, existence of the real object, the mark or criterion of intentionality. This makes the relation of consciousness to its object more static for Føllesdal than it is for Husserl. While for Føllesdal the objectivity of the object is not constituted by consciousness, for Husserl the relation of consciousness to the object is an *act* of objectification, of constituting the objectivity. Since the object is extranoematic for Føllesdal, the relation of consciousness to the object must then be a type of correspondence or a mapping on to the object.

The being directed to or referring to an object, according to this view, is nothing but a kind of "picking out" of the object. That is, real objects, being spatio-temporal, are identifiable, individuated objects that can be located and picked out. Taken in this way, referring is a kind of mapping out and constitutes a finite act; the act of referring comes to an "end" when one has picked out the object referred to. It is akin to directing, say, someone to the water fountain—there is a point of arrival. It seems as if Føllesdal is saying that if an act of consciousness picks out an object in this way, then it can be said to be directed toward an object—otherwise it merely has a noema. According to Husserl, however, the object is identifiable only because of the noema. There can be no extranoematic identifiable object, for all identity requires the noema, an X with predicates, identity being a unity with predicates. The notion of reference as a point of arrival at an object cannot constitute the essence of intentionality, for it presupposes the noema, itself an intentional entity. For Husserl it is illegitimate to claim that consciousness is directed to an object only if the object of consciousness is a real object. According to Husserl, consciousness, whether filled or empty, is always directed to an object. Being directed to the object, however, is not a static relation to the object but a highly specific act of striving for truth—of striving to bring the object to evidence.

(g) Rethinking the Noema-*Sinn* Comparison

According to some philosophers the rapprochement between analytic philosophy and phenomenology draws its legitimation from the similarity between noema and *Sinn*. As Solomon writes:

> The noema as a *Sinn* or meaning now falls into alignment with
> the various concepts of linguistic meaning that have been for-
> mulated and debated in the seventy years since Frege's pio-
> neering efforts. And with this conceptual bridge between two
> initially different conceptions of meaning comes a bridge be-
> tween two philosophical disciplines that have seemed to be mu-
> tually incomprehensible and irreconcilable. [HEA 169]

In the discussions of intentionality as intensionality, of noema and *Sinn*,
generally no mention is made of a striving of the subject to constitute the
object in evidence, the very distinguishing mark of Husserl's notion of
intentionality. While this omission does not invalidate the comparison
between intentionality and intensionality, a closer comparison between
the philosophy of Frege and Husserl can be drawn if the notion of the
subject's striving for truth is taken into account. It will then be seen that
this notion is not only not alien to Frege's thesis of sense and reference,
but is fundamental to it.[19]

(h) Names not Paradigmatic of
Expressions Having Sense
and Reference

When the Fregean notions of sense and reference are discussed by philosophers, on the whole these notions are taken to comprise a thesis
about sentence *parts*. In the articles examined for this chapter,[20] for example, no mention is made of the reference of sentences—namely,
truth-values. *Names* (singular terms) are taken as paradigmatic of expressions having sense and reference: sense is equated with the meaning of
an expression, while the referent is understood to be "that extra-linguis-
tic entity with which the expression has been correlated or which it picks
out" (FTJ 42). But taking "names" to be paradigmatic of sense and reference gives a narrow, truncated view of sense and reference. As Sluga
argues, Frege's article on sense and reference is not fundamentally concerned with *names:* only about one-third (PW 56–62) of the article is devoted to the reference of names, the remaining two-thirds (PW 62–78)
being devoted to the reference of sentences. Its main concern, then, is
with the reference of *sentences*, with truth-values, in other words. "On
Sense and Meaning" was in fact not motivated by a concern with the
workings of ordinary language per se, but by the desire to develop a
formalized language of pure thought modeled after the language of

arithmetic (PW 29). In other words, the article does not even primarily embody a linguistic thesis (GF 158). This is why Sluga writes:

> While it is true that the doctrine of sense and reference and the issues it raises have been a major concern of recent analytic philosophy of language, it is important to keep in mind that Frege's interest in that doctrine differs from the current one in several respects. [GF 157]

Understanding Frege's interest in the doctrine and how this differs from the import recent analytic philosophy of language has ascribed to it is vital to a correct understanding of "sense" and "reference."

It is true that Frege sometimes compares sentences to names. This is so because sentences are saturated entities according to Frege (PW 32), and he sometimes uses the term "name" to mean a complete or saturated entity as opposed to an incomplete or unsaturated entity, such as functional expressions (PW 57). In *this* sense sentences constitute names, as opposed to functional expressions, which do not. But he also uses the term "name" in its more popular sense to mean a sentence part, to mean a singular term. When used in *that* way, equating sentences and names is a mistake, for in that case, although sentences and names are *similar* in that they are both saturated entities, they are not *identical* in nature, according to Frege (GF 160). The referents of sentences and names are, for instance, of different logical types. Furthermore, the reference of a name is dependent on the reference of a sentence and the former can be understood only in context of the latter.

According to Frege, words, including names, have meaning only within the context of a sentence, not in isolation (GA x). But he says that "that which the sign designates [i.e., the referent] . . . may be called the meaning of the sign" (PW 57). In other words, one cannot ask for the referent of a word in isolation. But since sense is the way to the referent—is "the mode of presentation" (PW 57) of the object, of the referent, of the meant, according to Frege—one cannot ask for the sense of a word in isolation either:

> The meaning of a proper name is the object itself which we designate by using it; the idea which we have in that case is wholly subjective; in between lies the sense, which is indeed no longer subjective like the idea, but is yet not the object itself. The following analogy will perhaps clarify these relationships. Somebody observes the Moon through a telescope. I compare the Moon itself to the meaning; it is the object of the observa-

tion, *mediated by the real image projected by the object glass in the interior of the telescope* [my emphasis], and by the retinal image of the observer. *The former I compare to the sense* [my emphasis], the latter is like the idea or experience. The optical image in the telescope is indeed one-sided and dependent upon the standpoint of the observation; but it is still objective, inasmuch as it can be used by several observers. At any rate it could be arranged for several to use it simultaneously. But each one would have his own retinal image. [PW 60]

From this passage it is clear that the sense is the way to the referent, for Frege speaks of the sense as a mediation to the observation, to that which is meant, the referent, which in this case is the moon. Since sense *essentially* is a vehicle, a means to the referent, it cannot be understood without this relation to the referent. As it is in effect the *means* whereby the word is linked with its referent, the sense of a name includes knowledge of its referent; hence, one can no more ask for the sense of a word in isolation than one can ask for the meaning or referent of a word in isolation.

Although sense is the means whereby the word is linked to the referent, the movement from sense to referent everywhere comes about only due to truth. Consider the words of Frege:

The fact that we concern ourselves at all about what is meant by a part of the sentence indicates that we generally recognize and expect a meaning for the sentence itself. . . . But now why do we want every proper name to have not a sense, but also a meaning [i.e., a reference]? Why is the thought not enough for us? Because, and to the extent that, we are concerned with its truth-value. . . . *It is the striving for truth* [my emphasis] that drives us *always* [my emphasis] to advance from sense to the thing meant [i.e., to reference]. [PW 63]

From the above quotation it is clear that the notion of reference cannot be understood without the notion of striving for truth, since the latter motivates the act of referring; it makes the act of referring come about, as it were. But the striving for truth always occurs via or in the sentence. This means that the notion of reference, whether of names or of sentences, must be understood in terms of the workings of the sentence, in terms of the reference of a sentence. The latter are truth-values in Frege's theory. In fact, Sluga argues that "in the *Grundgesetze* he [Frege] singles out the introduction of truth-values as the most significant achievement of the theory of reference" (GF 158). This means that for

Frege the reference of names is subordinate to the reference of sentences. This is also how Tugendhat interprets Frege:

> The significance of the parts of sentences, and in particular of
> names, consists in their contribution to the truth-value of the
> sentences into which they may enter. . . . In this case we
> should have to take the significance of sentences as primary.
> Instead of transferring the characteristics of the significance of
> names to that of sentences, we should reverse the order and
> try to define the significance of names by means of the concept
> with which the significance of sentences is defined. [MBF 180]

It can be appreciated why the name/bearer relation cannot be
taken as paradigmatic of reference in Frege's theory. According to the
name/bearer model, the bearer, however tacitly, is understood to be an
object in the world. The object's identity is afforded by spatio-temporal
predicates. The referent, in other words, is an object with specific identifiable properties. But in Frege's theory the reference of names is in effect "defined" by means of the reference of sentences, and for Frege the
referents of sentences, truth-values, are not objects in the ordinary sense
of the term; they are not entities with determinate qualities (an "X" with
predicates); they are not objects spatio-temporally determined. A truth-
value is a very peculiar sort of entity. Writes Frege:

> Truth is not a quality that answers to a particular kind of sense-
> impressions . . . Being true is not a sensible, perceptible, prop-
> erty. [FLI 5]

In fact, according to Frege:

> In the meaning [i.e., reference] of the sentence all that is spe-
> cific is obliterated. [PW 65]

Furthermore, if it were maintained that Frege construed the sen-
tence-referent relation according to the model of name/bearer, it would
mean that Frege subscribed to a correspondence theory of truth, something he in fact does not:

> It might be supposed from this that truth consists in a corre-
> spondence of a picture to what it depicts. Now a correspon-
> dence is a relation. But this goes against the use of the word

"true," which is not a relative term and contains no indication
of anything else to which something is to correspond. [FLI 3]

And:

In any case, truth does not consist in correspondence of the
sense with something else, for otherwise the question of truth
would get reiterated to infinity. [FLI 4]

The reference of sentences is not to be construed on the model of
linguistics described previously, in which the name "maps onto" or corresponds to an extralinguistic entity. In the reference of sentences there
is no mapping onto or corresponding to anything at all. "The cat is on
the mat" is a categorial object, formed only *in* the judgment. To assert its
truth or falsehood one does not map the sentence onto any object or
state-of-affairs. One cannot say, for example, that one maps the judgment "the cat is on the mat" onto the state-of-affairs that the cat is on the
mat, for the state-of-affairs is also a categorial object, formed in the judgment. One must *judge*—that is, form the judgment— to affirm its truth
or falsehood.

Dummett disagrees with Tugendhat's claim that the reference of a
name is subordinate to the reference of a sentence, for he believes that it
does away with the equation of the referent of a name with its bearer, an
equation Dummett takes to be the prototype of reference. "The equation of the referent of its name with its bearer is just what Tugendhat has
thrown overboard" (DU 201), writes Dummett. He goes on to state:

What constitutes our conceiving it [an object] as a part of external reality is that we take it as being the *referent* of an expression: and "the referents of our words are what we talk *about*."
For Tugendhat, replacing the notion of reference by that of
truth-value potential, all this is lost. [DU 202]

Dummett seems to think that in Tugendhat's position reference
to the real world is *forsaken* in favor of reference to truth-values. But
Tugendhat neither denies the referent of a name to be an object, nor
"replaces" the notion of the reference by that of truth-value potential.
That Tugendhat has no intention of denying that the referent of a name
is an object should be clear from his following assertion:

The significance is, in the case of names, the object referred to.
[MBF 181]

In a footnote to this sentence he adds:

> As has been pointed out to me by Mr. Dummett, it is not
> strictly correct to say that the truth-value potential *is* the object
> referred to. All we claim is that two names that refer to the
> same object have the same truth-value potential. Consequently,
> it would be preferable to say that the truth-value potential of a
> name is, *rather than the object referred to, its reference to that object*
> [my emphasis]. [MBF 181, n. 1]

Tugendhat plainly states, then, that the referent of a name is an
object. He does not want to assimilate the reference of a name to that of
a sentence, but wants, rather, to put the reference of a name into perspective. It is strict adherence to Frege's most important dictum, that the
unit of meaning is a sentence, that motivates Tugendhat's claim that the
reference of names is subordinate to the reference of sentences:

> Thus the fact that the interpretation of significance as truth-
> value potential[21] is adequate while its interpretation as refer-
> ence is inadequate sheds light on the nature of sentences and
> their composition: it can be taken as evidence for the claim
> that the primary semantic unit is the sentence and it can also
> be used to protect this claim from misunderstanding. The con-
> tention that the sentence is the primary unit of meaning does
> not exclude its divisibility into meaningful parts; it only claims
> that the significance, and consequently the sense, of words can-
> not be understood in isolation, but rather consists in their con-
> tribution to the significance or sense of sentences, respectively.
> [MBF 183]

Tugendhat's claim, that although a name can and sometimes *does*
refer to an object, it can do so only via the sentence, accords with Sluga's
interpretation that for Frege there can never be a bare association of a
word and its object. Sluga denies that the name/bearer relationship
could be paradigmatic of reference, because it would assign to empirical
objects a basic role that Frege had not given them, and adds that Frege
"does not regard empirical objects as items of acquaintance that can be
simply named or described" (GF 159). After all, Frege is not a Millsian—
he does not have an associationistic theory of meaning. Needless to say,
Dummett realizes this. But then the manner in which a word does refer
to its object needs to be spelled out and made viable (in a non-Millsian
manner).

The only way to avoid a Millsianism is by saying that in the case of the perception of empirical objects a logical activity has already taken place. This, according to Sluga, is what Frege maintains:

> He [Frege] does not regard empirical objects as items of acquaintance that can be simply named or described. "Observation itself already includes a logical activity" (F, p. 99). It has been one of Frege's assumptions against physiologically oriented psychologism that sensation never presents us with material objects. In the late essay "The Thought" he argues that sensory impressions are necessary but not sufficient for seeing things. Something non-sensory must be added to the impressions and only with that addition do we gain access to the empirical world with its empirical objects (KS, p. 360). [GF 159]

And in Frege's words:

> Sense-perception indeed is often thought to be the most certain, even the sole, source of knowledge about everything that does not belong to the inner world. But with what right?. . . . Sense-impressions alone do not reveal the external world to us. . . . Having visual impressions is certainly necessary for seeing things, but not sufficient. What must still be added is not anything sensible. And yet this is just what opens up the external world for us; for without this non-sensible something everyone would remain shut up in his inner world. [FLI 26–27]

This nonsensory element that must be added to impressions is a logical component. Saying, as Frege does, that observation itself includes a logical activity, is in effect saying that perception is *intentional*. But logical activity occurs in the judgment. Hence the object always occurs in the judgment. As explained in chapters 1 and 2, this is exactly what Husserl argues. It is the nonsensory element at work in the perception of objects that the notion of the reference of the sentence tries to capture. The object occurs in the judgment, and the judgment is guided by and understood in terms of the ideal of the object, the object given in totality.[22] Truth, that to which the sentence refers, is the idea of the object given in its totality. The notion of truth, and, indeed, the function of asserting truth, is motivated by the idea of "filling out" the object: I can only affirm that "the cat is on the mat" is true if I have an idea of how the object is to be filled out.[23] The idea of filling the object out in turn necessarily has within it the ideal of perfect completion, the ideal of the object filled out completely. In other words, truth, the referent of a sentence, is motivated by the idea of the object given in its totality. Truth, then, is an ideal. This point is expressed both clearly and poetically by Amstutz:

> Wenn wir als Kinder die Voralpen sahen, schienen diese uns die Grenze unserer Welt zu sein. Doch als wir wandernd einst auf den Voralpengrat hinaufgekommen waren, sahen wir jenseits tiefer Täler die Hochalpen, und von den nördlichen Hochalpen erblickten wir später die südlichen, usw. Der Horizont ist unabschliessbar. . . . Auch Jaspers hat als Wesen des Bewusstseins gesehen, dass es immerfort transzendiert, weiter und weiter schreitet.
> Die Ausführungen Husserls zeigen nun, dass sein erkenntnistheoretischer Subjektivismus eine Neigung zur Zusammenhangstheorie der Wahrheit hat. "Eine Aussage ist wahr, wenn, und nur wenn sie Teil eines allumfassenden Zusammenhangs von Aussagen ist," so sagt diese Theorie. Und die subjektivistische Erkenntnistheorie mit ihrer Beobachtung von weiteren und weiteren Horizonten kann darum sehr leicht mit dieser Wahrheitstheorie einverstanden sein, sofern nur nie vergessen wird, dass "der allumfassende Zusammenhang von Aussagen" nie als Ganzes und abschliessend erfasst werden kann. Um die Zusammenshangstheorie der Wahrheit diesem erkenntnistheorischen Subjektivismus restlos annehmbar zu machen, müssten wir diese Wahrheitstheorie etwas anders formulieren; etwa so:
> Eine Aussage ist wahr, wenn, und allein wenn sie Teil eines nach Allumfassung strebenden Zusammenhangs von Aussagen ist. [DEJ 7]

It was said, then, that truth comes about via the idea of the object given in its totality. But, as explained in chapter 2, saying that the idea of the object guides any individual judgment concerning an object sounds like idealism. Indeed, the divergent interpretations of Frege's notion of reference can be traced back to a debate in Frege scholarship as to whether Frege was a realist or idealist. Dummett believes that Frege was a realist who "had for idealism not an iota of sympathy" (DU 684), and who in his writings was attempting to counteract and criticize the idealism prevalent in philosophical thought at the time—namely, Hegelianism. According to Dummett, "Frege's realism" played an important part "in bringing about the downfall of Hegelian idealism":

> It is undoubtedly true that the overthrow of Hegelianism was a precondition of advance in philosophy, and, in so far as Frege's realistic philosophy played a part in that, that is also an

ingredient in its historical importance. It is also true that
Frege's realism would have been viewed by Frege himself as
one of the essential features of his philosophical system, and
that his work represents a classic statement . . , of a realistic
theory of meaning [DU 683]

Sluga, on the other hand, refutes this and denies as well that Frege was
either a realist or an anti-idealist. After a careful historical analysis, Sluga
concludes:

Frege's thought was conceived in opposition to this form of
scientific naturalism,[24] and not to a dominant Hegelianism or
idealism, as Dummett has claimed.
    In opposing themselves to scientific naturalism the philoso-
phers of the late nineteenth century were often in sympathy
with some doctrines of the idealists. That is why idealist and rationalist elements can be found in Frege's writings. . . . And
Frege was concerned neither with the formulation of an anti-
idealist philosophy nor with a defence of realism. [GF 14–15]

Sluga's position on Frege's ontological commitment is that the latter had
a realism that was not antithetical to idealism:

If Frege's theory of objectivity can be interpreted in this Kantian sense, we can credit him with an understanding of the
shortcomings of metaphysical realism or Platonism while holding on to the belief in the objectivity of logic and mathematics.
There is a sense in which that position can be called realism
but its realism is not incompatible with idealism: it is itself a
form of idealism. [GF 107]

It is perhaps Dummett's concern to prove Frege to be a naive
realist—that is, one who excludes an idealism—which leads him to take
the name/bearer relation as the prototype of reference.[25] As Sluga argues, "the claim that after 1891 the name/bearer relationship is the paradigm of Frege's semantics and that his theory of sense and reference is
primarily meant as a theory of referring expressions has the effect of
assigning a basic role to empirical objects." He adds that "it seems
doubtful that such objects could ever have played an important role in
Frege's thought" (GF 159).

Dummett's belief that Frege is a realist leads him to see Tugendhat as eradicating any realistic strand in Frege. That is, Dummett
has not worked out a notion of realism that does not exclude idealism; to

him realism and idealism mutually exclude each other. He cannot conceive of the type of realism Sluga speaks of, a realism that "is itself a form of idealism." That Dummett has no articulated version of a viable idealism is clear from his writing the following:

> In Frege's day the kind of idealism that was everywhere prevalent in the philosophical schools was infected with a psychologism through and through: it was not until it had been decisively overthrown that it became possible to envisage a nonpsychologistic[26] version of idealism. *(Indeed, it is not even yet certain that such a version is possible)* [my emphasis]. [DU 684]

So, when Dummett sees idealist trends in Tugendhat's interpretation of Frege, he cannot help but feel the threat of an idealism that excludes realism.

If we are to remain true to Frege's texts, we must keep in mind the dictum that the unit of meaning is the sentence, and work from whole to part, and not vice versa. It is in this way that we must observe and articulate the interdependence of the reference of names and sentences. Tugendhat admirably captures this point:

> Granted on the one hand that names and sentences form two different semantic categories and on the other hand that they have something in common, we must require of an adequate account of what they have in common that it should not obliterate their differences. This requirement is only met by the present account. Why is this so? Why is it that if we interpret the significance of sentences setting out from names, one cannot help assimilating sentences to names, whilst names are not assimilated to sentences when we interpret the significance of names setting out from sentences? The reason is that we have here an instance of a functional connection between part and whole. In any such instance, for example a tool, machine, or organism, the part can only be defined by its relation to the function of the whole and not *vice versa*. Since the relation of part to whole is functional, the reference to the whole in the definition of the part does not result in the assimilation of the properties of the part to the properties of the whole. On the other hand, any attempt to define the whole by means of its parts is bound to result in a non-functional account of the whole which either assimilates its properties to the properties of the part or defines it as a mere conglomeration of its parts, or both. [MBF 183]

In speaking of a *striving* for truth (PW 63), Frege introduces a "subjective," purposive element into the notions of sense and reference.[27] That is, saying that we *strive* for truth implies that we aim for *achieving* truth, and this implies that we can discern when we do and do not "have" truth, that, at least in principle, we *know* when something is true. While for Frege truth is objective—independent of human acts of judging and asserting—and a claim is true or false whether we know it or not (LI 25), we cannot *know* a thought to be true or false "apart from making an act of judgment or assertion" (GF 115). In other words, the striving for truth is a subjective act that allows us to *know* a sentence to be true. Striving for truth is actualizing truth, which is a bringing to evidence, or, to use a Husserlian phrase, is a "filling out." According to Frege—and this is so for Husserl as well—going from the thought, the sense of the sentence, to truth, the referent of the sentence, is an act of going from one level to a higher level:

> The relation of the thought to the True may not be compared with that of subject to predicate.
> Subject and predicate (understood in the logical sense) are just elements of thought; they stand on *the same level* [my emphasis] for knowledge. By combining subject and predicate, one reaches only a thought, never passes from sense to meaning [reference], never from a thought to its truth-value. One moves at *the same level but never advances from one level to the next* [my emphasis]. A truth-value cannot be part of a thought, any more than, say, the Sun can, for it is not a sense but an object. [PW 64]

This striving, this dynamic aspect, is embodied in many notions of Frege's system, for his is a well-integrated system in which each concept is intricately linked with the others. It can be seen, for instance, in Frege's notion of *function*. Sluga writes that "the characterization of truth-value as *Bedeutung* (references) of sentences is . . . inseparable from the characterization of concepts as functions" (GF 145).

(i)   Function

Frege divides the sentence into saturated and unsaturated components—that is, into complete and incomplete components, respectively. By dividing a sentence into saturated and unsaturated components, Frege solves the problem of how sentence parts are "held together."

Incomplete or unsaturated components Frege calls functions, a term he borrows from mathematics but modifies.[28] According to Frege, a function is not an inert entity: it *connects* and *correlates* (GF 141). Specifically, just as a mathematical function correlates numbers with numbers, a functional expression in a sentence correlates objects with truth-values (GF 141). In effect, then, a function has truth as its *aim*. This means that a "subjective" act of judging is implied in the notion of function, no less than in the notions of sense and reference, for function too is involved with a striving for truth. This is to be expected, for while functions correlate objects to truth-values, presumably they do not do so on their own accord—that is, they cannot correlate themselves. Somehow, "somebody" must do the correlating. Indeed, in his earlier use of the term "function" Frege meant *operation*, which suggests an operator. But a treatment as to "who" does the correlating is lacking.

Dummett suggests that the notion of function cannot be introduced "without simultaneously introducing that of application of a function to an object" (DU 253), and he adds that some authors consider that "the notion of the application of a function to an object" is "spurious and mythical" (DU 255). While Dummett does not consider this a spurious or mythical notion, he does nothing to dispel its mythical nature, for he gives no satisfactory account of the process of application. He is probably unable to do so, because this would require an appeal to a "subjective" process. To avoid falling into a psychologism, appeal would have to be made to a *transcendental* subjectivity. But Dummett would probably take an appeal to *any* subjective act, even a transcendental act, to be indicative of idealism, or of psychologism. Hence, we find him writing:

> And how are we to explain the notion of "application"? What curious property does an object have to render it capable of "yielding" a number when *"applied to"* [my emphasis] a number? We know that water will produce steam when poured on to a fire: but *obviously* [my emphasis] we are not meant to think of the application of a function to a number as something that *we do* [my emphasis] to it, nor as its yielding a number as something that it does when brought into contact with an argument. [DU 251]

But this "we" that Dummett speaks of could be a transcendental subject. In other words, here Husserl's phenomenology could complement Frege's logic, for the latter has left the notion of function ungrounded, something that an explicit appeal to transcendental subjectivity would remedy. As discussed throughout the present work, grounding logic in a transcendental subject, properly understood, does not imply psychologism or idealism. Such an approach would not be incongruous with Frege's basic stance, for while Frege does not appeal to a transcendental subjectivity per se, he *does* seem to have an *implicit* transcendentalism. According to Angelelli "Frege gives some hints of weak or transcendental subjectivity" (SO 234). What prevented Frege from appealing to transcendental subjectivity outright is his difficulty in conceiving of a subjectivity that is not empirical. Dummett is quite like him in this respect. According to Angelelli:

> Frege usually characterizes *subjective* as that which is *verschieden für verschiedene Menschen*. . . . This is precisely *psychological* subjectivity as opposed to transcendental subjectivity. . . . Psychological subjectivity is also the *strict* sense of "subjective." . . . I think it is appropriate to call this the "strong" sense as well. It seems that Frege has understood "subjective" only in this way, leaving aside the minor exceptions we refer to in the present section. "Subjective" means for Frege *psychology, personal sensations, personal feelings*, and so on. . . . GED indicates that this was Frege's understanding of that term until the end of his life. [SO 245, n. 20]

Other authors too have noted the necessity of a transcendental account in Frege's work specifically and in the analytic tradition generally. Bell, for example, writes the following:

> We have introduced what might be called a *transcendental* element into our account. Frege's approach, by contrast, was essentially *mundane*. . . . In this general approach Frege has set the tone, the aims, and the methods in virtually all subsequent work in philosophical logic and semantics, at least in the English-speaking world. Russell and the early Wittgenstein, and later Quine, Tarski, Carnap, Church, and Davidson, with only minor deviations, have trod the Fregean path. The major exception has been the author of the *Philosophical Investigations* (though one ought to mention here those, like Grice and Strawson, who have been strongly influenced by him). [FTJ 78–79]

And:

> [Wittgenstein] showed that such an approach [a transcendental approach] must needs assume there is a community of lan-

guage users whose linguistic activities are not cut off from other, non-linguistic habits, customs, and activities. Language, Wittgenstein maintained, is not a formal calculus but a human tool whose construction and function become incomprehensible when it is divorced from the "forms of life" in which it is used. It is indeed precisely in order to restore the notion of a language to the context in which it belongs, from which it has been removed by philosophers, and wherein only it can be adequately understood, that Wittgenstein introduces the notion of a "language-*game*." [FTJ 79]

Bell goes on to write that "Hintikka has recently complained that the 'transcendental point of view,' which concentrates upon the human activities essentially involved in our obtaining whatever information we have, 'is notoriously absent from recent philosophizing' " (FTJ 79).

In sum, while in the Frege-Husserl comparison Frege's notion of *Sinn* is compared to Husserl's notion of noema, these notions are generally treated in a static manner. In this chapter it has been argued that both Fregean *Sinn* and Husserlian noema are dynamic notions that express a striving of the subject for truth. Not only is a subject implied in Frege's logic, but there are hints of transcendental subjectivity in Frege. Once this is appreciated, a closer affinity between Husserl's work and that of Frege can be seen. Such a comparison, which is more palatable to the phenomenologist because it does not ignore the reduction, deepens the understanding of certain logical notions found in Frege's thought, for the reference to transcendental subjectivity allows them to be grounded. This would also lend credence to the claim that transcendental logic is the ideal of formal logic.

Epilogue

T his work concerns itself with reconciling Husserl's description of phenomenology as a rationality, a purely formal, apodictic science, with his description of phenomenology as a science that understands itself through the *life-world* and as a science that deals with *life*.

In order to bring out the truly formal dimension of phenomenology, Husserl's characterization of phenomenology as a transcendental logic was presented first. It was explained how, in Husserl's view, traditional formal logic, implicitly presupposing the world and experience, had not achieved the ideal of purity under which it labored. It is transcendental logic that achieves a purity by taking its analysis to the foundation of logic where no world is presupposed, by taking its analysis to the pure transcendental ego. But if traditional formal logic aims at a purity that transcendental logic will supply, then transcendental logic is the idea of traditional formal logic.

It was shown how, according to Husserl, the pure transcendental ego that grounds logic is also the center of *life*. It was explained that, unlike Kant, Husserl is able to achieve a true transcendentalism by taking into account *life*, for only in the life-world is all objectivity overcome. For Husserl the pure transcendental ego is literally living; it involves the living body. This introduces a subjective experiential factor into logic, which to many formal logicians spells the threat of psychologism, the reduction of logical laws to empirical, de facto laws. It was shown that when speaking of the laws of logic, even when grounded in experience, it is not a matter of describing what the psyche as a matter of fact does, but rather a matter of describing necessary laws.

It was then demonstrated how Husserl's position differs from a kind of Kantian idealism in which the ego imposes a necessity on experience. For Husserl, the ego's necessity is part and parcel of experience. The transcendental ego is necessary *being* and its being is the *act* of experiencing. In other words, the necessity of mind does not destroy facticity in general, but necessity and facticity are interwoven in Husserl's philosophy. The essential interinvolvement of facticity and necessity in phenomenology was demonstrated by resolving the apparent conflict that Carr brings to light between the teleological-historical and the essential approaches in Husserl's phenomenology, as well as by resolving the apparent conflict brought out by Bachelard between Husserl's description of the transcendental ego as self-criticism and as absolute being. It was shown that the necessary status of the ego can accommodate life phenomena, phenomena that would seem to destroy the absolute, pure status required of an ego that is the source of logical laws. Specifically, it was demonstrated that the notion of pure transcendental ego can accommodate the phenomenon of the alter ego, of death, and such phenomena associated with the living body as the unconscious and desire, phenomena presented in Freudian psychology. In the process it was shown that in the notion of transcendental ego, logic and psychology come together, that phenomenology is both a logic and a pure psychology.

In short, the present work argues that the theoretical stance Husserl's phenomenology embraces, the ego-cogito-cogitatum, is not divorced from life. The .structure of the cogito was shown to be the structure of life; the "ego-cogito, ergo sum," an expression of *life*.

In reconciling the purely formal with the life aspects of phenomenology, the genetic and static phenomenological methods were contrasted. It was explained that the genetic approach is a second-order reflective act, which has the first phenomenological reflection as its object. It constitutes a phenomenology of phenomenology. While a static approach relates objectivities to the transcendental ego, a genetic approach asks that this relating be inserted into our living intentions. The genetic approach, then, expresses the phenomenological method par excellence, for it is an active seeing—a seeing of what we were intending— a seeing explication of our cognitive acts. The living realm, in which objectivity is overcome, and the formal objective realm, the realm at which self-understanding is expressed, can be related properly only by means of the genetic method, for only in the genetic approach does the *preobjective* level become properly understood. In other words, our analysis cannot merely "end" with the preobjective level, but the preobjective level too is in need of understanding. In inserting our act of relating objectivities to the transcendental ego into our living intentions, the preobjective level itself becomes properly understood.

For instance, from a static perspective the description of the transcendental ego as the nonwakeful, preobjective living ground of the objective will seem to contradict the description of the transcendental ego as self-criticism, as self-understanding, as the latter is necessarily wakeful and reflective. This is so because from the static perspective, the transcendental will seem to be one level. Viewed from the genetic phenomenological perspective, however, the transcendental is understood to be not one level, but an interplay of levels. A truly transcendental approach, the genetic approach, shows that the transcendental *is* an activity, not a "point," and shows the transcendental to involve an interplay of preobjective and objective levels. Hence, as the preobjective transcendental ego is the ground of the objective, it is implicated in the objective, it is not cut off from the objective. In effect the transcendental is also the objective, but *the objective properly understood* in terms of its preobjective ground. When the objective is understood transcendentally, it is no longer that which alienates pure subjectivity. In understanding the object the transcendental ego understands and hence constitutes itself.

In the true transcendental perspective, then, paradoxically, method and object merge: the transcendental ego is a mode of understanding whereby it constitutes itself. The transcendental is a mode of understanding and the transcendental ego actualizes itself in the act of understanding:

> Phenomenology will be primarily a clarification of the transcendental ego. But the latter subsists only in the actual intentional experience. [DeM 335]

And:

> The ego is therefore the primordial fact, the *Urtatsache*, and the absolute transcendental foundation, but its determination remains an infinite task. The flow of experience is what must effectively realize this task, and the transcendental ego will be at the point of its constitutive fullness when the object is at the point of its intuitive fullness, i.e., when reason and truth are correlatively realized. The ego therefore needs to live in rational acts which affirm its constitutive autonomy and hence its freedom. [DeM 336]

Cogito is not a static structure or utterance, but a project, a mode of Being, which must be constantly revived and brought to ever-new levels of actualization.

Since the transcendental ego actualizes itself in the act of understanding, understanding is an act of self-responsibility. But the cogito that was shown to have the structure of life was also shown to reflect the structure of intersubjectivity. In its very being, then, the ego embraces an ethics. Its was argued that self-knowledge does not go against freedom, spontaneity, or creativity, but is in fact essential to them, that to divorce rationality from life is to rob both life and rationality of their significance, their power as well as their beauty. In short, an attempt was made to present the holistic concept of rationality that Husserl's writings embody.

It was argued also that Frege's logic contains elements of transcendental subjectivity, which brings it closer to Husserl's holistic concept of rationality than is generally believed and lends credence to de Muralt's claim that "formal logic is the factical example which enables intentional analysis to anticipate the ideal exemplar, transcendental logic" (DeM 355).

Notes

Introduction

[1] The term "soul" is here not to be understood in an objectivistic, naturalistic sense. "Phenomenology," says Husserl, "frees us from . . . the idea of an ontology of the soul which could be analogous to physics" (C 265). In other words, phenomenology intends a "definite removal of the objectivistic ideal from the science of the soul" (C 257). See also chapter 4, section f, in which the relation between psychology and phenomenology is discussed.

[2] See for example C. Perelman's *The New Rhetoric and the Humanities*, chapter 4 (NRH 62–71). Husserl's phenomenology would fall into what Perelman calls a monism. But phenomenology is a monism that, if properly understood, is at once a pluralism. That is, a genuine pluralism is a position open to various standpoints. This openness to various standpoints requires a transcendental ego:

> One requires, however, if I am able to speak of alternate conceptual schemes, that I must be able to translate the others into my own; or mine into someone else's. This requirement has nothing to do with the primacy of the English language or, for that matter, of any other language. What it requires is that the languages must be mutually translatable. But when I assert this, I am not taking the "internal" standpoint, but rather the "external" standpoint of a transcendental ego, for whom any language is as good as any other, before whose gaze all possible worlds are spread out and none is more his own than any other. The transcendental ego's is no standpoint: all possible standpoints are arraigned before its gaze. The transcendental ego has no "home" language. [PTP xxviii]

And:

> But to be able to survey all possible points of view, conceptual

frameworks, languages objectively—as making sense to each other, therefore as commensurable (and mutually translatable), one needs to take up a stance, which is none other than that of a transcendental ego. [PTP xxviii]

3 Husserl writes in the *Crisis* that the "crisis" of European culture was due to "the *apparent failure of rationalism*" (C 299), and that "the reason for the failure of a rational culture . . . lies not in the essence of rationalism itself but solely in its being rendered superficial, in its entanglement in 'naturalism' and 'objectivism' " (C 299). We can take Husserl to consider Nazism, which is an instance of totalitarianism, to be a manifestation of the European crisis. Husserl says that the crisis of Europe has only two escapes, one of which is "the downfall of Europe in its estrangement from its own rational sense of life, its fall into hostility toward the spirit and into barbarity," the other being "the rebirth of Europe from the spirit of philosophy through a heroism of reason" (C 299). The former of these two escapes characterizes Nazism aptly.

4 It is certainly not a powerful enough motive for building a just society. As Robert Solomon states, "The problem with all such justifications [that appeal to prudence or enlightened self-interest] . . . is that they tend to fail just when they are needed most" (MGL 22). Perhaps to some, though, prudence is the only acceptable reason.

5 This is how *Plato* portrays the Sophists. There are, however, more sympathetic portrayals of the Sophists and one can even argue that there is truth to what the Sophists say. But this will be touched on briefly later (p. 129 and footnote 14 of chapter 5). For now , it is sufficient to characterize them in this way to show what Plato was reacting against.

6 While Plato agrees with the Sophists that natural science of the time did not yield knowledge, this is so, according to him, because it was not genuine science or rationality at all. Natural science did not meet the ideal of science on two counts: (i) it was not in touch with real Being—it did not have as its domain the ideas, but phenomena—and (ii) its ultimate premises were not first principles, but were claims concerning phenomena.

7 Such speculative accounts may or may not be true—that is, founded on insight—but they can only be *verified*, in Husserl's view, through descriptive analysis.

8 While the link is pointed out on pp. 209ff., in a sense this entire work is concerned with working out the relation between science and value in a nonmetaphysical manner.

9 In other words, Husserl thinks *value* can be an object of knowledge in the strict sense.

10 See also pp. 173ff.

11 Concerning this notion of all being and knowledge being on par, see the quotation from Koyré's *From the Closed World to the Infinite Universe*, p. 174.

12 But even after forging the link between world and ego via God, it is still a matter of *inferring* knowledge of the world from knowledge of the existence of

the ego. In other words, in proving that the ego is the ground of all knowledge, Descartes already appeals to the method that he is to ground—i.e., inference is part of the scientific method.

[13] Fink's cautionary essay in the *Crisis* (C 385ff.) regarding the unconscious is dealt with in chapter 4, section g.

[14] This is explained in chapter 4, section g, esp. pp. 108ff., and chapter 6, section h, esp. pp. 198ff.

[15] When Husserl is charged with Platonism, it is precisely such a separation of fact and essence that he is being accused of. See, for example, the quotation from Palmer's work on p. 207, n. 27, in which he criticizes Husserl's essentialism. According to Palmer, Husserl denies "the temporality of being itself and assert[s] a realm of ideas above the flux" (P 127).

[16] On pp. 136ff. it is explained how Husserl's phenomenological method reflects this belief.

[17] For support of this claim and a response to the possible objection that this makes of Husserl's phenomenology a speculative system not unlike that of Hegel, see pp. 160ff.

[18] This will be discussed in chapter 5 where professor Carr's claim that the hermeneutic method is not only foreign to Husserl's philosophy but is contrary to his method of "essential seeing" is also considered. Carr's claim, one shared by many Husserl scholars, is crucial because it transposes Husserl into a Platonist, which precludes a proper grasp of Husserl's notion of rationality.

[19] See chapter 5, section k, and chapter 6, section f.

[20] See pp. 161ff.

[21] This is touched upon in chapter 5, section k.

[22] Phenomenology of phenomenology constitutes the genetic approach to phenomenology (see pp. 202ff.). For a brief overview of the consequences of the genetic approach, see the Epilogue.

Chapter One

[1] "The whole of formal consequence-logic, the logic of analytic necessities, can be seen from the point of view of noncontradiction" (FTL 331 [290]).

[2] For Kant, who introduced the terms "analytic" and "synthetic," "analytic" was not synonymous with "a priori" or "necessary," for synthetic claims could also be a priori or necessary; e.g., "every event has a cause." Hence, Kant maintained a distinction between analytic and synthetic claims on the one hand, and necessary and contingent claims on the other. However, in present-day logic, the two distinctions tend to be collapsed, and it is generally assumed that "analytic propositions are necessary and . . . all non-analytic propositions are contingent" (ITL 161).

[3] It has not achieved scientific status because it has not analyzed certain of its basic concepts to their source. For Husserl the ideal of science is one in which none of its concepts is taken for granted.

⁴ Some authors, such as Carr, deny that Husserl employs the hermeneutic approach in *Formal and Transcendental Logic*, maintaining that Husserl's phenomenology, being a philosophy of *essences*, is incompatible with hermeneutics. This is discussed in detail in chapter 5.

⁵ Husserl begins his analysis of the term "logos" by looking at the role it plays in Plato's thought. But according to Husserl, for Plato logic as theory of science was not a discipline distinct from the act of philosophizing.

⁶ According to Kneale and Kneale, "The word 'logic' did not acquire its modern sense until some 500 years later, when it was used by Alexander of Aphrodisias; but the scope of the study later called logic was determined by the contents of the *Organon*" (KK 23).

⁷ One might argue that this is a naive reading of Plato's theory of Ideas. Nevertheless Aristotle's critique of the theory of Ideas *is* based on this interpretation of the theory.

⁸ This gives rise to an unavoidable ambiguity in the use of the word "logic." Logic is at once a science and a theory of science. So "logic" could refer to the broader "motive," i.e., theory of science, or to the narrower products of this motive, such as, apophantics, the formal study of the judgment, formal ontology, and so forth.

⁹ In the *Categories* Aristotle writes:

> All substance appears to refer to some particular thing. In the
> case of primary substances, it is unquestionably true that it
> does so, since what it refers to is a single individual [PA 141]

See also book Λ of the *Physics*. According to Ross, in this book "more perhaps than any other book . . . he [Aristotle] emphasizes the primary reality of the individual thing" (AS xviii). While from the Husserlian perspective Aristotle is correct in making primary substance the individual, he is wrong in not having "purified" the notion of individual. Further, while Husserl considers him correct in having made "life" his concern, he considers Aristotle to have failed in purifying that notion also.

¹⁰ In the *Metaphysics* Aristotle writes, "that which is primarily and *is* simply . . . must be substance" (AS 64). But primary substance in his view is the concrete individual, the living individual. Hence in effect he takes living nature as the paradigm of reality. In the *Categories* (PA 137), for instance, he gives as examples of primary substance "a particular man" and "a particular horse."

¹¹ According to Bambrough, Aristotle's "search for true substance is the search for what *must* be the logical subject of a proposition if it is to be accorded the status in thought and speech that belong to it in the order of being" (PA 26).

¹² It must be understood that Aristotle is not being criticized for wanting to study logic within the context of disclosing reality, for Husserl too ultimately sees logic within the context of truth. But what Aristotle is being criticized for is deciding too quickly what reality is. Whereas for Aristotle reality is the concrete individual, for Husserl this individual is not the grounding reality but is itself constituted. In other words, Aristotle moves back to truth and reality too

quickly, as it were. On page 29 it is pointed out that although it may seem as if Husserl, like Aristotle, says that S and p are linked in the judgment because they are linked in the world, an explanation as to why this is not so follows on pp. 29ff. See also chapter 2, section 1.

[13] Bochenski writes that "generally speaking they [the Stoics]everywhere show traces of the same spirit as Aristotle's, only in a much sharper form, that spirit being the spirit of *formalized* logic" (HFL 108).

[14] The notion of a purely formal logic was, of course, developed simultaneously by Husserl's contemporary, Frege, but he seems to have misunderstood what Husserl was doing (SO 97) and was critical of Husserl's method, claiming that it psychologized logic in the *Philosophy of Arithmetic.*

[15] Of course, the concept of a purely formal logic was alien neither to the Stoics, nor to Duns Scotus, but the insight did not prevail, as Husserl points out (FTL 49 [43]; 82 [72]). In other words, there are, as it were, two histories of thought: the history of individual thinkers and that which is emphasized over time, which becomes the "tradition."

[16] For a fuller discussion of this method, see pp. 52ff., chapter 5, sections f and g, pp. 127–40.

[17] Not that complete legitimation is in fact possible, but if it were, *this* would not be the way to achieve it.

[18] That is, they generally ignore a "subjective" doing. At times objective notions in the tradition may be explained by appeal to a subjective doing, but it is not recognized as such.

[19] In present-day texts on formal logic, there is a tendency to consider propositions in their purely objective formal dimensions. It is generally accepted that there are such "entities" as propositions and that logic deals with propositions in their purity on at least three levels: syntax, semantics, and truth. Legitimation of speaking of propositions and their various levels does not, on the whole, form a part of the texts on formal logic. At most the proposition is identified by contrast to the sentence, e.g., by pointing out how different sentences can express the same proposition. Legitimation in any deeper sense must find expression outside the texts on formal logic and is left to "philosophical logic." One expects that introductory texts on formal logic reflect what formal logic is in the eyes of contemporary philosophy, its function, its importance, and so forth. Hence one gets the sense that legitimation does not form part of formal logic per se, that logic can be "mastered" and "practiced" by the student without legitimation of its basic concepts, and that legitimation is of interest and concern to the "professional philosopher" only. For Husserl this is unthinkable. In his view formal logic, of too great an importance to be left to the professional philosopher, is in principle of fundamental importance to every person. Husserl, then, would maintain that for those who study formal logic legitimation must accompany introduction of the notions of logic.

[20] That is, since the true aim of logic or apophantics is the method of *science*, a method that reveals truth, its interest lies in the conditions of truth, i.e., the distinct judgment as a condition of possible truth.

²¹ Chapter 2, sections f to k.

²² Examples of nonsense and countersense are, respectively, "king and or because" and "this circle is a square."

Chapter Two

¹ It makes no difference whether we use judging, dreaming, imagining, or perceiving, for example, to study the nature of mind qua mind (Husserl's aim), for all these acts are acts of mind and as such will display the essence of mind. However, it will be shown later (chapter 2, section i) that using the judgment as example is rather fortuitous because it is in fact *the* mode of intentionality. Had we studied intentionality by examining, say, dreaming, we would have been led back to the judgment, for the judgment, understood in its proper, phenomenological sense, is found within *all* mental acts, according to Husserl. Husserl writes:

> This teleological structure of intentional life, as a universally
> Objectivating life, is indicated by the fact that object and judg-
> ment (in the widest sense) belong together, and by the univer-
> sality with which we can freely submit any already-given object
> to our categorial actions. For that reason moreover (and this is
> another index of that same teleology), the predicative judg-
> ment gains universal significance for psychic life. [FTL 263–64
> (232)]

(See also TIHP 62ff.) This will be considered also in chapter 4, section g, when the link between life and the judgment is worked out. The study of the judgment as a means of studying the mind qua mind is fortuitous too in that the judgment has been studied *formally* and mind qua mind must be studied *formally* (FTL 212) as well, since its properties are not tied to any particular content per se, yet are revealed in all its contents.

² According to Husserl the judgment *always* has a modality (belief character), but this need not be explicitly stated. Modalities are ego-decisions for Husserl (EJ 271).

³ This is not a question Brentano asked himself, for he was satisfied that matter was the mark of intentionality. But for Husserl, as will be explained shortly, presentation or matter is not the essence of intentionality but is itself the result of a deeper intentionality.

⁴ Karl Popper, "What is Dialectic?," *Mind*, n.s., 49, 1940.

⁵ In other words, Husserl here sounds like Aristotle.

⁶ Intentional analysis aims precisely at an analysis of such a history of sense genesis (FTL 207ff. [184ff.]). This is why phenomenological analysis is sometimes compared to archeology, since the former, like the latter, involves a type of

unearthing. The sense genesis that phenomenology aims at is, of course, a *logical*, not a psychological, genesis.

⁷ Intentionality, turning toward something and making that something the explicit object of attention, is an act that can be reiterated. Reiteration is part of the essence of objectification.

⁸ We get only a glimpse here. Later (pp. 47ff.) this will be discussed in more detail.

⁹ That being related to an object is a striving conforms to Husserl's claim that the transcendent object is truly transcendent, i.e., transcendence expresses itself as a *striving* instead of a having once and for all. "Where the dator intuition is of a *transcending* character, the objective factor cannot come to be adequately given; what can alone be given here is the *Idea* of such a factor," writes Husserl (I 367 [298]).

¹⁰ Husserl says the same in FTL 285 [251] and FTL 234 [207].

¹¹ Husserl cautions us, however, against understanding this in the Humean way. Belief is not based on the mere force of a datum, but is based on thematic or structural considerations. While a hallucination may, for example, be as forceful as a sense perception, it will nevertheless not be confused with reality, because it does not fit into the broader structure of our sense experience.

¹² Contrary to Brentano, presentation, which is an act of predication, is not the lowest act of intentionality, according to Husserl. Hence, Husserl maintains that intentionality must be characterized differently than the way in which Brentano characterizes it.

¹³ See chapter 6, section i.

¹⁴ That is, the lower levels constitute the field to which the ego can direct its attention and on which it can exert its acts of objectification to achieve ever-higher levels of objectivity.

¹⁵ Cf. Carnap: "objects on higher levels are not constructed by mere summation, but . . . are *logical complexes*. The object *state*, for example, will have to be constructed in this constructional system out of psychological processes, but it should by no means be thought of as a sum of psychological processes" (A 9).

Chapter Three

¹ This is not a position in which all truths are reduced to necessary truths, in which nothing truly new ever confronts one. It is not the case that one knows everything implicitly from the start, that the given in its totality, or even in part, is implicitly known. Rather, what is given "*contains*" something "implicit," which one can draw out or make explicit by *looking* at it. Thus the given qua given truly has the sense "something new for me."

² Nicolai Hartmann's "Gesetz des Gegenstandes der Erkenntnis" might be mentioned as a modern example of objectivism:

Von hier aus kann man nun . . . das Gesetz des Gegenstandes

der Erkenntnis so formulieren: der Gegenstand der Erkenntnis
geht in seinem Gegenstandsein nicht auf, seine Seinsweise ist
eine übergegenständliche. Oder auch: er ist, was er ist,
unabhängig von seinem Gegenstandsein, er ist es an sich. Darin
eben unterscheidet er sich vom Gegenstand des Denkens, des
Urteils, der Meinung, der Phantasie. [KS 19]

3 The aim in this chapter is to present what *Husserl* understands the effect of
these philosophers to have been on the history of thought, rather than attempt
to understand what these philosophers "really meant." The latter approach
would involve us in so many intricacies of the respective philosophies that it
would require an in-depth, independent study of each. Hence throughout this
chapter *Husserl's* description of what these philosophers maintained will be frequently cited, rather than the philosophers themselves. It might be pointed out
in passing that according to Husserl all philosophers really aim at the same
thought: all philosophy aims to become phenomenology, according to him.
Hence Husserl reads Descartes, Hume, Kant, and others, as "really meaning" to
achieve phenomenology. Even his own phenomenology is not yet true phenomenology but is striving to become genuine phenomenology, according to Husserl.
It is interesting to note that Simone Weil as well thinks that all philosophy aims to
express the same thought:

One generally sees only conjectures in philosophy. What produces this opinion are the contradictions between the systems
and within each system. It is generally believed that each philosophy has a system that contradicts all others. Now, quite far
from this being the case, there exists a philosophical tradition
that is truly as ancient as humanity and that, one must hope,
will last as long as humanity will; from this tradition, as from a
common source, are inspired, it is true, not all those who call
themselves philosophers but several among them, so that their
thought is nearly the same. Plato is no doubt the most perfect
representative of this tradition; the *Bhagavad-Gita* is inspired
by the same tradition, and one can easily find Egyptian and
Chinese texts that can be named alongside these. In Europe in
modern times one must cite Descartes and Kant; among the recent thinkers, Langneau and Alain in France and Husserl in
Germany. This philosophic tradition is what we call philosophy.
Far from being able to reproach it for its differences, it is one,
eternal, and not susceptible to progress. The sole renewal of
which it is capable is that of expression, when a man expresses
himself to those around him in terms that are related to the
conditions of the epoch, the civilization, and the environment
in which he lives. It is desirable that such a transformation take
place from age to age, and this is the only reason that makes it

worth the trouble to write on this subject after Plato wrote.
[SW 406]

⁴ For reasons to be discussed later in this chapter, of the three he considers Hume to have come closest to phenomenology.

⁵ It will be shown later that in all three cases this includes the meaning of rationality with its various concepts and notions, including the pure categories.

⁶ Spiegelberg, in his glossary of phenomenological terms, "defines" the different levels of constitution in the following manner:

> Constitution, phenomenological: the act by which an object is
>   built up in consciousness; also what is so constituted 71,
>   99, 130–31, 706–8
>   —, active and passive 130–31
>   —, transcendental: constitution originating in transcenden-
>   tal consciousness 130–31
>   See also Urkonstitution [PM 741]

And:

> Urkonstitution, primal constitution (Husserl): the prime level of
>   constitution, i.e., the constitution of inner time 131 [PM
>   755]

⁷ While a radical skepticism is found in Augustine's philosophy, unlike Husserl, St. Augustine does not build his philosophy on that skepticism.

⁸ Husserl's use of the term "apparently" can be explained as follows. The body as physical object is constituted by the ego through the living body. The ego is not identical to the physical body it has constituted, and hence in a *certain* way *is* an abstraction from the pure physical body. But this claim can be safely made only if it is understood that the ego has an inextricable link to the body, that the ego "in" the living body constituted the physical body in the first place, and this Descartes does not see.

⁹ Cf. Martin Buber: "So they build their ark or have it built, and they name the ark *Weltanschauung*, and seal up with pitch not only its cracks but also its windows. But outside are the waters of the living world" (DL 90).

¹⁰ In maintaining that the sense of the world is constituted by the ego, the phenomenologist is able to avoid this position. Hence the ego always has its bond with the world, the ego is always "at" the world, according to the phenomenologist.

¹¹ Husserl writes the following:

> This *evidence is . . . related to the whole life of consciousness.*
> Thanks to evidence, the life of consciousness has an *all-perva-*

sive teleological structure, a pointedness toward "reason" and even a pervasive tendency toward it. [FTL 160 (143)]

¹² Although Hume is dealing with various objective categories such as "cause and effect," what is basically at issue is the notion of "object." That is, Hume's claim that there is no necessary connection between cause and effect is basically an expression of his belief that objects do not have essences. Indeed, if objects had essences, the latter would determine the necessity of connections between objects, analogous to the way in which the meanings of ideas determine the necessity of the connection between ideas. In short: if objects had essences their interaction would be essential. Hence that the argument in this chapter is sometimes framed in terms of "cause and effect," and at other times in terms of the notion of "object," is not indicative of a discontinuity in the train of thought. The same issue is fundamentally being addressed.

¹³ That is, he did not think that any of the objective categories, categories used to describe reality, pertained to the ego.

¹⁴ Kant only partially follows Hume's transcendental turn, according to Husserl (C 97). Kant does not share Hume's extreme skepticism and so his questions do not display the radicalism necessary to achieve a true transcendentalism (C 97).

¹⁵ Very minimally, that which is combined must lie within one and the same understanding.

¹⁶ If the "I" *were* known, it would be known *before* we knew the external world, for the transcendental unity of apperception *precedes* knowledge of the external world and is its a priori ground or condition. In that case, self-knowledge would be a condition of knowledge of the world, for the latter would be known only via the former. The former would be immediate: we would know the self as it is in itself, for there is nothing between its being and our knowledge of it—while knowledge of the world would be mediate. We would not have knowledge of the object *in itself*, for *it* would always be known mediately via knowledge of the self. But this would imply that there is a "gap" between self-knowledge and knowledge of the world, a gap in need of bridging. This occurs in Descartes's system where self-knowledge is superior to knowledge of the external world, in which the gap is bridged by *deducing* knowledge of the external world from knowledge of the self. That gap allows skepticism to creep in, for there is always the possibility of bridging it in a *false* way—one thinks here of Hume's claim that the objective categories do not apply to the world. Hence for Kant it is important to prove that knowledge of the world and of the self are given at *once*, and are of the same status. And indeed in his "Refutation of Idealism" Kant makes it clear that he does not maintain that the ego is better known than the external world. He maintains that just as we do not have knowledge of objects as they are in themselves, we do not have knowledge of self as it is in-itself, i.e., "in the synthetic unity of apperception I am conscious of myself, not as I appear to myself, nor as I am in myself, but only that I am" (CPR 168 [B 157]).

¹⁷ This will be explained in chapters 4 and 5.

¹⁸ Compare Carnap's words: "the object and its concept are one and the same" (A 10).

¹⁹ Compare the words of Fichte:

> Sensible objects, therefore, exist for you only in consequence
> of a particular determination of your external senses: you
> know of them only as a result of your knowledge of this deter-
> mination of your sight, touch, etc. Your assertion, "these are
> objects external to me," depends upon this other—"I see,
> hear, feel, and so forth." [VM 36]

Chapter Four

¹ The *transcendental subject* is the *idea* of the *object in general*," writes de Muralt (DeM 359).

² Recall that in chapter 2 it was explained that not only do judgments intentionally refer back to experience, but reference to experience forms part of the sense of judgment.

³ Actually, a stronger claim will be made in this chapter. As will be explained on pp. 128ff., one can look at experience only by experiencing, so one can achieve a theory of experience only by an act of experience, by attending to the act of experience as one experiences. Hence, logic must be grounded in an act of experience.

⁴ Hume sharply distinguishes between belief and knowledge. According to him we have knowledge only when we know something with absolute certainty, when its opposite is inconceivable. Statements of fact produce only belief or opinion, for their denial is always conceivable. Only the relation between ideas produces knowledge, according to Hume:

> It appears, therefore, that of these seven philosophical rela
> tions, there remain only four, which depending solely upon
> ideas, can be the objects of knowledge and certainty. [THN 70]

And:

> All certainty arises from the comparison of ideas, and from the
> discovery of such relations as are unalterable. [THN 79]

⁵ Note the title of section 62 in *Formal and Transcendental Logic*: "The Ideality of All Species of Objectivities over against the Constituting Consciousness. The Positivistic Misinterpretation of Nature is a Type of Psychologism" (FTL 165 [148]).

⁶ Hume realizes that the notion of real object involves ideas to which no sense

impression corresponds, such as the notion of identity over time and that of substance. Such ideas he calls *fictions*. (See, for example, THN 200–201.) One could argue that he maintains these notions to be ideals, i.e., what is not real must be ideal.

7 That Hume regarded sense data as criteria of reality can be seen from his "copy principle." According to this principle the truth or reality of an idea is determined by whether or not it corresponds to an impression of the senses. Hume writes that "all our ideas are copy'd from our impressions" (THN 72) and that "it must be some one impression, that gives rise to every real idea" (THN 251):

> When we entertain, therefore, any suspicion that a philosophi-
> cal term is employed without any meaning or idea (as is but too
> frequent), we need but enquire, *from what impression is that sup-*
> *posed idea derived?* And if it be impossible to assign any, this will
> serve to confirm our suspicion. By bringing ideas into so clear
> a light we may reasonably hope to remove all dispute, which
> may arise concerning their nature and *reality* [my emphasis].
> [THN 22]

8 Mohanty (PTP 231) writes that "the transcendental subjectivity that is revealed through the Kantian enquiry remains the formal principle that it is."

9 The dream, a primitive mode of thought closely related to the body, is filled with contradictions. For example, in a dream it is not unusual to find ourselves interacting with someone knowing all the while that that person is actually deceased. Nor is it unusual for one and the same person to be both young and old in the dream.

10 Pp. 79ff.

11 Ricoeur, for example, has said that the problem of other selves is the "touchstone for the success or failure not only of phenomenology but also of the implicit philosophy of phenomenology" (HAP 195). The problem of the alter ego is dealt with in chapter 6.

12 Husserl's phrase "being-sense" *(Seinssinn)* expresses his thesis that sense or meaning and being are essentially related, that all being is essentially imbued with meaning. This it achieves in virtue of transcendental subjectivity. See pp. 127ff.

13 It will be shown below (p. 131) that, as Descartes established, it is indubitable that I am.

14 Neither the term "part" nor "aspect" should be understood in a reified sense.

15 Fichte writes:

> You are here, not for idle contemplation of yourself, or for
> brooding over devout sensations—no, you are here for action;

your action, and your action alone, determines your worth.
[VM 84]

[16] In chapter 6 it will be shown that according to Husserl our essence involves an ethical dimension. This concrete doing, then, will involve ethical actions. This is once more similar to the philosophy of Heidegger. In his article on Heidegger Amstutz writes:

Darin nun, dass das Sein den Menschen beauftragt liegt verborgen eine vollständige *Ethik*. [MUS 6]

[17] This is the reason why the terms "life" and "body" are interchanged in this work.

[18] However, in chapter 5, section f, it will be shown, that, contrary to Carr, the Cartesian way is indispensable to phenomenology in certain respects.

[19] Biemel interpolates "tied to pure experience." I would say that Husserl meant more observant of the phenomena, i.e., more empirical. The latter would lead to pure experience.

[20] It is interesting to note that Noam Chomsky in effect expresses the same critique against empiricist thought—namely, that *it*, rather than the rationalistic psychologies and philosophies of mind, suffers from dogmatism and apriorism because it fails to be truly empirical. Chomsky writes:

It is important to emphasize that seventeenth-century rationalism approaches the problem of learning—in particular, language learning—in a fundamentally nondogmatic fashion. It notes that knowledge arises on the basis of very scattered and inadequate data and that there are uniformities in what is learned that are in no way uniquely determined by the data itself. . . . Consequently, these properties are attributed to the mind, as preconditions for experience. This is essentially the line of reasoning that would be taken, today, by a scientist interested in the structure of some device for which he has only input-output data. In contrast, empiricist speculation, particularly in its modern versions, has characteristically adopted certain a priori assumptions regarding the nature of learning (that it must be based on association or reinforcement, or on inductive procedures of an elementary sort—e.g., the taxonomic procedures of modern linguistics, etc.) and has not considered the necessity for checking these assumptions against the observed uniformities of "output"—against what is known or believed after "learning" has taken place. Hence the charge of a priorism or dogmatism often leveled against rationalistic psychology and philosophy of mind seems clearly to be misdirected. [CL 65]

²¹ A philosophy that considers consciousness, in whatever form (as cogito, as ego, or as transcendental ego) to be the foundation of all meaning/being Ricoeur calls a "philosophy of the subject." In Ricoeur's words, a philosophy of the subject is one that "claim[s]that the subject's reflecting on himself or the positing of the subject *by* himself is an original, fundamental, and founding act" (CI 237).

²² In *Conflict of Interpretations* Ricoeur in effect maintains the same position. "It is notable that, even when Freud speaks of instinct, it is always in and based on an expressive level, in and based on certain effects of meaning which lend themselves to deciphering and which can be treated like texts: oneiric texts or symptomatic texts," writes Ricoeur (CI 263). It is not clear, however, why Ricoeur maintains that we cannot read Freud in this fashion from the start, but that we can do so only after taking the detour of semiotics, that what we need is a "re-reading of psychoanalysis in the light of semiology" (CI 263).

²³ Later (pp. 108ff.) it will be made clear that by "thoughtlike" is not meant the empirical ego, the concrete psyche, or the explicit ego as Descartes uses the term.

²⁴ Desire is not something alongside meaning. It *is* meaning. Contrary to Ricoeur, libido *is* symbolic, not *related to* the symbolic (CI 264).

²⁵ The relation between seeing and evidence, that to see X is to have evidence of X, has been discussed in chapter 2, section h.

²⁶ We are reminded of Parmenides, fragm. 3 and 8: τὸ γὰρ αὐτο νοεῖν ἐστίν τε καὶ εἶναι

²⁷ The argument here is against Palmer, according to whom Husserl posited a realm of ideas above the flux of experience:

> Husserl had observed the temporality of consciousness and
> furnished a phenomenological description of internal time con-
> sciousness, yet his eagerness for apodictic knowledge led him
> to translate this temporality back into the static and presenta-
> tional terms of science—essentially to deny the temporality of
> being itself and assert a realm of ideas above the flux. [P 127]

For Husserl ideas are not above the flux of experience, but are *lived* and *felt*. This claim will be reinforced in the next chapters.

²⁸ After all, intentionality aims to describe the essence of *mind* and all three— unconscious, preconscious, and conscious—are phenomena of mind.

²⁹ Although Freud changes the model (F 195–96) after the text cited here, even in its earliest conception it is described dynamically.

³⁰ The only thing that *is* irreducible is the division between the stream of experience and attention.

³¹ This will be demonstrated again in chapter 6, section h, where it will be worked out in more detail.

³² This point is argued at length in chapter 3, section f. Consider also the following:

> Kant did not set up a genuine intentional psychology, in oppo-
> sition to *sensualist* "psychology" . . . *a fortiori*, he did not set up
> a psychology as, in our sense, an apriori eidetic theory. He
> never submitted the psychology of Locke and his school to a
> radical criticism, one that would affect the underlying sense of
> that psychology's sensualism. His own dependence on Lockean
> psychology was still too great. And, connected with this depen-
> dence, there is the additional fact that he never worked out the
> profound sense of the difference between *pure psychology* (solely
> on the basis of "internal experience") and *transcendental phe-
> nomenology* (on the basis of transcendental experience, which
> originates from "transcendental-phenomenological reduction")
> and therefore did not work out the deepest sense of the tran-
> scendental problem of *"psychologism."* [FTL 257–58 (227–28)]

And:

> Perhaps a deeper critique could show that Kant, though he at-
> tacks empiricism, still remains dependent upon this very empir-
> icism in his conception of the soul and the range of tasks of a
> psychology, that what counts for him is the soul which is made
> part of nature and conceived of as a component of the psycho-
> physical human being within the time of nature, within space-
> time. Hence the transcendentally subjective could certainly not
> be [identical with] the psychic. [C 115]

And:

> A true beginning, achieved by means of a radical liberation
> from all scientific and prescientific traditions, was not attained
> by Kant. He does not penetrate to the absolute subjectivity
> which constitutes everything that is, in its meaning and validity,
> nor to the method of attaining it in its apodicticity, of interro-
> gating it and of explicating it apodictically. [C 199]

Chapter Five

[1] It is also the question of dogma versus openness.

[2] Unless otherwise stated, in this work by "phenomenology" is meant Husserl's phenomenology.

[3] The concept of transcendental ego as radical self-examination reflects the
openness of phenomenology.

[4] Although at one point (C xlii) Carr suggests that the two approaches are

compatible, it does not seem that he seriously considers it. In any case, he does not see the structural reason for their compatibility.

⁵ As examples of transcendent essences Husserl gives the following: "thing," "spatial shape," "movement," "color of a thing," "man," "human feeling," "soul," "psychical experience" (experience in the psychological sense), "person," and "quality of character" (I 161 [114]).

⁶ Husserl writes that it took him a long time to see this important point:

> At least for me the second stage was very difficult, even after the first. Today that cannot escape an attentive reader of the *Logische Untersuchungen*. . . . The fact is that the beginner in phenomenology finds it difficult to acquire a reflective mastery of the different focusings of consciousness with their different objective correlates. [I FK 140–41 (117)]

⁷ Again there is a similarity between Husserl's position and that of Buber. Writes Buber: "He knows no security yet is never unsure; for he possesses steadfastly that before which all security appears vain and empty: direction and meaning" (DL 92). Direction and meaning are the essential characteristics of intentionality.

⁸ This gives rise to the paradoxical hermeneutic circle.

⁹ See also the quotation from *Formal and Transcendental Logic* on p. 122.

¹⁰ It will not do to say that Descartes *explains* the cogito's apodicticity by the notion of clear and distinct ideas, for Descartes himself felt the latter notion to be in need of grounding. He attempts to prove the status of clear and distinct ideas by appeal to the benevolence of God.

¹¹ It has already been explained in a previous chapter how in Husserl's view evidence is not a blind feeling but is intelligible.

¹² As Buber writes, "it is immediacy which alone makes it possible to live the realizing as real" (DL 78).

¹³ If it be objected that the cogito is only mental being, and not physical, the reader is referred to chapter 4, in which it is discussed how the cogito involves the body.

¹⁴ One could take the Sophists to be saying something like this when they say there are no principles one can appeal to in the search for truth (cf. pp. xxxv).

¹⁵ An analysis of memory might allow us, for example, to conclude the following apodictically. My experience is given to me as a continuous succession—it has the form past, present, future. The ever-present sensory experience of my living body defines for me my present, the "now." This "now" is always "filled"; it is the "moment" in which all my experiences originate and all experience, both past and present, carries within it an implicit reference to this "now," for it is in virtue of this that they all implicitly have the sense of being "my" experiences, and in virtue of which they are unified. Recollection is made possible because the ray of attention is not "tied" to any particular sense experience, but is "transparent" and free to move throughout all experience. When recalling, the ray of

attention may partially withdraw from the current flow of sensory impressions. Memory, like perception, has a horizon to which I can turn my attention. I may recall a particular event and go on to recall earlier or later events, for example.

¹⁶ See page 32.

¹⁷ What is meant by "immanent object" is explained in chapter 5, section f.

¹⁸ The world is not a necessary object, but a factual object. While the world as a matter of fact is, it might not have been. Cogito, however, is a necessary Being. Husserl writes:

> I myself or my experience in its actuality am *absolute* Reality *(Wirklichkeit)*, given through a positing that is unconditioned and simply indissoluble.
>
> *The thesis of my pure Ego and its personal life which is "necessary" and plainly indubitable, thus stands opposed to the thesis of the world which is "contingent." All corporeally given thing-like entities can also not be, no corporeally given experiencing can also not be:* that is the essential law, which defines this necessity and that contingency.
>
> Obviously then the ontic necessity of the actual present experiencing . . . is the necessity of a fact *(Faktum)*, and called "necessity" because an essential law is involved in the fact, and here indeed in its existence as such. [I 131]

It is interesting to compare this to the words of Buber:

> To neither the joinings of human need between birth and the grave, however, nor to the fate of all life that is scattered abroad in the world, nor to all the counterplay of the elements, nor even to the movement of the stars themselves, not to all these investigated and registered things may I grant the name of necessity, but only to the directed soul. [DL 57 (18)]

¹⁹ And here lies the ground of the principle Husserl insisted upon since the time of his *Philosophy of Arithmetic*, namely, that a "subjective" doing is the most radical way of grounding statements of science. Frege strenuously objected to this, considering it an expression of psychologism. But according to Husserl, it is the only way to yield scientific statements, for the ideal of science is precisely that of a radical grounding (FTL 279 [246]).

²⁰ Iso Kern writes the following:

> Mit Recht wurde Husserl in manchen Kritiken vorgeworfen, dass er dem Eigensein der fremden Subjektivität in seiner phänomenologischen Philosophie nicht Rechnung zu tragen vermöge. Diese Kritik hat aber—so müssen wir wiederum

vorausnehmend sagen—nur vom Gesichtspunkt des Catesiani-
schen Weges ihr Recht, der den eigentlichen Sinn von Husserl's tranzendental-phänomenologischer Reduktion nicht
erreicht. [IK 205]

21 This is the reason why Iso Kern (IK 203–4) writes that, unlike Descartes in
his doubting, Husserl does not lose the world in the reduction.

22 So too in the case of mathematical objects. Husserl did not want to *reduce*
them to the cogito even in his *Philosophy of Arithmetic*, but wanted to see what
meaning they presuppose.

23 On the difference between phenomenology and deductive science, de
Muralt writes the following:

Geometry and phenomenology are both eidetic sciences; but
the deductive method is a deduction of essences, while the
phenomenological method is a direct intuition of essences.
[DeM 76]

And:

Factical science, tending toward its own ideal perfection, always
remains in tendency toward its idea. Hence we have a necessarily *dynamic* point of view, that of realization of the idea by development, which contrasts with the static point of view of
deduction. Even if the idea is analogous to an axiom, definition
of science by its idea is not the definition of science's object
but of its own development as science. This development is, to
be sure, a "consequence" of the idea, since it is motivated a
priori by it. But it is not deduced from its idea as the analytic
consequences of a geometric axiom are deduced from the axiom. [DeM 73]

24 This point is articulated by Gadamer too when he says that every question
implies or presupposes knowledge (TM 326).

25 The reference is to Richard Palmer's *Hermeneutics: Interpretation Theory in
Schleiermacher, Dilthey, Heidegger, and Gadamer* (Evanston: Northwestern University Press, 1969).

26 Palmer's presentation of the debate will be used in this chapter because he
expresses clearly the main points of contention between the two camps, at times
more so than members of either camp do. Although Palmer favors the approach
of Gadamer and Heidegger, he presents the other side with laudable fairness.

27 Their critique of Gadamer's hermeneutics is the same as the critique of Carr
put forth above in chapter 5, section b.

28 The second reason is perhaps the most telling for our purposes, for it gives
rise to a more significant set of undesirable consequences.

²⁹ This will be discussed in chapter 6, section h.

³⁰ This has already been dealt with (pp. 108ff.), but there will be occasion to go over this again in chapter 6, section h to j.

³¹ That is, Hegel saw clearly that the Subject-Object dialectic was irreducible. In this respect Husserl is close to Hegel, for the former too insists that phenomenology is correlational research, that subject and object occur together.

³² This is brought out beautifully in Heinrich von Kleist's *Über das Marionettheater* (MT 9–16).

³³ What is novel is the extent to which Beethoven's music expresses "raw" emotion, something not found previously. The tradition has no way of conveying to us the way in which his music is to be performed; it has no way of conveying the peculiar blend of explosiveness and tender restraint that mark his music. This is Beethoven's "stamp" on music and in part it reflects his personality.

³⁴ By "conscious mind" is here meant "self-consciousness."

³⁵ Again, compare the words of Buber:

> Realization has nothing to promise. It says: If you wish to become mine, you must descend into the abyss. What wonder is it if the choosing man hands himself over to the friendlier mistress [orientation] and only now and then, in the rare hours of self-recollection, casts a melancholy glance at the other [realization]? [DL 96 (44)]

And:

> Security—thus you name the breath of your first life. But that was not the security of those who protect themselves and know their way about. That was the security of the sleepwalker. Children are sleepwalkers in the world. They pass through all abysses unharmed, for they do not see them.* The direction that guides their steps is dreamlike, the meaning in which everything fulfills itself for them is dreamlike. Dreamlike they realize their life-experience. It is granted them to realize without risk because they are unaware of the inner duality and therefore all things also offer themselves to them undivided. Everything harmonizes with them like a roundelay, and the contradiction itself joins in the play. . . . Then comes the hour of awakening. It can come late. There are men whose realizing power is so great that it outlasts childhood in its first form— the dreamlike simplicity. No matter: it happens that an abyss that one has countless times passed by suddenly looms at his feet. [DL 95–96 (43–44)]

---

*I would say that not all children "pass all abysses unharmed."

[36] For Buber also the artistic act is one that is not only *ordered* but *comprehended* (DL 75 [30]). Writes Buber:

> The primitive man and the child are *still*, the creative man
> *newly* master of reality. A moonbeam lies on the forehead of
> the former like the mirroring of a forgotten paradise, but the
> latter shines with the fire that it has stolen from heaven. [DL
> 71 (27)]

[37] This is explained and further textual reference is given on pp. 198ff.

[38] *"Untergründe der Welt."*

[39] *"Untergründ und die Geburtsstätte des Wortes."*

[40] By tragedy is meant: "a concrete manifestation of Dionysiac conditions, music made visible, an ecstatic dream world" (BT 89; K 92 [91]).

[41] It must be stressed that what is meant by "madness" here is *not* psychosis. As Trilling argues:

> The doctrine that madness is health, that madness is liberation
> and authenticity, receives a happy welcome from a consequen-
> tial part of the educated public. . . . But who that has spoken,
> or tried to speak, with a psychotic friend will consent to betray
> the masked pain of his bewilderment and solitude by making it
> a paradigm of liberation from the imprisoning falsehoods of an
> alienated social reality? [SA 171]

Chapter Six

[1] For philosophy in general, its importance is twofold. If one maintains that philosophy has implications for those actions that concern one's dealings with one's fellow human beings, then one must deal with philosophy's problem of the alter ego. It is hard to conceive how a discipline for which the existence of other selves constitutes not merely a difficulty, but, to use Merleau-Ponty's expression, an "outrage" (PhP 349), can be a form of social activity. Secondly, our *values* are based on our essential nature. If the relation to others is at the heart of our Being—that is, if our relation to others forms part of our essence—then a philosophy for which the alter ego is a problem, a philosophy that does not touch the heart of our Being, our essence, is a philosophy that is bankrupt in terms of *value*. Such a philosophy, to borrow Husserl's phrase, will have nothing to say to us. Hence, philosophy's problem of other selves is a problem of *values*.

[2] See chapter 3, section c.

[3] According to a metaphysics of presence, Being is understood exclusively in terms of the temporal present and subjectivity is considered as an absolute self-presence. According to "presence by clearing" Being is understood, not in terms

of mere presence, but in terms of what is *not* present—past and future. A metaphysics of presence grasps Being as what is "now," while a metaphysics of "presence by clearing" sees Being as a *project* into what is not yet, springing from a ground of which we are forgetful.

4 This bears certain moral consequences, about which more will be said in chapter 6, section j.

5 See chapter 3, section b.

6 Repeatedly instituting the reduction is in effect to ask at each successive stage what meaning "X" has for the ego. If we institute the first reduction, we see that all meaning is constituted by the ego. Another way of saying this is that the first reduction yields the ego with its essences. But a second reduction applied to the results of the first reduction—that is, applied to the ego and its essences— separates transcendent and immanent essences. The second reduction reveals the immanent essences of the pure constituting activity of the ego. In short, the ego of the first reduction is itself constituted by a deeper ego—namely, the pure transcendental ego with its temporal synthesis (see pp. 63, 66, and esp. 118).

7 Objectivism is to be distinguished from objective thought. The concept of life-world marks the antithesis of objectivism, but not of objective thought.

8 See chapter 3, section f.

9 Merleau-Ponty means by "constituting consciousness" the notion of consciousness entertained in intellectualist theories—namely, the notion of consciousness as a constituting entity or agency, of consciousness as substrate, as interiority.

10 As Husserl urges, there is another stream in Descartes's thought that suggests a more phenomenological understanding of the ego-cogito.

11 One thinks of the different theoretical approaches to color that Goethe and Newton had. Whereas Goethe's concern in his theory of color is with the lived experience of color, Newton's is with the quantfication of color.

12 It should be clear from the quotation that Merleau-Ponty's criticism of the intellectualist thesis is not to be taken as a critique of Husserl's phenomenology. The theory Merleau-Ponty criticizes here is one in which the relations between world, own body, empirical self, and transcendental ego "remain what they were in empiricism: causal relations" (PHP 208).

13 Duhem argues that translation of a concrete fact into symbol is often not even a straightforward (one-step) translation. Indeed, very often, because of the fact that physical theories become quite complex, in order to effect the translation of a practical fact—that is, in order to use a measuring instrument—an appeal to further, *already established*, theories is required. Interpretation may be involved in the very use of a measuring device. Duhem writes, for example, that while "any man can . . . follow the motions of a spot of light on a transparent ruler, and see if it goes to the right or to the left or stops at such and such a point," unless he knows the theory of electrodynamics, "he will not . . . be able to measure the resistance of the coil" (ASPT 145). In other words, experimentation in physics does not deal with concrete facts per se, but with theoretical facts, which at times cannot be translated back into concrete facts in one step, but

which must be translated back by a *chain* of theoretical symbols, "by long and complicated theoretical intermediaries."

14 In chapter 5 (pp. 131) it was explained how nothing is lost in the *epochē*, however.

15 It must be understood that a complete absence of causal relationship between the perceived and the percept is not being claimed here. The causal relation between the perceived and the percept is illustrated by the phenomenon of blindness, for example. What *is* being claimed, however, is that the causal relation itself is parasitic upon the constituting activity of consciousness. This is not to invalidate causality anymore than saying that consciousness constitutes the world is to invalidate the world. In Mohanty's words: "intentionality characterizes the constituting order, real, natural causality the constituted" (PTP 73).

16 It was explained in chapter 3 that since they do not concede of experience outside the objective categories, both Descartes's ego-cogito and Kant's transcendental ego are objectivistic notions, according to Husserl. It is interesting to note that in *The Concept of Nature in Marx* (CNM 25), Schmidt makes the same point concerning Kant as does Husserl.

17 In chapter 5, sections f and g, it was explained that according to Husserl, the ego-cogito is apodictic because the ego is given to itself *nonobjectively*. In other words, for Husserl, unlike for Descartes, the cogito is *act*, not representation. Hence consciousness is never pure presence for Husserl; because consciousness is activity, something of myself always escapes me. I am *never* given to myself in totality. The transcendental reduction, then, can only *point* to the activity of consciousness, to its intentional life; reflection can never coincide with it (S 179; I 214 [160]).

18 In *The Structure of Behaviour* Merleau-Ponty deals with consciousness seen from the outside," whereas in the *Phenomenology of Perception*, he deals with it from "the inside." In other words, in the former he is concerned with discussing the problem of consciousness from a scientific standpoint and in the latter from a phenomenological standpoint. He writes in the *Phenomenology of Perception:*

> We have pointed out elsewhere that consciousness seen from
> outside cannot be a pure *for itself. (La Structure du Comporte-
> ment*, pp. 168ff.). We are beginning to see that the same applies
> to consciousness from the inside. [PhP 215, n. 2]

19 If the intellectualist thesis were correct, there would remain no opaque element to experience. That is, if behavior were the execution of the intentions of consciousness, consciousness would ultimately know everything, having given rise to these intentions in the first place.

20 According to Merleau-Ponty, while empiricism cannot see that we need to know what we are looking for, intellectualism cannot see that we need to be ignorant of what we are looking for (PhP 28).

21 See chapter 3, section f, esp. pp. 78ff.

22 These dicta are (i) overturning of the idea of thing and world (see chapter 6,

section c) and (ii) overcoming the notion of transcendental ego as constituting *agency* in favor of a notion of transcendental ego as constituting activity (see chapter 6, section d).

23 Compare the words of Carnap: "the object and its concept are one and the same. This identification does not amount to a reification *(Substantialisierung)* of the concept, but, on the contrary, is a 'functionalization' of the object." (A 10)

24 To name something, that something must have determinations or characteristics; it must have an identity. If there are no determinations, there are no characteristics for identity. Hence, anonymity.

25 This is the problem of methexis (μεθέξιζ), participation of the thing in the idea, that Plato struggled with.

26 It may seem like a contradiction that association is described as passive and as an act. Yet Husserl maintains that there are such things as passive acts. The contradiction disappears if we realize that passivity is here to be understood in terms of degrees, rather than in absolute terms. Writes Husserl:

> Accordingly, there is not only a passivity *prior* to the activity, as passivity of the originally constitutive temporal flux, which is only *preconstitutive*, but also a passivity erected on this, a passivity which is truly objectivating, namely, one which thematizes or cothematizes objects; it is a passivity which belongs to the act, not as a base but as act, a kind of *passivity in activity*.
> This formulation shows that the distinction between passivity and activity is not inflexible, that it is not a matter here of terms which can be established definitively for all time, but only of means of description and contrast, whose sense must in each case be recreated originally with reference to the concrete situation of the analysis—an observation which holds true for every description of intentional phenomena. [EJ 108]

27 By "thinking" Husserl means objective processes.

28 What is usually stressed concerning Freudian theory is how the superego can be a shackle to the ego. The superego can indeed rage against the ego to the point of crippling the ego. But it is important to realize that the ego is also dependent on the superego for its being, according to Freud.

29 This will be addressed again on pp. 210ff.

30 Concerning the wakeful ego, see also chapter 2, section i.

31 See chapter 5, section g.

32 Ibid.

33 This is *not* to be confused with the thesis that maintains that rationality is *agreement*. The latter is held, for instance, by Perelman in his *The New Rhetoric and the Humanities*.

34 See the Epilogue concerning the apparent contradictory ways of characterizing the transcendental ego as nonwakeful and as self-criticism.

35 See pp. 95ff.

[36] The term "forgetfulness" may be a bit of a misnomer, however, for we can forget only that which we knew, and we are not, to begin with, explicitly aware of the transcendental realm. The transcendental is originally *lived* and not reflectively had. It would be more accurate to speak of its *absence* from thetic consciousness.

[37] "Contagion" would be a better translation of *Gefühlsansteckung* than "contamination."

[38] This is why any investigation into cognition is always *correlational* research, according to Husserl.

[39] While in principle one would *be* without the other, one would not be self-conscious, one would have no concept of ego and so one would not be an *ego*, for as mentioned above, ego is created every time I conceive of ego. Hence, the mere fact that I am alive does not make me an ego, but only a potential—that is, unconscious ego. Psychology bears this out, for it observes cases, such as in autism, in which an ego does not develop. Lack of ego in autism is indicated by the lack of use of the term "I," for ego is such that if it were constituted or formed it would be cathected and thus enjoy a certain narcissism, which would automatically lead it to self-assertion.

[40] In footnote 1 to this chapter it was stated that philosophy's problem of other selves mocked the claim that philosophy is social in nature. Within phenomenology's framework the problem of the alter ego is solved and the social nature of philosophy is once more brought out:

> Philosophy is indeed, and always, a break with objectivism and a return from constructa to lived experience, from the world to ourselves. It is just that this indispensable and characteristic step *no longer transports it into the rarefied atmosphere of introspection* or into a realm numerically distinct from that of science. It no longer makes philosophy a rival of scientific knowledge, now that we have recognized that the *"interior" it brings us back to is not a private life but an intersubjectivity that gradually connects us ever closer to the whole of history* . . . philosophy has a dimension of its own, *the dimension of co-existence* . . . as the milieu and perpetual event of universal praxis. [EW 80]

Chapter Seven

[1] As was discussed in chapters 1 and 2, the germ of the critique is found *within* the tradition—it is not a critique *ab extra* or *von oben her*—and is usually experienced as a sense of shortcoming within the tradition. See also pp. 239ff.

[2] To some extent it is undesirable to speak of *the* tradition of formal logic, since the tradition is a *varied* one. Still, since the tradition *is* composed of certain broad, unified themes, there is some justification for talking of "the tradition."

³ In his *Philosophie der Arithmetik* one finds the rudiments of the method of legitimation by appeal to "subjective" experience. See page 11, and chapter 5, n. 18.

⁴ Cf. Smith and McIntyre (IVI 543).

⁵ HNN.

⁶ Bell (FTJ 25) realizes this, however.

⁷ Pp. 147ff.

⁸ It is interesting to note that Jaakko Hintikka understands this point. However, he fails to capitalize on it and discusses the noema without relating it to the noesis.

⁹ Although Husserl says that the noema, "despite its dependence [on the noesis], permits of being considered on its own account" (I 265 [206]), he makes this claim on the understanding that any account that focuses explicitly only on the noema must nevertheless reflect an understanding of the essential relation of the noema and the noesis.

¹⁰ Nor, it will be argued in chapter 7, section h, can Frege's concept of *Sinn*.

¹¹ This is how objectivism is overcome, after all.

¹² Langsdorf in her paper on Føllesdal makes the same point.

¹³ The notion of quality touches on the *nature* of the subjective relation to the noematic *Sinn*, the relation of noesis to noematic core and object. In the *Logical Investigations* quality is still considered noetic, while in *Ideas* and later it is considered noematic but pointing to a noetic act.

¹⁴ Compare the words of Brand:

> Intentionality, therefore, is not a static consciousness-of, but a dynamic process through which consciousness continuously transcends itself. Intentionality is not just *being*, but, rather, *functioning*. That is why Husserl calls it "functioning intentionality." [IRI 197–98]

¹⁵ Pp. 32ff.

¹⁶ Chapter 2, section g.

¹⁷ This is tantamount to taking the complete noema to be the core of the noema *(Sinn)*, for the core of the noema is the *idea* of the object given in adequation, is the idea of the object filled out completely.

¹⁸ See pp. 54ff.

¹⁹ This aspect of the theory was not overtly stated or worked out by Frege, because of his trouble with the notion of subjectivity. See below, pp. 235ff.

²⁰ Articles that were the foundation of the *Sinn*-noema comparison.

²¹ This is another phrase for his theory of reference.

²² See chapter 2, section h.

²³ This does not mean that the assertion "maps onto" the idea. The idea is a rule of procedure, not an image to be mapped onto.

²⁴ A position that stressed "observatîonal and experimental techniques" and rejected "the deductive methods of the idealists," according to Sluga.

[25] One could ask whether it is not the other way around, i.e., is it not the name/bearer relation as the prototype of reference that leads Dummett to conclude that Frege is a realist? However, taking the name/bearer as paradigmatic of reference is not supported by Frege's doctrine (see chapter 7, section h) and so must find its motivation elsewhere, such as in the desire to prove Frege to be a realist.

[26] Nonpsychologistic idealism is an idealism in which thoughts, etc., are not "in" the mind and are not merely empirical events.

[27] This purposive element is found in sense as well as in reference because sense necessarily implies reference and hence shares in this striving for truth.

[28] Examples of mathematical functions are: $y = x + 2$, $x = 2y + 5$, etc. Examples of functions in language: the capital of _____ , this tree is _____ , _____ is green.

Bibliography

Amstutz, Jakob. "Das Erkenntnisverhalten C. G. Jungs." *Akademie für Ethische Forschung*, Nr. 12, Jan. 1984.

————. "Der Mensch und das Sein." *Schweizerische Theologische Umschau* (Bern), 5/6, 1957.

Angelelli, Ignacio. *Studies on Gottlob Frege and Traditional Philosophy*. Dordrecht: D. Reidel, 1967.

Aristotle. *Metaphysics vol. 1 and 2*. Introduction and Commentary by W. D. Ross. Oxford: Clarendon Press, 1924.

Ayer, A. J. (ed.). *Logical Positivism*. New York: Free Press, 1959.

Bachelard, Suzanne. *A Study of Husserl's "Formal and Transcendental Logic."* Translated by Lester E. Embree. Evanston: Northwestern University Press, 1968. *La Logique de Husserl: Étude sur Logique formelle et transcendentale*. Paris: Presses Universitaires de France, 1957.

Bambrough, R. (ed.). *The Philosophy of Aristotle*. New York: New American Library, 1963.

Barral, Mary. *Merleau-Ponty: The role of the Body-Subject in Interpersonal Relations*. Duquesne University Press, 1965.

Bell, David. *Frege's Theory of Judgment*. New York: Oxford University Press, 1979.

Bettelheim, Bruno. *Freud and Man's Soul*. New York: Alfred Knopf, 1983.

Bochenski, I. M. *A History of Formal Logic*. Notre Dame: University of Notre Dame Press, 1961.

Brand, G. "Intentionality, Reduction, and Intentional Analysis in Husserl's Later Manuscripts," in J. Kocklemans (ed.). *Phenomenology*. Garden City, N.Y.: Doubleday, 1967, pp. 197–217.

Brentano, Franz. *Psychology from an Empirical Standpoint*. Oskar Kraus (ed.). Translated by Antos C. Rancurello, D. B. Terell, and Linda L. McAlister. New York: Humanities Press, 1973, *Pyschologie vom empirischen Standpunkt*. Leipzig: Duncher & Humbolt, 1874.

Buber, Martin. "Daniel: Gespräche von der Verwirklichung," in *Werke*, Bd. 1, Schriften zur Philosophie. Munich: Kösel-Verlag; Heidelberg: Verlag Lambert Schneider, 1962. *Daniel: Dialogues on Realization*. Translated,

with an introductory essay, by Maurice Friedman. New York: Holt, Rein-
hart and Winston, 1964.

Cairns, Dorion. *Conversations with Husserl and Fink*. The Hague: Martinus
Nijhoff, 1976.

Camus, Albert. *The Myth of Sisyphus and Other Essays*. Translated by J. O'Brien.
New York: Alfred Knopf, 1975. *Le Mythe de Sisyphe, essai sur l'absurde*.
Paris: Gallimard, 1942.

Carnap, Rudolf. *The Logical Structure of the World*. Translated by R. George.
Berkeley: University of California Press, 1967. *Die logische Aufbau der
Welt*. Berlin: Welt Kreis, 1928.

———. *The Logical Syntax of Language*. Translated by Amethe Smeaton Countess
von Zeppelin. London: Kegen Paul Trench, Trebner, 1937.

Chomsky, Noam. *Cartesian Linguistics: A Chapter in the History of Rationalist
Thought*. New York: Harper & Row, 1966.

Descartes, René. *Discourse on Method and Meditations*. Translated, with an Introduction, by F. E. Sutcliffe. Middlesex: Penguin, 1977.

———. *The Philosophical Works of Descartes*. In 2 vols. Translated by Elizabeth S.
Haldane and G. R. T. Ross. Cambridge: Cambridge University Press,
1967.

Dodds, E. R. *The Greeks and the Irrational*. Los Angeles: University of California
Press, 1971.

Duhem, Pièrre. *The Aim and Structure of Physical Theory*. Translated by Philip P.
Wiener. New York: Atheneum, 1977.

Dummett, Michael. *Frege: The Philosophy of Language*. New York: Harper & Row,
1973.

Elliston, F., and P. McCormick (eds.). *Husserl: Expositions and Appraisals*. Notre
Dame: University of Notre Dame Press, 1977.

Fancher, Raymond E. *Psychoanalytic Psychology: The Development of Freud's
Thought*. New York: Norton, 1973.

Fichte, Gottlieb J. *The Vocation of Man*. Edited with an Introduction by Roderick
M. Chisholm. New York: Bobbs-Merrill, 1956.

Føllesdal, Dagfinn. "Husserl's Notion of Noema." *The Journal of Philosophy*, 20,
Oct. 16 (1976): 680–87.

Frege, Gottlob. *Foundations of Arithmetic*. Translated by J. Austin. Oxford: Basil
Blackwell, 1959.

———. *Logical Investigations*. New Haven: Yale University Press, 1977.

Freud, Sigmund. "A Note on the Unconscious in Psychoanalysis." *A General Selection from the Works of Sigmund Freud*. John Rickman (ed.). Garden City,
N.Y.: Doubleday, 1957, pp. 46–53.

———. *Civilization and its Discontents*. Translated and edited by James Strachey.
New York: Norton, 1962.

———. "The Ego and the Id." *A General Selection from the Works of Sigmund
Freud*, pp. 210–35.

———. "On Narcissism: An Introduction." *A General Selection from the Works of
Sigmund Freud*, pp. 104–23.

————. "Beyond the Pleasure-Principle." *A General Selection from the Works of Sigmund Freud*, pp. 141–68.

Friedman, R. M. "Merleau-Ponty's Theory of Subjectivity." *Philosophy Today*, 19 (1975): 228–42.

Gadamer, Hans-Georg. *Philosophical Hermeneutics*. Berkeley and Los Angeles: University of California Press, 1976.

————. *Truth and Method*. London: Sheed and Ward, 1975.

Geach, P. T., and Max Black (eds.) *Translations from the Philosophical Writings of Gottlob Frege*. Totowa, N.J.: Rowman and Littlefield, 1980.

Hartmann, Nicolai. *Kleinere Schriften, Band I, Abhandlungen zur systematischen Philosophie*. Berlin: 1955. (First published in *Deutsche systematische Philosophie nach ihren Gestaltern*, Hermann Schwarz [ed.], 1933).

Hintikka, Jaakko. *The Intention of Intentionality and other New Models for Modalities*. Dordrecht: D. Reidel, 1975.

Horowitz, Joseph. *Conversations with Arrau*. New York: Alfred Knopf, 1982.

Huertas-Jourda, José. "On the Threshold of Phenomenology: A Study of Edmund Husserl's *Philosophie der Arithmetik*. PhD Dissertation, New York University, 1969.

Hume, D. *A Treatise of Human Nature*. Edited, with an analytical index, by L. A. Selby-Brigge. Oxford: Clarendon Press, 1975.

Husserl, Edmund. *Cartesianische Meditationen*. The Hague: Martinus Nijhoff, 1950. *Cartesian Meditations: An Introduction to Phenomenology*. Translated by Dorion Cairns. The Hague: Martinus Nijhoff, 1973.

————. *Erfahrung und Urteil: Untersuchungen zur Genealogie der Logik*. Ludwig Landgrebe (ed.). Prague: Academia, 1939. *Experience and Judgment: Investigations in a Genealogy of Logic*. Revised and edited by Ludwig Landgrebe. Translated by James S. Churchill and Karl Ameriks, with a Foreword by Ludwig Landgrebe and an Afterword by Lothar Eley. Evanston: Northwestern Unviersity Press, 1973.

————. *Formale und transzendentale Logik. Erster Band. Versuch einer Kritik der logischen Vernunft*. Husserliana vol. 17. Paul Janssen (ed.). The Hague: Martinus Nijhoff, 1974. *Formal and Transcendental Logic*. Translated by Dorion Cairns. The Hague: Martinus Nijhoff, 1969.

————. *Ideen zu einer reinen Phänomenologie und phänomenologischen Philosophie. Vol. 1: Allgemeine Erführung in die reine Phänomenologie*. The Hague: Martinus Nijhoff, 1950. *Ideas: General Introduction to Pure Phenomenology*. Translated by W. R. Boyce Gibson. London: Collier Macmillan, 1975.

————. *Die Krise der europäischen Wissenschaften und die transzendentale Phänomenologie*. The Hague: Martinus Nijhoff, 1954. *The Crisis of European Sciences and Transcendental Phenomenology: An Introduction to Phenomenological Philosophy*. Translated, with an Introduction, by David Carr. Evanston: Northwestern University Press, 1970.

————. *Logische Untersuchungen*. 2 vols. 4th ed. Tübingen: Max Niemeyer Verlag, 1928. *Logical Investigations*. Translated, with an Introduction, by J. N. Findlay. 2 vols. New York: Humanities Press, 1970.

————. *Pariser Vorträge*. The Hague: Martinus Nijhoff, 1950. *Paris Lectures*. Translated, with an Introductory Essay, by Peter Koestenbaum. The Hague: Martinus Nijhoff, 1975.

————. *Philosophie der Arithmetik*. The Hague: Martinus Nijhoff, 1970.

Kant, Immanuel, *Critique of Pure Reason*. Translated by Norman Kemp Smith. New York: St. Martin's Press, 1956.

Kern, Iso. *Husserl und Kant*. The Hague: Martinus Nijhoff, 1964.

Kneale, William, and Martha Kneale. *The Development of Logic*. Oxford: Clarendon Press, 1978.

Koyré, Alexander. *From Closed World to the Infinite Universe*. Baltimore: Johns Hopkins University Press, 1974.

Landgrebe, Ludwig. *Der Weg der Phänomenologie*. Gütersloh: Gerd Mohn: Gütersloher Verlagshaus, 1963.

Langsdorf, Leonore. "The Noema: An Analysis of its Structure." Paper read at the Husserl Circle Annual Meeting (Waterloo, Canada: May 8–10, 1981).

Levinas, Emmanuel. *The Theory of Intuition in Husserl's Phenomenology*. Translated by André Orianne. Evanston: Northwestern University Press, 1973. *Théorie de l'intuition dans la phénoménologie de Husserl*. Paris: J. Vrin, 1963.

Merleau-Ponty, Maurice. *The Essential Writings of Merleau-Ponty*. Harcourt, Brace and World, 1969.

————. *Phenomenology of Perception*. Translated by Colin Smith. New York: Humanities Press, 1962. *Phénoménologie de la perception*. Paris: Gallimard, 1945.

————. *The Primacy of Perception and Other Essays in Phenomenological Psychology, the Philosophy of Art, History and Politics*. Edited, with an Introduction, by James Edie. Evanston: Northwestern University Press, 1964.

————. *Signs*. Evanston: Northwestern University Press, 1964. *Signes*. Paris: Gallimard, 1960.

————. *The Structure of Behaviour*. London: Methuen, 1965. *La Structure du comportement*. Paris: Presses Universitaires de France, 1942.

Mitchell, David. *An Introduction to Logic*. London: Hutchinson, 1968.

Mohanty, J. N. *The Possibility of Transcendental Philosophy*. The Hague: Martinus Nijhoff, 1985.

de Muralt, André. *The Idea of Phenomenology: Husserlian Exemplarism*. Translated by Garry L. Breckon. Evanston: Northwestern Unviersity Press, 1974. *L'Idée de la Phénoménologie: L'Exemplarisme Husserlien*. Paris: Presses Universitaires de France, 1958.

Neurath, Otto. "Sociology and Physicalism." *Logical Positivism*. A. J. Ayer (ed.). New York: Free Press, 1959.

Nietzsche, Friedrich. *The Birth of Tragedy*. Translated by F. Golffin. New York: Doubleday Anchor, 1956

————. *The Birth of Tragedy and the Case of Wagner*. Translated, with Commentary, by Walter Kaufmann. New York: Random House, 1967. "Die Geburt der Tragödie oder Griechenthum und Pessimismus." *Nietzsche Werke*.

Kritische Gesamtausgabe. Bd. 1, Abt. 3. Berlin and New York: Walter de Gruyter, 1972. "Der Fall Wagner," ibid., Bd. 3, Abt. 6, 1969.
——. "The Spirit of Modernity." *The Philosophy of Nietzsche*. Edited, with an Introduction, by Geoffrey Clive. New York: New American Library, 1965. "Unzeitgemässe Betrachtungen." *Nietzsche Werke*. Ibid., Bd. 1, Abt. 3, 1972.
——. "Thus Spoke Zarathustra." *The Portable Nietzsche*. Selected and Translated, with an Introduction, Prefaces, and Notes, by Walter Kaufmann. New York: Viking Press, 1970. "Also Sprach Zarathustra." *Nietzsche Werke*. Ibid., Bd. 1, Abt. 6, 1968.

Palmer, Richard E. *Hermeneutics: Interpretation Theory in Schleiermacher, Dilthey, Heidegger, and Gadamer*. Evanston: Northwestern University Press, 1969.

Payzant, Geoffrey. *Glenn Gould: Music and Mind*. Toronto: Van Nostrand Reinhold, 1978.

Perelman, Chaim. *The New Rhetoric and the Humanities: Essays on Rhetoric and its Applications*. With an Introduction by Harold Zyskind. Dordrecht: D. Reidel, 1979.

Pétrement, Simone. *Simone Weil: A Life*. Translated by Raymond Rosenthal. New York: Pantheon Books, 1976.

Richman, H. P. (ed. & translator). *W. Dilthey: Selected Writings*. Cambridge: Cambridge University Press, 1976.

Ricoeur, Paul. *The Conflict of Interpretations: Essays in Hermeneutics*. Don Ihde (ed.). Evanston: Northwestern University Press, 1974. *Le conflit des interprétations*. Paris: Seuil, 1969.
——. *Husserl. An Analysis of his Phenomenology*. Evanston: Northwestern University Press, 1967.

Rosenberg, Jay, and Charles Travis (eds.). *Readings in the Philosophy of Language*. Englewood Cliffs, N.J.: Prentice-Hall, 1971.

Ross, W. D. (ed.). *Aristotle Selections*. New York: Charles Scribner's Sons, 1955.

Sarte, Jean Paul. *Being and Nothingness: An Essay on Phenomenological Ontology*. Translated by Hazel E. Barnes. New York: Philosophical Library, 1956. *L'être et le néant: Essai d'ontologie phénoménologique*. Paris: Gallimard, 1964.

Scheler, Max. *The Nature of Sympathy*. Translated by P. Heath. London: Routledge and Kegan Paul, 1970. *Wesen und Formen der Sympathie*. Bonn: Cohen, 1923.

Schmidt, Alfred. *The Concept of Nature in Marx*. Translated by Ben Fowkes. London: NLB, 1971.

Sluga, Hans D. *Gottlob Frege*. London: Routledge and Kegan Paul, 1980.

Smith, Donald, and R. McIntyre. "Intentionality via Intensions." *The Journal of Philosophy*, vol. 68, no. 18, Sept. 16, 1971.

Solomon, Robert. *Morality and the Good Life: An Introduction to Ethics through Classical Sources*. New York: McGraw-Hill, 1984.

Spiegelberg, H. *The Phenomenological Movement. A Historical Introduction*. 2 vols.

3rd revised and enlarged edition. 2nd impression. With the Collaboration of Karl Schumann. The Hague: Martinus Nijhoff, 1984.

Stigen, Anfinn. *The Structure of Aristotle's Thought. An Introduction to the Study of Aristotle's Writings*. Oslo: Universitetsforlaget, 1966.

Trilling, Lionel. *Sincerity and Authenticity*. Cambridge: Harvard University Press, 1972.

Tugendhat, Ernst. "The Meaning of 'Bedeutung' in Frege." *Analysis*, 30, 6, June (1970).

Veatch, Henry. *Intentional Logic*. New York: Anchor Books, 1970.

von Kleist, Heinrich. "Über das Marionettentheater." *Kleists Aufsatz über das Marionettentheater*. Berlin: Erich Schmidt Verlag, 1967, Translation by Jane Volkert (Geneva, 1967).

Zaner, Richard. *The Problem of Embodiment*. The Hague: Martinus Nijhoff, 1964.

Index

Actualization, 37, 238

Adequation, 14, 26, 27, 28, 39, 40, 41; and concrete science, 21; concern for, in logic as theory of science, 8; and quality of the noema, 222; as a theme of logic, 17

Amstutz, Jakob, 98, 235

Analogical reasoning, and the problem of other selves, 167–69, 188–89, 191, 193–94, 208

Angelelli, Ignacio, 240

Antiscientism, 144

Apodicticity, 61–62; of the cogito, 126–39, 171; Descartes's notion of, 63, 70; and evidence, 127, 131–33; Hume's notion of, 68, 75; Husserl's notion versus Descartes's notion of, 125–34; Kant's notion of, 75; and relativism, 124–25; and the teleological-historical approach, 125–26

Apollonian, 163

Aristotle, 4–5, 100; and the implicit idea of pure logic, xlviii, 6; and the science-value link, xxxvi

Arrau, Claudio, 157–58, 159

Art, and the new rationality, xlix, 157–60, 163–64

Artistic act: and ecstasy, 158; and objectification, 158–59; and self-reflection, 157–60; and will, 156–59

Association, 112, 191–94, 197–98

Attention, 34, 47–52, 54; and the explicit cogito, 109; and topography (Uncs, Pcs, Cs), 110–11

Augustine, Saint, 61

Authority: Husserl's notion of, 151–52; Nietzsche's notion of, 152. *See also* Tradition

Bachelard, Suzanne, xxxv, xlix, 8–9, 18, 115; and the threat of an infinite regress in transcendental subjectivity, 114, 121; and genetic analysis, 52; and Husserl's notion of operation, 221

Being: and Aristotelian logic, 4, 7; and apodicticity, 127; forgetfulness of, 206; and objectification, 159; plentitude of, 152; pure transcendental ego as ground of, 104, 112–13, 165; qua being, 6; and the quest for purity in logic, 4, 9; reflection as a function of, 161–62; as seeing, 108, 129, 138, 161–62; temporal dimension of, 190; and will, 162

Being-in-the-world, 144, 153, 155

Being-sense: and the cogito, 131; in Heidegger, 144; and the implicit cogito, 110; pure transcendental ego as ground of, 92, 104, 112, 113–14; and subjectism, 143

Belief: datum of, 33–34, 44; intentionality as an act of, 67

Belief, passive, 44–45, 222

Bell, David, 240–41

Berkeley, George, 68

Bettelheim, Bruno, 164–65

Betti, 140, 141, 142, 148

Bochenski, I. M., 6

Body, 99–100, 102, 106–9, 112; as the bearer of a dialectic, 185; Descartes's notion of, 62–63, 65,

intersubjective, 209; Descartes's influence on Husserl's notion of, 170; and mathesis universalis, 21; as a new rationality, xiv, 151, 164, 200–201, 245; phenomenology of, xlix, 203–4; and psychoanalytic theory, 107–12, 195–207; psychology as a way into, 100, 101–4; pure psychology as, 102–12; as pure transcendental logic, xxv, 103; as radicalization of traditional logic, xxxiv, 2; and the rapprochement with analytic philosophy, 227; as self-analysis, 137; significance of the problem of other selves for, 168; and the teleological-historical (hermeneutic) method, xlix, 115–17, 119–24; tension of facticity and necessity in, 113–33, 160; traditional logic as a way into, 101

Plato: Aristotle's critique of, 4, 100; concept of science in, xxxiv–xxxvi, xl–xli, xliii, 173–74; and logic (dialectic) as a theory of science, xxxiii

Popper, Karl, 28

Positivism. See Objectivism

Possible world, 28, xlviii

Preconscious, 110–11

Presentation, mere, 23–25, 33, 35; as implying nominalization, 36–38

Psychologism, xxv, 56, 86, 97, 112, 114, 142, 146–48, 213; characterization of, 86, 145; and the concept of intentionality, xxvi, xlix; and the denial of the subject, 11, 149–50; and empiricism, 86, 88, 146; and Frege, 11, 239, 240; Husserl's extension of the notion of, 87; and idealism, 87–88, 146–48; in Kant, 86, 99; and the necessary status of logical laws, 88; in Palmer's hermeneutics, 145–50

Psychological genesis, 53

Psychology, 96–97, 100–102; empirical, 94

Pure analytic apophantics. See Formal apophantics

Pure mathematics, 18–19, 20

Pure ontology. See Formal ontology

Quality, primary and secondary, 175. See also Judgment quality

Rationality: Descartes's failure to ground, 66–67, 71, 127; differing theories of, xli; as a form of relativity, 122; Husserl's new sense of, xlv, 151–52, 153, 201–4, 164; preobjective, 198, 201; as a prerequisite for a liberal society, xxv; pure transcendental ego as ground of, 209; of the transcendental realm contrasted with rationality of empirical realm, 201; of the wakeful ego, 200, 201, 202

Rationality, new: Husserl's sense of, xlv, 151–52, 153, 164, 201–4; in Nietzsche, 164–65; in Socrates, 164–65

Reality: in Aristotle, 7, 16; in Brentano, 32; criterion of, 45, 131; and the ego in Freudian theory, 200; primacy of, in Husserl, 33; "as-if," in Hume, 69, 72, 73

Reality-in-itself, 173, 174, 177

Reason, xxviii, 150, 151, 153

Reduction. See Phenomenological reduction

Reference, 37, 227, 228; name/bearer model of, 214–15, 228; name/bearer model of, and reference in Frege, 231–33; of names, subordinate to references of sentences, 231–33, 237; of sentences, 228, 230–35; and striving for truth, 230. See also Consciousness, Intentionality

Reflective thought, 200, 210. See also Cogito

Reiteration, 16

Relativism, 124–25

Renaissance, science in, xxxvi–xxxvii

Resistance, 111

Ricoeur, Paul, 2, 62, 103, 104, 105, 107, 110, 130; and the ego-cogito, 170–71; and the problem of history for an absolute philosophy,

About the Author

Johanna Maria Tito was born in the Netherlands and received her early education there. She did undergraduate work in philosophy and psychology at York University and received her M.A. and Ph.D. in philosophy from McMaster University. This is her first book.